Steps Toward Making Every Vote Count

Steps Toward Making Every Vote Count

Electoral System Reform
in Canada and its Provinces

EDITED BY
HENRY MILNER

UNIVERSITY OF TORONTO PRESS

Copyright © University of Toronto Press 2015
Higher Education Division

www.utppublishing.com

Library and Archives Canada Cataloguing in Publication

Steps toward making every vote count : electoral system reform in Canada and its provinces / edited by Henry Milner.
Previously published under title: Making every vote count. Previously published by Broadview Press.
Includes bibliographical references.

ISBN 978-1-55111-648-8

1. Elections — Canada. 2. Voting — Canada. 3. Representative government and representation— Canada. I. Milner, Henry

Jl193.S74   2004   324.6'3'0971   C2004-903481-2

We welcome comments and suggestions regarding any aspect of our publications—please feel free to contact us at news@utphighereducation.com or visit our Internet site at www.utppublishing.com.

North America
5201 Dufferin Street
North York, Ontario, Canada, M3H 5T8

2250 Military Road
Tonawanda, New York, USA, 14150

ORDERS PHONE: 1–800–565–9523
ORDERS FAX: 1–800–221–9985
ORDERS E-MAIL: utpbooks@utpress.utoronto.ca

UK, Ireland, and continental Europe
NBN International
Estover Road, Plymouth, PL6 7PY, UK
ORDERS PHONE: 44 (0) 1752 202301
ORDERS FAX: 44 (0) 1752 202333
ORDERS E-MAIL: enquiries@nbninternational.com

Every effort has been made to contact copyright holders; in the event of an error or omission, please notify the publisher.

The University of Toronto Press acknowledges the financial support for its publishing activities of the Government of Canada through the Canada Book Fund.

Printed in the United States of America

Contents

[5]

List of Tables and Figures

Tables

Figures

Notes on Contributors

Karen Bird is an associate professor at McMaster University, where she teaches comparative politics and research methods. She has been a visiting research fellow at the Institut de sciences politique at Grenoble, at the University of Paris VII, and at the University of Aalborg. Her current research examines the political representation of women and ethnic minorities in advanced democracies.

John C. Courtney is a professor of political science at the University of Saskatchewan. His most recent book is *Commissioned Ridings*, published by McGill-Queens University Press in 2001. *Do Conventions Matter? Choosing National Party Leaders in Canada* (McGill-Queen's University Press) was short-listed for the Harold Adams Innis Prize in the Social Sciences in 1996.

John Andrew Cousins is a Prince Edward Islander and a member of the Nova Scotia Bar. He is the author of the discussion paper "Electoral Reform for Prince Edward Island," released by the Institute of Island Studies in 2000.

Brian Doody is a Ph.D. candidate in political science at the Université de Montréal. He has also worked in Ottawa for several departments and agencies of the Canadian government.

Murray Faure is a professor in political sciences at the University of South Africa, Pretoria, South Africa. He also headed that department for 15 years. He has published widely in the fields of political theory, comparative politics, and electoral systems.

Larry Gordon is a co-founder and executive director of Fair Vote Canada. He has worked in senior communications and marketing positions in the non-profit and co-operative sectors, both in Canada and the United States, over the past 25 years.

Steven Hill is a senior analyst of the Center for Voting and Democracy and managed the 1996 campaign for choice voting and the 2002 campaign for instant run-off voting in San Francisco. He is author of *Fixing Elections: The Failure of America: Winner Take All Politics* (Routledge Press, 2002).

Harold J. Jansen is an assistant professor of political science at the University of Lethbridge. One of his primary research interests is the use of the single transferable vote and the alternative vote in provincial elections in Manitoba, Alberta, and British Columbia.

Richard S. Katz is a professor of political science at Johns Hopkins University in Baltimore, Maryland. He has published widely on electoral systems and on political parties. His most recent book is *Democracy and Elections*, published by Oxford University Press.

Lawrence LeDuc is a professor of political science at the University of Toronto. His recent publications include *Comparing Democracies 2: New Challenges in the Study of Elections and Voting* (with Richard G. Niemi and Pippa Norris; published by Sage) and *The Politics of Direct Democracy: Referendums in Global Perspective* (Broadview Press, 2003).

Peter Lynch is a senior lecturer in politics at the University of Stirling. He is author of *Scottish Government and Politics* (Edinburgh University Press, 2001) and *SNP: The History of the Scottish National Party* (Welsh Academic Press, 2002). His research interests are in the areas of regionalism, devolution, and political parties.

Louis Massicotte is associate professor of political science at the Université de Montréal. He co-authored *Le scrutin au Québec: Un miroir déformant* (Hurtubise HMH, 1985) and (with André Blais) *Establishing the Rules of the Game: Election Laws in Democracies* (University of Toronto Press, 2003). He is currently advising the minister of electoral reform in Quebec.

Henry Milner teaches political science at Vanier College. He is adjunct professor at Laval University, Visiting Professor at Umeå University in Sweden, Visiting Fellow at the Institute for Research in Public Policy, and co-editor of *Inroads*. He has studied electoral reform in New Zealand and published extensively on Scandinavian institutions.

Jack H. Nagel is Stephen F. Goldstone Endowed Term Professor of Political Science at the University of Pennsylvania. A former Fulbright lecturer at the University of Canterbury in Christchurch, he has written numerous articles on New Zealand politics, as well as on elections and electoral reforms in the United States.

Dennis Pilon is a doctoral candidate at York University and has written extensively on Canada's experience of voting system reform.

Robert Richie, after working on three winning congressional campaigns, has been executive director of the Center for Voting and Democracy since its founding in 1992. He has contributed articles to numerous book collections and frequently represents the Center at conferences and in the media.

Norman Ruff is an associate professor of political science at the University of Victoria. He has published widely on British Columbia politics.

Alan Siaroff is an associate professor of political science at the University of Lethbridge. He is the author of *Comparative European Party Systems: An Analysis of Parliamentary Elections Since 1945* (Garland Publishing) and various articles on democratization, electoral systems, party systems, political economy, and women's representation.

Albert Venter is a professor and former chair in political studies at the Rand Afrikaans University, Johannesburg, South Africa. He has published widely in the fields of political theory, South African politics, the politics of deeply divided societies, and political risk analysis.

Preface

In *Making Every Vote Count: Reassessing Canada's Electoral System*, which came out in 1998, I began the preface by asking how I came to be editing a book on electoral system reform for Canada. The answer was that there was a need for a readily accessible book on the subject, and, as I elaborated, a number of unrelated factors made me especially well placed to meet that need. "The outcomes of the 1993 and, especially, 1997 Canadian federal election, which graphically demonstrated how our electoral system can regionalize political party representation in Parliament, prompted numerous columns and editorials questioning the appropriateness of our 'first-past-the-post' (FPTP) system; but, in the absence of sufficient 'resonance,' the discussion subsided rather quickly." The book was therefore needed to help develop a "sufficiently wide public understanding of what an electoral system is, and the effects that it has."

Without the backdrop of an aircraft carrier, I nevertheless lay fair claim to asserting "mission accomplished." *Making Every Vote Count* was read by many of the people who should have read it. Its chapters were cited not only in academic publications but, on occasion, in newspaper articles and columns, on the floor of Parliament, and even by the Supreme Court in the portentous *Figueroa* decision (see the chapter by Larry Gordon). It can thus take a little bit of the credit for the remarkable change in attitude in a short period of time borne out by the chapters in this book. Electoral system reform has gone from the subject of policy institute seminars to a series of concrete actions being contemplated and, quite possibly, implemented in half the provinces.

Intervening events, in particular the Québec election of 1998, which was won by the party that came in second, and the 2001 election in British Columbia (BC), which resulted in a legislature with effectively no opposition representation, have propelled this development. Events have moved so quickly that the planned second edition of *Making Every Vote Count* has evolved into a second and entirely different volume. Though eight of the 18 authors in this volume also contributed chapters to the first edition, every chapter in this second edition is new.

While it is by no means necessary to read the first volume before reading this book, they do follow a natural sequence. *Making Every Vote Count* responded to the needs at the time, setting out the arguments for and against the various electoral systems being proposed in the context of a growing sense that the FPTP system was serving Canadians poorly. Since no action was being contemplated at that time, the alternatives presented tended to be more abstract. Now, they are placed in the context of concrete developments in several provinces.

The international context has also evolved. In *Making Every Vote Count*, the only relevant example of an FPTP country with parliamentary institutions moving to proportional representation was New Zealand, which had its first proportional representation (PR) election in 1996. Now New Zealand has had two more elections under its mixed-member proportional (MMP) form of PR, and MMP has been adopted elsewhere, most notably in Scotland.

The federal elections of 1993 and 1997 were fresh in people's minds when *Making Every Vote Count* came out, and the analysis therein stressed the connection between FPTP and the regional distortions they produced in the composition of Parliament. It is fair to say that it is now common knowledge among those who should know that FPTP distorts outcomes not only in favour of stronger parties, but also regionalizes those outcomes. The 2000 Canadian federal election confirmed this; it also confirmed the fact that voter turnout was in free fall. The relationship of this decline to our FPTP electoral system is a complex one, but it is real and adds another dimension to the current concern over the effects of the electoral system. I take up this question in the Introduction.

While the content is new, the approach taken has not changed. I have again selected the contributors and edited the contributions in an effort to attain the same blending of form and content characterized as follows by one British reviewer of *Making Every Vote Count*: "Options are explored, objections raised and difficulties faced without recourse to the shallow rhetoric so often associated with the subject when it enters the everyday political domain; and yet each chapter is highly readable and never unduly technical."[1] Underlying this approach are the words set out in the introduction to the earlier volume:

> The editor of this collection is not neutral on the subject. But this does not mean that what follows is biased or lacking objectiv-

ity. For the goal of this collection is not to sell MMP, or even electoral reform as such. It is to make the point that institutions matter—in this case, the institutions by which we elect people to office. Institutions affect outcomes by framing the choices we make. If we care about the policy outcomes that are the results of those choices, it is nothing less than folly to ignore the institutions through which policies are developed and decided.

Whatever success this endeavour will meet will reflect the quality of the work of those whose names appear on the list of contributors. One name missing is that of Broadview publisher Michael Harrison, who has supported this project from the beginning. Special thanks to Frances Boylston and Brian Doody for their careful reading of the text. Others whose help contributed to this project being realized include (in alphabetical order): Peter Aimer, Doug Baillie, André Blais, Ken Carty, Bob Chodos, Paul Cliche, Jean Crete, Bill Cross, Svante Ersson, Patrick Fournier, Gordon Gibson, Brian Gibb, Julian Green, Paul Harris, Greg Hill, Tom Kent, Jeannie Lea, André Larocque, Vincent Lemieux, Nick Loenen, Ed McDonald, Paul-André Martineau, Arthur Milner, Maria Neil, John Richards, Mercedez Roberge, Hugh Segal, Leslie Seidle, Eric Shaw, Donley Studlar, Brian Tanguay, Hugh Thorburn, Jack Vowles, and Julian West.

Henry Milner
Montreal, March, 2004

Notes

1. British political scientist James Connelly in *British Journal of Canadian Studies*, Vol.4, 2003, p. 278.

INTRODUCTION

Political Drop-Outs and Electoral System Reform

Henry Milner

Canadians are entering a period of intense debate, and perhaps action in several provinces, on the question of changing to an electoral system based on a form of proportional representation (PR). Among the political institutions inherited from our British past — known as the Westminster model — is the system by which we elect people to office. This system, in which all the members of Parliament obtain their positions by virtue of having gained the highest number of votes in a district, is still referred to by a metaphor whose origins lie in the British passion for horse-racing: first-past-the-post (FPTP). Yet among the main Westminster countries only Canada retains FPTP for all its regional (provincial) as well as national elections.

Not for much longer, apparently. This debate began in earnest after the 1997 federal election, and *Making Every Vote Count* contributed to it. The discussion in that volume was largely theoretical, at least as far as Canada was concerned, and looked mainly to New Zealand, which had just reformed its electoral system, for concrete developments. Its main contribution was to describe, in language understandable to interested lay Canadian readers, the workings and effects of the different systems — should the day come when we would be ready to adopt one of them here.

Now that day has come. The chapters that follow here have been selected to address this new and decisive stage of the debate. The most important purpose of this book is the most straightforward: to assemble information on what is happening in the different regions of the country. Five provinces — BC, Québec, Prince Edward Island, Ontario, and New Brunswick — are moving more or less resolutely towards PR; chapters in Part III provide comprehensive, up-to-date reports on developments and prospects in the first four of these provinces while the mandate of the nine-member commission set up very recently — December 2003 — in New Brunswick to report by the end of 2004 is reproduced in Appendix I.

The New Brunswick Commission was instructed "to examine and make recommendations on implementing a proportional representation electoral system for the New Brunswick Legislative Assembly, and propose a specific model best suited for our province that ensures fairer representation, greater equality of votes, an effective legislature and government, and a continued role for directly-elected MLAs [members of the Legislative Assembly] representing specific geographic boundaries." Only one electoral system, what the New Zealanders call mixed-member plurality (MMP), which is based on principles developed in Germany, corresponds to this mandate. And that is neither an accident nor an exception. To the extent that they are considering electoral systems with outcomes approaching proportionality, provinces are turning their attention primarily, if not exclusively, to MMP. As I elaborate below, among proportional systems, only MMP, which retains the relationship between the voter and a single representative, has any realistic chance of being accepted by the people in a country like Canada that is used to FPTP. In the context of possible implementation, the discussion needs to transcend the abstract consideration of the theoretical merits of alternative electoral systems and focus on the practical merits of those potentially under consideration. Hence, when PR is presented as a practicable alternative to the status quo in the pages to follow, it is generally the MMP variant that is being evoked. There is no general discussion comparing workings, advantages, and disadvantages of the various electoral systems used in democratic countries. The reader seeking more detailed information is advised to consult *Making Every Vote Count* as well as the websites of the various organizations and agencies in Appendix II and the texts listed in the References at the end of this book.

One of those links is to the website of the Law Commission of Canada. There the reader will find the Commission's interpretation of its legislative purpose as "directing it to examine critically even the most fundamental principles of the Canadian legal system and to evaluate the performance of those institutions by which these principles are put into practice." In keeping with this mandate, and in light of the growing perception that a "democratic malaise" has begun to characterize the political landscape in Canada, the Commission undertook to analyze Canada's voting system. As this book was being completed, the Commission produced its report calling for the replacement of Canada's FPTP system by an MMP system. The report provides a useful complement to this book, especially in its historical account of the discussion of electoral reform in Canada. Also useful is its detailed exposition on the form of MMP seen as best suited for Canada, going so far as to set out suggested boundaries of the electoral regions from which the list MPs that constitute one-third of the total would be selected.

While advocates of change will disagree over the number of list MPs and the boundaries of the electoral regions, the Law Commission's position reflects the growing consensus over MMP for reasons noted above and set out below. And it sets the stage for the effort in this book to go beyond principles to practices, to the concrete implications of electoral system reform. Beginning with the Canadian federal scene in Part One, we proceed in Part Two to a number of countries with relevant recent experience. We catch up first on important recent events in New Zealand and the United Kingdom (Scotland in particular) in order to assess the consequences of applying different variants of the MMP model in a Westminster environment. We then go to four quite different non-Westminster countries — South Africa, Japan, France, and the United States — each selected for the particular light it casts on the discussion. South Africa adopted the pure list system for its non-racial elections in the 1990s; in discussing what has happened there under this system, Murray Faure and Albert Venter make the case for changing to MMP. Japan's experience with its partially proportional system, as recounted by Lawrence LeDuc, suggests that trying to mix opposing elements results in mixed outcomes. Rob Richie and Steven Hill explain the American electoral reform movement's failure to make a real dent into that country's electoral system, leaving in place its dismal consequences on the workings of American democracy.

In this introductory chapter I shall first briefly describe MMP and summarize the basic case for adopting a Canadian variant. I summarize rather than spell out, since the various elements of the discussion are taken up in detail in the chapters in Part I. Louis Massicotte, John Courtney, and Richard Katz assess the implications of bringing MMP to Canada from three perspectives, setting Canadian experience in comparative context. Katz is the most critical, followed by Courtney; Massicotte the most favourable. The attention given to MMP, even when critical, is further evidence that the real debate about electoral system reform in Canada is, more and more, about MMP. Of course, other formulas have been proposed; but these are hybrids or compromises intentionally falling quite far short of proportionality. Just how short, and what this would mean in terms of regional representation, emerges from the empirical simulations by Harold Jansen and Alan Siaroff.

The concluding and longest section of this introductory chapter focuses on the effects of the electoral system on voter turnout, an aspect which has grown in importance as evidence of turnout decline has piled up[1] (and on which my own comparative research has focused). This dimension is especially relevant to Canada, given the recent steady and sharp decline in voter turnout (from 75 to 61 per cent between the federal elections of 1988 and 2000), and adds a note of urgency to the call for institutional reforms to reduce the "democratic deficit." While the comparative evidence of a positive relationship between the proportionality of the electoral system and voter turnout is solid, it turns out to be a far more complex proposition to assess the degree to which adopting such a system will address the — generation-linked — causes of the current turnout decline.

A Brief Case for MMP in Canada

Under MMP the voter casts two votes — a party vote for the list of a party and a district vote for a constituency representative. After constituency winners are decided by plurality — just as under the FPTP system — its party vote determines the total number of seats to which each party is entitled. The constituency seats it has won are subtracted from its overall total in order to establish the number of MPs drawn from its lists. Constituency candidates can also be nominated to have their names placed on the lists, as is common in Germany, New Zealand, and Scotland. The overall result is proportional, though the extent to which the outcome diverges from perfect proportionality is affected by three factors. The first is the threshold used to discourage the proliferation of small parties: in New Zealand, for example, to qualify for list seats a party must either receive at least 5 per cent of all party votes or win at least one district seat. The second is the percentage of overall seats available for purposes of compensation. In Germany this is 50 per cent; in both New Zealand and Scotland it is about 42 per cent. New Zealand's outcomes are more proportional than Scotland's since the territory covered by the party lists is large (the entire country), while in Scotland each list covers a regional district with approximately one-eighth of the population. The result is an effective regional vote threshold that somewhat reduces overall proportionality.

As noted, if willing to consider a proportional electoral system, Canadian voters would likely choose MMP over the single-vote, list-based PR systems used in much of Europe because, as in New Zealand and the UK, they would insist on continuing to have a single MP represent them. I suspect also that Canadians would insist on a high real or effective threshold to limit the number of parties winning seats to, typically, four to six and that they would also insist that the electoral law specify, as it does in Germany, that placing on the list is determined by party members (or their elected delegates) and not by party officials. Canadians might wish to add an element of "openness" to the lists, so that, as in Sweden for example, a popular candidate low on the party's regional list is moved to the top if he or she receives the "personal vote" of more than 8 per cent of the party's supporters in the region. These aspects, and other more technical ones, such as the actual mathematical method for allocating seats,[2] can be "made to measure" depending on local circumstances. Hence, MMP can work for electing members of parliament and of legislatures in provinces large and small, though the specifics of the two systems would differ in many respects.

If MMP is the appropriate "fix" for Canada's electoral system, we must first determine if the current one is broken. In *Making Every Vote Count* and many other documents published before and since, the system's failings have been spelled out both generally and particularly in Canada, which is becoming a political science textbook case of the kind of distortions that can occur under FPTP. Here are some of the more blatant recent manifestations of these kinds of distortions:

- *One-party dominance.* While the Liberals averaged around 40 per cent of the overall vote in the 1993, 1997, and 2000 federal elections, no other party could win nearly enough seats to form any kind of effective opposition or government in waiting.
- *Decimation of parties.* In 1993, the voters repudiated the ruling Progressive Conservatives, but in the process the electoral system decimated what had been Canada's oldest party. Rather than the 46 MPs that a system in which parties elected a number of legislators proportional to their support (PR) would have given them, the PCs managed to seat only two.
- *Regionalization of parties.* In 1997, two-thirds of all the Liberal MPs were elected from Ontario, where the Liberals won only 48.5 per cent of the vote but 101 of 103 seats. This left almost none for Reform, although Reform received many more votes in Ontario than it did in Alberta where it won 92 per cent of the seats with 55 per cent of the votes.
- *Feeble opposition.* Recent elections in PEI and BC (see chapters 14 and 11 by John Andrew Cousins and Norman J. Ruff, respectively) ended up kicking the party in power not just out of the government, as the voters wanted, but — effectively — out of the legislature.
- *Loser wins.* In the Québec election in 1998, with their support concentrated in non-francophone ridings, the provincial Liberals garnered the

most votes (43.6 to the Parti Québécois' 42.9 per cent) but elected only
48 MNAs compared to the PQ's 76 (see Chapter 13, by Brian Doody
and Henry Milner).

- *Hyperpolarization.* In that same election, no room was left for parties
  representing the middle group of Quebeckers who prefer a compromise short of sovereignty and do not define themselves politically
  along the federalist-sovereignist fault line. The Action démocratique,
  which takes such a position, was effectively marginalized, averaging
  two seats (of 125) in the last three elections despite being supported
  by about one-sixth of Quebeckers. At the same time, in Ontario (see
  Chapter 12 by Dennis Pilon) successive elections produced majority
  governments ideologically more extreme than the majority of Ontario
  voters — first, Bob Rae's New Democratic Party (NDP) on the left,
  then Mike Harris's PCs on the right — though neither won anywhere
  near the support of 50 per cent of the voters.

Harris's conservative policies were reminiscent of those of New Zealand's
National (conservative) Party between 1990 and 1993. As recounted by Jack
Nagel in Chapter 5, New Zealanders came to understand that electoral institutions needed to be changed if they wished to avoid narrow, ideology-driven
agendas imposed by a governing party with a majority of seats but a minority
of votes. A New Zealand Royal Commission proposed, and the people
in 1992 and 1993 referenda ratified, MMP. Like any form of proportional
representation, MMP makes single-party majority government effectively a
thing of the past. Nagel shows how New Zealanders, severely disappointed
by the first MMP-produced coalition, became more comfortable with the
second and now third one. After New Zealand, MMP came to the UK, most
importantly to the new Scottish Assembly (see Chapter 6 by Peter Lynch)
as well as the Welsh Assembly and Greater London Council. And there are
even rumours that the long-stalled negotiations between Tony Blair's ruling
Labour party and the Liberal Democrats for changing the system for electing
members to Westminster are to recommence in 2004.[3] Given Scotland's status
as a regional government operating within wider Westminster institutions, it
comes as no surprise that the Canadian provinces looking at electoral system
reform are showing special interest in the "Scottish Model."

Since Australia has long had a type of PR system for electing its federal and
state upper chambers (as well as the single chamber of the state of Tasmania),
Canada remains the only significant Westminster country with elections
limited to FPTP. While this is likely to soon change in more than one prov-

ince, our federal legislature, where change is needed most, has been slowest to act. Despite urging from prestigious bodies like the Law Commission of Canada and new Prime Minister Paul Martin's commitment to reducing the democratic deficit, the ruling Liberals refuse to consider changing a system from which they benefit greatly to one in which they would probably have to share power. If pressed, they stress the risk of instability that results from minority government.

However, these days a minority government would have little fear of being defeated in Parliament since the other parties (the new Conservative Party, the NDP, and the Bloc Québécois) have so little in common. Of course, it would have to work harder, its majority not always guaranteed in advance. Indeed, the Liberals' own experience suggests that Canada can do worse than being governed by a minority government. Of the nine federal elections that took place between 1957 and 1979, six resulted in minority governments. The Canadian Press, on May 30, 1997, quoted from the memoirs of Pierre Trudeau (who was a minister in one minority government, led another, and headed the Opposition in a third): "They were exciting times, akin to canoeing through seething rapids. A leader learned how to live dangerously, how to savour the pleasures of running risks and overcoming perils.... If you can't do that when you are in a minority government, you shouldn't be in politics." And there is a distinct possibility that a minority government may emerge after the federal election expected in 2004 in light of the scandal evoked by the auditor general's revelations early that year of the diversion of $100 million to Liberal-friendly public relation firms. This possibility, especially given the position of the NDP in support of some form of PR (see Chapter 15 by Larry Gordon), could bring voting system reform to the federal political agenda earlier than anyone might expect.

Beyond its effect on party politics, a change toward PR will increase the chances of women and members of visible minorities being elected to the government. Although the magnitude of the effect will vary depending on particular circumstances difficult to know in advance, there will be some effect due to the simple fact that PR systems use lists from which — unlike winnable single-member districts — it is hard to exclude women or identifiable minorities. To go further toward achieving gender equity, under MMP Canada could impose quotas on the lists, as is done in France. Karen Bird, in Chapter 9, weighs the circumstances under which such a measure can prove beneficial. The quotas turn out to be really effective, she finds, only at the French municipal level where lists are used in a quasi-PR system.

Until recently, the advantages of more equitable representation by women and ethnic minorities, as well as of supporters of different parties — incontestably an advantage of PR systems — were set against what have been seen to be the disadvantages accruing from the absence of single-party majority governments. As Massicotte argues in Chapter 2, there is mounting evidence that such adverse effects are exaggerated. Meanwhile, a new concern has taken centre stage in the analysis of political institutions — namely, what has increasingly come to be known as the democratic deficit. Observers point to the apparently negative effect of existing institutions on voting and other forms of citizen participation, especially on at-risk groups defined by ethnicity, class, gender, and, most of all, age. This is the issue we will now explore.

Will PR Shelter Us from Declining Voter Turnout?

The great advantage of PR systems is that they bring more sectors of the community under the umbrella of democratic institutions by facilitating entry of their representatives into the legislature, thus enhancing their role in the governing process. This applies both to groups linked by ascribed characteristics such as gender and to those united by program objectives, such as environmentalists. This greater representativeness, moreover, begins to explain the well-documented fact of higher average voter turnout in countries using list and MMP systems of PR.[4] The overall logic is clear: votes count. Under PR, citizens are more likely to be able to find parties that stand for policies and principles that they — or the groups with which they identify — support, a support they can expect to be translated into legislative representation.[5] This is obvious with regard to minor parties but applies also to mainstream parties whose supporters can, under FPTP, find themselves living in constituencies in which their vote is certain to be wasted since their party has no chance of winning the seat, an extremely common occurrence in congressional districts in the United States.

The incentives different electoral systems place on citizens to exercise their franchise is but the tip of the iceberg of the relationship between electoral institutions and voter turnout. Since voters under PR or in competitive FPTP districts know that the chance that the outcome would have been different had they not voted is minuscule, the direct turnout effect of the voter's no longer being in an uncompetitive district under PR is limited. More important is the indirect effect that results from the incentives different electoral systems place on the strategy adopted by political actors. By making all votes count, PR places fundamentally different incentives on political parties and candidates than FPTP, the effects of which are crucial. Parties under PR seek to mobilize support everywhere, rather than concentrate resources on marginal districts as under FPTP. And fundamental to mobilization, especially when the electoral rules encourage this, as they tend to do in PR countries (Bowler, Carter, and Farrell 2000), is the task of informing potential voters.

Yet there are more, and more complex, incentive effects built into different electoral systems. Under FPTP, parties know that the choices of a relatively small number of voters can make the difference between monopolizing political power and having none whatsoever. With politics as a zero-sum game, distorting the opponent's position (through appeals to emotion, negative advertising and the like), while keeping one's own policies vague, tends to pay off (Amy 2002). This is not the case with PR where cooperation among parties is necessary and commonplace. All aspects of party strategy are affected, often with a real, if imperceptible, effect on voter participation.

Consider, for example, the relationship between the incentives on party strategy built into FPTP and the dramatic decline in democratic participation in the UK (18 per cent fewer citizens voted in 2001 than in 1992). To defeat Margaret Thatcher's Conservative government policies, Tony Blair pushed Labour firmly to the centre throughout the 1990s, thus creating "New Labour." Yet the powerful Conservative majority was in fact an artefact of the electoral system, highly vulnerable to defeat by a Labour-Liberal Democratic coalition, had the elections been fought under PR and not FPTP. A Liberal-Labour government would have earlier enacted centre-left policies similar to those of New Labour. However, there is a profound difference between Blairite policies that may have emerged as a compromise program of government between parties of the centre and left rather than from a party transformed almost beyond recognition. In the former case, normal under PR, a formal or informal coalition government implements a compromise program reflecting the expressed choices of a majority of voters, but constituent parties retain programs reflecting the evolving expectations of party supporters. Supporters need not, as under FPTP, renounce principles at the core of their attachment to the party, a renunciation that stokes increased cynicism toward politics and that, in due course, discourages voters.

Even more important in the long term than the effect on attitudes, I contend, is the far less well-known effect on knowledge — in other words, how the interplay of these and other incentives affects the political knowledge of citizens. Transforming Labour into New Labour alters the political map, changing the settings on the citizen's political compass. Especially in the context of an FPTP environment in which parties concentrate mobilization efforts — including providing information — on voters in marginal districts, for the citizen with limited knowledge this can mean no longer being able to make the basic distinctions necessary for meaningful choice. (In surveys, this is typically expressed as the assertion that "all politicians are the same.") In my current work (Milner 2002), I argue that the crucial missing link between PR and higher turnout is political knowledge. Based on various indirect measures from secondary sources in advanced democratic countries, my research shows that countries with PR-based political institutions consistently show a greater proportion of politically informed citizens — what I term a higher level of civic literacy. And, of course, politically informed citizens are more likely to vote.[6]

The data are far from ideal since there is, as yet, no single general set of political knowledge questions used in international surveys. Nevertheless, it is possible to derive insights from the responses to the political knowledge questions in recent national election surveys in democratic countries. These surveys, coordinated by the Comparative Study of Electoral Systems (CSES), include at least three knowledge questions about political institutions and actors.[7] A useful recent compilation is provided by Grönlund (2003) who combines the results for 19 CSES countries without compulsory voting[8] to test the relationship between political knowledge, voting and non-voting, and the electoral system. The data confirm the importance of political knowledge when it comes to turnout: respondents with low education levels but a high level of political information reported turning out at 83 per cent, more than 5 per cent above the overall average.[9]

Grönlund asks if the electoral system has something to do with this. He compares the 32,000 respondents from the 12 countries with PR electoral systems with the 17,000 in the seven countries with FPTP and other non-proportional (majoritarian) systems. As expected, reported turnout proved higher among respondents in countries with proportional systems (79.7 per cent) than with majoritarian systems (77.2 per cent), though the difference was lower than in the official electoral data in those countries (72 per cent in the proportional countries and 65 per cent in the majoritarian ones). Though the CSES data cannot be applied to nation-to-nation comparisons of political knowledge since political knowledge questions differ, there is no reason to believe the questions are harder or easier on average in the proportional or non-proportional countries. Hence Grönlund's finding that political knowledge is less dependent on formal education in PR countries is very suggestive (the correlation between years of education and political knowledge is significantly higher in the non-PR countries — .32 — than in PR ones — .24).

The finding that people with low educational resources are more informed under PR goes against conventional thinking but confirms my argument. FPTP defenders claim voting under that system is a simpler proposition since FPTP typically delivers a choice between keeping the incumbents in and kicking them out. This views voters as living outside time and space. In reality, it is PR systems that enhance the political knowledge of those with marginal educational resources because such systems provide them with a political map that is relatively clearly drawn and stable across time and space on which to plot their political paths. Since parties under PR are not subject to the volatility of FPTP, which blows up their strength when they do well and shrivels it when they do poorly, there is a relative stability to the features of the political map. Furthermore, under FPTP, which turns setbacks into routs, parties are discouraged from risking operating at levels — national, regional, and local — other than the one at which they are best organized. PR electoral systems thus play an important direct and indirect role in enhancing the cohesion, stability, and consistency of political parties. They make it easier for the potential voter to identify with a political party and to use that identification as a guide through the complexities of issues and actors at various levels of political activity, both over time and over space, that is, from the local up to the regional, national, and intergovernmental. By thus simplifying a complex political reality and enhancing partisanship, PR fosters political participation especially at the lower end of the education and income ladders where information is at a premium.

Political Knowledge and the Generational Factor

There is no mystery, then, to the higher overall levels of voter turnout under PR. But does this guarantee that adoption of MMP in a low turnout country like Canada will stem the decline we have witnessed? That is a more difficult question. International data is not a sure guide. FPTP UK and Canada were the mature democracies that suffered the greatest degree of turnout decline in the 1990s, but some PR countries like Finland also experienced a real decline.[10] In an effort to control for such differences, Andreas Ladner and I examined data from Switzerland, the only country without compulsory elections using a variety of electoral systems in local elections. We found that PR municipalities had higher turnout than non-PR ones, but that PR provided no shelter against the turnout decline experienced at all levels in Swiss elections in the 1990s (Ladner and Milner 1999). Jack Nagel's analysis in his chapter on New Zealand (Chapter 5) is also revealing. The effect of PR can be described as a spike, pushing turnout in 1996 upward to the level from which the decline that had begun in the 1980s resumed in 1999. The results recounted in Peter Lynch's analysis of Scotland in Chapter 6 are no more encouraging, suggesting that PR could not shelter voting for the Scottish Assembly from the negative effects of plummeting participation in Westminster elections.

Hence, it is not enough to show higher turnout under PR: to appreciate if and how changing our electoral system could affect voter turnout we need first to understand why it has been plummeting. We know that fewer people are voting today than in previous decades in almost all the advanced democracies; and we are learning that this is largely an age — or, rather, generational — factor. Not long ago, the International Institute for Democracy and Electoral Assistance (IDEA) published a report analyzing the political activity of young people in 15 western European countries (1999). While young people have, on balance, historically voted less than their elders, by the early 1990s the gap between average turnout for citizens 18 to 29 and those over 30 had grown to 12 per cent. In virtually all countries, though some clearly more than others,[11] somewhere in the latter 1980s significantly fewer young people were arriving at voting age ready to exercise the franchise.

In Canada, a detailed study carried out for Elections Canada revealed that only 26 per cent of those 18 to 24 turned out to vote in the 2000 federal election (Pammett and LeDuc 2003). The Canadian Election Study has been following the four most recent cohorts in its latest surveys. It finds a life-cycle effect amounting to an increase of about 15 points between the ages of 20 and 50,[12] but generation is replacing life-cycle as the key element in the absence of young people among voters. "At the same age, turnout is 3 or 4 points lower among baby boomers than it was among pre-baby boomers, 10 points lower among generation X than it was among baby boomers, and another 10 points lower among the most recent generation than it was among generation X at the same age. This translates into a total generational effect of over 20 points" (Blais *et al.* 2002: 48). While the generation Xers consistently vote less than the two older groups, the post-Xers not only vote less than all others, but have actually been increasing in the proportion of abstainers over the past few elections.

We are in fact witnessing the manifestation of two phenomena: the decline in young people's sense of a civic duty to vote[13] and the decline in their political knowledge. The two are closely related: a decline in the sense of civic duty means that young people are less inclined to seek the information needed to vote meaningfully. Since we do not know how to boost civic duty, we must concentrate our efforts on the political knowledge side of the equation. What do we know about the relationship of age to declining political knowledge? While not always the case, there is nothing new in the fact that young people, though somewhat more educated than their elders, know less about politics. Other things being equal, young people have less experience and fewer responsibilities, hence less reason to inform themselves. But the numbers are worrisome, especially at the lower educational levels. Grönlund's CSES data confirms that at all levels of education, 18- to 35-year-olds are less knowledgeable in political matters.[14]

This phenomenon has been explored in depth in the United States[15] where the differences in age groups' attentiveness to news is well documented. The Pew Research Center Biennial News Use Survey (of 4,002 adults and taken in spring 1998) revealed that only 33 per cent of Americans aged 18 to 29 made an effort to keep up with the news compared to 68 per cent of seniors (Bennett 1998). In the United States, at least, this appears to be almost entirely a generational phenomenon. The Times Mirror Center (1990) analyzed survey results from the 1940s through the 1970s revealing that previous generations of young people knew as much as, if not more than, their elders.[16]

There has been a comparable decline in the level of political knowledge among young Canadians in the last 15 years. In a 1990 survey carried out for the Royal Commission on Electoral Reform and Party Financing (1991), 56 per cent of 18- to 29- year-olds were able to answer at most one of three political knowledge questions correctly (Who is the PM? Who is the Liberal leader? Who is the NDP leader?) For the survey sample as a whole, the figure was 40 per cent. By 2000, as reported by Paul Howe, the younger group was lagging further still: when asked to identify the prime minister, finance minister, and official opposition party, fully 67 per cent of 18- to 29-year-olds scored no more than one out of three compared to 46 per cent for the sample as a whole (Howe 2001). In a later paper, Howe (2002b) penetrated more deeply into this phenomenon. He compared data from 1956 Gallup polls testing political knowledge with those from the political knowledge items in the 2000 Canadian Election Study.[17] Age differences turn out to be important in both periods, but significantly more so in 2000. Most affected are those with no more than a high school education, among whom those under age 30 are 30 percentile points less politically knowledgeable than the same group aged 50 plus. "Not only are the young less informed about politics today than they were forty-five years ago," Howe concludes, "they are also more likely to allow this condition to influence at least one important element of political behaviour, the decision to vote or not to vote" (Howe 2002b). In 1956, the difference in reported turnout level between the groups at the lower and upper ends of the knowledge scale was 17 percentage points; moreover, for the youngest age group (21 to 29 years), the figure was actually lower — only 12 points separated the groups. In the 2000 election study, the overall gap in turnout between the knowledgeable and ignorant had risen to 32 points; moreover, a significant transformation had taken place. "A 43 point gap separates the least and most knowledgeable respondents in both the 18 to 20 and 21 to 29 age groups. With increasing age, this relationship weakens, to the point that among those 50 and older, only thirteen points separate the two groups" (Howe 2002a).

Can Electoral System Reform Bring Back the Political Drop-Outs?

Where does the electoral system fit into the fact that young people vote less and know less of politics than earlier generations? In examining the factors accounting for differences in turnout level for voters between 18 and 29 years old in 15 western European countries, the International IDEA (1999) report cited earlier suggested that the most significant factor was whether the electoral system facilitated access to representation in parliament for small parties. In countries using such PR systems, IDEA estimated the youth turnout rate to be almost 12 percentage points higher than elsewhere. Political knowledge, as argued above, has something to do with this relationship, if we are to go by the results of a comparative test of young people. In 2003, the National Geographic-Roper Global Geographic Literacy Survey assessed 3,250 young adults in nine countries on their awareness of geographical aspects of current events. Out of 56 questions that were asked across the countries surveyed, young Americans on average answered 23 questions correctly, with young people in Canada (with 27) and the UK (28) — the other two FPTP countries in the survey — faring almost as poorly. The two PR, high-turnout countries, Sweden (with 40) and Germany (38), led, followed by the countries with more mixed systems, Italy (38), France (34), and Japan (31).[18]

These comparative differences in political knowledge under PR and FPTP help explain the significant turnout variation under the two systems, but they also oblige us to be modest in expecting positive turnout effects from adopting PR. Electoral system effects on political knowledge can only occur gradually and through consistent experience of the system over time and space. This is the case in continental Europe, but in New Zealand, PR has only made it in fits and starts to local elections,[19] while Scotland, which operates in the context of Westminster's FPTP environment, is only now moving to introduce the single transferable vote (STV) system for local elections (see Chapter 6). Thus, it is unrealistic to expect the adoption of MMP in a given Canadian province to have the political knowledge effects needed to perceptibly boost turnout. To be more specific about what we can expect, we need to understand the reasons underlying the development that has caused Canada's dramatic decline in voting, namely, young people dropping out politically.

A useful way to characterize youth non-voting is as a manifestation of four related phenomena, only two of which are susceptible to the direct influence of the electoral system. First, there is a group of knowledgeable young people who feel unrepresented by the parties that can win seats under FPTP but who can be expected to vote under PR since the parties they support — most often Green or anti-globalization, but also libertarian — have a real chance of winning representation. This is the group the IDEA data pointed to, and its existence helps explain the turnout "spike" in New Zealand's first MMP election in 1996 (Karp and Banducci 1998). If Canada were to adopt a form of PR, it is fair to say that a certain number of these young non-voters would be drawn to the ballot box, though, given their educational and political knowledge levels, their abstention appears to be mainly a life-cycle phenomenon and most will vote in any case when their political views moderate with age. Moreover, their numbers appear not to be large enough to perceptibly boost overall turnout levels. Young Canadians are at least as "mainstream" in their political attitudes as their elders.[20] In their study for Elections Canada, when they asked abstainers why they failed to vote in the 2000 election, Pammett and LeDuc (2003: 17) found respondents 18 to 24 had the lowest tendency (27.3 per cent versus 34.4 per cent overall) to cite a failing in the political process as a reason.

There is an indeterminate second group whose abstention is the consequence of arriving at voting age at a time when there has been effectively only one national political party. The group is small, if we are to judge by the 6.5 per cent of respondents 18 to 24 who gave the absence of a contest as reason for non-voting, compared to 9 per cent of all abstainers (Pammett and LeDuc 2003: 17). Nevertheless, some of the young abstainers who gave as a reason general lack of interest in politics (28 versus 25 per cent of abstainers overall) might have had their attention drawn, and thus made interested enough to vote, if the election were a real contest. Given the importance of habits developed when young (see below), more competitive elections — which PR elections would bring — could have a marginal but long-term effect of developing the habit of voting among a greater proportion of young people.

This brings us to the two other factors underlying the phenomenon of political drop-outs, factors impervious to a change of electoral system. Rather than political, these are socio-economic and socio-cultural in origin. There is no shortage of data to show that political knowledge and political participation is lower among those lacking basic economic resources. For example, a recent American study found the voting rate of persons below the poverty line to be 25 per cent, compared to 65 per cent for those above it (Leighley and Nagler 2000:1). And the difference, once we exclude temporarily poor students, is greater among the young. Howe's data shows it is among young, relatively poorly educated Canadian males that voting has most dropped off since the 1950s (Howe 2002a). A similar phenomenon has been identified in high civic-literacy Finland — where youth unemployment rates spiked to 25 percent during the economic crisis of the early 1990s — to account for its sharp decline in turnout in legislative elections, from 77.3 percent in 1987 to 65.2 in 1999[21] The turnout gap between those 19 to 24 years of age and the overall average rose to 17 percentage points in 1999 (Martikainen 2000).

If wide-scale abstention is becoming the norm among poorly educated young men, it raises the question of whether the traditional pattern of "life experiences … dampening the biases in patterns of political participation attributable to socioeconomic status" (Strate *et al.* 1989: 456) still holds. During the high mobilization period in the United States in the 1960s and 1970s, political participation increased only marginally for the best educated, but significantly (from 20 to over 50 per cent) among the least educated Americans (Wolfinger and Rosenstone 1980). The evidence is that this was temporary, that sociological change has transformed non-voting among young, poorly educated males from a life-cycle to a generational phenomenon. To put it simply, they increasingly fail to act as political citizens because they feel excluded from social citizenship. They lack what their counterparts in the 1950s and 1960s had, namely, the economic and educational resources to regard themselves as potential full citizens, able to contribute to family and community. Hence, to enhance the possibility of potential political drop-outs becoming political citizens instead, society must address the factors that deny them social citizenship — a tall order well beyond the reform of electoral institutions and the concerns of this book.[22]

Thus, we arrive at the final and most elusive aspect of the phenomenon, namely, what we might term a generational culture. Increasingly, though in some places more than others, it is becoming normal, and accepted as such, for people to be "tuned out" to everything connected to politics. This apolitical youth culture is the product of a spillover from the three phenomena described above combined with the subtle but powerful effects of the new electronic information technology. If politics is boring, uninteresting, uncool, irrelevant, and not "where it's at," then political inattention and ignorance is not a reflection of any failing on the part of the young citizen. If it is anyone's fault, it is that of the politicians for making their world less exciting than those of (other) celebrities, those whose worlds can be entered at the push of a button on a TV remote controller, computer mouse, or playstation joystick. Gauging the pervasiveness of this culture is an immensely complex enterprise well beyond our capacity here, but, clearly, changing the electoral system will not transform it from apolitical to political.

Overall, therefore, Canada's adoption of MMP cannot be expected to markedly augment the vote of the 18- to 24-year-olds, and, thereby, noticeably boost overall turnout. As noted, there should be a positive but marginal effect: a small but nevertheless meaningful number of young people who would otherwise not do so may be expected to develop the habit of voting if the first elections in which they can vote were held under PR. Yet we need not leave it quite at that, since electoral reform need not take place in a vacuum. The small dent that adopting PR should make in the democratic deficit could be enlarged if another reform were introduced along with it.

Getting to the 16- and 17-year-olds

The reform proposed to address the democratic deficit is to reduce the age of eligibility to vote from 18 to 16, an idea endorsed by Canada's chief electoral officer, Jean-Pierre Kingsley, who told members of Parliament in late March 2004 that decreasing the voting age to 16 could help stop further declines in participation rates among young voters. The idea seems more than dubious on the face of it: if young people don't vote at 18, why should they vote at 16?

In itself, the vote at 16 won't meaningfully help turnout. But combined with a new approach to civic education and PR elections, it just might. Current comparative research reveals that paying attention to the political world, and thus being sufficiently informed to vote when an election is called, is in good part a matter of habit. If, in the first few years that one is first eligible to vote, one is preoccupied with things to the extent of fully excluding any attention to politics and public affairs, not only is abstention almost certain, but the habit of non-voting is more likely to be established. As Franklin, following Plutzer (2002), puts it: "voting is costly and the costs of learning to vote are considerably raised if a person's first election falls during the period immediately after leaving high school [since] the four years that follow are fraught with the problems of early adulthood ... years in which young adults are only starting to establish the social networks that will ultimately serve to guide their political choice and motivate their vote" (Franklin 2003: 8). Franklin's argument is based on evidence of the secular decline in turnout after the minimum age was reduced, typically to 18, in different countries. His explanation is that those aged 18 to 20 are typically in a period of transition, in the process of withdrawing from their home and traditional school environment without fully settling into another. Most become voters later in life, but some do not, and, he argues, some of these would have done so had their first opportunity to vote been later, when they were in a better position to develop the habit. This same logic applies today, but in the reverse direction, to 16- and 17-year-olds, mainly because parents can more easily set an example for 16-year-olds than for 18-year-olds.

Would reducing the age of eligibility to 16 get more young Canadians to the polls? Increased parental influence should have some effect, but that effect often needs to be stimulated and reinforced in the schools. The far from simple[23] question is how. It is a matter of taking advantage of the fact that, if the voting age is lowered, many potential political drop-outs will still be in school at the moment of their first chance to vote. Not all civics courses are the same. For example, American courses increasingly stress volunteering, which seems to have no effect on attentiveness to politics and, thus, the decision to vote.[24] Timing appears to be crucial as well. There is little in the literature to suggest that civics courses given during adolescence have an appreciable lasting effect.[25] The exception appears to be civics courses given at the end of the period of secondary education. An interesting case in point here is Sweden where the IDEA study on Youth Voter Participation (IDEA 1999) found a low turnout level gap between 18- to 29-year-olds and all others of only 4.3 per cent. In Sweden civics courses are taken at or near the age of 18 when young people are in a position to soon put the information into concrete application as new voters.[26] Compared to Canada, however, Swedish secondary students are older and drop-outs are few,[27] so that, given in the last year of school, the civics courses address a significantly larger fraction of the cohort than would be the case in Canada and most other countries, where, by age 17 and 18, those most at risk of dropping out of school have already done so.

To have civics courses reach a comparable group in Canada, we would thus need to offer them at ages 15 and 16. Moreover, for the courses to, potentially, have a similar effect, we would simultaneously need to lower the voting age to 16. In designing the courses, we could also learn something from the Swedish approach, in which the courses give an important place to the positions taken by the different parties on relevant issues, at the local, regional and national level, and regularly invite the parties' representatives into the classroom,[28] especially in the period leading up to an election or referendum. This is a more natural option in a PR environment in which each party has a relatively stable political presence at each level. Moreover, the partisanship fostered in such an environment, compared to the volatility under FPTP, has a positive effect since parental partisanship is known to be a key factor boosting the political participation of young people (Plutzer 2002). In sum, the fit between targeting 16- and 17-year-olds still in school and adopting PR is a natural one.

The underlying logic is to seek to establish among young people a "habit of citizenship" as they arrive at the age of voting. Such courses could profit from the experience of the "Kidsvoting" program set up during the 2003 provincial election in Ontario, which brought candidates to the schools and the issues to the classrooms. The program allowed Ontario students in grades nine to 12 to vote in their schools using ballots supplied by Elections Ontario just like those being cast by their parents in polling booths. About three-quarters of Ontario public high schools participated, and, in all, over 43 per cent of Ontario high school students cast a ballot. The ballots were collected and tabulated, and the results were presented next to the adult vote on CBC television. Table 0-1 below reproduces the results from www.kidsvotingcanada.com.

Table 0-1
Ontario Election Results October 2, 2003 (809 schools reporting)

Party	# Seats Elected	Popular Vote Count	Popular Vote Per cent
PC		56,259	18.031
Liberal	93	141,022	45.198
NDP	9	67,473	21.625
Green	1	33,314	10.677
Other		12,928	4.469
Totals	103	312,008	100.000

From all reports, the students generally took the exercise seriously and used it to inform themselves, with civics or history classes often taking the lead in engaging the student body during the campaign. The relatively strong showing of the Greens and NDP, and the weakness of the PCs, seems to well reflect the preoccupations of young people cast in partisan terms.

There are plans to extend the kidsvoting program to the entire country in the 2004 federal election, which, if nothing else, will advance the debate over measures to enhance youth participation, including allowing 16-year-olds to vote. And if that election results in a minority government dependent on NDP support, the institutional reform that this book examines, adopting a PR system of elections, could make its way to the federal political agenda. Though by no means a panacea for the decline in voter turnout in Canada, the application of a strategy targeting 16- and 17-year-olds with a civic education program focused on bringing the issues to their classrooms and giving them — and the rest of us — the chance to vote under a new electoral system in which those parties and their supporters can expect to be represented fairly would undoubtedly make a difference.

There is, of course, much more to changing an electoral system than getting young people — or, indeed, older people — to vote, and it is time to turn to these matters in the following chapters.

Notes

1. An analysis of turnout in 20 countries found an average decline of 5 per cent, from 83 per cent in the 1950s to 78 per cent in the 1990s (Dalton 1996: 44-45; see also Franklin 2002 and Wattenberg 1998).

2. There are two quota methods used: Hare, which sets the quota at V (votes) divided by S (seats) and Droop (V divided by S+1). There are also two divisor methods: D'Hondt, successively dividing the votes of each party by 1,2,3 …, and Saint-Lague (divisor is 1,3,5….).

3. Reported by Marie Woolfe, in *The Independent*, 23 December 2003.

4. See, e.g., Lijphart, 1999; also Milner 2002, chapters 5 and 6. In Chapter 4 of this book, John Courtney shows that Canada's historical experience with STV does not confirm expectations that PR boosts turnout. At least in part, I contend, this is due to the nature of STV, which in important ways operates differently from other forms of PR. This is why I do not favour the STV alternative supported by some proponents of electoral system change in Canada.

5. On the effect of this factor on turnout in New Zealand's first MMP election in 1996, see Karp and Banducci 1998.

6. One example among many: a study of 1,500 respondents by the *Washington Post*, Kaiser Foundation and Harvard University in late 1995 found "those in the highest third of the survey in terms of political knowledge were twice as likely to have voted in the 1994 presidential election as those in the lowest third" (Morin 1996:7; see also Popkin and Dimock 1999, and Junn 1995).

7. Each CSES (Comparative Study of Electoral Systems group, based at the University of Michigan) team independently determines the content of their three political knowledge questions, making an effort that their content be such that they could be answered correctly, respectively, by roughly two-thirds, one-third, and one-half of respondents.

8. Compulsory voting boosts turnout (by 11 per cent; Franklin 2003:28), but it also reduces the incentive on parties to "get out the vote." One analysis, which compared the turnout in Australian states and in the Commonwealth in the election before and after the introduction of compulsory voting, found an increase averaging 23 per

cent, varying from a low of 12.4 per cent to a high of 37.8 per cent (McAllister and Mackerras 1998: 2).

9. There are similar findings for Canada. We know, from an analysis of the 1997 Canadian Election Survey data, that the more politically knowledgeable were 9 per cent more likely to have voted, a percentage higher than all the other 19 tested variables, including level of education and political interest, except age (Coulson 1999).

10. Indeed, the four Nordic countries, which share key aspects of culture and institutions, differ significantly. Denmark most closely maintains the traditional Nordic model of participation; Norway has seen a serious, largely generational, decline but has apparently replaced it to a significant degree with non-mainstream forms of participation; Finland and Sweden seem to have both followed the general trend of secular decline, except that Sweden is among the slower paced (Goul Andersen and Hoff 2001: 32), and Finland joins the UK and Canada among those where the decline has been most rapid. According to IDEA (1999), turnout based on potential voters went down 12 per cent in Finnish parliamentary elections between 1987 and 1999.

11. According to the American national election survey, turnout among those aged 18 to 24 went down from 50 per cent in the 1972 presidential election to about 32 per cent in 1996, while overall turnout fell by only 6 per cent. Non-voting in Finnish parliamentary elections has increased most markedly among the young: the turnout gap between those 19 to 24 years of age and the overall average rose to 17 percentage points in 1999 (Martikainen 2000). For Norway, Bjorklund (2000) finds particular effects of age upon turnout in local elections, the level at which there has been a significant and worrisome decline. In 1999, only 31 per cent of those born after 1975 voted, a number rising steadily by age cohort to 72 per cent for those born between 1930 and 1945. Similar figures are reported by the British election survey for verified voter turnout. In 1997, turnout among those 18 to 24 was more than 25 per cent lower than for those over 25 (Campbell 2002). As for Spanish non-voters, Anduiza found them to be significantly younger than voters: "They have paid less attention to the campaign and they have talked little about politics during the campaign" (Anduiza, 2002: 9).

12. "The propensity to vote increases by 7 or 8 points from age 20 to age 30, by 4 to 6 points from age 30 to age 40, and by 2 or 3 points from age 40 to age 50. From age 50 to age 70, the propensity to vote remains stable, but then starts to decline from age 70" (Blais *et al.* 2002: 48).

13. This is a phenomenon to be found in otherwise disparate countries like the United States and Norway. In a survey of 1,500 Americans between the ages of 15 and 25 commissioned by the Council for Excellence in Government's Center for Democracy and Citizenship and the Partnership for Trust in Government, in cooperation with the Center for Information and Research on Civic Learning and Engagement (CIRCLE) in fall 2001 (after September 11 when patriotic feelings were at a maximum), 49 per cent said voting is of little or no importance to them. Twenty per cent described it as a responsibility, and only 9 per cent as a duty (http://www.civicyouth.org/research/products/national_youth_survey.htm). Looking at Norway, Bjorklund stresses a change in attitudes toward voting. He signals a "dwindling support for voting as a form of civic virtue.... The difference between cohorts is pronounced. It is the youngest cohort that most often sticks to the [voting as] self-interest alternative" (Bjorklund 2000: 19).

14. Holding education constant, Grönlund finds that for those with less than completed secondary education, the average score on the three or more CSES political

knowledge questions was .40 for the 18- to 35-year-olds, compared to just under .50 for the 34- to 55-year-olds, and .53 for those 55 and over. For those with secondary or vocational school completed, the disparity is essentially the same, with the youngest groups' score rising to .53. Only when we get to those who completed university is the disparity reduced by roughly half, with the youngest group averaging .65 right answers (Grönlund 2003). This is confirmed by numerous recent national studies. For example, Chiche and Haegel (2002: 280) show that 18- to 29-year-old French men and women are over 10 per cent less politically knowledgeable than those above 30, while Rose (2003: 6) found that when it came to local political actors, institutions, and policies in Denmark and Norway that "older people, in short, display higher levels of political knowledge, regardless of their educational attainment."

15. Looking at the results of one Pew survey, Parker and Deane (1997) note that 26 per cent of young people were able to answer campaign-related questions correctly, compared to 38 per cent of those 30 to 49 and 42 per cent of those 50 and over, while on national politics, the average per cent correct were, respectively, 32, 44 and 48.

16. A study of first-year college students (reported in the *New York Times*, 12 January 1998: A10), found "a record low of 26.7 percent thought that 'keeping up to date with political affairs' was a very important or essential life goal, compared with 29.4 percent in 1996 and a high of 57.8 percent in 1966."

17. The 1956 Gallop surveys showed respondents a list of 10 prominent political figures, of which two were Canadian, and asked them to identify the country and position of each, as well as a list of Canada's ten provincial premiers and asked them to identify their province. The 2000 CES included an unprecedented number of knowledge items: the names of the leaders of the Liberals, PC, Alliance, and NDP, the name of the federal finance minister, and the name of one's provincial premier.

18. <http://geosurvey.nationalgeographic.com/geosurvey/download/Roper Survey.pdf>.

19. A new law allows local authorities to run elections under STV as well as FPTP. For the 2004 municipal elections, only 10 have chosen the former. (See <http://www.dia.govt.nz/diawebsite.nsf/wpg_URL/Resource-material-STV-Information-Index?OpenDocument#four>.)

20. Canadian data shows that young people, though less attentive and informed, are in fact more supportive of "politics as usual" than older Canadians. O'Neil found 18- to 27-year-olds to be roughly ten per cent more satisfied with Canadian democracy and elections than other age groups and comparatively even more willing to view the federal government as fair and effective. Nor are they any less distrustful of multinational corporations than older Canadians. In fact, they are less prone to see them as too powerful than all groups except those in the 28- to 37-year age group (O'Neill, 2001).

21. For presidential elections the drop was lower, from 85.2 per cent in 1988 to 76.8 in 2000.

22. I hasten to add, however, that at a more profound historical level, political institutions are related to socio-economic outcomes. I show elsewhere (Milner 2002: Part IV) that, in effect, excluding those with low resources from informed political participation makes it less likely that policies will be chosen to address their socio-economic needs and vice versa: a classic vicious circle.

23. We have noted that the relationship between education and voting is much weaker than that between political knowledge and voting. We note, also, at the aggre-

gate level, that higher educational standards appear to count for little when it comes to political participation. Canada is already doing relatively well, preceded only by Finland — both countries with high levels of youth political disaffection — in the latest international test. The Program for International Student Assessment (PISA), a 32-country survey which tested the skills and knowledge of 15-year-old students, assessed three literacy domains: reading, mathematics, and science (OECD 2001).

24. For example, one study found that service experiences did not change "the students' assessments of the value of elections" nor their "definitions of what civic responsibility is and should be" (Hunter and Brisbin 2000: 625).

25. A recent American study finds practically no positive effects on later voting of exposure to various forms of civics related courses in high school (Lopez 2003). Civics courses taken one hour per week from grade 7 or 8 by practically all German students (Händle *et al.* 1999) seem to have little effect on the adolescents, while in the Dutch case, there was a correlation only for the less than 10 per cent of students (Hahn 1998: 15) who took the civics course (called "society") as a part of their formal program leading to the final examination (Dekker 1999), suggesting that its effects are likely to prove short-lived.

26. Westholm, Lindquist and Niemi (1989) found that upper secondary students taking civics courses were more likely to retain knowledge about international organizations (11 per cent more) and international events (6 per cent more) when retested two years later than those in a control group.

27. In Sweden, only 2 per cent leave school at the end of compulsory schooling at age 16 (Skolverket 1998).

28. A useful comparison can be drawn with the United States, where it is reported that the Corporation for National Service, a major funder of service learning, explained its refusal to allow participants in Americorps to attend the "Stand for Children" rally in Washington, DC, as follows: "National Service has to be nonpartisan ... it should be about bringing communities together by getting things done. Strikes, demonstrations and *political activities* can have the opposite effect" (Cited in Walker 2000; emphasis added).

PART I

The Pros and Cons of Reforming the Canadian Electoral System

CHAPTER 1
Regionalism and Party Systems: Evaluating Proposals to Reform Canada's Electoral System

Harold J. Jansen and Alan Siaroff

Over the years, political scientists, government commissions, and think tanks have proposed potential replacements for Canada's single-member plurality (SMP) electoral system. There has been a wide variety of proposals; indeed, it would be difficult to find an electoral system that has not been proposed for Canada at some point. Most of the proposals, however, involve injecting an element of proportional representation (PR) into Canada's electoral framework. All of them attempt to address perceived shortcomings in the SMP system and the way it affects the dynamics of the Canadian party system.

The closest thing to a consensus in the literature on the Canadian electoral system is the observation that the SMP system contributes to the regionalization of Canada's party system. In a seminal article, Alan Cairns (1968) drew attention to the way the SMP system distorts the parliamentary representation of large parties, underrepresents small parties with diffuse support, and over-represents those parties with a narrowly defined regional base of support. Of course, no electoral system can compensate a party for weak or non-existent voter support in a region of the country, but Cairns demonstrated the way the electoral system amplified regional variations in voter support and failed to reward parties for the support they did have. Since then, most (though certainly not all) proposals to reform Canada's electoral system have to a large extent targeted this concern.

A particular preoccupation has been the representation of the various regions of the country within the governing caucus, which has intensified since the mid 1970s due to the failure of the SMP system to translate Liberal votes in western Canada into seats in Parliament. The weakness of western representation in the government caucus plagued both the Trudeau and

Table 1-1
Share of the Popular Vote, 1980 and 2000 (%)

1980	Lib	PC	NDP	Social Credit (SC)	Rhino	Other
Newfoundland	47.0%	36.0%	16.7%			0.4%
PEI	46.8%	46.3%	6.6%			0.3%
Nova Scotia	39.9%	38.7%	20.9%		0.2%	0.4%
New Brunswick	50.1%	32.5%	16.2%		0.5%	0.6%
Québec	68.2%	12.6%	9.1%	5.9%	3.0%	1.2%
Ontario	41.9%	35.5%	21.9%	a	0.2%	0.6%
Manitoba	28.0%	37.7%	33.5%		0.4%	0.4%
Saskatchewan	24.2%	38.9%	36.3%	a	0.1%	0.4%
Alberta	22.2%	64.9%	10.3%	1.0%	0.7%	0.9%
BC	22.2%	41.5%	35.3%	0.1%	0.4%	0.5%
Territories	37.2%	30.6%	31.5%		0.7%	
Canada	44.3%	32.5%	19.8%	1.7%	1.0%	0.7%

a. voter support of less than 0.1%.
Source: Elections Canada report

Chrétien Liberal governments and led to concern that western interests were not adequately being heard. The extent to which this concern drives the electoral reform agenda in Canada can be seen in the timing of proposals for electoral reform. The late 1970s and the 1980s saw the first flurry of electoral reform proposals, coinciding with the almost complete lack of representation of the West in the government caucus. The second modern period of interest in electoral reform began with the regionalized Parliament resulting from the 1993 federal election. Once again, questions of regional representation have been central in the debate. As Gibbins and Berdahl (2000: 178) correctly point out, interest in and momentum for parliamentary electoral reform faded during the years of the Mulroney Progressive Conservative (PC) government. In the 1984 and 1988 elections, the PCs elected a government caucus with representation from across Canada. Hence, the electoral reform debate has been enlarged to include non-regional dimensions of political identity (e.g., gender, race), though these arguments remain less prevalent than those that focus on regional representation (Studlar 1999 is a notable exception).

In this chapter, we review the various electoral system proposals that have been proposed since the mid 1970s from this perspective. This review is obvi-

Table 1-1 (continued)

Share of the Popular Vote, 1980 and 2000 (%)

2000	Lib	PC	NDP	BQ	CA	Green	Mari-juana Party	Other
Newfoundland	44.9%	34.5%	13.1%		3.9%			3.7%
PEI	47.0%	38.4%	9.0%		5.0%	0.3%		0.2%
Nova Scotia	36.5%	29.1%	24.0%		9.6%	0.1%	0.4%	0.3%
New Brunswick	41.7%	30.5%	11.7%		15.7%		0.1%	0.2%
Québec	44.2%	5.6%	1.8%	39.9%	6.2%	0.6%	1.0%	0.7%
Ontario	51.5%	14.4%	8.3%		23.6%	0.9%	0.3%	1.0%
Manitoba	32.5%	14.5%	20.9%		30.4%	0.2%	0.1%	1.4%
Saskatchewan	20.7%	4.8%	26.2%		47.7%	0.4%		0.2%
Alberta	20.9%	13.5%	5.4%		58.9%	0.5%	0.2%	0.6%
BC	27.7%	7.3%	11.3%		49.4%	2.1%	0.7%	1.5%
Territories	45.8%	8.6%	26.8%		17.6%	1.0%		0.2%
Canada	40.8%	12.2%	8.5%	10.7%	25.5%	0.8%	0.5%	0.9%

ously not exhaustive, but we have tried to select proposals that represent the major approaches to electoral reform in Canada. After describing each proposal, we then simulate what would have happened if that system had been in place in the 1980 and 2000 federal elections. Our rationale for choosing those elections is that they represent two different party systems in Canadian political cal history, each with a different pattern of voter support. A robust electoral system should perform well in either party system. Furthermore, at the time of writing this chapter (March 2004), the party system has changed, with the merger of the Canadian Alliance and the Progressive Conservative parties into the new Conservative Party of Canada. The emerging party system will likely come to resemble the party system through 1980, with multiple parties, but only two main parties competing for power.

Table 1-1 reports the vote shares for the most significant parties in the 1980 and 2000 Canadian federal elections. The seats awarded by the SMP system are reported in Table 1-2. The 1980 election turned out to be the last of the era of two-and-a-half-party politics that had existed for decades federally. In the 1980 election, the Liberals and PCs won almost 90 per cent of the seats between them. The NDP came a distant third, winning seats in only four provinces. No other parties won any seats, the Créditistes having lost all of theirs from the previous election(s). The outcome was a "standard" manufactured

Steps Toward Making Every Vote Count

Table 1-2

Seats, 1980 and 2000

	1980				2000					
	Lib	PC	NDP	Total	Lib	PC	NDP	BQ	CA	Total
Newfoundland	5	2		7	5	2				7
PEI	2	2		4	4					4
Nova Scotia	5	6		11	4	4	3			11
New Brunswick	7	3		10	6	3	1			10
Québec	74	1		75	36	1		38		75
Ontario	52	38	5	95	100		1		2	103
Manitoba	2	5	7	14	5	1	4		4	14
Saskatchewan		7	7	14	2		2		10	14
Alberta		21		21	2	1			23	26
BC		16	12	28	5		2		27	34
Territories	2	1		3	3					3
Canada	147	103	32	282	172	12	13	38	66	301

Source: Elections Canada Reports

majority, in that the Liberal plurality—but not majority—in the popular vote translated into a workable majority of seats (12 more than the combined opposition). The Liberal majority in seats, however, was totally based on central and eastern Canada. The party won only two seats in all of western Canada (and the territories), these two seats coming in Manitoba. In the three westernmost provinces the Liberals won no seats, although the party got above 20 per cent of the vote in each province. Conversely, the Liberals won all but one of the seats in Québec even though over 30 per cent of Quebeckers voted for other parties. Of course, the Québec pattern was paralleled in Alberta, where the PCs won every single seat—even though over 30 per cent of Albertans voted for other parties. Only in PEI could the seat breakdown (of four seats) be said to accurately reflect the provincial vote distribution.

Although the 2000 election also produced a regionalized pattern of party representation in the House of Commons, the situation was more complicated than in 1980 by virtue of the more fragmented party system. As in 1980, the Liberals formed a majority government but, unlike 1980, they had at least one MP from each province. As in the previous two elections, their majority was due largely to their almost total domination of the province of Ontario (100 of their 172 seats came from Ontario). Overrepresentation of Liberal support in

Ontario was mirrored by underrepresentation in Alberta and BC. Conversely, the Canadian Alliance, which formed the official opposition following the election, dominated the seats from Alberta and BC but earned only two seats in Ontario, despite having earned almost a quarter of the vote there. The 2000 election also saw the Bloc take a majority of Québec's 75 seats for the third consecutive election, even though their share of the popular vote had declined to below 40 per cent of Québec's voters (and less than the Liberals' 44 per cent of the vote). The NDP and PC parties reflected the challenges small parties with national appeal face under SMP systems. Both barely retained the 12 seats needed to retain official party status in the House of Commons, despite taking over 20 per cent of the national vote between them.

Any attempt to recreate what would have happened if the elections had been conducted under alternative electoral rules faces one intractable problem. To do so we must assume that voters would vote the same way under the proposed system as they did under the SMP system. Given the differing strategic incentives for parties, local candidates, and voters under different electoral arrangements (Cox 1997), this is a problematic assumption. It is, however, even more problematic to simulate how these actors might have changed their behaviour under the proposed system. Our simulations thus focus on the mechanical effects of electoral systems (the translation of votes to seats), not on their psychological effects.

The Proposals

I. PARTY LIST PROPORTIONAL REPRESENTATION

Despite the popularity of party list proportional representation in the world, it has hardly ever been proposed for adoption in Canada. Former policy secretary to Lester Pearson Tom Kent (1999), one of the few people to do so, proposes list PR for the House of Commons, to be combined with electing the Senate through SMP. Kent does not provide details of how he would implement list PR; details such as the district magnitude and the exact PR formula used can influence the results (Taagepera and Shugart 1989: 112-25; Lijphart 1994b: 21-25). We treat each province as one electoral district with the same number of seats they have currently in order to avoid having to draw artificial boundaries for multi-member districts.[1] We assume the use of a largest remainders list system with a Droop quota,[2] commonly used in similar circumstances and described by Lijphart (1994b: 24) as being neither the most nor least proportional of PR formulas. We also assume that there would be no

Table 1-3

Hypothetical Seats under List PR, 1980 and 2000

1980	Lib	PC	NDP	Cred	Rhino	Total
Newfoundland	3	3	1			7
PEI	2	2				4
Nova Scotia	5	4	2			11
New Brunswick	5	3	2			10
Québec	52	10	7	4	2	75
Ontario	40	34	21			95
Manitoba	4	5	5			14
Saskatchewan	3	6	5			14
Alberta	5	14	2			21
BC	6	12	10			28
Territories	1	1	1			3
Canada	126	94	56	4	2	282

legal threshold that parties have to reach to earn seats. Table 1-3 reports the results of our simulations of the 1980 and 2000 elections.

In 1980, the results would have been, as the system implies, highly proportional. The Liberals would not have won a majority of seats. In particular, they would have won 22 fewer seats in Québec and 12 fewer in Ontario. On the other hand, the Liberals would have won seats in every province, including a total of 18 in the four western provinces and one in the Territories. The PCs would also have won fewer seats, in particular fewer seats in Alberta, BC, and Ontario. In return, they would have won ten seats instead of one in Québec. On balance, the NDP would have been the biggest winner from this system, gaining overall 24 more seats nationally. The party would have won seats in every province except for PEI, winning 21 instead of five seats in Ontario (though winning slightly fewer seats in each of BC, Saskatchewan, and Manitoba). Beyond these three parties, two others would also have won seats: the Créditistes would have won four seats and, much more dubiously, the Rhinoceros Party two seats, in Québec.

In 2000, list PR would also have reduced the Liberals to a minority. Almost all of those seat losses would have been in Ontario, although the Liberals would still have held a majority of the province's seats, reflecting their voter support there. Some of the losses would have been offset by a higher number of MPs from Alberta and BC (tripling their representation in Alberta, dou-

Table 1-3 (continued)
Hypothetical Seats under List PR, 1980 and 2000

2000	Lib	PC	NDP	BQ	CA	Green	Mari-juana	Total
Newfoundland	3	3	1					7
PEI	2	2						4
Nova Scotia	4	3	3		1			11
New Brunswick	4	3	1		2			10
Québec	34	4	1	30	5		1	75
Ontario	53	15	9		25	1		103
Manitoba	5	2	3		4			14
Saskatchewan	3		4		7			14
Alberta	6	3	1		16			26
BC	10	2	4		17	1		34
Territories	2		1					3
Canada	126	37	28	30	77	2	1	301

bling it in BC). The Canadian Alliance would have been affected more profoundly, losing seats in the two westernmost provinces, but earning 25 seats in Ontario, as well as breaking through with five seats in Québec and three in Atlantic Canada. Both the NDP and PCs would have seen their parliamentary representation increase substantially and their national support reflected more faithfully, the PCs earning seats in every province but Saskatchewan and the NDP winning seats everywhere but PEI. Finally, list PR would have aided smaller parties, with the Greens winning two seats and the Marijuana party earning a seat in Québec.

2. MIXED-MEMBER PROPORTIONAL REPRESENTATION

Most proposed electoral reforms for Canada would combine elements of PR with SMP. Increasingly popular in Canada is the mixed-member proportional (MMP) system that would elect roughly half of Canada's MPs in single-member districts using SMP while the other half would be allocated in such a way as to compensate parties for the distortions of the SMP system. Voters would still have a particular MP who is "theirs," while the system would produce proportional results overall. In the first wave of electoral reform, Irvine (1979) proposed a system modelled after the German electoral system. More

Table 1-4

Hypothetical Seats under Mixed-Member Proportional, 1980 and 2000

	1980				2000					
	Lib	PC	NDP	Total	Lib	PC	NDP	BQ	CA	Total
Newfoundland	3	3	1	7	3	3	1			7
PEI	2	2		4	2	2				4
Nova Scotia	5	4	2	11	4	3	3		1	11
New Brunswick	5	3	2	10	4	3	1		2	10
Québec	57	10	8	75	34	4	2	30	5	75
Ontario	40	34	21	95	54	15	9		25	103
Manitoba	4	5	5	14	5	2	3		4	14
Saskatchewan	3	6	5	14	3		4		7	14
Alberta	5	14	2	21	6	3	1		16	26
BC	6	12	10	28	10	3	4		17	34
Territories	1	1	1	3	2		1			3
Canada	131	94	57	282	127	38	29	30	77	301

recently, Milner (1999) has proposed that Canada follow New Zealand's lead and switch to MMP. We simulated the 1980 and 2000 elections using Milner's proposal, which also imposes a 5 per cent threshold that parties have to reach in order to qualify for compensatory list seats. Following the New Zealand example, we also award list seats to any party that earns a seat under SMP. We assume that half of the seats are elected using SMP and that those seats would have been divided among the parties in the same proportion as they were in the actual elections. The overall results are calculated using the largest remainder-Droop formula we used for list PR. The results of our simulations can be found in Table 1-4.

Under a system of MMP, the results in almost every single province in both elections would have been the same as under list PR. The main difference under MMP is that the national thresholds would have prevented either the Créditistes or the Rhinoceros Party from winning a seat in 1980 and would have shut out the Green and Marijuana parties in 2000. The Liberals would have been the primary beneficiaries of this. Thus, the Liberals would have done slightly better under MMP than under list PR (although still well short of a majority), and the overall result would have been slightly less proportional than under list PR. That said, the same modifications would have occurred under list PR if there had been a national vote threshold of 5 per cent, or even 2 per cent.

Table 1-5
Hypothetical Seats under Dobell Partially Compensatory System,
1980 and 2000

	1980					2000					
	Lib	PC	NDP	Cred	Total	Lib	PC	NDP	BQ	CA	Total
Newfoundland	5	2	1		8	5	2	1			8
PEI	2	2			4	3	1				4
Nova Scotia	5	6	1		12	4	4	3		1	12
New Brunswick	7	3	1		11	6	3	1		1	11
Québec	74	4	2	1	81	36	3	1	38	3	81
Ontario	52	38	11		101	100	3	1		5	109
Manitoba	3	5	7		15	5	2	4		4	15
Saskatchewan	1	7	7		15	2		3		10	15
Alberta	2	21			23	3	2	1		23	29
BC	2	16	12		30	7	1	2		27	37
Territories		2	1		3	3					3
Canada	153	106	43	1	303	174	21	16	38	75	324

3. DOBELL'S PARTIALLY COMPENSATORY SYSTEM

Both list PR and MMP are real-world systems in use in other countries. They share one feature that many would-be electoral reformers find troubling: they would eliminate manufactured majorities. In other words, unless a party achieved a majority of the vote, it would not earn a majority of the seats and the political stability associated with this. One feature of the debate over electoral systems in Canada is the attempt by some to adapt or develop systems tailor-made for Canada, which would reduce the extent of regionalism while producing majority governments (at least most of the time). Dobell's (1981) "limited corrective" system is one such proposal. In its mechanics, Dobell's proposal works similarly to MMP, but with considerably fewer list seats available for compensation. Dobell proposes that each province be granted one list seat for each million people (rounding up initially), up to a maximum of six.[3] The limited number of extra seats (21 in 1980 and 23 in 2000) is intended to produce a result that is slightly more proportional but only rarely failing to produce a majority government where one would have occurred under SMP. Table 1-5 shows our simulation of the two elections.

In 1980, the Liberals would have won six additional seats, all in western Canada: one each in Manitoba and Saskatchewan and two each in Alberta and

BC. Indeed, these would have been every single compensatory seat in the West. The Liberals would thus have had at least one seat in every province. More generally, under the Dobell formula the Liberals would have—just barely—maintained their overall seat majority (with three seats more than the combined opposition). The PCs would have won only three compensatory seats, all in Québec. The NDP would have gained the most—11 compensatory seats in five provinces, with six of these seats being in Ontario (indeed, all six from Ontario). The NDP would still have been shut out in Alberta and PEI, though. Finally, under the Dobell formula the Créditistes would have won a seat, but just the one seat, in Québec.

In 2000, the Liberals would have earned two additional seats (gaining one in Alberta and two in BC, while losing one in PEI), retaining a (reduced) majority of the seats. The Dobell model would thus have only very modestly improved the regional representativeness of the government caucus in 2000. It would, however, have given the parliamentary caucuses of the three national opposition parties a much more national profile. The PCs would have been the main beneficiaries of this system and would have earned nine additional seats, including seats in provinces where they were shut out (PEI, Ontario, and BC). The NDP would have earned seats in provinces where they had no representation (Newfoundland, Québec, and Alberta), while the Alliance would have earned their eight additional seats in central and eastern Canada.

4. WEAVER'S PARTIALLY COMPENSATORY SYSTEM

In a similar vein, Kent Weaver, a senior fellow at the Brookings Institution, proposes a system that would partially correct the distortions of the SMP system using list seats (Weaver 1997). Weaver differs from Dobell in the apportionment of the list seats between provinces: he would give each province roughly 10 per cent additional seats, and he does not cap the large provinces at six additional seats.[4] Furthermore, he would award the compensation seats in each province sequentially, starting with the party that earned the largest number of national votes, then the second largest, and so on. Each party would receive enough of the compensation seats to bring its seat proportions in that province in line with its vote proportions. We simulated the results of the 1980 and 2000 elections using the Weaver system; Table 1-6 reports the results of our calculations.

Under the roughly 10 per cent additional seats proposed by Weaver, the changes from the actual outcome would not be as dramatic as under MMP or list PR. Nevertheless, in 1980, the Liberals would have fallen short of a major-

Table 1-6
Hypothetical Seats under Weaver System, 1980 and 2000

	1980				2000					
	Lib	PC	NDP	Total	Lib	PC	NDP	BQ	CA	Total
Newfoundland	5	2	1	8	5	2	1			8
PEI	2	2		4	4					4
Nova Scotia	5	6	1	12	4	4	3		1	12
New Brunswick	7	3	1	11	6	3	1		1	11
Québec	74	9		83	36	4		38	5	83
Ontario	52	38	15	105	100		1		12	113
Manitoba	3	5	7	15	5	2	4		4	15
Saskatchewan	1	7	7	15	3		2		10	15
Alberta	2	21		23	5	1			23	29
BC	3	16	12	31	8		2		27	37
Territories		2	1	3	3					3
Canada	154	111	45	310	179	16	14	38	83	330

ity, albeit by just two seats. However, with their additional provincial seats they would now have had representation from every province. Their one seat in Saskatchewan would still not have been near the three seats of true proportionality, since under the Weaver formula there would be only one compensatory seat for Saskatchewan (and all the other smaller provinces). However, for the largest provinces there would have been enough extra seats to make a difference: the PCs would have gone from one seat to nine in Québec, and the NDP would have gone from five seats to 15 in Ontario. Yet the NDP still would have had no seats in Québec (or Alberta or PEI).

Unlike in 1980, the 2000 election would have seen the Liberals retain a majority government, though a reduced one. Their seven additional seats would all have come in the three westernmost provinces, improving the regional representativeness of the governing caucus. The Canadian Alliance stands as the major beneficiary of the Weaver system, earning 17 additional seats, all in central and eastern Canada. The Alliance thus would have earned a proportion of the seats almost exactly proportional to their vote share and one that more accurately reflects their national appeal. In contrast to the Dobell formula, the Weaver proposal is far less favourable to the PCs and NDP. The NDP would have earned only one additional seat (in Atlantic Canada, where the party is already strong) and the Conservatives would have earned four,

Table 1-7
Hypothetical Seats under Task Force on Canadian Unity System,
1980 and 2000

1980	Lib	PC	NDP	Cred	Rhino	Total
Newfoundland	5	2				7
PEI	2	2				4
Nova Scotia	5	6	1			12
New Brunswick	7	3				10
Québec	74	12	3	1	1	91
Ontario	59	46	12			117
Manitoba	4	5	7			16
Saskatchewan	3	7	7			17
Alberta	6	21	1			28
BC	9	16	12			37
Territories		2	1			3
Canada	174	122	44	1	1	342

including three in Québec. In sum, the Weaver proposal tends to achieve better regional balance than SMP, but with a decided bias towards larger parties.

5. THE PARALLEL SYSTEM OF THE TASK FORCE ON CANADIAN UNITY

Besides systems that attempt to compensate the seat distortions of SMP with party list MPs, either fully (MMP) or partially (Dobell and Weaver), there are those that elect a set of list MPs separately from those MPs elected by SMP. In these systems, the list MPs provide a set of representatives who run parallel to those elected by SMP. There have been two prominent proposals of this type, one published by the Canada West Foundation (Elton and Gibbins 1980) and the other proposed by the Task Force on Canadian Unity (Canada 1979). Based on Irvine's (1985) endorsement in his study for the Macdonald Commission, we chose the Task Force proposal as representative of this kind of system. The Task Force's description of their proposal is frustratingly ambiguous, but Irvine (1979: 64-67, 86-89; 1985: 86-89) has fleshed out the proposal. The Task Force would allocate 60 additional seats to the House of Commons. These would be divided between the parties according to their share of the national popular vote. Each party's seats would be divided between provincial party lists for each party in a way that took account of the

Table 1-7 (continued)
Hypothetical Seats under Task Force on Canadian Unity System,
1980 and 2000

2000	Lib	PC	NDP	BQ	CA	Green	Total
Newfoundland	5	2					7
PEI	4						4
Nova Scotia	4	4	3				11
New Brunswick	6	3	1				10
Québec	47	1		45	3		96
Ontario	100	6	5		14	1	126
Manitoba	5	1	4		4		14
Saskatchewan	2		2		10		14
Alberta	8	1	1		23		33
BC	13	1	2		27		43
Territories	3						3
Canada	197	19	18	45	81	1	361

party's existing representation from that province. Table 1-7 shows the results of our simulations.

Interestingly, the Task Force model does not predetermine the total number of seats for each province (as do the previous models). Indeed, these seats essentially would go to the largest provinces: 54 of the 60 seats in 1980 would have gone to the largest four provinces, with 38 of these 60 seats going to just Ontario and Québec. In 2000, all 60 of the additional seats would have gone to the largest four provinces, and 44 of those seats would have gone to Ontario and Québec. In other words, the Task Force system corrects for deviations from the principle of representation by population that have been accumulating over time due to the operation of the Senate floor and grandfather clause rules in seat apportionment.[5]

In 1980, 45 per cent (27 seats) of the 60 list seats would have gone to the Liberals, and 55 per cent (33 seats) to other parties—reflecting of course the national vote shares. This six-seat difference in favour of the other parties would not have been enough to have cost the Liberals their majority, but it would have cut said majority in half, from 12 seats (147 versus 135) to six seats (174 versus 168). The additional Liberal seats would have been allocated to five and only five provinces: BC (nine seats), Ontario (seven seats), Alberta (six seats), Saskatchewan (three seats), and Manitoba (two seats). In contrast, the PCs would have been given additional seats in only two provinces: Québec (11 seats) and Ontario (eight seats). As for the NDP, its additional seats would have been spread across four provinces: seven in Ontario, three in Québec, one in Alberta, and one in Nova Scotia. Finally, the Créditistes and the Rhinoceros Party would each have received a seat based on their national vote share.

Similar effects would have been seen in 2000. The Liberals would have earned 25 of the additional seats, which would have slightly reduced the scope of their majority in the House of Commons. All of their additional seats would have come in Québec (11 seats), Alberta (six seats), and BC (eight seats). The Alliance would have gained an additional 15 seats, all in Ontario and Québec. The built-in correction for representation by population would have meant that there would be no list seats available for the Alliance in Atlantic Canada, limiting the capacity of the Task Force system to reduce regionalism. The system is one of the few reform proposals that would have augmented the Bloc's representation; indeed, the proposal preserves the overrepresentation of that party. The Task Force proposal would have been less favourable for the PCs and the NDP than many of the other proposals we have examined. They would have earned six seats and five seats, respectively, all in Ontario. In 2000, then, the Task Force proposal would have corrected some of the regionalism in the party system, but the addition of seats only to the largest provinces limits the capacity of the system to correct for regional imbalances.

6. SMILEY PROPOSAL

All of the preceding systems embrace some degree of proportional represen-tation by using party lists to improve the seats-to-votes correspondence within all or most provinces. There have been some electoral reformers, however, who explicitly do not do this. One such suggestion is that of Donald Smiley (1978: 84-87). He proposes to add 100 seats to the House of Commons, giving one to PEI and dividing the rest proportionately among the other provinces. These seats would be filled by the candidates "who had received the highest proportion of popular votes to the winning candidates" (Smiley, 1978: 85). In other words, he would award those seats to the "losing" candidates who have received the highest proportions of the vote of the winning candidates in their districts. Our simulation found that though the Smiley system appears to go some distance to improve the regional representation within fairly large national parties, it does little to improve the lot of small national parties or to dampen the influence of regional parties. Since the Smiley proposals were never picked up in subsequent discussions, in the interests of brevity we will not present details of the simulation here.

7. THE ALTERNATIVE VOTE

Finally, one reform proposal that is increasingly discussed is the alternative vote (AV). University of Calgary political scientist Tom Flanagan (1999) has led the calls for this system. Unlike the other systems discussed, the AV does not focus on improving the regional representativeness of party caucuses or the proportionality of results; rather, its proponents focus on its ability to reward or even induce cooperative behaviour between parties (Flanagan, 1999: 89-90). We include it in our simulation because it is the major non-proportional alternative to SMP. AV would require voters to rank the candidates in single-member districts. The candidate who wins a majority of the vote is declared elected. If a majority is not achieved by any one candidate, the candidate with the fewest votes is dropped, and the ballots given to that candidate are allocated to the other candidates according to the second preferences indicated on them. This process continues until one candidate wins a majority of the vote. Simulating AV elections is particularly difficult, because it requires some knowledge of the second and subsequent preferences of voters. Furthermore, we cannot guess what kind of arrangements for preference exchanges between candidates might have been made. Given that this is more speculative, the results of these simulations (Table 1-8) should be approached with additional caution.

For 1980, we assume that the Liberal candidate generally would have been the preferred second choice of those who would have expressed a second preference. In particular, even if we assume that half of NDP supporters would not have expressed a second preference, and that some of the second preferences expressed would have been PC, there still would have been enough NDP second preferences for the Liberals so that nationally the Liberals likely would have taken 20 seats from the PCs—12 of these in Ontario. (Remember that the 1980 Liberals under Pierre Trudeau were certainly campaigning on the left.) Also, although more hypothetically, we suspect that the NDP would have gained two seats from the PCs in ridings where the Liberals were third and seemed more left-leaning. Overall, then, under AV the PCs would have only lost seats, gaining none. Thus, they would have come out much worse than under the current system, the NDP would have done very slightly better, and the Liberals much better. Consequently, both the Liberal seat share and their resulting majority would have been much higher. However, the Liberals

Table 1-8

Hypothetical Seats under Alternative Voting, 1980 and 2000

	1980				2000					
	Lib	PC	NDP	Total	Lib	PC	NDP	BQ	CA	Total
Newfoundland	5	2		7	5	2				7
PEI	3	1		4	4					4
Nova Scotia	7	4		11	6	3	2			11
New Brunswick	8	2		10	5	4	1			10
Québec	75			75	41	1		33		75
Ontario	64	26	5	95	103					103
Manitoba	2	5	7	14	5	1	4		4	14
Saskatchewan	1	6	7	14	2		2		10	14
Alberta		21		21	2	1			23	26
BC	1	14	13	28	5		2		27	34
Territories	1		2	3	3					3
Canada	167	81	34	282	181	12	11	33	64	301

still would have remained underrepresented in western Canada—and still would not have won a single seat in Alberta.

For 2000, we are fortunate in that the Canadian Election Study[6] asked voters their second preferences. Using a process similar to that of Bilodeau (1999), we were able to approximate the outcome of an AV election that year. The results of AV in 2000 are similar to those in 1980. The Liberal party's status as the most common second choice of most non-Liberal voters gives them an advantage over other parties in this scenario. Our analysis suggests that the Liberals would have increased the size of their majority, taking a few close seats away from the Bloc due to their superior ability to attract second preferences. The Liberals would also likely have swept Ontario, but AV would have done little to improve their regional representation in the West. The adoption of AV would have done little to help the Alliance and likely would have cost them their only seats outside of western Canada. The NDP would likely have been reduced to less than the 12 seats required for party status in Parliament. Set against this negative effect, the only potential contribution to reducing the regionalization of the party system would have been a reduction in the number of seats given to the Bloc.

8. OTHER SYSTEMS

There have been two additional systems proposed to reform Canada's electoral system, but we were unable to simulate those results. One perennial favourite is the single transferable vote (Loenen 1997). We could not reasonably simulate those results because to do so requires a combination of detailed information about voter preferences and the imposition of a system of hypothetical electoral districts on the existing electoral map. Too many assumptions would have to be made to simulate the results meaningfully. To the extent that a single transferable vote (STV) system uses relatively large multi-member districts (at least five members) and that voters are reasonably disciplined in transferring their ballots within their preferred party—which cannot necessarily be assumed for Canadian voters—the results of an STV election could be expected to be reasonably similar to that of a list PR or MMP system.

Less common are calls for run-off elections (Lovink 1998; Lovink 2001) between the top two candidates one week later in constituencies where no candidate won a majority of the vote. We could not meaningfully simulate the results of run-off elections because of the changes in voter participation between the first ballot and the run-off. Some voters will choose not to participate in the second ballot; others might choose to participate only in the second ballot. Furthermore, parties and candidates might announce support for one another in the intervening week, complicating the situation. To the extent that success in run-off elections requires attracting the second preferences of supporters of other parties and candidates, we believe that the results would be broadly similar to those under AV, favouring the Liberals.[7]

The Impact on Regionalism

Table 1-9 provides summary values of various measures of interprovincial variations in parliamentary representation for each of the main parties, both for the actual results and for the various simulations. Note that we are only looking at the percentage support in each province, thus excluding the territories. What are most useful for comparing across the electoral systems are the range of support and the standard deviation for each party. This is the main issue here. However, if one wishes to compare across the parties for a given system, we would suggest the standard deviation divided by the mean.

That said, one cannot forget the obvious point that even under completely pure proportionality, there would be interprovincial variations in support for

Table 1-9

Measures of Regionalization, 1980 and 2000

		1980			2000			
		Lib	PC	NDP	Lib	PC	NDP	CA
Vote shares (actual results)	Range	46.04	52.25	29.72	52.89	33.61	23.14	55.03
	Std. Deviation	14.20	12.20	10.49	15.14	11.64	7.44	19.18
	Deviation/Mean	0.364	0.317	0.508	0.381	0.593	0.560	0.754
SMP (actual seat shares)	Range	98.67	98.67	50.00	92.31	36.36	28.57	88.46
	Std. Deviation	33.37	24.14	21.61	34.78	13.90	10.69	35.74
	Deviation/Mean	0.825	0.540	1.459	0.651	1.280	1.229	1.325
	Magnification	2.35	1.98	2.06	2.30	1.19	1.44	1.86
List PR (simulated seat shares)	Range	47.90	53.33	35.71	54.13	50.00	28.57	61.54
	Std. Deviation	14.77	13.02	11.85	15.08	15.59	9.57	20.78
	Deviation/Mean	0.374	0.328	0.591	0.372	0.759	0.747	0.816
	Magnification	1.04	1.07	1.13	1.00	1.34	1.29	1.08
MMP (simulated seat shares)	Range	54.57	53.33	35.71	54.13	50.00	28.57	61.54
	Std. Deviation	17.04	13.68	12.20	15.16	15.33	9.35	20.78
	Deviation/Mean	0.427	0.348	0.585	0.373	0.736	0.717	0.816
	Magnification	1.20	1.12	1.16	1.00	1.32	1.26	1.08

all parties, simply because there are interprovincial variations in their vote shares![8] For the Liberals and the NDP, these variations were lower in 2000 than they were in 1980, but they are still there. For the Canadian Alliance, the interprovincial variation in votes was far and away the highest of any party in 2000. Thus, to be clear, the issue is the extent to which any given electoral system *magnifies* or conversely (and perhaps ideally) *lessens* these interprovincial vote variations. This effect we have assessed by dividing the standard deviations for the parties under a given electoral system by the standard deviations of the vote proportions, a variable we call "magnification." A value of "1" for this variable indicates that the regional variation in voter support is reflected accurately in the seat distribution; a value of more than that indicates that the electoral system is magnifying the regionalization of party support in the seat totals.[9] Our findings are mitigated somewhat by the fact that in 2000, regardless of the electoral system, there was little change in interprovincial variations for the PCs and relatively little for the NDP. Change was substantial in 2000 for both the Liberals and the Canadian Alliance, though, as it was for all three national parties in 1980.

Table 1-9 (continued)

Measures of Regionalization, 1980 and 2000

		1980			2000			
		Lib	PC	NDP	Lib	PC	NDP	CA
Dobell (simulated seat shares)	Range	84.69	86.37	46.67	81.40	33.33	26.67	79.31
	Std. Deviation	27.46	21.64	18.08	28.40	11.58	9.55	30.74
	Deviation/Mean	0.682	0.516	1.024	0.596	0.808	0.907	1.120
	Magnification	1.93	1.77	1.72	1.88	1.00	1.28	1.60
Weaver (simulated seat shares)	Range	82.49	80.46	46.67	82.76	33.33	26.67	79.31
	Std. Deviation	26.62	20.64	18.06	28.95	12.29	9.59	30.08
	Deviation/Mean	0.663	0.489	1.024	0.566	1.104	1.033	1.056
	Magnification	1.87	1.69	1.72	1.91	1.06	1.29	1.57
Task Force (simulated seat shares)	Range	63.67	61.81	43.75	85.71	36.36	28.57	71.43
	Std. Deviation	22.00	15.69	16.79	28.68	13.52	10.34	29.42
	Deviation/Mean	0.485	0.391	1.176	0.527	1.184	1.126	1.179
	Magnification	1.55	1.29	1.60	1.89	1.16	1.39	1.53
Smiley (simulated seat shares)	Range	67.26	57.52	44.44	86.93	35.71	22.22	74.29
	Std. Deviation	24.00	16.46	17.11	27.68	12.96	9.47	30.12
	Deviation/Mean	0.579	0.383	1.155	0.533	1.063	1.194	1.082
	Magnification	1.69	1.35	1.63	1.83	1.11	1.27	1.57
AV (simulated seat shares)	Range	100.00	100.00	50.00	92.31	40.00	28.57	88.46
	Std. Deviation	35.65	24.78	22.10	34.71	14.28	9.45	35.88
	Deviation/Mean	0.739	0.677	1.457	0.636	1.307	1.229	1.339
	Magnification	2.51	2.03	2.11	2.29	1.23	1.27	1.87

Magnification calculated by dividing standard deviation of seat shares by standard deviation of actual votes.

The findings suggest that the various electoral systems should be grouped into three categories. In the first category are the systems that most magnify the interprovincial variations in voter support. Here we find the actual system of SMP. For the Liberals, for example, SMP more than doubled their inter-provincial variations in support in 1980 and more than tripled these in 2000. We also find the other single-member system: the alternative vote. Indeed, for almost all parties regional imbalances would have been *worsened* if we adopted AV even (though slightly) more than under SMP. In the second, opposite, category are those electoral systems that do not — or only minimally — exaggerate interprovincial variations in support, at least for the largest parties.

List PR and MMP fall into this category. This is not surprising, as these two systems are the only two intended to be fully, or nearly fully, proportional. Finally, in the intermediate category are the remaining systems—Dobell, Weaver, the Task Force, and Smiley. These also would have clearly exaggerated interprovincial variations in party support—for all parties in 1980 and for the Liberals and Canadian Alliance in 2000—although not to the extent of SMP and AV. In 1980, the Task Force system appears to work a little better in reducing regional disparities than the Dobell or Weaver systems, at least for the PCs and Liberals, though those differences largely disappear in the 2000 election when they all reduce regionalism more or less similarly. As noted earlier, the Task Force proposal has the added problem (not reflected in Table 1-9) of doing little to correct the overrepresentation of the Bloc. Finally, it is interesting to note that, particularly in 2000, these intermediate category systems tend to perform better at accurately reflecting the regional support for the major opposition party than they do for the governing party. This is surprising given the electoral reform debate's emphasis on regional representation in the government caucus.

Conclusion

The regionalization of party support has been a fact of life in Canadian politics for decades. No change to the electoral system is going to eliminate that. Our analysis demonstrates, however, that the SMP system magnifies the problem of regional variation. The most proportional electoral systems—list PR and MMP—eliminate regional distortions most completely, although they do so better for larger parties than for relatively small parties (the NDP and the PCs in 2000). The four intermediate systems were generally designed with a dual objective: reducing regionalism while still maintaining majority governments. Generally, they all achieve these dual goals (the Liberals would have fallen just short of a majority in 1980 under Weaver's system), but none reduces regionalism to the extent that fully proportional systems do. Although the various electoral reform proposals vary in the extent to which they can correct regionalism, they all do reduce it at least somewhat—with the notable exception of AV.

Although in the aggregate these intermediate systems appear to differ little, they do have slightly different emphases. The Weaver system emphasizes correcting the regional disparities of the largest parties by awarding them compensatory list seats first. The Dobell system is more favourable for correcting the regional disparities of smaller parties. The combination of the

Task Force system with the increasing deviations from the principle of representation by population in Canada means that the Task Force system does a reasonably good job of correcting the seat imbalances in the most populous (and currently underrepresented) provinces, but does little to correct regionalization in less populous provinces.

Regionalism, however central to the debate on reforming Canada's electoral system, is just one of the criteria advanced for electoral reform. The extent to which other criteria—more balanced gender representation, encouraging ideological moderation, providing incentives for more cooperative behaviour, more accurately reflecting the partisan composition of the electorate, or maintaining stable government—are valued by Canadians and thus stressed in the debate will obviously play a role in the choice of electoral system.

Notes

1. We assume that the territories are one district with three seats.

2. See Introduction, note 2, for an explanation of the Droop quota.

3. PEI does not have enough population to qualify for an additional seat under this plan, but Dobell (1981: 77) reduces PEI to three constituency seats with one list seat. We treat the territories as three single-member districts. On the other hand, as noted, there would be more compensatory seats in Ontario and Québec than under Dobell's system.

4. Under Weaver's system, PEI does not earn any compensation seats, nor, presumably, would the territories.

5. This raises the question of whether the Task Force proposal would require a constitutional amendment. We agree with Irvine's (1985) assessment that it likely would not. Indeed, this appears to conform more closely to the principle of "proportionate representation" in Section 42 of the *Constitution Act, 1982*.

6. Data from the 2000 Canadian Election Survey were provided by the Institute for Social Research, York University. The survey was funded by the Social Sciences and Humanities Research Council of Canada (SSHRC) and was completed for the 2000 Canadian Election Team of André Blais (Université de Montréal), Elisabeth Gidengil (McGill University), Richard Nadeau (Université de Montréal) and Neil Nevitte (University of Toronto). Neither the Institute for Social Research, the SSHRC, nor the Canadian Election Survey Team are responsible for the analyses and interpretations presented here.

7. This is different than the conclusion Lovink (2001) reaches in his simulation. It should be noted, however, that his simulation was conducted without reference to data on second preferences.

8. As the Bloc ran candidates only in Québec, it cannot by definition have interprovincial variations and, hence, is excluded from this analysis.

9. To illustrate the concept of magnification in Table 1-9, the standard deviation of the Liberal vote shares in 1980 is 14.20 per cent, while the standard deviation of

the actual seat shares in that election is 33.37 per cent. The ratio of 33.37 to 14.20 produces a magnification effect of 2.35. In other words, the standard deviation of the seat shares in 1980 is 2.35 times greater than the standard deviation of the vote shares. On the other hand, the provincial distribution of the simulated seat results under list PR would have magnified the standard deviation of provincial vote shares by only 1.04.

CHAPTER 2

That Bleak? Fathoming the Consequences of Proportional Representation in Canada[1]

Louis Massicotte

Introduction

Given the developments described in this book, electoral system reform is no longer inconceivable in Canada. It is thus useful and timely to explore the likely consequences of proportional representation (PR) on crucial features of the Canadian political system. To be concrete, we will focus on a system based on electoral regions, a feature of any option that can fulfill at the same time the hopes of those who want fairer results and deplore regional polarization, low turnouts, and the underrepresentation of women. In this system, seats are allocated to parties in proportion to their vote in four- to ten-seat constituencies. In addition, if for no other reason than because Canadians are unlikely to accept any electoral system that does not allow them to have a single member of Parliament (MP) to represent them, I add the features of a German-style mixed system in which about half of MPs are elected in single-member districts, but where the remaining, regional district-based seats are distributed in such a way as to bring the total distribution of seats among parties in proportion to the votes cast for each.

Adopting a PR electoral system would have direct consequences on the shape and size of electoral districts, on the work of members of the House of Commons, and on the representation of political parties and minorities. But it would also likely affect the position of the prime minister, as well as alter the way cabinets are formed and operate, their composition, and their relation with both Houses of Parliament. The federal-provincial balance might be affected as well. We should make no mistake about it: along with responsible government and disciplined parties, the first-past-the-post (FPTP) system is one of the three crucial variables that have shaped Canada's Westminster system of governance, both federally and provincially, and replacing it with PR is likely to have sweeping consequences.

Moreover, not all consequences of PR can be anticipated. We can simulate what the result of previous elections would have been, by assuming voters would have voted the same way. Such exercises are helpful, but the conclusions that can be derived from them remain somewhat fragile, insofar as we cannot know what the distribution of the popular vote *at future elections* will be. It is even more difficult to anticipate with certainty the impact of PR on Canada's system of governance, an impact that will result from the combined effects of decisions made by a myriad of political actors.

We can gain insight into these matters from the experience of countries where PR has been operating for generations, though it should not be transposed slavishly. The "real world" of PR encompasses dozens of countries, from the inauspicious cases of Italy or Israel to the more reassuring examples provided by Germany and the Scandinavian countries. We should resist the temptation to systematically assume rosy scenarios, if only because the sometimes wild expectations of reformers have often been shattered by the actual operation of the systems they ardently advocated.[2] This said, I now proceed to examine the likely consequences of adopting a PR electoral system under 15 headings.

Fifteen Consequences of Adopting a PR Electoral System

I. A MORE REPRESENTATIVE PARLIAMENT

Parliament, meaning here the House of Commons, would be more closely representative, insofar as the number of seats won by political parties would match more closely their electoral support. The number of political parties represented in the House would probably be higher than it now is, not necessarily because PR would lead to the fragmentation of existing parties, but because the threshold of inclusion for new movements like the Greens would be lower. The range of political views represented in Parliament would be broader and could include viewpoints that Canadians find innovative and engaging as well as others they might find objectionable.

Existing minority parties whose electoral support is widely spread would no longer be disadvantaged compared with parties with equivalent electoral support concentrated in specific areas. This would benefit the Conservatives and New Democratic Party (NDP).[3] As far as the representation of women is concerned, countries with PR systems normally have a higher proportion of women in legislatures than countries with plurality or majority systems, which has led many activists and scholars to advocate the introduction of PR as a kind of affirmative action measure to augment the presence of more women legislators (Rule 1994).

This should not be exaggerated. The FPTP system does not "block" access of women to Parliament. The number of women in the House of Commons now hovers around 20 per cent, a significant increase compared with the all-male House elected at the 1968 election. Important variations in the number of women among PR legislatures shows that PR alone cannot guarantee the presence of women legislators and has led the Jenkins commission to conclude in its 1998 report that the evidence linking PR to women MPs was "not over-whelmingly strong" (Jenkins 1999: par. 39). Much will depend on the extent to which political parties will give priority to the inclusion of women on their slate of candidates. In the short term, there will probably be more women in Parliament, though the percentage of women is likely to increase in the future whichever electoral system is used.

The representation of "multicultural Canadians" would be affected, since they would lose the advantage they now derive from their concentration in certain metropolitan ridings. To compensate, however, they could seek a degree of assured representation on party PR lists.

2. LESS REGIONAL POLARIZATION IN PARLIAMENT

PR would ensure that party caucuses will include some representatives from most major provinces, provided of course they secure some minimum electoral support there. More specifically, it would break the Liberals' present monopoly over Ontario seats that has been a crucial factor in their consecutive majority victories in 1993, 1997, and 2000.[4] It would allow the Conservative Party of Canada (which has resulted from the merger of the Canadian Alliance with the Progressive Conservative Party), while losing some seats in the West, to win seats in Canada's largest province and to some extent shed the image of the former Reform Party as a purely western party.[5]

PR would provide all parties but the Bloc Québécois (the Bloc) with more regionally balanced caucuses in Parliament. It would become more difficult for Ontario or Québec MPs to secure within the ruling party caucus the inflated weight that Québec Conservative members achieved in 1988 — one-third of the caucus — Québec Liberals achieved in 1980 — one-half of the caucus—or that Ontario Liberals enjoyed following the 1997 election with two-thirds of the ruling party caucus.

This in turn would encourage parties to develop policies more palatable to all regions rather than giving up on any region, as the PCs did, following the Gordon Churchill strategy, *vis-à-vis* Québec in 1957. On election night, regional electoral variations would be merely reflected in the distribution of seats, rather than being exaggerated as they have often been, notably in 1979, 1980, and 1997.

PR would address the deep-seated problem of regional polarization at federal elections, a recurring phenomenon that the Pépin-Robarts Commission claimed to be a harbinger of the break-up of federations (Canada 1979: 105). After the 1984 election, many thought the problem had gone away following Brian Mulroney's selection as PC leader and his sweeping victory over John Turner's Liberals, with a majority of both votes and seats in each and every province and territory. Yet this proved to be a short interlude, with polarization resurfacing with a vengeance. Polarization comes and goes, but also goes and comes back. (This preoccupation was a major factor in the decision taken in 1899 to introduce PR in Belgium and was successful for a long time in reducing the polarization that had previously existed under a majority system between Flemish Catholic and Walloon Liberal or Socialist areas.)[6]

The results of the German election of 2002 illustrate very well how regional polarization would be reduced by PR. Of the half of the membership of the Bundestag elected by FPTP (as in Canada), the Social Democrats won 57 per cent of the seats. Without the corrective seats from regional lists, the country would have been electorally polarized on north-south lines. Under FPTP, the opposition Christian Democrats would have been shut out in no less than six of Germany's 16 *Länder* (provinces), all located in the north. In the second largest province, Bavaria, in the south, the ruling party would have won only a single seat out of 44. The operation of personalized PR resulted instead in the Social Democrats winning 27 per cent of Bavarian seats, while the Christian Democrats were able to win seats in every *Land*.

This is not to say that PR will solve the crisis of Canadian federalism. The strong presence of a region within the federal executive, bureaucracy, and judiciary does not necessarily dampen aspirations for regional autonomy, as shown by the rise of separatism in Québec over the past 30 years. Many regional champions expect far more than mere inclusion in federal decision-making circles. Nevertheless, the presence of a sizable group of cabinet ministers from these regions is likely to weaken their case: how committed to federalism would Québeckers have remained had their presence in the federal cabinet continuously been reduced to what it was for a brief time after the 1957 and 1979 elections?

3. A REDUCED MP'S ROLE IN THE CONSTITUENCY?

Would PR change the job description of MPs? Though pure PR would substitute large multi-member districts for the smaller single-member districts, German-style PR would mean—assuming the total number of seats in the House would remain around 300—that at least half of MPs would continue to be returned from single-member districts, but that these districts would be up to twice as large as existing districts. The PR members would likely be returned from province-wide districts, except in Ontario and Québec, and perhaps BC and Alberta, where the creation of regional "top-up areas" would probably emerge as the most appropriate solution.

Clearly the job description of MPs would be affected, but to a different degree. MPs elected in larger multi-member districts would find it more difficult to control their district associations than their present smaller single-member district associations. Constituency work, an activity that absorbs much of the energies of MPs and enhances the self-esteem of many, would be affected by PR. A German-style system would maintain the close relationship between constituency MPs and the voters in their enlarged constituencies but would also create a second layer of representation. As such, it is open to the often-made (but rarely substantiated) charge that there will be two "classes of MPs" warring in the bosom of a single parliament. How the two categories would interact with each other cannot be predicted with absolute certainty, but it is worth pointing out that in the two dozen countries with mixed systems, very few tensions are reported between the two groups of MPs (see Massicotte and Blais 1999: 341-66).

In the case of Germany, where a mixed system has existed now for over half a century, the very existence of such tensions is explicitly denied by the literature (See Roberts 1988: 114; Jesse 1987: 446; Jesse 1988: 120; Burkett 1985: 130).

One important reason is that, in practice, list MPs are strongly encouraged to conduct "surgeries" in a constituency, usually the one in which they stood unsuccessfully. In New Zealand, though PR members are perceived by some as "second-class MPs," in reality there is little to substantiate that perception (Ward 1998).[7]

4. LESS PARTY DISCIPLINE?

Members are now constrained by party ties, and some of them, together with many observers of Parliament, find party discipline too constraining and push for a higher number of free votes. Would PR lead to a relaxation of party discipline? Not very much should be expected on that front. There is no clear-cut correlation between party discipline and single-member districts systems, as exemplified by the contrast between the American House of Representatives and the Canadian House of Commons. In the former, parties exhibit much less cohesion at congressional roll-calls than members of other legislatures, a pattern of behaviour that has prevailed for over a century (see Brady *et al.* 1979). In Canada, the same electoral system now coincides with relatively tight—though decreasing—party discipline, yet our parties were much less cohesive during the second half of the nineteenth century (Massicotte 1998; Wearing 1998).

There is no reason to believe that individual MPs would have much more freedom and clout if PR was introduced. Disciplined parties appear to be the norm in all democratic countries except the United States, irrespective of the electoral system used (Colliard 1978). Party discipline is no less stringent within Canadian governing parties in minority than in majority situations (Massicotte 1997). Indeed, it becomes at times more stringent in the former. The practice in PR countries is for interparty negotiations to take place at the cabinet level, with MPs from all sides expected to accept the outcomes reached by their leaders. If candidates were elected depending on their party-determined position on party lists, parties would arguably be in an even better position to exact conformity from their followers in Parliament. Further, MPs breaking with their respective parties would have more difficulty getting re-elected as independents in substantially enlarged districts.

5. THE END OF SINGLE-PARTY MAJORITY GOVERNMENTS

If the past is any guide, single-party majority governments like those we have had for most of our history would become exceptional occurrences. The experience of PR countries suggests that single-party majority governments are rare interludes in a long succession of minority and coalition governments. Indeed, in countries where coalition government is the norm, it is not infrequent for a party having secured a majority on its own to maintain its earlier alliance with smaller parties, in anticipation of a return to the standard pattern.

Though Canadian parties have some experience of single-party minority governments (eight of the 24 elections held since 1921 have produced such outcomes), the latter would probably not become the standard government formula. So far, they have been resorted to as a kind of least—and tempo-rary—evil solution, in the hope that the ensuing election would produce a majority. The latter scenario is plausible under the FPTP system (in fact, three elections[8] since 1921 resulted in a majority for the incumbent minority government); in fact, under FPTP gaining only a few percentage points of popular vote may well be enough to reach a majority of seats. Under PR, this is unlikely.

The experience of PR countries suggests that coalitions would be more fre-quent than minority governments. For the years 1945-87, Laver and Schofield found an almost two-to-one such ratio in European cabinets (see, e.g., Laver and Schofield 1990). In this regard, much would depend on the constitutional rules governing cabinet formation. It is easier for minority governments to be formed and to endure if no formal vote of investiture in Parliament is required for a new cabinet to be appointed or if, by the same logic, mechanisms are in-troduced like that provided by Article 49 of the French Constitution, whereby cabinets can be censured only by an absolute majority of the Assembly's membership. (Only the votes in favour of censure are counted, which means that members abstaining are implicitly counted as supporting the cabinet, thus facilitating the survival of minority administrations.)

If coalitions became the norm, Canadians would find little guidance in their own parliamentary history as to how to operate them. Ottawa's experience with coalitions is uninspiring, being limited to the Borden Unionist coalition of 1917-20. Ontario had a coalition of United Farmers and of Labour under Drury (1919-23). BC was ruled by a coalition of Liberals and Conservatives in 1941-52 under John Hart and afterwards Byron Johnson. Saskatchewan had a Conservative-dominated "Cooperative" coalition during the Depression years under Anderson (1929-34), while a Liberal joined the NDP cabinet following the inconclusive 1999 election. Bracken's premiership in Manitoba included a long period of coalition government. Incidentally, an encouraging feature is that most of these coalition governments lasted for the full life of a legislature.

Despite our own limited experience in this field, coalition government is well entrenched in most democratic countries, including some with majority systems like France and Australia, and Canadians could derive inspiration from the practices that have been developed elsewhere (see, e.g., Boston 1998).

6. LESS DURABLE CABINETS

Our experience with minority governments strongly suggests that they would be less durable. Since 1867, minority governments in Ottawa lasted an average of less than 20 months, compared with more than 50 months for majority governments. There is no reason to believe that minority governments, if they were formed in a PR context, would be any more lasting. Thus, we must turn to the experience of other countries to see whether coalition governments would be more lasting than in Canada's history.

In their study, Laver and Schofield found single-party minority governments to have lasted an average of 19 months in office, compared with 33 for (minimal winning) coalitions and 45 for majority governments,[9] and no evidence that coalitions had become more durable over recent decades (Laver and Schofield 1990: 148-52). True, one can quote examples of cabinets in PR countries lasting for the full duration of a legislature, of heads of governments serving aggregate terms comparable to those served by many Canadian prime ministers,[10] or even of coalitions lasting for decades (like the Swiss four-party coalition that has run the country without interruption since 1959). Yet the possibility remains that party fragmentation and the presence in Parliament of parties deemed "extremist" by the others and consequently excluded as coalition partners may combine to produce a succession of short-lived governments under PR. Cases like Israel, Italy, and the French Fourth republic, where governments have on average been short-lived,[11] are relatively rare, but they can happen.

Coalitions are inherently more fragile than single-party majority governments, are more likely to break up during the life of the parliament, or lead to early elections. When an unpopular decision has to be made, it is tempting for the junior partner to withdraw support in the hope of escaping voters' vengeance. When an unforeseen issue arises, coalition partners may find their respective positions irreconcilable and dissolve their partnership. It is difficult to gauge how Canadians would react to this new pattern of parliamentary politics. Much criticism has been voiced in recent decades against governments having too much power, the executive dominating Parliament and the prime minister behaving like an elected monarch (see Savoie 1999). Hence PR would likely make governments more fragile, but this may be what Canadians, or at least many of them, actually want, if it means governments were more willing to listen and to compromise. It is striking that Australia, the country where the working of the Westminster model arouses the least criticism, is also the only one where the power of the ruling party or coalition is checked by a PR-elected second chamber that the government party or coalition rarely controls.

Cabinet formation and survival, assuming that future elections return the same parties we now have, would be made more complex by the presence of the Bloc, a party created in order to highlight the deficiencies of the Canadian federation, not to support, or be part of, the federal cabinet. In the present context, it seems doubtful the Bloc would be a willing coalition partner or would be accepted as such by the other parties. The new Conservative Party would probably be more eager to join a coalition. How other parties would react is uncertain. The presence of the Bloc reduces the range of potential government formulas, making cabinets more fragile.

7. WEAKER PRIME MINISTERS

In the long run, PR would most likely erode the authority of the prime minister within cabinet. At present, prime ministers enjoy a very strong position and are acknowledged to be far more than *primus inter pares*. Contrary to their counterparts in the UK, Australia and New Zealand, Canadian prime ministers have stayed longer in office and have been less vulnerable to successful cabinet, caucus, or rank-and-file revolts,[12] probably because their status as party leaders derives from elected delegates at a party convention or (more and more) from direct election by party members, rather than from a caucus decision.

This ascendency results from their position as leaders of the sole ruling party and from the existence of crucial powers commonly acknowledged to be their personal prerogatives, like recommending the convocation or dissolution of Parliament and recommending appointments to the bureaucracy, the judiciary, and the Senate.

These prerogatives would survive intact in minority single-party cabinets, though the more precarious position of the cabinet as a whole would affect their use. In coalition cabinets, many ministers would belong to a party other than the prime minister's and would have more complex loyalties. The list of the prime minister's personal prerogatives is then likely to diminish. Junior coalition partners are unlikely to tolerate in the long run that appointments to the bureaucracy, the Senate, the governor generalship, or the bench continue to be made ultimately— and secretly—by a single individual. They are likely to insist on some kind of sharing of order-in-council appointments. They might even have a veto on the prime minister's appointment.[13] To the extent that one thinks prime ministers wield too much power, therefore, PR would

likely make our cabinet system more collegial and less monarchic in its operation and style.

8. THE RELATIONSHIP BETWEEN ELECTION RESULTS
AND GOVERNMENT FORMATION

It has been argued that FPTP empowers the electorate to select rulers "directly," insofar as elections normally result in a clear majority for one party with
a recognized leader and policy position, instead of leading to negotiations
between parties as to what kind of coalition will be formed, who will lead it,
and what that government will do.

There is much truth in that argument, though most of the time a "clear-
cut outcome" reflects the will of only a plurality of the electorate. However,
malapportionment of electoral districts or excessive concentration of a party's
vote in certain districts at times leads to majority governments that do not
even rest on a plurality of the popular vote, as was the case in Québec in 1998
and BC in 1996, which unquestionably amounts to a serious distortion, some
would say a denial, of the voters' will.

Under PR, voters would have a less direct say in government formation
than they now do. Governments would be formed after the election through
negotiations between parties, taking into account each party's respective
strength. Leaders may state in advance of polling day which party they would
ally—or not ally—with, but there would be no legal obligation for them to
do so. I have found in the literature no systematic survey determining to what
extent, in PR countries, parties had given such indications. Yet it seems to be
a fairly common practice, since, in the absence of such indications, the feeling may develop in the electorate that the people's role at elections amounts
merely to "reshuffling the cards" among political elites. An even worse
scenario is acted out when pivotal parties choose to ally with other parties
in defiance of their own pre-election public statements (as occurred in New
Zealand in 1996), or switch sides in the middle of the life of a parliament (as
the West German Free Democrats did in 1982).

Yet these occasions are rare. Not unrelated is the fact that (as in these two
cases), the "slippery partner" suffered losses at the ensuing election, thus
deterring politicians who would be tempted to emulate this behaviour.

9. NO EVIDENCE THAT GOVERNANCE WOULD BE WORSE

It is still largely accepted in Canada, especially among political elites, that the FPTP system, while distorting to some extent the representation of parties in Parliament, should be maintained because the stable and effective cabinets it produces ultimately ensure better governance.

Most Canadian elections have resulted in majority governments. Parliaments with no single-party majority have been typically short interludes managed by a single-party administration biding its time before it could call another election and get a majority. Except in the 1920s and in the 1960s, there have been few "back-to-back" minority parliaments that might have, in the long run, entrenched minority governments or coalitions as standard government formulas. Since 1980, no election has failed to return a majority government.

In such cabinets, decisions can be made quickly. It is easier to reach consensus within the confines of a cabinet composed of people belonging to a single party. Decisions that are unpopular in the short term can nevertheless be made and be allowed to produce their long-term advantages. The conventional wisdom is that our present system produces "firm and decisive leadership." For many Canadians, this is to be equated with good governance.

Until the 1970s, this was the accepted wisdom among students of comparative government. The Westminster system was widely acknowledged as the most successful variant of parliamentarianism. After all, it originated from one of the most powerful countries in the world, one where democracy had successfully withstood the challenges of the interwar period.

However, more recent literature casts serious doubts on the advantages the governance of countries supposedly derives from single-party majority governments. Simple assumptions that used to be deemed self-evident and were accepted without question have been recently tested and found wanting. The argument advanced by perceptive observers of French politics before 1958 like André Siegfried and Raymond Aron—namely, that cabinet instability, while exposing a country to ridicule, is less harmful for governance than many assume—has been reinforced. Instead, there is no statistical evidence that economic growth in majoritarian countries is higher, or that inflation and unemployment are lower. On the whole, cabinets are more stable in majoritarian countries than in PR countries, but there is no evidence that cabinet durability results in better outputs.

In a major article published in 1994, and in a book published in 1999, Arend Lijphart has attacked the conventional wisdom that assumed the existence of a trade-off between accurate representation and good governance (Lijphart 1994a; 1999). He reaffirmed that PR coincided with a more accurate representation of parties in the legislature, a higher proportion of women, and a higher electoral turnout. He did not deny that executive durability was higher in countries with majoritarian electoral systems; rather, he presented evidence that PR countries did not perform less well than countries with plurality systems on a number of important indicators. On average, plurality systems had a lower incidence of political riots but a higher incidence of political deaths than PR countries. On crucial economic indicators like economic growth, inflation, and unemployment, countries with majoritarian systems were not found, on average, to outperform PR countries. In other words, there was evidence that PR led to less durable executives, but no evidence that durable executives produced better policies. Indeed, some data pointed in the opposite direction. "Majoritarian governments," Lijphart wrote, "may be able to make decisions faster than consensus governments, but fast decisions are not necessarily wise decisions"(Lijphart 1994: 12).

Lijphart's findings are an important milestone in the age-old debate between supporters of PR and majoritarian systems, a debate that had become largely repetitive by the 1980s. The argument is grounded on the analysis of up to 36 stable democracies, small and large; in contrast, the conventional wisdom tended to overfocus on a few large and dysfunctional PR countries. In addition, the argument is based on empirical indicators rather than on impressionistic evidence. Lijphart's 1994 article has not only won praise (Schmidt 1997: 193-95) but, to my knowledge, has met with no systematic rebuttal by supporters of the Westminster model.

Other recent works have also offered a more positive assessment of governance under non-majority administrations. Kaare Strom has analyzed the working of minority governments in 15 democratic countries between 1945 and 1987. He found that minority governments, either coalitions or single-party governments, were frequent, accounting for almost 35 per cent of all cabinets formed. Looking at their performance, he concluded that contrary to conventional wisdom, minority governments do not perform particularly poorly in office. While minority governments are less durable than majority coalitions, they fare better at the polls and resign under more favourable circumstances. They perform best in those political systems where they are most common, and least well where they are most rare.

After examining in detail the record of minority governments in Italy and Norway, he concluded that "at least in these countries, minority governments are just as effective as majority coalitions" (Strom 1990: 239).

The thrust of this is that many Canadians' instinctive preference for majority governments and distaste for coalition or minority governments rests on foundations that are shakier than they appear. Even if cabinets were shorter-lived than they are now, it is far from certain that Canada's governance would perforce be worse.

10. THE FEDERAL/PROVINCIAL BALANCE

Any reflection as to the consequences of introducing PR federally must take into account the fact that Canada is a federation with powerful provinces, in which federal-provincial relations tend to be conducted in an adversarial mode, and which has to deal with a strong secessionist movement. In 1983, Canada's preeminent mandarin, Gordon Robertson, described Canada as "the most quarrelsome" among major federations, and this stands true today.

Would a succession of relatively short-lived administrations in Ottawa, facing strong single-party majority administrations in the provinces (an unlikely prospect to be sure, given that the provinces are well ahead on electoral system reform), weaken the federal government? It is difficult to derive significant insights from the experience of other federations, because the same electoral system tends to prevail at both levels in federal countries, either because such congruence is constitutionally mandated, as in Austria, or because the federal and state legislatures have freely opted for the same kind of system, as in Switzerland (see Massicotte, 1999).

It is plausible to infer that PR would result in less assertive federal cabinets in the field of federal-provincial relations. One can point out, for example, that Ottawa's most prolonged succession of minority administrations (1962-68) coincided with a more accommodative attitude with the provinces, as exemplified by the pensions deal of 1964, the abortive Fulton-Favreau formula which granted *every* province a constitutional veto, or the setting up of the Bilingualism and Biculturalism Commission. On the other hand, Trudeau's attitude towards provincial governments, as manifested in the National Energy Policy (NEP), does not appear to have been markedly softer while he was heading a minority cabinet in 1972-74. Further, Mulroney's very large majority in the House of Commons during his first term coincided with one of the most accommodative eras in federal-provincial relations, one which saw the mothballing of the NEP and the signing of the Meech Lake Accord. One is tempted to conclude that, in this field, much more depends on the character and beliefs of the federal prime minister than on the extent of his or her support in the Commons.

Moreover, the possibly increased weakness of federal cabinets might be counterbalanced by an increase in their representativeness. More broadly based federal cabinets will weaken some premiers' claims to be the true spokespeople of their provinces since they will no longer be facing a federal cabinet including no minister from that province. William Irvine, a leading advocate of electoral reform in the late 1970s, argued that PR, by increasing the representativeness of the federal government, might spare Ottawa massive transfers of powers to the provinces (Irvine 1979).

11. QUÉBEC AND FRANCOPHONES

How would PR affect francophones in general and Québec in particular? PR would not change the proportion of seats from Québec, which would remain governed by section 51 of the Constitution Act, 1867. However, it would alter the shape of political representation in that province as well as in others. Bakvis and Macpherson have documented the fact that Québec's "block vote" made a substantial difference in the outcome of many Canadian elections throughout the twentieth century (Bakvis and Macpherson 1995). This resulted not only from the sheer weight of Québec seats (25 to 29 per cent of the total, depending on the election) but also from the fact that Quebeckers tended historically to massively support a specific political party, thus enhancing the chances of that party to form the government. An extreme illustration of this occurred in 1980 when all but one of Québec's 75 seats went to the Liberals, allowing that party to form the government while trailing in all other provinces combined. As a result, for the next four years, more than half of the ruling party caucus came from Québec. While the Liberals' share of the vote in Québec was already high (68 per cent), only the FPTP system could translate it into 98.6 per cent of the seats. In this sense, PR would reduce Québec's clout—or for that matter the clout of any major province indulging in "block voting."

Before rushing to the conclusion that PR would hurt Québec, two notes of caution must be added. First, block voting is a risky game, as any region that puts all its eggs in the same basket could end up with, instead of strong representation within the winning party (as Québec usually achieved), very weak representation, as occurred notably in 1917, 1957, and 1979. In the latter scenario, Québec can expect few cabinet seats and must rely on expedients like choosing ministers from the Senate, which in retrospect does not seem to have proved effective, either for Québec (1979-80) or for the western provinces (1980-84). PR, on the other hand, would guarantee each major party a minimum number of seats from Québec and would substantially reduce the likelihood that the province would be severely underrepresented in cabinet.

Second, it is far from certain that Québec will again send massive one-party contingents to Ottawa. The Liberals maintained their traditional dominance of federal elections in Québec during the 1970s and the early 1980s because supporters of Québec sovereignty, until 1990, chose to stay away from the federal arena. This factor appears to have contributed strongly to Trudeau's lopsided victories, at a time when the Parti québécois (PQ) was doing well on the provincial scene but was unwilling to divert its energies to federal elections. Many PQ supporters abstained, deliberately spoiled their vote, voted for freak parties like Rhinoceros, or dispersed their vote more or less strategically among the PCs, the Créditistes, the NDP, or even the Liberals.

Now supporters of Québec sovereignty have their own party on the federal scene, one fully backed by their provincial allies. A return to Liberal ascendancy in Québec and the election of massive Liberal contingents from that province appear unlikely unless the sovereignty option vanishes completely from the Québec political scene. The most likely scenario for the predictable future is that the electorate in Québec will remain fragmented and that there will continue to be a substantial number of Bloc members in the House of Commons.

PR would have been helpful to the Bloc had it existed in the 1970s, but is likely to be detrimental now. First, PR would eliminate the advantage the Bloc has derived at the previous three elections from the division of the federalist vote between the Liberals and the PCs. It would increase the likelihood of prominent Québec federalists being elected in heavily francophone areas, thus impairing the Bloc's ability to claim they speak for Québec's francophones. PR would also diminish a handicap that afflicts the Liberals and helps the Bloc, namely, the excessive concentration of Liberal support in English-speaking areas in Québec. This phenomenon, which is replicated to an even higher degree on the provincial scene, largely explains why in the 1997 election the near equality between the Bloc and the Liberals in the province (37.9 versus 36.7 per cent of the vote respectively) was not matched in terms of seats (44 Bloc versus 26 Liberals). In 2000, the bias became even clearer, with the Bloc securing two seats more than the Liberals while trailing them by four points in the popular vote. In both cases, a look at the massive majorities won—and thus, votes wasted—by the Liberals in Western Montreal provides the explanation.

On the other hand, PR might reduce the likelihood of francophones being elected from provinces other than Québec. The reasoning here is that PR requires much larger electoral districts and that much would depend then on the willingness of parties (not only national leaders, but also local activists) to include French-speaking candidates in top positions on their lists. For example, under its present boundaries and linguistic profile, Ottawa-Vanier can be expected to return a francophone MP, but the same result would be less certain if the constituency comprised metropolitan Ottawa, where francophones make about ten per cent of the population. A single New Brunswick PR constituency electing ten members might result in less Acadian representation than it now does in single-member districts, depending on decisions made by parties while preparing their lists of candidates. This is why a German-style mix, by keeping single-member seats, would help to preserve the representation of Acadians.

12. THE ROLE OF THE SENATE

Two important constraints influence the impact of the Senate on the political process. The first one—that Senators are appointed rather than directly elected—diminishes the clout of the Senate since most Canadians believe it is illegitimate for a chamber so constituted to oppose the government on major issues. This would not be affected by PR. The second constraint is whether the Senate is dominated by the government or the opposition: experience suggests that the Senate is much more likely to be assertive when the government has no majority "up there," as exemplified by the behaviour of Senators in 1984-90—over the Goods and Services Tax and free trade in particular—and to a lesser extent in 1994-96. As long as the Senate continues to include members from both traditional parties almost exclusively, coalition governments composed of those parties can expect a cooperative attitude from senators. Like any new government, coalitions excluding those two parties can expect a rough time in the Senate until they have appointed enough of their own in that chamber. This should happen gradually since junior coalition partners will insist on some share of Senate appointments, thus leading to a more broadly representative Senate than at present.

13. THE GOVERNOR GENERAL

Governors general are appointed, and may be dismissed, by the monarch at the personal request of the prime minister. Their political influence is extremely modest, notably because most elections produce clear-cut results and because, even in minority contexts, refusing to follow the prime minister's advice in the use of the reserve powers is assumed—rightly—to be a highly risky attitude. It is conceivable further that junior partners in coalition cabinets might challenge the right of the prime minister to personally recommend appointments to Rideau Hall.

Would PR, by multiplying hung parliaments, provide an opportunity for the governor general to play a more active role in the selection of the prime minister, as do parliamentary presidents in some PR countries? Probably not. The trend in the latter, including New Zealand, is for party leaders to negotiate between themselves and for the head of state to be informed of their conclusions and to act accordingly. Contrary to hereditary monarchs or to directly or indirectly elected presidents, the governor general may be dismissed by the monarch at any time on the recommendation of the prime minister. This should dampen any temptation by the governor general to act as a player, either in cabinet formation or with regard to the dissolution of Parliament.

14. THE JUDICIARY

The relative position of the judiciary in the Canadian political system would not be directly affected by PR, as it derives from constitutional provisions. The only possible influence has to do with the appointment of judges. Junior coalition partners will probably insist either on having a more decisive input in judicial appointments or on a more open selection procedure involving public hearings by Commons committees.

15. NO THREAT TO THE SURVIVAL OF DEMOCRACY

Some still fear that PR would endanger the very survival of democracy. A quick succession of short-lived cabinets, they fear, might give the public the impression that anarchy prevails at the highest level of the state, and the country may become a laughing-stock abroad. At worst, the working of parliamentary government under PR might be unfavourably contrasted by the public with the firm and decisive leadership of monarchs or dictators, thus discrediting democracy itself. In reality, the argument that PR is conducive to democratic breakdown, quite popular in the 1940s and 1950s, is itself now discredited, though it may have some value for emerging democracies (Blais and Dion 1990). This argument was inspired by an analysis that focused excessively on the experiences of Weimar Germany or interwar Italy. It overlooked the fact that, at the same moment, in many PR countries like Switzerland, the

Low Countries, and Scandinavia, democracy had survived the challenges of the interwar period quite well. A recent survey of historical works on democratic breakdowns during the interwar period revealingly makes no mention of PR (Ertman 1998).

Conclusion

There is no perfect electoral system, as evidenced by the continuing presence of both PR and of majority or plurality systems in established democracies, as well as by the spread throughout the 1990s of mixed systems that try to secure the best of both worlds. It is significant, however, that contrary to the experience of many countries (France, Ireland) in the 1950s, current PR systems suffer little challenge in most of the countries where they exist, while plurality systems and the Westminster model have been frequently challenged, sometimes successfully, in most established democracies where they prevail.

On balance, in this country and at this time, I believe the benefits of PR outweigh its disadvantages. Party caucuses would become regionally more balanced, no region would appear to have an overwhelming say within the government party, and the formation of regionally representative cabinets would be facilitated. The chief downside—that large electoral districts would be less appropriate for constituency work as Canadian MPs traditionally practice it—would be offset to a large extent by opting for a German-style mixed system, with 50 or 60 per cent of members being elected in single-member districts.

Our cabinet system would be profoundly transformed by PR. Party elites, rather than the straight will of a plurality (most of the time) of the electorate, would select the government. Single-party majority governments would almost disappear, and coalitions would become the standard government formula, though the formation of single-party minority governments should not be ruled out. Cabinets would be less durable, and prime ministers would lose some of the dominance they now enjoy.

Contrary to a widely held view, there is no evidence at all that PR would necessarily lead to a negative economic performance or to bad governance. Governments would devote more time to cabinet discussions in order to reach an agreement between coalition partners, but the decisions so arrived at may prove to be wiser than some decisions taken impulsively by a prime minister after minimal discussion within cabinet.

Notes

1. This is an abridged and updated version of a paper written for the Institute of Research on Public Policy (IRPP) and published in 2001 under the title *Changing the Canadian Electoral System*. Alterations necessitated by the 2000 election have been incorporated in the text. The permission of the Institute is gratefully acknowledged. No account has been made for the fusion between the PC and Canadian Alliance parties which was still in the process of being ratified at the time of writing.

2. For example, New Zealanders were promised the best of all worlds in the early 1990s when the introduction of the mixed-member proportional system (MMP) was under debate, and this, combined with almost universal scorn for the existing political class, contributed to the victory of MMP at two referendums. A few years later, the actual operation of MMP had proved so disappointing, even to some of its promoters, that public opinion turned sharply against it, and New Zealand started to be cited as an example of the drawbacks of PR, to the point of making people forget about the real improvements it brought in the area of representation. Since then, however, the successful operation of MMP in subsequent elections has swung public opinion to a more favourable view.

3. In 1993, the Reform Party and the Bloc, with respectively 18.7 per cent and 13.5 per cent of the vote, secured 52 and 54 seats, while the PCs, with 16.0 per cent, got only two. The Bloc reached Official Opposition status while ranking fourth in terms of popular vote. It should not be overlooked that the Bloc fielded only 75 candidates and Reform 207, while the PCs had candidates in all 295 seats.

4. Since 1993, Ontario has been, in terms of representation in the House of Commons, a one-party province, with the Liberals sweeping all but one of Ontario's 99 seats (1993) and all but two of 103 seats (1997), though the Liberal share of the Ontario vote never exceeded 53 per cent in either case.

5. In 1997, 40 per cent of Reform's votes came from non-Western provinces (35 per cent from Ontario alone), but brought no seat.

6. Belgium initially had a two-ballot majority system in multi-member districts. At the 1894 election, held prior to the introduction of PR, the Catholic party won all seats in Brussels and 71 of the 72 Flemish seats, but only 14 of the 62 seats in Wallonia. See Mabille 1986: 194. Incidentally, this result illustrates how little a two-ballot system can do to mitigate regional polarization.

7. This source revealingly concludes that "the problem is less one of reality than of inaccurate perception" (Ward 1998: 143).

8. The elections of 1958, 1968, and 1974 provided an incumbent minority government with a majority of seats.

9. The median duration of minimum winning coalitions (35 months) was higher than the mean.

10. For example, Tage Erlander served as prime minister of Sweden without interruption from 1946 to 1969, a total of number of years (23) that exceeds the number served by Mackenzie King, the most durable of Canada's prime ministers. In recent years, Felipe Gonzalez was president of the Spanish government for 14 years, while Helmut Kohl led Germany for an uninterrupted 16 years.

11. From 1945 to 1995, there have been 42 cabinets in Israel (starting from 1948) and 55 in Italy. The French Fourth Republic saw 28 cabinets in its 13 years of existence. See Woldendorp, Keman, and Budge, 1998.

12. One was attempted against John Diefenbaker in 1963, but failed. There was a successful revolt against Jean Chrétien's leadership in August 2002. Significantly, unlike all other such coups known to the author, the leader was able to secure a reprieve for an additional 18 months.

13. Australian political history offers at least two examples of this. After the 1922 election, the Country Party, whose support had become a precondition for the continuance in office of the Nationalist Party government, insisted not only on an almost equal number of cabinet ministers, but also blackballed incumbent Prime Minister Hughes, thus obliging the Nationalist Party to select a new leader as prime minister. In 1967-68, following the death of Liberal Prime Minister Holt, Country Party Leader John McEwen similarly vetoed the appointment of William McMahon as prime minister on the ground that he did not trust him personally.

CHAPTER 3

Problems in Electoral Reform: Why the Decision to Change Electoral Systems is Not Simple

Richard S. Katz

The 1990s witnessed an unusually large number of major electoral reforms, with long-standing national systems replaced in Italy, Japan, and New Zealand, and novel (at least for them) systems introduced into the UK for the election of members of the European Parliament, the Scottish Parliament, the Welsh Assembly, and the London mayor—not to mention the numerous reforms occasioned by the transitions to democracy in eastern and central Europe, as well as in other regions of the world. A variety of predictions were made, and justifications offered, by the reformers, some of which have been verified by experience and others not. In some cases, the reforms themselves have been reformed, but in virtually all cases it is still too early to say what the long-term consequences of these reforms will be.

As a number of Canadian provinces begin seriously to consider reforming their electoral systems, and with the issue looming, perhaps not quite as immediately, on the national agenda as well, a variety of claims and counter claims about the political consequences of electoral laws undoubtedly will be raised—including in this volume. Without myself taking a position regarding the desirability of electoral reform for Canada, in this chapter I want to suggest a note of caution regarding the arguments advanced. The history of electoral reforms is rife with examples of wishful thinking and of the law of unintended consequences. The potential effects of electoral reform are very far-reaching; it is a process that, like marriage, "should not be entered into unadvisedly or lightly, but ... deliberately" and with considerable caution.

Paths to Electoral Reform

People who are dissatisfied with the outcome of electoral politics often call for electoral reform. On one hand, particularly for those whose dissatisfaction stems from the results obtained by the parties they support, blaming the electoral system externalizes the fault. It is not that their cause is unpopular or that they campaigned badly, but rather that the rules are unfairly biased against them and that brought about the disappointing outcome. On the other hand, regardless of whether the dissatisfaction is partisan or systemic, electoral reform is likely to be seen to provide a tractable strategy for achieving their objectives.

In some cases, the connection between the electoral system and the immediate cause of reformers' dissatisfaction is direct and obvious. The party or political orientation that they support may have representation in parliament that is significantly less than that to which its share of the popular vote appears to entitle it. Alternatively, parties that they do not support may appear to have too much bargaining power in parliament relative to their electoral support. If one believes that parliamentary representation should be proportional to popular support, that parliamentary power should be proportional to parliamentary representation (and hence also to popular support), and that the electoral system is the primary mechanism through which popular support is translated into parliamentary representation and then parliamentary power, these results lead to a prescription of electoral reform—and in particular, at least in the first case, to a call for a more proportional system[1] (Amy 1993; Lakeman 1982).

In some cases, the connection between the electoral system and the unsatisfactory outcome is less direct and also less obvious. The proportion of elected officials who are women or members of some ethnic, religious, or racial group may be markedly less than the proportion of citizens who have the same demographic characteristic. Even if representation in the parliament as a whole accurately reflects the composition of the citizenry, particular regions or demographic groups may be radically over- or underrepresented in the governing coalition. Here calls for electoral reform are predicated on the belief that an alternative system would, for example, either alter the nominating strategies of parties so that more members of the underrepresented groups would be elected or change the geographic mix in the parliamentary party delegations (Young 1994; Rule and Zimmerman 1994; Weaver 1997).

For some would-be reformers, the connection between electoral system and the ill to be remedied may not be direct at all, and indeed the call for reform may simply reflect the fact that institutions are easier to change than are culturally based practices or attitudes. Claims that electoral reform is necessary as a cure for political corruption or for declining levels of political information or participation among the public are of this type.

All of these real or potential complaints about the operation of the single-member plurality electoral system have been raised in Canada. The complaints have not been without justification. Nationally, in 2000 the Liberals formed a majority government on the basis of only 40.9 per cent of the vote, and that was (in proportional terms) an improvement over the majority government they formed in 1997 after winning only 38.5 per cent of the vote. In the same elections, the PCs won only 4 per cent (2000) and 6.6 per cent (1997) of the seats, although they had 12.2 per cent and 18.7 per cent of the votes. In the 2000 election, the Liberals won 18.2 per cent of their total vote in the provinces west of Ontario (which altogether represent roughly 29 per cent of the total votes and seats in Canada), but MPs from those provinces were only 8 per cent of the Liberal caucus. At the end of 2001, only 20.6 per cent of the members of the House of Commons were female, although women make up roughly half of the electorate. Even more disproportional results are common in provincial elections. In 2003, the PCs in PEI won 87 per cent of the Legislative Assembly seats with only 54 per cent of the votes, a result similar to the 2001 election in BC in which the Liberals turned 57 per cent of the votes into 97 per cent of the seats, while the BC Greens won no seats at all though they took 12.4 per cent of the vote. The 1999 election in Saskatchewan left the three Liberal members of the Legislative Assembly (MLAs) elected (with 20 per cent of the vote) in a position to determine whether the NDP would be able to form a majority coalition government or have to govern with exactly half of seats—notwithstanding that the Saskatchewan Party had more votes, but won three fewer seats, than the NDP. Other examples from the last 25 years of one party winning a majority of the legislative seats although another party had more votes include Newfoundland (1989), Québec (1998), Saskatchewan (1986), and BC (1996).

At the same time, however, it should be recognized that to cite many of these outcomes as valid grounds for complaint depends on a variety of contestable assumptions. Some of these assumptions concern the primary function of an election (e.g., to give the voters a direct choice of governing party and thus also of prime minister, or to represent the diversity of the public's views in Parliament, or to choose local ombudsmen). Others concern the acceptable level of proportionality between votes and seats (ranging from insistence on nearly perfect proportionality of representation even for very small parties, through insistence on proportional representation for "significant" parties but toleration of underrepresentation or exclusion of splinters, ultimately to acceptance of a system that does no more than guarantee a majority of the seats to any party that wins an absolute majority of the votes); the level of minor party power that is appropriate (ranging from justifying a small party's holding the balance of power through to a belief that small parties have no place in the legislature in the first place); and the necessary levels and locus (in Parliament, in the government caucus, in the cabinet) of representation for minorities and regions.

Unsurprisingly, these "unsatisfactory" (to some) outcomes have led to a variety of calls for electoral reform, including most prominently calls for an elected Senate and proportional representation (perhaps in the form of MMP) in the House of Commons, or, somewhat less radically, the introduction of the Alternative Vote (which would retain single-member districts), or a more limited system of compensatory seats particularly designed to increase the geographic diversity of membership in the major party caucuses (Weaver 1997; Flanagan 1999). For the most part, these calls have appeared in academic books and journals. When they have been raised in more political arenas, as with the report of the Pépin-Roberts Commission in 1979, the government has lost no time in making it clear that far-reaching changes to the electoral system would not be considered. Given a record of much study but no action, the Royal Commission on Electoral Reform and Party Financing (Lortie Commission), set up in 1990, decided not even to address the question of fundamental electoral reform.

With the adoption of the Canadian Charter of Rights and Freedoms, however, an alternative route to electoral reform, not so directly under the control of the party that was winning under the existing electoral arrangements, was opened up—the courts. If, rather than convincing elected officials (either directly or by first convincing the voters) that electoral reform was desirable, would-be reformers could instead convince the courts that the status quo was incompatible with the higher law of the Charter, that status quo system could be declared void, thereby forcing the government to enact a reformed system. The earliest attempts to use this strategy to force reform concerned the (mal)apportionment of legislative seats. Building on the success of these efforts, the same strategy was used successfully to challenge the section of the Canada Elections Act mandating that a party nominate candidates in at least 50 election districts in order to qualify for some benefits (*Figueroa v Canada (Attorney General)*, 2003 SCC 37).[2] These reforms might be understood to be concerned primarily with improving the implementation of the basic

Canadian SMP electoral system rather than with its replacement, although the boundary between improved implementation and fundamental change is, of course, fuzzy.

More recently, however, the Green Party of Canada, with the assistance of the Constitutional Test Case Centre of the University of Toronto, has sought to use the courts to force Parliament to adopt some form of proportional representation based on the claim that the current system of single-member plurality election violates rights guaranteed by the Charter in two respects (*Joan Russow and the Green Party of Canada v The Attorney General of Canada, The Chief Electoral Officer of Canada and Her Majesty the Queen in Right of Canada*; see Russow 2001). On one hand, the applicants claim that the Canada Elections Act denies citizens equal and effective representation by giving the geographically dispersed supporters of small parties fewer MPs per vote (in general, no MPs at all) than larger parties in contravention of their understanding of Section 3's guarantee of the right to vote. On the other hand, they claim that the Canada Elections Act disadvantages women and minority candidates, in contravention of their reading of Section 15's guarantee of equal protection and equal benefit of the law.

The correct interpretation of the guarantees of Sections 3 and 15 is a question properly left to Canadian judges and lawyers, not American political scientists, and I will not address it in this chapter. Rather, I will use the Russow application to exemplify the kinds of empirical claims often raised by advocates of electoral reform, whether in the specific context of court proceedings or not, in order to address three closely interrelated questions of more general relevance. First, what sort of evidence is used to make the claim that the problems complained of actually should be attributed to the electoral system that the reforms seek to change? Second, on what grounds, and with what confidence, can the claim be supported that the change sought in the electoral rules would substantially ameliorate those problems? Third, supposing the desired benefits did result from electoral reform, might there be other consequences that would not be desirable — perhaps even from the perspective of those advocating the original reform? In other words, is electoral reform about finding the best electoral system, or is it about compromise and trade-off among competing visions of the good?

Problems of Evidence

The evidence adduced to support the claim that an electoral system is unfair generally falls into three basic types. With the first type, the outcome of elections, or the political situation more widely, under the system to be reformed is compared to some absolute ideal. This is the standard used, for example, when the Russow applicants complain that "supporters of the Bloc Québécois won a seat for every 34,186 votes whereas each Conservative MP spoke for 1,058,211 Canadians,"[3] or when the complaint is raised that the proportion of women or members of visible minorities (or of any other identifiable group) among elected officials is substantially less than the proportion of the same group in the population at large. The ideal is perfect proportionality, whether between seats and votes or between MPs and the whole population, and any departure from that ideal is cause for complaint.

With the second type of evidence, the outcomes of elections in the polity in question and in other polities with similar electoral arrangements are compared to the outcomes of elections in polities using the electoral system to which change is proposed. As an example of the deployment of this type of evidence, the Russow applicants observe that "the percentage of women who have been elected to the House of Commons varies between one quarter and one-half of the percentage of women elected to the national legislatures of countries like Sweden, Norway, and Germany." The implications that one is intended to draw is that the difference between the Canadian outcomes (and those of other countries using SMP) and those in Sweden, Norway, and Germany (and other countries using PR) can in significant measure be attributed to those electoral institutions, and even more that were Canada to reform its electoral system in favour of PR there would be an increase in the female proportion of Parliament as a direct consequence.

The deployment of these types of evidence is hardly unique either to Canada or to litigation. In broad terms, it underlies all of the social sciences and indeed all of the non-experimental sciences, whether social or not.[4] It is widely recognized in those scientific communities that evidence of these types must be interpreted with caution and that those interpretations can only be made with reference to a range of unverifiable assumptions. Often when the debate leaves the academy (and sometimes before that as well), the importance of the implicit caveats is lost.

One can identify three problems of this type in the claims of the Russow applicants. The first might be identified as the problem of "idealism," and relates most directly to the comparison of current Canadian outcomes to the standard of perfect proportionality. Implicit in the citing of SMP's departure from perfect proportionality as grounds for declaring its use to contravene the Section 3 guarantee is the assumption that PR would deliver perfect proportionality—and indeed this assumption is made explicit in the claim that "Although there is considerable variation in how PR systems operate in different countries, they all share the common characteristic of ensuring each vote carries the same weight in the assignment of seats in the legislature." The truth of this statement depends, of course, on the meaning of the phrase "the same weight," and the voluminous American jurisprudence on the subject makes clear that there is at least a reasonable interpretation of the phrase that is entirely compatible with SMP. But even taking the standard used by the applicants (that the quotients computed by dividing national total number of votes received by the number seats won be the same for each party), the claim of absolute proportionality clearly is false. Most simply, no electoral system can deliver perfect proportionality because legislative seats must be assigned in whole numbers, and the arithmetic will not work out.[5] More generally, once the "considerable variation in how PR systems operate" is taken into account—including, especially, differences among PR formulas, the imposition of statutory thresholds, and the (possibly mal-) apportionment of representatives among constituencies with differing numbers of seats—it is clear not only that some implementations of PR are likely to be more proportional than others, but also that there may be implementations of PR that yield outcomes that actually are less proportional than those generated by some SMP systems.

When realized, this possibility then illustrates the second problem. Comparison of outcomes under alternative electoral systems generally focuses on the means of the two distributions. But distributions with quite different means may still overlap to a very significant degree. While it clearly is true that the average proportion of women MPs in parliaments elected in countries that use PR is larger than the average proportion of women MPs in parliaments elected in countries that use SMP, this fact cannot be unequivocally translated into the statement that "women ... are represented in significantly smaller numbers in legislatures elected through SMP systems than those elected under electoral laws that are based on the principle of proportionality." The latter locution suggests that the parliament of *every* PR country has a higher proportion of women than is found in *any* SMP country, and this is not true. In fact, the data presented by the Russow applicants show Canada to have a proportion of women in the House of Commons that actually is greater than the average percentage of women in the parliaments of countries using PR that were listed as "free" by Freedom House. On the other side, Ireland, Malta, and Greece (the first two using STV, which generally is regarded as a variant of PR, and the last using list PR) all had proportions of female MPs that were below the average percentage for SMP systems.

A third concern inherent in the use of these types of data may be called the *ceteris paribus* problem. The advantage of comparing averages rather than individual cases lies in the presumption that differences among cases other than those that define the populations to be compared will "average out," so that extraneous factors can be "held constant" statistically, rather than being held constant literally as in an experimental setting. For this to work, however, requires that two conditions be satisfied. First, the number of cases in each of the categories must be large. Second, the cases must be assigned to the categories randomly, or failing that, there must be good reason to believe that there is no systematic connection between any of the factors supposedly being held constant and the location of the cases in one or another of the categories being compared. Unfortunately, in considering electoral reforms, neither of these conditions is very well met. What might be called the "canonical" set of cases—the established democracies of Western Europe plus Australia, Canada, Israel, Japan, New Zealand, and the United States—number less than 25, of which only Canada, the UK, and the United States use SMP. Even if pre-1993 New Zealand (SMP), France (single-member majority), and Australia (alternative vote) are added, there are only six systems that use single-member districts. While the number of cases can be increased by considering all of the currently "free" countries, using, for example, the 2000 categorization of Freedom House only increases the total number of cases to 85, of which only 21 (24.7 per cent) use the SMP electoral system. Moreover, far from having the appearance of random assignment, nearly every country that uses SMP is an English-speaking former colony of the UK.

The third type of data involves estimating the consequences of a proposed reform by applying the proposed new electoral system to the results of previous elections held under the old system. "If Canada had been using PR in 2000, the Liberals would have won...", estimated by applying some PR formula to the party vote totals actually recorded (most likely at the provincial level), would exemplify this type of evidence. It has, however, two major problems.

The first problem is a variant of the problem of "idealism" already discussed. On one hand, in order to make these calculations, the analyst is forced to decide which PR formula to apply. On the other hand, unless one assumes that the PR formula will be applied either at the national level or provincial level, the analyst also is forced to specify district magnitudes and, what is even more problematic, district boundaries. Even if one assumes (and it is a highly questionable assumption) that PR districts would simply be combinations of the existing single-member districts, this can be done in a very large number of ways, many of which will suggest quite different outcomes.

The other problem is even less tractable. In applying a new formula to the results of an old election, one is assuming that behaviour would not change. There is, however, a large body of theory (e.g., the "wasted vote thesis" or the "psychological factor," and theories concerning strategic voting; see Cox 1997) and survey research that suggests that voters would have voted differently in a PR election than they did in an SMP election (e.g., Butler and Stokes 1969: 329). It is also likely that the parties would have adopted different strategies as well: nominating candidates in areas that are "hopeless" under SMP but which would contribute to their national or provincial totals; allocating campaign resources differently; perhaps even modifying their programs. In fact, each of these behavioural changes is sometimes advanced as a reason why PR should be adopted, but unless they can be taken into account, they leave projections based on past elections of very dubious value.

Problems of Causal Inference

The *ceteris paribus* problem is particularly significant because it limits the possibility of drawing causal inferences from the correlational data. While differences between outcomes under different electoral systems may be of considerable scientific interest in their own right, their interest in debates about electoral reform lies in the claim that changing the electoral system will *cause* a change in the outcome. In the case of the Russow applicants, the claim is that were Canada to adopt some form of PR, then, as a direct result, the problems of which they complain—devaluation of the votes of geographically dispersed supporters of minor parties and the underrepresentation of women and visible minorities—would be reduced. Similarly, advocates of reform in Italy claimed that a more majoritarian system would produce more stable governments, increase the accountability of MPs to their constituents, and reduce the power of the "party barons" (Katz 1996). In Japan, it was claimed that replacing the single non-transferable vote (SNTV) system would reduce factionalism, the importance of money, and ultimately the endemic corruption that had come to characterize Japanese politics (Reed and Thies 2001). To what extent can claims such as these concerning the causal power of electoral reform be sustained?

The first answer must be that it depends on the kind of claim being made. Where the complaint can be expressed in purely mathematical terms, it is relatively easy to design electoral institutions that will necessarily solve the problem. The American experience with reapportionment, for example, shows that problems of malapportionment can be effectively eliminated altogether—provided that one defines malapportionment solely in terms of population disparities among districts, that one need not respect local boundaries, and that one is prepared to accept the accuracy of the census or registration data on the basis of which the district boundaries are to be set.[6] The Israeli and Dutch experiences show that one of the more proportional forms of PR applied at the national level with a large parliament and without any additional statutory threshold can guarantee a highly (albeit not perfectly) proportional outcome that is not sensitive to the geographic distribution of parties' support. The Indian, Lebanese, and Fijian experience with reserved seats shows that representation of minority (or other groups) can be guaranteed simply by making membership in specific groups a legal requirement for election to specific seats.

Where the objective is less simply quantifiable or directly mandatable (e.g., more accountability or less corruption), or where one chooses not to be so institutionally high-handed as to directly mandate an outcome like gender parity without regard to the voters' preferences, or where one cannot do so for constitutional reasons (e.g., equipopulous parliamentary ridings on the national level in Canada cannot be mandated so long as the constitution itself mandates unequal allocation of seats among the provinces), the ability of electoral reform to produce the desired outcome must be more questionable.

The first question is whether one can conclude with confidence that the problem to be corrected is the result of the electoral system, even if its incidence is correlated with the electoral system. Simply, correlation does not establish causation. On one hand, it is possible that the cause and effect have been reversed. One of the on-going debates in the study of electoral systems asks whether the correlation between PR and multiparty politics (and between SMP and two-party politics) known as Duverger's Law came about because PR encourages multipartism, or because PR was adopted in countries that already had multi-party systems (Blais and Dobrzynska 2000; Boix 1999; Riker 1982; Grumm 1958). Clearly, if party number is the cause rather than the effect, the impact of changing the electoral system on the number of parties may not be directly predictable from a theory that postulates party number to be the effect. And indeed, notwithstanding confident predictions based on Duverger's Law that the reform of the Italian electoral system to a system dominated by SMP districts would reduce the number of parties in Parliament, the result was to increase their number (D'Alimonte 2001: 326).

On the other hand, the correlation between outcome and electoral system may be spurious, reflecting the fact that both have been caused by some prior factor, even though there is little or no direct causal connection between current institutions and outcomes. If, for example, there is something about the Anglo-American political culture that leads to a bias in favour of two-party politics or against the election of women, then the fact that SMP systems are found almost exclusively in countries whose politics have been strongly shaped by that culture could generate a strong correlation. More generally, looking over the range of free countries shows that the percentage of the population that is Protestant has a considerably higher correlation with female inclusion in Parliament than does the electoral system. While there may not be anything in Protestant theology that directly inclines countries with large numbers of Protestants to elect women to Parliament, it is certainly plausible to imagine that Protestantism is involved in a complex cultural pattern, some element of which does make countries both more prone to elect women to public office and more likely to have adopted a PR electoral system.

The reference to plausibility in the previous paragraph points to a further problem in causal inference in non-experimental settings. While it is plausible for the Russow applicants to claim that "women are nominated much less frequently in SMP countries because there is an incentive for parties trying to win a plurality of votes in each district to nominate candidates they regard as the safest and least controversial," ultimately both elements of this claim—that parties want uncontroversial candidates and that they perceive men to be less controversial than women—depend more on their conformity to "widely accepted" understandings than on solid evidence. Even more, claims that the Italian or Japanese systems of intraparty choice caused the corruption that afflicted those systems were predicated primarily on the plausibility of the causal chain between electoral exigencies and the need for money and then between money and corruption. Of course arguments that seem plausible often are correct, but they are not always correct. Indeed, it is sometimes possible to construct two incompatible, but each plausible, accounts of the same phenomenon, or two plausible accounts that begin with the same premise but end with different conclusions. For example, the subservience of backbench MPs to their party leaders in the UK frequently has been attributed to the SMP electoral system, while one of the claims made in the debate surrounding the move toward SMP in Italy was that this would free backbench MPs from subservience to their party leaders.

The second question concerning the causal connection between electoral institutions and outcomes is, even if one grants that the electoral system was in some sense the underlying cause of the status quo, how, how much, and over how long a span of time, would changing the electoral system alter the status quo? Again, at least two problems can be raised. Both ultimately relate to the question of whether electoral systems should be understood to cause behaviour or rather to more or less severely constrain or facilitate behaviour.

In one of the earlier formulations of Duverger's Law, Duverger (1986: 70; citing Duverger 1955) himself said that "proportional representation tends to lead to the formation of many independent parties.... the plurality rule tends to produce a two-party system." In these directly causal terms, identified as "sociological laws," it would follow that a change from SMP to PR would cause an increase in the number of parties, while a change from PR to SMP would cause the number of parties to be reduced, ultimately to exactly two. Unfortunately, the evidence, including in particular the evidence from Canada, does not support the law-like status of Duverger's Law. This led Sartori (1986) to recast the hypothesis in terms of "facilitation" rather than "production," with the result that the numerous cases in which the law does not fit no longer provide adequate grounds for its rejection.

The implications of the shift from production to facilitation are more widely relevant, however. Of particular relevance to the Russow application, this shift suggests a quite different interpretation of the observed correlation between electoral formula and female representation. If PR is a facilitative factor in the increase in women's representation (perhaps because it lowers the cost to parties of taking risks, or because it gives central party offices more control over nominations, or simply because it tends to be associated with higher rates of turnover in office and therefore with more opportunities for new candidates, including women, to be elected),[7] then one would expect a universal tendency toward gender parity to be reflected faster and, at least in the early stages of this development, more strongly in PR systems. But unlike the implicit claim by the Russow applicants that PR is necessary for the achievement of anything approaching gender parity in Canada, this suggests merely that the increase in women's representation that will occur in any case will take a bit longer with SMP. And indeed the evidence shows that although the rate of women's representation has increased more rapidly in PR than in SMP systems, the rate is increasing in both categories.

The other problem is that of path dependence. Changes in electoral systems do not take place in a vacuum and do not simultaneously replace either the players (parties and politicians) in electoral politics or cultural expectations concerning elections. Thus, the result to be expected when a functioning polity adopts a new electoral system may be quite different from the result to be expected had that system been chosen originally. One explanation for the increase in the effective number of parties in parliament after Italy abandoned PR stems from this fact. Exactly as its advocates predicted, the reform created strong pressure toward the formation of two national electoral alliances. But because the overriding concern for the leaders of those alliances was to win a majority of the parliamentary seats for the alliance, the small parties were able to use their blackmail potential to negotiate allocations of single-member constituencies that were particularly favourable to themselves in a way that would have been impossible had they not already been established under the old system.

Unintended and Collateral Consequences

The conclusion so far is that both the attribution of causality and the prediction of results are far more problematic than advocates of electoral reform customarily recognize. There is, however, an additional set of problems associated with electoral reform that is at least as serious. This is the possibility that the reform will not only have its intended consequences, but that there also will be other consequences that are neither intended nor desired. In part, these negative outcomes may be the result of miscalculations on the part of the reformers, but in part they are the inevitable consequence of the fact that there is no ideal electoral system because there can be no ideal democracy. Rather, any electoral system embodies a series of compromises among competing values, all of which are desirable but which are not entirely compatible with one another.

These unintended or collateral outcomes can stem from any aspect of an electoral system (for example, internet voting may have the intended consequence of increasing turnout, but also the unintended consequence of increasing fraudulent voting),[8] but since the primary question for Canada today, and the one raised by the Russow case, is the replacement of SMP with PR, this section will focus on that potential reform. If one assumes that PR were adopted for elections to the House of Commons with constituencies electing between five and ten MPs each but still allocated among the provinces as at present, or alternatively assumes that MMP implemented at the provincial level would be adopted, one could be reasonably sure that the partisan balance in the House of Commons would more closely reflect the national distribution of votes among the major parties than is true at present. One might also imagine that parties currently without representation would win a seat or two. But what other potential consequences should reasonably be taken into account?

One possible consequence (and it should be emphasized, in keeping with the lessons of the two previous sections, that it is extremely problematic to assert with any certainty that these consequences either will, or will not, occur) is a breakdown of the ties between individual MPs and local constituencies. At best (from the perspective of local ties being important), PR constituencies would have to be twice as large, both geographically and in population, as current parliamentary ridings.[9] Moreover, this increase in size might be expected (on the basis of experience in countries using PR) to involve a process of candidate selection and list construction that would be far more centralized and far more under the control of party operatives than is true at present.

A second, and virtually certain, consequence would be the end of single-party governments. This is, of course, not necessarily bad in itself, but it raises four possibilities that generally would be considered undesirable. The first is that a coalition government would be dependent on small parties. For example, if the popular votes cast in 2000 had been translated perfectly into seat share in the House of Commons, one might imagine a majority coalition consisting of the Liberals (40.9 per cent), the NDP (8.5 per cent), and the Greens (0.8 per cent). On one hand, this suggests that the Greens could demand at least one cabinet post (3 per cent of the total, assuming a cabinet of 33 ministers—and there is reason to expect that one consequence of coalition governments would be an expanding cabinet; see Mershon 2002). On the other hand, the Greens would be in a strong position to demand policy concessions from the larger parties because, although they would under this scenario have only two or three seats in the House, they could deny the government a majority at any time.

The second potential consequence of the end of single-party government would be a permanent Liberal hegemony. The more common complaint about coalition governments is that they are unstable, and indeed it is the case that coalition governments tend to have shorter lives than single-party majority governments (Katz 1997: 164-65). The less often noted problem with coalition governments is that, if one looks to partisan composition rather than the identity of the prime minister, they may appear to be immutable. It was, for example, widely noted that Italian governments in the PR era (1948-93) were very unstable, with 49 governments in 46 years. What is sometimes ignored is that one party, the Christian Democrats, dominated every one of those governments, even when they ceded the prime ministership to one of their allies. Even more, although the presidency of the Swiss government changes annually, the last time the partisan balance of the Swiss executive changed was in 1956, notwithstanding changes in electoral support for the parties. Regardless of whether dependence on small parties would make Canadian governments unstable under PR, given the central position of the Liberals it is likely that they would be the indispensable senior partners in every conceivable coalition government.

The third potential consequence is that the people would no longer directly choose their government. Instead, they would choose a parliament, and then the party leaders would negotiate among themselves to choose the government. While there are some systems, such as Italy after 1994, in which potential coalitions are decided and announced in advance, so that voters can be said to be voting for a particular government when they vote for any of the parties that have pledged to support it, in many PR-based systems, coalitions are decided only after the composition of the parliament is known. Moreover, even when coalitions are signalled in advance, those commitments are not always honoured in the immediate post-election government formation process and certainly cannot be regarded as binding for the life of the parliament.

The fourth potential consequence is to break the connection between electoral popularity and the likelihood of inclusion in government. It is certainly possible for a party to lose votes and remain in government, as the Liberals did in 1997 when they lost 2.8 per cent of the vote and 8.5 per cent of the seats, but still retained a majority; and it is possible for a party to gain votes and remain outside of government, as the Canadian Alliance did in 2000, when it increased its vote by 6.4 per cent but still had only 66 seats in the House. It is less easy to reconcile situations in which a party in government gains votes in an election but then finds itself on the opposition benches or in which a party in opposition loses votes but enters the government with the idea that elections are the way in which voters hold parties accountable. Yet these situations, perhaps equally perverse as the SMP situation in which one party wins a majority of the seats even though another party had more votes, are not at all uncommon in PR systems.[10]

Although each of these possibilities is worth considering in its own right, more generally they all point to a fundamental dichotomy in the way in which one understands the purpose of elections in democratic societies. While both sides of this dichotomy have attractive features, they are fundamentally incompatible both institutionally and philosophically. In one view, roughly the model Lijphart (1999) identifies as "consensus democracy," elections are about the choice of representatives, and democracy is best served by the formation of broad centrist coalitions. In the other view, roughly Lijphart's "majoritarian democracy," elections are about the choice of governments, and democracy means that clear-cut decisions are made on the basis of majority rule. Lijphart's analysis of these two models of democracy suggests two dimensions. One he identifies as a "Federal-Unitary" dimension, along which

Canada's position near the federal (consensus democracy) end is not in question. The other dimension he identifies as "Executives-Parties." Although an electoral system per se is not part of the definition of consensus democracy, three of the five characteristics that define the parties (consensus democracy) end of the dimension (effective number of parliamentary parties, minimal winning one-party cabinets, and electoral disproportionality) are generally regarded—and specifically regarded by the Russow applicants—to be consequences of electoral formula. In these terms, to change an electoral system cannot be seen unambiguously as a decision to improve democracy. Rather, it must be understood as a decision to alter the character of democracy—not a better democracy, but a different democracy. While there may be reasons to prefer a more consensual version of democracy, it is important to recognize that the choice of an electoral system is also implicitly a choice among competing democratic values.

Notes

1. Logically the converse results should also lead to calls for reform, but in practice reformers rarely complain about too much representation for their friends or too little power for their opponents.

2. Similarly, appeal to the Federal Constitutional Court was used to force extension of public subsidies to German parties that receive as much as 0.5 per cent of the vote.

3. This, and all other quotations attributed to the Russow applicants, comes from the applicant's Factum, available at <http://www.law-lib.utoronto.ca/testcase/gpfactum.pdf>.

4. For example, much of the evidence used in epidemiological research compares two naturally occurring populations that are distinguished by some characteristic hypothesized to be of causal importance.

5. Even the Weimar system of giving a party one seat for every 60,000 votes or remaining quota over 30,000 votes meant that a party with 89,900 votes would "pay" nearly three times as much for its one seat as a party with 30,100 votes.

6. As the American experience also shows, if additional criteria, such as racial or partisan "fairness," are also considered, the problem may become intractable; if one must respect local boundaries (in the American case, the boundaries between states), this may seriously limit the possibility of uniform district populations. If carried to extremes, the requirement of equal populations can effectively become ludicrous, with disparities that are only a small fraction of the recognized margin of error in the original data being disallowed.

7. It should be noted that each of these explanations has been advanced, and is advanced in one or another of the documents supporting the Russow application, to explain the greater representation of women in PR systems.

8. The most widely feared avenue for vote fraud with internet voting is that some hacker will either alter the vote totals or violate the secrecy of the vote without the voter's consent. There is, however, a less widely recognized danger—that internet (or

postal) voting will allow the voter intentionally to violate the secrecy of the ballot. By making this possible, internet voting undermines one of the primary justifications for the secret ballot, that it makes bribery and intimidation less likely because the briber or intimidator cannot be sure that the voter acted as directed.

9. This assumes that the form of PR adopted would be MMP, with half of the seats still filled from single-member districts. Were a form of simple PR to be adopted, the constituencies would have to be at least three to five times the size of current ridings.

10. Looking at changes in government in Belgium, Denmark, Finland, Germany, Ireland, Italy, the Netherlands, Norway, and Sweden between the second election after World War II and 2000 (through 1992 in Italy), 103 parties left government immediately after elections, of which 74.8 per cent had lost votes, but 25.2 per cent had gained votes relative to the last election. Conversely, 116 parties entered governments after an election, of which 65.5 per cent had gained votes, but 34.5 per cent had lost votes.

CHAPTER 4

Reminders and Expectations about Electoral Reform[1]

John C. Courtney

By early 2004, there can be little doubt that the "electoral reform issue" has once again heated up in Canada, possibly to a greater extent than at any point in Canadian history. A spirited House of Commons debate took place at the end of the previous year on an opposition member's motion to hold a national referendum on proportional representation. Although defeated by the government in a vote of 144 to 76, the motion was the first to make it to the floor of the Commons since the 1920s. Several conferences sponsored by major public policy institutes have been held on electoral reform in the last half-decade. Websites, electoral reform organizations such as Fair Vote Canada, and internet chat groups have been created to encourage public discussion of the topic. A year after the Green Party of Canada launched a court challenge against plurality voting in 2001, the Law Commission of Canada released a discussion paper on electoral reform (Law Commission 2002, Russow 2001). Possibly of greatest significance was the fact that five provinces had undertaken investigations of various kinds to explore alternative methods of election. Other provinces may follow suit.

The speed with which the discussion of electoral reform has proceeded might create the impression that the issue is so clear-cut that it is only a matter of time until PR replaces plurality voting throughout Canada. In the excitement over the possibility of changing electoral systems, however, it is prudent to recall some of the elements of the issue that might otherwise go unheeded. We will explore these in two broadly defined categories. The first, relating to parties, voters, and institutional transference, is simply labelled "three reminders." All three stem from the fact that every electoral and political system contains its own distinctive elements. We then look at the likely consequences of an electoral system chosen to replace plurality voting under the heading of "three expectations." These are the claimed effect of a different electoral system on voter turnout, the representation of women in Parliament, and the election of governments with reformist/progressive agendas.

Three Reminders

First, political parties find it "rational" to pursue strategies that maximize their chances of converting votes into seats. Because the incentives contained in any method of casting and aggregating votes differ from one electoral system to another, party electoral strategies will also differ according to the incentives present. Canadian history has demonstrated that the principal incentive for any party intent on winning a federal election under plurality voting has been to bridge the country's regional, linguistic, and racial cleavages with policies, leaders, and candidates that appeal to a wide cross-section of voters. The model of broadly based, accommodative parties has, as a general rule, been one of the hallmarks of Canada's party system since Confederation. Where federal governing parties have abandoned that model, most famously in their handling of such controversial issues as the Manitoba Schools Question, World War I conscription, and the National Energy Policy, their electoral defeat soon came at the hands of an erstwhile opposition party that successfully created a "big-tent" coalition of its own (Courtney 1980).

It is no accident that the long-term dominance on the national scene of Macdonald's Conservatives, Laurier's Liberals, and Mackenzie King's/St. Laurent's Liberals owes much to the accommodative skills of the parties and their leaders. Those skills were honed in a highly regionalized and socially diverse country that employed the plurality vote to elect its governments. There is no guarantee that party strategists hoping to win federal office would see a non-plurality vote system as offering the same incentive to forge inter-regional, bilingual, and multicultural parties. They may, instead, find that proportional voting offers an electoral premium on winning the support of particular interests based overwhelmingly in one or two regions rather than of a wider cross-section of interests and voters in all parts of the country. The fact is, even taking into account the variety of proportional voting schemes available, it is not known how proportional voting would impact on our parties' capacity or willingness to fashion intra-party coalitions of diverse interests and regions. This could have profound implications for parties and, ultimately, for governance in Canada.

Second, just as each electoral system provides various incentives to parties and encourages particular electoral strategies on their part, each system also enables voters to pursue different strategic options. Voters' strategic choices are influenced by the number of votes they have been allocated, by the way preferences may (or may not) be ordered, and by the manner of distributing (or redistributing) votes among the candidates. Therefore, different electoral systems may prompt different voting behaviour. Any claim that *y* number of seats would have been won by a party in a *hypothetical* election under one set of rules, given that it won *z* share of the votes in an *actual* election under another set of rules, must be treated with suspicion. Just because parties A, B, and C received, for example, 40 per cent, 35 per cent, and 25 per cent respectively of the total popular vote under plurality does not mean they would have received that level of support under, let us say, some form of PR. Preference ranking among candidates presents the individual voter with choices that are simply not available when a single "X" is all that can be placed on the ballot. This serves to remind us, once again, that institutions, of which electoral systems are among the more visible, affect outcomes (Cox 1997: chaps. 2 and 3).

It is an article of faith among electoral reform proponents that the distortions in the vote/seat relationship under plurality elections would be corrected by PR. What is often missing from that claim is any detailed discussion of *which* proportional vote system would be better at minimizing the distortions. This is a not insignificant oversight given the range of alternative voting systems that exists and their varying capacity to distribute votes into seats more-or-less proportionately.

Past election results frequently serve as the database used to support calls for PR. Not surprisingly, of recent federal elections the one in 1997 has proved a favourite. The Chrétien Liberals were returned to office with a slim majority in the Commons even though they won slightly less than 39 per cent of the popular vote. Although the two main opposition parties (Reform and the Bloc) switched places in the Commons, Parliament once again was fractured among five parties each over-dependent on a single region for its representation. Two parties (Reform and PC) whose share of the national vote was virtually identical (19.4 per cent and 18.8 per cent respectively) had a 40-seat difference between them in Reform's favour. The NDP, with a slightly larger share of the vote than the Bloc (11 per cent versus 10.5 per cent), won only half the seats of the Québec-based party. Thus, there was much grist for the reformers' mill in 1997.

Because voter choices in an election are fashioned by, among other things, the strategic options that a system provides, the projection of future election outcomes based on past electoral results is problematic. It would be unwise to claim that (drawing on the 1997 figures) the Liberals under PR would have won 39 per cent of seats and the parliamentary representation of the other parties would have mirrored their respective shares of the 1997 vote. Such a claim overlooks the fact that the share of popular vote received by each of the parties might have gone up, down, or remained the same under an electoral system providing voters with alternative strategic choices. Arguments framed in favour of PR should not overlook that fact.

Third, institutional transference does not take place in a vacuum. As each political system is unique, there is no guarantee that the method of election judged to be a success in one country will suit another equally well. A change from one electoral system to another can be expected to have an impact (possibly quite a considerable one) on essential parts of a country's representational and governance institutions and processes. Those most subject to change under different electoral rules would include parties, the representative system, and cabinet government. (The latter, of course, would itself include the possibility of coalition governments composed of two or more parties.) As these are major components of any political system, the impact that a method of election may have on them should be fully understood before one voting system is replaced in favour of another.

Should an alternative electoral system replace the plurality vote at the federal level in the years ahead, it must be one that ensures the continuation of the fundamental cornerstones of our parliamentary system. These include Canada's essential constitutional principles: cabinet secrecy and solidarity, Commons' confidence votes on issues of critical public policy, responsible government, and (however shop-worn this concept may have become) individual ministerial responsibility.

Our constitutional-federal-parliamentary systems have deep roots in this country. Collectively they are the source of our entire machinery of government. They have contributed to and helped to shape our political culture, the expectations that the electorate holds about the political process and parliamentary government, and the internal organizational and authority structures of our parties. Too much is at stake both constitutionally and institutionally to introduce changes to the electoral system that might compromise or endanger the carefully crafted set of arrangements we have established to govern ourselves. Thus, the fundamental principle that must be adhered to if Canada decides to "transport" a seemingly better electoral system from abroad into its federal electoral process is that it proves to be compatible with our constitutional, federal, and parliamentary systems.

Three Expectations

Electoral reformers hold out a variety of hopes about what would be accomplished if Canada had a more proportional electoral scheme. Doubtless the objective of electoral reform about which there is no disagreement is the prospect of greater "electoral fairness" in converting votes into seats under PR. Naturally the degree of fairness would vary from one method of voting to another, but the goal of bettering the relationship between votes and seats is common to those who call for change. Beyond that there are several (sometimes competing) expectations held out on behalf of a different electoral system.

Among the claims offered in support of a switch to a proportional system are three that we will examine. It is said that with proportional representation voter turnout would rise, the number of women in Parliament would increase, and governments of a progressive/reformist bent would become more frequent. How realistic are these expectations? That question, of course, is impossible to answer with precision, but a few observations can be offered.

I. IMPROVED VOTER TURNOUT

On the face of it, the case for an increased level of citizen interest in politics and voter participation under proportional elections makes a good deal of sense. If electors support a candidate or party that is clearly going to lose, or so certain to win that an "extra" vote would be unnecessary, the value of a single vote can easily be cast into doubt. In those situations, voter turnout could reasonably be expected to decline. Conversely, levels of voter interest and turnout should go up when the "utility" of the vote is seen as greater. Under a scheme in which a party's share of seats reflect in some measure its share of votes, each individual vote could be perceived as more determinative of the final outcome. Thus, parties would have an incentive to encourage their own supporters to participate, and voters would have less reason not to vote. One study found that, all other things being equal, voter turnout tended to be roughly 7 per cent higher in countries with some form of proportional representation than in those with plurality voting (Blais and Carty 1990).

The problem, however, is that all other things are not always equal. It is not possible to predict in which direction voter turnout will go following electoral reform. That a drop in the level of electoral participation cannot be ruled out is demonstrated by the experiences of two Westminster-styled parliamentary jurisdictions that moved from plurality voting to a proportional scheme. The first example draws from the comparative electoral history of Manitoba and Saskatchewan over the past 80 years and the second from New Zealand's experience since 1996 with MMP. Neither of these cases confirms that an increase in turnout under proportional elections is necessarily a "done deal."

Over the course of its 35-year history with the AV and STV between 1920 and 1955, Manitoba experienced a sharp drop from its previous levels of voter turnout. Prior to the introduction of preferential voting, Manitoba's voter turnout averaged 82 per cent. Under AV and STV, when governing coalitions became the norm and the number of acclamations (a measure of inter-party competition) over the course of nine elections reached 16 in 1941 and 15 in 1949, voter turnout slumped by about one-quarter to 63 per cent. Since the return to FPTP, average turnout in Manitoba has yet to reach its pre-1920 levels, although it has reversed slightly from what it had been during the proportional voting period to 68.5 per cent (n = 13 elections).

By contrast, in Saskatchewan (a neighbouring province with many social and economic similarities to Manitoba) the nascent party system in the early years of the twentieth century generated far less voter participation than the province's later, highly competitive two- and three-party elections. Prior to the provincial election of 1921, voter turnout in Saskatchewan averaged 67 per cent, which was 15 percentage points below Manitoba's participation rate for the same period. But during the following decades during which Manitoba experimented with PR, Saskatchewan's turnout jumped to 79 per cent, an average that disguises the fact that for seven of those nine elections (1921-56), the range was between 80 and 85 per cent. In 12 subsequent elections, turnout figures in Saskatchewan have averaged close to 80 per cent even though, like much of the rest of the country, they have declined to the 60-70 per cent range over the past decade.

These figures suggest different party development patterns in the two provinces, which can in part be explained by how parties maximized their strategic opportunities under the respective electoral systems. In Manitoba from 1922 to 1958, the Progressives were never out of office. They were the central player in the formation of every government, whether it was coalition or single party. Until the return to true party competition in the late 1950s, there was a reduced level of inter-party rivalry and a heightened tendency to nonpartisanship in the province as a whole. Both of those features of Manitoba's party system led to reduced voter interest and partisanship, which ultimately contributed to the decline in voter turnout (Donnelly 1957: 20-32). Voters in such a context might have asked, why bother voting if the results are relatively easy to predict in advance, if the major governing party never changes, and if the incremental value of one vote will likely make little or no difference to the outcome?

In Saskatchewan, by contrast, the party system has been highly competitive following its early formative years, and the shares of votes of the two principal parties have been much closer to one another than was ever the case in Manitoba under AV and STV. Saskatchewan's system can best be described as a competitive two-party one, although the two parties have changed over time; the list has included the Liberals, PCs, Cooperative Commonwealth Federation (CCF), NDP, and Saskatchewan Party. Voter turnout has averaged ten to 15 percentage points more than Manitoba's. In that period seven governments have been defeated in an election, with the principal opposition party at that point taking over as the new government.

The contrasting experiences of these two provinces was later repeated by New Zealand's experience with voter turnout after its switch in the 1990s from FPTP to MMP elections. In 1993 New Zealanders agreed through a referendum to replace their plurality vote system with their own variant of the MMP scheme (see Chapter 5). It was anticipated, in the words of the royal commission whose report served as the basis for the change, that "a turnout higher than under plurality" would result from MMP elections (Royal Commission on the Electoral System 1986: 56-57). That justification for moving away from FPTP was echoed by the media and throughout the debate leading up to the adoption of the new electoral system.

The reverse, in fact, has proved to be the case. The turnout level in the first MMP election (1996) was 78 per cent. Although this level was a slight improvement over the previous two FPTP elections (1990 and 1993), it nonetheless fell short of the roughly 85 per cent average under plurality voting of the previous 75 years. From 78 per cent in 1996, to 75 per cent in 1999, and 72 per cent in 2002, New Zealand's voter turnout has now declined to its lowest level in the country's history. (A different way of measuring voter turnout in New Zealand confirms the same phenomenon. It shows a 15 percentage point drop in participation rates from an average of 92 per cent throughout the 1980s to 77 per cent in 2002.) One expert on the impact of electoral change in New Zealand has concluded that the decline in voter turnout is a direct result of weaker party identifications and reduced party campaign contacts with voters under MMP (Vowles 2002a: 599; turnout figures from Vowles 2002a: 588-89; LeDuc and Pammett 2003: 2; and the University of Auckland's New Zealand Election Study data, provided to the author 29 October 2002).

The voter differences in Manitoba, Saskatchewan, and New Zealand cannot be explained solely on the grounds of electoral systems. Cultural, representational, social, and political variables are all at play here in what is ultimately a complex matter. Voter turnout is itself a function of many variables, only one of which is an elector's perceived value of an incremental vote or the true level of inter-party competitiveness in an election. Nonetheless, these examples demonstrate the complexity of the question of electoral reform and confirm that changes in methods of election cannot be certain to attain anticipated goals. They also hint at the possibility that the decline in voter turnout that has been so pronounced over the past decade in the great majority of liberal democracies may well be independent of the electoral system.

2. GREATER ELECTORAL SUCCESS FOR WOMEN

Electoral reform advocates in Canada expect that the distribution by gender and race of those elected to Parliament and legislatures would change under a more proportional voting scheme. They point to, among other things, some comparative studies of methods of election that confirm a positive link between proportional elections and increased election of females (e.g., Rule 1994).

Can the election of relatively few women to Parliament be laid at the feet of FPTP? There is no question that intra-party structures at the federal, provincial, and local levels were in Canada's past overwhelmingly the preserve of white men. This, in turn, reduced a party's capacity or willingness to recruit female candidates for public office. Women have fared far less well in gaining party nominations than men and, accordingly, have been underrepresented on the ballots and elected assemblies. When they have been nominated, women have often had to run in seats that are from their party's standpoint more difficult, if not impossible, to win.

Of course, none of these hurdles is totally independent of the method of election, which as we learned earlier affects parties' strategic behaviour. Nonetheless, it would be a mistake to conclude that the fault line in mirror representation has stemmed exclusively from plurality voting. Cultural, historical, and institutional norms and practices must also form a part of the explanation.

Some studies support the claim that one way to correct for representational imbalances of women in legislative assemblies is to replace FPTP with a more proportional method of election. According to one authority, list PR (in which voters in multi-member districts accept either a party's set ordering of candidates or indicate their own preferences within a single party's list or among lists of the various parties) offers the most "woman-friendly" electoral system (Rule 1994). Political parties in a proportional system are claimed to have more incentive to produce a "balanced ticket" than in plurality elections (Bogdanor 1984: 113-14). Parties have an opportunity to appeal to the greatest number of voters by putting forth lists containing a demographically and socially wide cross-section of society. Thus, so the argument goes, women and minorities would be positioned high enough on a party's list to ensure their election in greater numbers than would be the case under FPTP.

The difficulty with the generalized proposition that PR systems lead to greater female and minority representation is that not all parties or countries use PR elections to promote a greater measure of "mirror representation" in their assemblies. The likelihood of women gaining legislative seats under list PR is well established in Sweden, Denmark, Finland, Norway, Netherlands, and Iceland. These countries rank highest in the world for the share of women in their parliaments. They are followed by Germany and New Zealand, two countries whose MMP electoral systems offer some of the same incentives as list PR for parties to construct diversified lists of candidates. But compare such other list PR countries as Israel (ranked 47 in number of female legislators), Greece (77), and Brazil (95); or a modified-MMP country such as Italy (68); or STV countries such as Ireland (54) and Malta (73). Despite their more proportional electoral systems they all fall well behind countries like Canada (26) and the UK (33) that use FPTP (Inter-Parliamentary Union 2001: 1-5).

How do we account for the differences? History and political culture help to answer that question. Women were given the vote and played a significant role in public affairs in the Nordic countries earlier than in other Western democracies. In fact women's relatively early political socialization in Scandinavia stands in stark contrast to the experience of women elsewhere. Moreover, gender quotas were established either by the states or the parties to guarantee the election of a predetermined share of women in local and parliamentary elections (Bystydzienski 1994: 62; Bystydzienski 1995: 20; Zimmerman 1994: 4-10). Canadian lawmakers have eschewed setting fixed quotas on grounds of gender and race. So too have the parties, with rare exceptions such as the federal NDP in the occasional recent election. Should governments or parties wish to impose such quotas, FPTP offers no institutional impediment. Quotas may be more difficult to institute in single-member districts than in list or MMP systems, but PR is not an absolute necessity for affirmative action policies in candidate nominations.

The representation of any group in an assembly is the result of a complex mix of institutional variables such as the electoral system, electoral incentives, political strategies, and cultural norms. The six countries at the top of the list of female parliamentarians share a number of distinctive features. They are all developed, territorially small, northern states with a history of women playing an important part in public affairs well before that was true elsewhere. Although it shares many social values in common with them, Canada is both structurally and politically different from Sweden, Denmark, Finland, Norway, Netherlands, and Iceland. Ours is a territorially vast, multicultural, officially bilingual, and ethnically diverse federation with a unique representational and party history. How our parties would try to reflect that social diversity in their selection of candidates under a more proportional electoral scheme cannot be foretold with precision.

3. INCREASED LIKELIHOOD OF REFORMIST/PROGRESSIVE GOVERNMENTS

It has long been known that PR elections are more likely than plurality elections to produce "minority parliaments," that is, an assembly in which no one party holds a majority of the seats (Hermens 1941; Lakeman and Lambert 1959). To some who favour PR, the increased chances of Canada having a government without majority support is seen as a strength. They reason that the increased probability of defeat in the Commons by the combined opposition forces enhances government accountability to both Parliament and the public and serves to "keep the government on its toes." Over the past half century, the record supports that claim. The only government defeats on the floor of the Commons that led to general elections being called all occurred when minority governments were in office — in 1963, 1974, and 1979.

The argument is pushed further, however, with the assertion that Canada's "most dynamic," reformist, and progressive governments are minority governments. For example, it is said, the establishment in the 1960s of two of Canada's most progressive pieces of legislation, medicare and the Canada Pension Plan, is explained by the fact that the Pearson government had only a minority of the Commons seats at the time.[2] At face value the claim would seem to make a good deal of sense. Governments lacking a majority of members in the House would be more willing (and anxious) to reach an understanding about their legislative agenda with at least some parties on the opposition benches in order to ensure their survival. Progressive legislation would seem a natural bargaining tool for that purpose.

But are progressive legislation and a dynamic government exclusively a function of minority parliaments? For that matter, can there by any assurance that minority governments would be of a reformist/progressive bent? A few illustrations from twentieth-century Canadian history provide an answer to those questions.

Some governments lacking a majority in the House (1925-26, 1962-63, and 1979 come to mind) have been indecisive, or out-of-touch with political reality, or both. As well, Canadian history has demonstrated that majority governments can advance a very progressive policy agenda. Unemployment Insurance (1940) and Family Allowance (1944) legislation came from a Parliament in which the governing Liberals held a sizeable majority. The same has been true at the provincial level. For instance, Canada's first hospitalization and medical care acts were introduced in Saskatchewan by CCF governments enjoying solid legislative majorities at the time. It can be taken as a virtual certainty that the Pearson government, had it been elected with majorities in 1963 and 1965 rather than with a minority of the Commons seats, would have pursued its reformist agenda. The Liberal party that Lester Pearson, Walter Gordon, and many others refashioned in the early 1960s was committed to progressive social policies, including the introduction of a national medical insurance plan (Smith 1973: chap. 4; Stursberg 1978: chaps. 4 and 5).

The point is not that a government has either a minority or a majority of an assembly's seats that defines it as "reformist" or, for that matter, "conservative." Rather, a government's policies are a product of many factors. These include its ideological predisposition (if any), the climate of public expectations, the mindset of the party's leadership, the jurisdiction's current financial health, and the larger political context. To urge the adoption of a more proportional electoral system on grounds that ensuring the election of minority governments would help to advance a progressive agenda, is to overlook the multitude of variables that go into shaping public policy. Minority government should not be taken as a synonym for progressive government.

Conclusion

Canadians early in the twenty-first century are being called upon to evaluate their method of voting. At the federal level the push to replace the plurality vote with some as yet undefined, but nonetheless more proportionate, electoral scheme is a direct result of the fallout from the last three parliamentary elections. Between 1993 and 2000 voter turnout declined steadily, a five-party parliament became the norm, a government was elected with a majority of the Commons' seats but less (sometimes substantially less) than a majority of the popular vote, and the four opposition parties had oddly mismatched shares of seats and votes. Several provinces, responding in some instances to wildly lopsided legislative election results and in others to a capricious tendency of FPTP to enable a party to form a majority government with fewer popular votes than its principal opponent, launched inquiries into alternative methods of voting.

If Canada's method of election were changed, parties and voters would be given the opportunity of employing different strategic options from those they had under FPTP. On the face of it, incentives seem to exist under PR that are absent under FPTP to increase voter participation, party inclusiveness, and system responsiveness in elections. Some form of proportional voting might give political parties a huge incentive to mobilize as wide and as varied an electorate as possible, that is, to be as inclusive of the population as possible. The logic is simple: a party's share of the vote determines its share of the legislative seats. For their part, voters might be given the incentive to vote because they have an interest in ensuring that their preferred party gets as large a share of the votes as possible in order to gain as many seats.

That proposition is logical, but expectations about what would occur once an electoral system is changed in the direction of proportionality are sometimes turned upside down. We saw that with respect to voter turnout in both New Zealand and Manitoba. Other factors and considerations muddy the electoral waters between expectation and reality. These include, but are not limited to, the possibility that the process of coalition formation in a more proportional system is unresponsive to public preferences and that weaker party competition and identification and reduced direct party campaign contacts with voters may result. The fact remains that electoral reform can promise a good deal. Much of this promise may be deliverable, such as the possibility of a greater sense of voter efficacy or of greater public trust in an electoral system that is seen to convert votes into seats in a fairer manner. But equally, at least part of the promise may be unrealizable and may, in turn, lead to public disaffection with politics over unmet expectations.

No electoral system is neutral, which means that it is not hard to find faults with an electoral system (*any* electoral system) on grounds of both governance and representation. The faults differ, of course, both in kind and magnitude from one system to another. What is critical in any evaluation of the costs and benefits of moving from one method of election to another is to know where the trade-offs will have to be made. As Canadians begin seriously debating alternative electoral systems in the years ahead, the long-term implications of change on governance and representational practices at both the federal and provincial levels should be at the centre of their considered attention.

Notes

1. Parts of this chapter appear in my *Elections: Canada's Democratic Audit* (Courtney 2004).

2. Doris Anderson, "PR would have saved the PCs," *Globe and Mail* 2 January 2004: A11.

PART II

Recent Experience in Other Countries

CHAPTER 5

Stormy Passage to a Safe Harbour? Proportional Representation in New Zealand

Jack H. Nagel[1]

In a 1993 referendum, New Zealanders voted to replace their Canadian-style first-past-the-post (FPTP) parliamentary elections with a new mixed-member proportional (MMP) electoral system. The island nation thus became the first English-speaking country to adopt a form of proportional representation (PR) based on party lists. MMP has since been employed in three national elections—1996, 1999, and 2002. Following a supportive review by a parliamentary select committee in 2001, the new system appears securely established.

Three aspects of New Zealand's experience may be of special interest to Canadians:

1. As subsequent adoptions in Scotland and Wales also suggest, MMP is the PR variant with greatest appeal to countries with traditional single-member electorates (ridings), because it retains constituency representation by individual MPs while also producing a high degree of proportionality among parties. The version of MMP used in New Zealand incorporates an additional element relevant to Canada—a unique system of dual constituencies that guarantees seats for the indigenous Maori minority.

2. New Zealand adopted MMP despite opposition from most leaders of both major political parties. The process by which reform unexpectedly triumphed offers insights to would-be reformers in Canada and elsewhere who also must overcome politicians with a vested interest in the status quo.

3. The performance of MMP through three electoral cycles provides evidence against which to judge claims of its advocates and opponents. Which expectations have been fulfilled, and which must be more carefully restated? What transitional difficulties have been revealed, and what problems remain unsolved?

Basic Elements of MMP in New Zealand[2]

As background, it may be helpful to review a few basic political and demographic comparisons between New Zealand and Canada. The two former British colonies share a heritage of Westminster institutions and long histories of representative government. With a far smaller land area and population (barely four million in 2003, about one-eighth of Canada's), New Zealand has no need for federalism. After provinces were abolished in 1876, a vestigial upper house of Parliament lingered on until 1950, when the legislature became fully unicameral. Despite its size, New Zealand has significant ethnic diversity. About 15 per cent of the population are at least part Maori. The Maori are acknowledged constitutional partners of the *pakeha* (European) majority, by virtue of the 1840 Treaty of Waitangi, but they also were victims of superior military force in later wars over land. The Maori are sufficiently dispersed across New Zealand that secession or other forms of territorial self-government are unlikely options; and, despite efforts to revive the Maori language in recent decades, English remains the everyday tongue for most Maori. Because they are the indigenous people, the situation of the Maori is comparable in some respects to that of the First Nations in Canada. Since 1977, a process of awarding reparations to Maori for land and other claims, overseen by the Waitangi Tribunal, has been politically and economically important. Adding to the demographic mix, New Zealand over several decades has experienced significant immigration by Pacific islanders and Asians. Each of those groups comprised about 7 per cent of the 2001 census.

Continuously from 1914 through 1993, and predominantly before then, New Zealand used plurality rule in single-member electorates (constituencies) to choose members of the House of Representatives, which had 99 MPs in 1993, the last FPTP election. The MMP system approved in the 1993 referendum increased the size of the House to 120 members and established two types of MPs — 65 to be elected from single-member electorates, and the other 55 to be chosen from nationwide party lists. Under a formula designed to preserve 16 electorates for the South Island (where the population is declining relative to the North Island), the share of electorate seats has subsequently increased, reaching 69 in the 2002 election.

MMP gives each elector two votes—one for a political party and the other for a constituency representative. After electorate winners are chosen by simple plurality, party votes determine (using the Saint-Laguë formula) the *total* number of seats to which each party is entitled, including *both* electorate and list members. In other words, seats a party wins from electorates are subtracted from its overall total in order to establish the number of MPs drawn from its list. This "compensatory" allocation of list seats makes MMP a truly proportional system, relative to the party vote, which thus becomes crucial in determining the strength of parties in Parliament.[3] The system is not perfectly proportional, because very small parties are excluded by threshold requirements. To qualify for list seats, a party must either receive at least 5 per cent of all party votes or win at least one electorate seat.

Most of the features just described simply transfer to New Zealand's smaller, non-federal setting basic principles of MMP as developed in West Germany after World War II. However, New Zealand's version of MMP also includes an original element—the adaptation to MMP of a distinctive dual-constituency (DC) system that has guaranteed representation of Maori since 1867. The DC system can be visualized as a map with two overlays, one dividing New Zealand into numerous "general" (formerly "European") electorates and the other apportioning the same territory into a smaller number of geographically larger Maori electorates. Thus, every place in New Zealand is simultaneously located in a general and in a Maori electorate. Through the "Maori option," individuals of Maori descent can choose every five years, before legislative redistricting, whether to register on the general roll or on the Maori roll and thus whether to vote for an MP representing a general or a Maori electorate. The number of Maori seats is calculated using a formula that multiplies the Maori census population by the proportion of Maori electors who opt for the Maori roll, and then divides the product by the same population quota as is used to apportion general seats. As a result of campaigns by Maori organizations encouraging Maori to opt for their own roll, the number of Maori seats has risen steadily since MMP was adopted—from four in 1993 to five in 1996, six in 1999, and seven in 2002 (Comrie, Gillies, and Day 2002). Thus the Parliament elected in 2002 consisted of seven members representing Maori electorates, 62 representing general electorates, and 51 chosen from party lists.

The Surprising Victory of Radical Electoral Reform[4]

The winner-take-all nature of FPTP tends to reduce the number of serious competitors in each electorate down to two. In New Zealand, regional differences are less sharp than in Canada, so the same two parties, National and Labour, were the chief contenders in most districts nationwide from 1935 through 1993.[5] Following every election in that period, one or the other held a majority in Parliament and formed a single-party government. National was in power for 32 of those years, and Labour for 26. Because a switch to PR would predictably result in a multi-party parliament and coalition governments, both of the competing duopolists had a stake in maintaining FPTP. The system became still more secure in 1956, when Parliament stipulated that key provisions of the Electoral Act could be repealed or amended only by a 75 per cent vote of all MPs or by a majority vote in a national referendum. The super-majority provision meant that Parliament itself would not enact any major electoral reform unless it had bipartisan support. The referendum option established an alternative route to reform — one that eventually proved crucial — but even that path could not be taken without the consent of a parliamentary majority.

Beneath the surface of duopolistic stability, political developments created awareness of deficiencies in the electoral system and fostered constituencies for reform. Chief among them were the rise of minor parties and increased unease about representation of Maori.

Deficiencies of FPTP elections become most apparent when three or more parties attract votes. In the 13 New Zealand elections from 1954 through 1990, minor parties won an average vote share of 13.5 per cent. The first and most persistent third-party contender was Social Credit, but nine nominally different minor parties won at least 2 per cent of the popular vote a total of 18 times. In contrast to Canada, no minor party in New Zealand benefited from geographically concentrated support, so the FPTP system treated them all very shabbily. Their efforts were rewarded with a grand total of seven parliamentary victories, only 0.6 per cent of the seats available. As minor parties siphoned off votes, governing parties won smaller vote shares, never attaining an absolute majority after 1951 and twice falling below 40 per cent. Contrary to New Zealanders' majoritarian ideology, it became apparent that the electoral system manufactured parliamentary majorities and that governments' electoral bases were only pluralitarian and sometimes not even that.[6]

By the 1970s, in the context of growing worldwide sensitivity to racial discrimination, New Zealand's century-old provisions for separate Maori representation became a source of embarrassment to liberal whites and a focus of discontent among increasingly militant Maori. From 1867 until the 1993 reform, the number of Maori seats was fixed at four, an allotment that became increasingly inadequate as both the relative size of the Maori population and the number of general seats in Parliament grew. Reforms in 1967 and 1975 gave Maori candidates the right to contest general constituencies and Maori voters the option of choosing to vote on either Maori or general rolls, but those well-intentioned measures did little to solve the problem of underrepresentation. Only a few Maori candidates won general seats, and many Maori electors opted to remain on the separate roll. Meanwhile, the National Party, in power from 1975 to 1984, believed that all new Maori constituencies, like the old, would be safe Labour seats and therefore blocked any increase in their number.

Underrepresentation of minorities, disproportional allocation of seats in favour of larger parties, and pluralitarian outcomes are common structural or *inherent* defects of FPTP elections.[7] Such problems may motivate certain groups to favour reform, but by themselves they are insufficient to overcome power holders who benefit from FPTP. The infrequent triumphs of radical reform depend on *contingent* factors — human agency and historical circumstances that trigger, sustain, and empower successful reform movements.[8] The recipe for electoral reform in New Zealand included the six contingent ingredients summarized below, each of which was essential to the outcome.

1. COMPETING INTERESTS OF PARTIES WITH A STAKE IN THE STATUS QUO

The inherent problems of FPTP made Maori and minor-party supporters potentially receptive to PR, but they lacked the power to enact reform. Instead, the impetus to change began with a third defect of the old system, one that adversely affected a major party. In both the 1978 and 1981 elections, Labour received a plurality of the popular vote, but National won a majority of seats in Parliament and thus retained control of government.[9] The occurrence of such an anomaly in consecutive elections suggested that Labour faced a systemic disadvantage, because its votes were excessively concentrated in urban and Maori constituencies. Distressed by those losses, Labour pledged in its 1981 and 1984 manifestoes to establish a Royal Commission to conduct "an authoritative and exhaustive reappraisal of electoral law." Most Labour MPs expected and wanted the Commission to propose an incremental reform, such as a "supplementary member" add-on to FPTP that might prevent wrong-winner outcomes.

2. ABILITY TO SHIFT DECISIONS TO DISINTERESTED ACTORS

Decisions about electoral laws are usually controlled by legislatures. Having a huge stake in the electoral process, their members either block significant reform of the rules under which they won office or else produce bargained outcomes designed to protect their interests as much as possible. New Zealand's switch to MMP is remarkable for the absence of political influence or bargaining in the design and adoption of the new system. Its nearly immaculate conception occurred because, at two crucial junctures, power was transferred to disinterested actors whose careers did not depend on the electoral system. At the final, adoption stage, the disinterested decision-makers were the voters themselves, whose authoritative role was made possible by the provision in the Electoral Act for reform by referendum. At the initial, proposal stage, design of the plan ultimately presented to the people was entrusted to a prestigious, non-political body, the five-member Royal Commission on the Electoral System (RCES). Chaired by John Wallace, a judge of the High Court, its other members were John Darwin, a former government statistician; Kenneth Keith, a professor of constitutional law; Richard Mulgan, New Zealand's leading political theorist; and Whetumarama Wereta, a Maori research officer. Unlike similar commissions elsewhere, the RCES decided to ignore political feasibility and instead recommend whatever system it concluded would be best for New Zealand.[10] In partisan terms, the RCES was a runaway commission. Its choice of a radical plan that seemed a political non-starter made its quest appear quixotic. In the end, however, the Commission's dispassionate, thorough, and systematic effort, combined with the impressive quality of its book-length report (Royal Commission on the Electoral System 1986), gave its recommendation persuasive force and moral authority that ultimately led to a stunning political success.

3. PUBLIC-SPIRITED POLITICAL LEADERS

Most New Zealand politicians approached electoral reform, as one would expect, from the standpoint of partisan or personal interest. However, there was one major exception who played an essential role at the beginning of the reform process. Appointment of the Royal Commission and formulation of its mandate were largely the responsibility of the Minister of Justice (and Deputy Prime Minister), Geoffrey Palmer. A professor of constitutional law before entering Parliament, Palmer was an unusual politician, ultimately more dedicated to constitutional reform than to his political career or the fortunes of his

(Labour) party. Despite later speculation that he was committed in advance to PR, such a conclusion is not warranted by his own previous writings and the commissioners' consistent testimony (e.g., Wallace 2002) that they were neither pre-committed nor pressured. Nevertheless, Palmer opened the door to a recommendation favouring proportional representation, both in composing the wide-ranging mandate and by appointing individuals known for independent judgement. After the RCES issued its report in 1986, Palmer became a proponent of MMP but, even when prime minister in 1989-90, could not win consent from the Labour cabinet and caucus to proceed as the Commission recommended— "the greatest disappointment that I had in politics," he later wrote (Palmer 1992: 177). Nevertheless, Palmer's public position as well as support from several less prominent Labour and National MPs, helped give needed respectability to the reform cause.

4. DETERMINED GRASSROOTS REFORMERS

The Royal Commission's report inspired a poorly funded but vigorous and persistent grassroots movement, the Electoral Reform Coalition (ERC). Early on, the ERC made two wise strategic decisions. First, it avoided domination by, or excessive identification with, minor-party adherents who were the natural core supporters of PR. Second, members previously attracted to the single-transferable vote (STV) or other options agreed to unite behind the focal alternative established by the Royal Commission, MMP. Over six years when both major parties sought to put the genie of reform back in its lamp, the ERC's imaginative tactics never let the press, public, or politicians forget the RCES proposal for a referendum. In a country with a populist tradition and a long history of using referendums (albeit mostly to decide liquor laws), it was difficult for politicians to resist appeals to "let the people decide." When Parliament finally permitted a binding referendum in 1993, the ERC waged a David-and-Goliath struggle to overcome a sophisticated advertising campaign sponsored by the pro-FPTP Campaign for Better Government, which was lavishly funded by leaders of major corporations.

5. EXPLOITATION OF OPPORTUNE EVENTS

Taking "the current when it serves," the ERC benefited from mistakes and miscalculations by defenders of the status quo, as well as a fortuitous tide in the affairs of New Zealand that helped lift the reform cause to victory. The mistake was made by Labour Prime Minister David Lange during

a televised leaders' debate during the 1987 election campaign, when the
Royal Commission's MMP proposal seemed dead on arrival. In response
to a question from an ERC leader, Lange promised to hold a referendum as
recommended by the Commission. As an articulate former trial lawyer better
known for being quick on his feet than for preparing thoroughly, Lange may
have simply succumbed to the temptation to score points in a competitive setting, for his answer was contrary to the wishes of the Labour caucus and his
own personal preferences. Throughout the party's next term in power (1987-
90), the Labour caucus prevented Lange and even his pro-MMP successor,
Palmer, from fulfilling the ill-considered pledge.

The miscalculation occurred during the next election campaign. Breaching
promises is a cardinal sin in New Zealand politics, so Lange's self-described
"gaffe" and Labour's resulting embarrassment led to competitive bidding
in 1990, when—spurred on by backbench advocates of reform as well as by
the ERC—both National and Labour pledged a referendum. The parties
had not relented in their opposition to MMP, but—relying on contemporary
polls—they mistakenly believed reform would fail when put to a vote.

That expectation might have been fulfilled if it had not been for the confluence of electoral reform with a previously separate political tide that arose
from a wrenching process of market liberalization launched by Labour in
1984-90. The National Party, after returning to power in 1990, dashed the
hopes of many voters by intensifying rather than moderating the economic restructuring. Meanwhile, on the electoral reform front, National finally agreed
to hold the promised referendum in September 1992. In a rather obvious
attempt to divide reformers, the vote was complex and non-binding. Citizens
were asked, first, whether or not FPTP should be kept and, second, if it were
to be changed, which of four alternatives they preferred—MMP, STV, the
alternative vote, or a supplementary member system. The 1992 referendum
coincided with a trough of economic discontent, as the restructuring to that
point had failed to fulfill politicians' promises of improved welfare, delivering
instead high unemployment, declining real wages, and near-zero growth. The
outcome of the vote was devastating—84.7 per cent rejected FPTP, and in the
choice among reform options, MMP won 70.5 per cent. However, it would
be wrong to interpret that result as merely a backlash against economic policies and conditions. Electoral reformers successfully argued that the FPTP
electoral system had enabled zealous leaders to impose radically disruptive
policies without winning broad-based popular consent, as they pyramided
plurality elections, one-party rule, and party discipline to impose "elective
dictatorship." The Royal Commission's primary reasons for endorsing MMP

had been traditional pro-PR arguments—representational fairness for parties and minorities—but by the early 1990s, the ERC augmented those themes with a new appreciation for multi-party politics and coalition government as checks on arbitrary power.

6. PUBLIC EDUCATION

Electoral systems are an abstruse subject, even among political scientists, and the two New Zealand referendums posed daunting obstacles to informed public choice. The indicative poll in 1992 asked voters to answer two questions requiring judgements about five systems, including four that were unfamiliar and complex. The binding referendum in 1993 narrowed the options to just two, but the pro-FPTP Campaign for Better Government enjoyed a spending edge estimated at eight-to-one or more over the ERC. In votes on popular initiatives in California, such a financial advantage has virtually guaranteed victory for the side defending the status quo (Magleby 1984: 147-48). The playing field in New Zealand was rendered more nearly level before both referendums by government-funded education campaigns conducted under the direction of an ad hoc, independent Electoral Referendum Panel chaired by the Chief Ombudsman (Jackson and McRobie 1998: 234-51). In a notable contribution to civic literacy (Milner 2001), the panel teamed the communication skills of an advertising agency with advice on content from academic experts. Together they produced lucidly informative and sometimes entertaining TV and radio spots, videos, booklets, and pamphlets. Although scrupulously neutral, even to the point of not mentioning that the Royal Commission had endorsed MMP, the panel's work helped produce an impressive level of public awareness and understanding. Following the victory of MMP, government-funded public education continued under the auspices of the Electoral Commission, which was established as part of the 1993 reform. Led during its first ten years by Paul Harris, a political scientist who had been principal research officer for the RCES, the Electoral Commission (2003b) devoted particular attention to ensuring that citizens understood the importance of the party vote under MMP.

Three Elections and the Decision to Keep MMP

Through its first three elections, the course of MMP in New Zealand traced a stormy passage to what appears to be a safe harbour. In 1996, the first election using the method immediately fulfilled several major promises of proponents, and yet its popularity almost immediately plunged, leading to a widespread perception that the reform was a failure.[11] Nevertheless, after just one more election, MMP escaped unscathed from a mandatory parliamentary review. Following a relatively uneventful third election in 2002, the system appears secure for the foreseeable future.

Although partisan and individual political interests had almost nothing to do with the design and adoption of MMP, they explain a lot about its initial disrepute and subsequent acceptance. During the 1996 election campaign, the unpopular National government—elected with only 35 per cent of the vote in the last FPTP contest—came under attack from three opposition parties—Labour, the left-wing Alliance, and the centrist New Zealand First (NZF). In the election, National won 44 seats, more than any other party, but its three critics combined held 67, a comfortable majority of the 120-member Parliament. (See Table 5-1 for votes and seats won by parties in elections from 1984 through 2002.) Most supporters of the three opposition parties expected that they would cooperate to throw National out of power. The Alliance had pledged not to join a coalition in the absence of a pre-election pact (which Labour had been unwilling to make), but its leaders were ready to support a Labour-led minority government on votes of confidence and supply. NZF, however, exploited its pivotal numerical and ideological position by engaging in protracted bargaining with both Labour and National, before finally agreeing—nine weeks after the election—to join a coalition with National (Boston *et al.* 1997).

Prolonged uncertainty about a new government, the spectacle of a controversial minor party as king-maker, and a deal widely seen as opportunistic combined to disillusion many voters about MMP. In polls asking voters their preference between MMP and FPTP, the majority that had supported the proportional system before the election disintegrated. By June 1997, FPTP was preferred by a 54-30 margin. The sour response after 1996 included a strong element of partisan disappointment, as approval of MMP fell most among Labour and Alliance voters, who had "provided the backbone of support for electoral change" in 1993 (Vowles *et al.* 1998: 205-07). The standing of NZF also plummeted, as most of its voters had favoured a centre-left coalition and felt betrayed by the party leaders' choice of National. By late 1997, NZF support in polls reached a nadir of just 2 per cent, down from 13.4 per cent in the election.

The reputations of coalition government and therefore of MMP were further tarnished by the rocky and short-lived marriage of National and NZF. In November 1997, the National caucus replaced Jim Bolger with Jenny Shipley

Table 5-1

Parties' Vote and Seat Shares in New Zealand Elections, 1984-2002

	Values (1984)	Greens (1990–)	New Labour (1990)	Alliance (1993–99)	Progressive Coalition (2002)	Social Credit (1984)	Democrats (1987–)	Labour	United NZ (1996–99)	Future NZ (1999)	United Future (2002)	NZ First	National	New Zealand Party (1984–87)	ACT (1996–)	Others	Total Seats
1984	0.2					7.6		*39.0*					35.9	12.3		5.0	95
	0					2.1		*58.9*					38.9	0		0	
1987							5.7	*48.0*					44.0	0.3		2.0	97
							0	*59.8*					40.2	0		0	
1990		6.9	5.2				1.7	35.1					*47.8*			3.3	97
		0	1.0				0	29.8					*69.1*			0	
1993[a,b]				18.2				34.7				8.4	*35.1*			3.6	99
				2.0				45.5				2.0	*50.5*			0	
1996*		—		10.1			—	28.2	0.9			*13.4*	*33.8*		6.1	7.5	120
				10.8				30.8	0.8			*14.2*	*36.7*		6.7	0	
1999*[c]		5.2		*7.7*			—	*38.7*	1.6			4.3	30.5		7.0	5.0	120
		5.8		*8.3*				*40.8*	0.8			4.2	32.5		7.5	0	
2002*[d]		7.0			*1.7*			*41.3*			6.7	10.4	20.9		7.1	4.9	120
		7.5			*1.7*			*43.3*			6.7	10.8	22.5		7.5	0	

* Within cells, the top figure is the party's percentage of the popular vote (aggregated across electorates through 1993 and as measured by the party vote under MMP from 1996 on). The bottom entry is the party's percentage of parliamentary seats. Figures in italic type indicate the governing party or parties in the initial post-election period. Asterisks indicate MMP elections. With the exception of "Others," parties are arrayed from left to right according to positions usually attributed to them on the conventional ideological spectrum.

Source: Electoral Commission (2003a).

a. Greens were part of the Alliance in 1993 and 1996.
b. Democrats were part of the Alliance in 1993, 1996, and 1999.
c. United NZ and Future NZ were separate parties in 1999. Vote total shown is the sum of their party votes. United NZ won an electorate seat in both 1996 and 1999.
d. A rump Alliance party contested in 2002; its vote is included in "Others."

as party leader and prime minister, largely because Bolger was too closely associated with the unpopular coalition. Nine months later, Shipley removed NZF leader Winston Peters from his cabinet posts as deputy prime minister and treasurer. Most of the NZF caucus followed Peters into opposition, but seven MPs defected from his party to remain part of what was now a minority government sustained in office with help from two renegade independents and the free-market ACT party on the right.

Meanwhile, the opposition was suffering schisms of its own, as the Green Party, formerly a component of the Alliance,[12] decided to run under its own banner in the next election. Having drawn a lesson from voters' revulsion against post-election bargaining in 1996, Labour and the remainder of the Alliance agreed to govern as a coalition if voters would reward them with sufficient seats. In the 1999 election, Labour's vote rose sharply, as it benefitted especially from switches by former NZF adherents (Vowles 2002b: 89-90). Together, Labour and the Alliance won 59 seats, just two short of a majority. They proceeded to form a minority government with backing on confidence and supply from the Greens, who captured seven seats by finishing just above both thresholds.[13]

The 1999 election showed that MMP could hold unpopular incumbents accountable, result in quick formation of a new government, and bring the centre-left to power. As the new prime minister, Labour's Helen Clark, proceeded to lead a generally effective ministry, her party's standing in opinion surveys climbed. MMP also rose, but generally less markedly. The change in fortunes had come none too soon for the survival of MMP, because the 1993 reform legislation required a parliamentary review after the second election using the new system.

In 2000-01, a parliamentary select committee conducted the mandated review (Church and McLeay 2003). The committee, which included MPs from all parties except (by its own choice) NZF, was directed by the House to reach its conclusions on the basis of unanimity or near-unanimity, "having regard to the numbers in the House represented by each of the members of the committee" (MMP Review Committee 2001: 4). This charge, which practically guaranteed that the main features of the status quo would not be disturbed, reflected practical barriers to restoring FPTP or enacting any major change in MMP. Smaller parties, which owed their parliamentary existence to MMP, held enough seats (32 of 120) to block attainment of the 75 per cent supermajority required for Parliament to legislate major changes.[14] The two big parties, Labour and National, could have combined to form the ordinary majority needed to call a new referendum, but to do so, they would have had to overcome not only their traditional rivalry but also potential resistance from within their own ranks, because 25 of their MPs had been elected from lists. In any case, Clark, who previously opposed MMP, and her Labour colleagues now realized their party could thrive under the proportional system.

Thus the Labour, Alliance, Green, and ACT members of the committee joined forces to reject holding a new referendum on whether to keep MMP. In separate votes, the committee also upheld other key features of the 1993 reform. Defying a 1999 citizens-initiated indicative referendum that overwhelmingly endorsed a reduction in the size of the House to 99 members, committee members from the Labour, Alliance, and Green parties insisted on keeping the number at 120—a decision important to maintaining proportionality, because any decrease would surely have been at the expense of list seats. On the question of retaining separate Maori constituencies, only ACT sought abolition. The committee also left intact closed party lists and the one-electorate alternative threshold for list seats (MMP Review Committee 2001: 28, 29-30, 35, 19, 52, 50).

Ironically, MMP—originally imposed by voters on reluctant politicians—was now protected by politicians against potential repeal by a popular majority. A survey commissioned by the Review Committee showed "decisive support for a binding referendum" on whether to keep MMP, with 76 per cent in favour and only 17 per cent opposed. From November 1996 onward, tracking polls asking for a choice between MMP and FPTP found majorities favouring the old system, with the exception of a single poll just after the 1999 election. However, MMP had recovered considerably from its trough in 1997-98, when some polls found two-to-one margins in favour of FPTP; by February 2001, 40 per cent favoured MMP to 47 per cent for FPTP. Moreover, as the Committee noted, a more complex question elicited evidence that support for both systems was "soft" and arguably favourable to the basic idea of MMP. Given a three-way choice, 17 per cent preferred to keep MMP unchanged, 47 per cent wanted to stay with the basic structure of MMP but make some changes, and only 37 per cent desired a different electoral system altogether. There was also evidence that the most informed and intense opinion opposed change—of the 290 submissions the Select Committee received from individuals and groups, a substantial plurality favoured keeping MMP (MMP Review Committee 2001: 28, 78-79, 29).

With continuation of proportional representation thus assured, it seemed possible, paradoxically, that New Zealand might return to single-party rule. Labour's support in some polls during 2001-02 exceeded 50 per cent, while its coalition partner, the Alliance, split over whether to oppose the Clark government's decision to send special forces to assist the American invasion of Afghanistan. Hoping to exploit the advantage, the prime minister called an early election, but in the July 2002 balloting, Labour won only 41.3 per cent of the vote and 52 seats. Joined by the two MPs from the Progressive Coalition (a remnant of the Alliance), Labour formed a minority coalition government that could turn to any of three minor parties—the Greens, United Future, and NZF—in order to secure legislative majorities. Thus, in the early years of the twenty-first century, New Zealand under MMP settled into a Scandinavian pattern, in which a dominant party on the centre-left led minority governments while parties constituting a fragmented opposition were unable or unwilling to coalesce against it.

Evaluation of MMP

Mere survival of MMP under conditions conducive to its becoming "locked-in" does not constitute a reason for Canadians to take New Zealand's example as a model. Such a judgement should depend on a closer look at the performance of the system. Compared with arguments of its proponents in 1993, New Zealand's experience with MMP meets two major expectations, requires adjustment of several others, and disappoints one secondary hope. I shall begin with the clear successes.

REPRESENTATIONAL VALUES

Except for the threshold requirement, proportionality between votes and seats is built into MMP through the seat allocation formula, so it is not surprising that the new system quickly and consistently delivered the benefit of a much fairer allocation of seats to political parties. This can be seen by comparing vote and seat shares across elections in Table 5-1, or more quickly from the summary measure of disproportionality in the first row of Table 5-2. For the three MMP elections, the index averages 6.3, only a small departure from perfect proportionality (an index of zero). In contrast, disproportionality in the last four FPTP elections averaged 19.6, comparable to recent Canadian levels.[15]

A second representational advantage attributed to list PR, election of more minorities and women, is less automatic, because it depends on parties' nomination strategies and voters' choices. The immediate leap forward by both groups under MMP is therefore truly impressive, even startling. The second and third rows of Table 5-2 summarize their gains. The average

Table 5-2

Analysis of New Zealand Elections, 1984-2002

	Elections under FPTP				Elections under MMP		
	1984	1987	1990	1993[a]	1996	1999	2002
Index of dispropor-tionality[b]	19.0	11.8	21.3	26.2	7.7	6.2	4.9
Minority MPs[c]	6.3%	5.2%	5.1%	8.1%	16.7%	16.7%	20.0%
Women MPs	12.6%	14.4%	16.5%	21.2%	29.2%	30.8%	28.3%
Number of parties in parliament	3	2	3	4	6	7	7
Type of government formed	one-party majority	one-party majority	one-party majority	one-party majority	majority coalition	minority coalition	minority coalition
Voter turnout[d]	87.7%	82.3%	78.2%	78.9%	80.8%	77.2%	72.5%

Source: Electoral Commission (2003a) or author's calculations from data provided there.

a. 1993 was a transitional election — conducted under FPTP, but with adoption of MMP widely expected. The referendum that approved replacing FPTP with MMP was held at the same time as this election.

b. Disproportionality equals the sum across parties of the absolute value of the difference between each party's share of seats and share of votes, divided by 2.

c. Maori, Pacific Islander, and Asian.

d. Turnout $= 100 \cdot \dfrac{\text{(valid votes + informal votes + special votes disallowed)}}{\text{(voting-age population)}}$

proportion of minority members almost tripled in the first three MMP parliaments compared with the last four elected by FPTP. The percentage of Maori MPs almost doubled between 1993 and 1996 and in 2002 reached 15.8 per cent, about equal to the proportion of Maori in New Zealand's population. Of the Maori members elected in 2002, nine were chosen from party lists, three were victorious in general electorates, and seven represented Maori electorates. In addition, the number of Pacific Islander MPs rose from one in 1993 to three in all the MMP parliaments, and New Zealanders of Asian descent gained representation for the first time under MMP, winning one list seat in 1996 and 1999 and two in 2002 (Electoral Commission 2003a: 182).

Women were already a force in New Zealand politics before MMP. They held major cabinet portfolios, and after the 1993 election, 21.2 per cent of

MPs were female, a higher proportion than in most FPTP systems. Shortly after that election, Helen Clark became leader of the main opposition party, Labour. Nevertheless, MMP gave an immediate boost to women's representation, with the percentage of female MPs fluctuating around 30 per cent after each of the three MMP elections. Women's initial gain in 1996 came entirely from party lists, but by 2002, women held nearly equal shares of electorate and list seats (27.5 per cent and 29.4 per cent, respectively) (Electoral Commission 2003a: 176-77). In November 1997, National MP Jenny Shipley became New Zealand's first female prime minister. With the Labour-Alliance victory in 1999, Clark replaced Shipley. Thus, for six of the first seven years under MMP, women led the government of New Zealand.

To avoid overstating the impact of MMP per se on representation of minorities and women, it should be noted that their gains were aided not only by the introduction of party lists but also by several reforms bundled with the new system: an increase in the size of Parliament from 99 to 120 members; a reduction in the number of general electorates from 95 to 60 (initially), which prompted the retirement (voluntary or otherwise) of many former MPs; and the decision to allow the number of Maori electorates, previously fixed at four, to vary according to the number of voters registered on the Maori roll. All of these changes opened up opportunities for entry of new participants into Parliament. As a result, of the 120 MPs elected in 1996, 45 were serving in the House for the first time.

A MULTI-PARTY SYSTEM AND COALITION GOVERNMENTS

In the 1993 referendum debate, reformers' most effective argument was that MMP would prevent narrowly-based one-party "elective dictatorships." By giving small parties their due, MMP would result in multi-party parliaments in which one party would seldom, if ever, enjoy an absolute majority. The leading party would therefore be compelled to reach accommodations with at least one other party, either through formal coalitions or ad hoc agreements on specific bills, or both. As Tables 5-1 and 5-2 show, these expectations were fulfilled after every MMP election. Each parliament included six or seven parties. A majority coalition formed after the initial MMP election, but following the breakup of NZF in late 1997, the National Party led a minority coalition, as did Labour after the next two elections. The leading parties in those governments had to satisfy not only a coalition partner but also one or more parties outside government in order to maintain confidence, vote supply, and pass legislation. Moreover, it may be that voters in 2002 used options given them by MMP deliberately to ensure such a check on government. A prominent interpretation attributes Labour's drop from majority support in pre-election polls to just 41.3 per cent on Election Day as a "voters' veto" on rule by a one-party majority (Vowles *et al.* 2004).

If MMP succeeded so quickly and even brilliantly in confirming the key arguments of its advocates, why were many New Zealanders disillusioned during the early years of the new system? Besides the disappointed partisanship already discussed, experience with MMP revealed three ways in which some supporters of the reform had too lightly dismissed potential problems or expected from it more than it could deliver.

TOO MUCH POWER FOR MINOR PARTIES?

After the 1996 election, many New Zealanders resented seeing NZF, which had won only 13.4 per cent of the vote, so obviously calling the shots about which government would form. That anger was compounded by two controversial features of NZF: First, its leader, Winston Peters, a charismatic hero to some, was widely disliked by others who considered him an irresponsible demagogue. Second, although NZF had deliberately staked out a centrist stance on economic issues, its positions on two other, cross-cutting dimensions were extreme. Capitalizing on Peters's half-Maori parentage, the party became the vehicle for a new group of Maori leaders, whose aggressive style one characterized proudly as "pushy, arrogant, loud, coarse, unrefined, in-your-face, and intolerant."[16] The main source of NZF support, however, was its strenuous opposition to immigration, which temporarily glued together an odd-bedfellows alliance of militant Maori and traditionalist, often elderly, whites.[17]

The charge that PR gives too much power to small and sometimes extremist parties is a familiar claim of FPTP defenders in New Zealand and elsewhere. In their preoccupation with proportionality between votes and seats, PR advocates too often forget that a party's power in a legislature is not necessarily (or even usually) proportional to its share of seats. After the 1996 election, NZF wielded far more power than its popular support justified. Nevertheless, supporters of MMP (or PR generally) have two rebuttals to the charge of excessive small-party power. First, they can point out that FPTP results in even worse misallocations. FPTP in New Zealand gave the National Party 100 per cent of parliamentary power in 1990 and 1993, and surveys indicate it would have done so again if used in 1996. The ratio of National's power to its popular vote would have been comparable to that of NZF, except that under FPTP National would have gained an absolute *monopoly* of power, not just a disproportionate *share*. Second, as the Royal Commission (1986: 49) argued, voters can punish any small party that pushes its bargaining advantage too far. That is exactly what happened to NZF. In 1999, its vote plummeted to 4.3 per cent, below the usual threshold, and it retained five seats only because Peters managed to hold on to his electorate with a 30.1 per cent plurality and a winning margin of 63 votes.

Indeed, with the exception of 1996, smaller parties under MMP have been weak, rather than too strong. ACT, more coherent ideologically than the other small parties, has enjoyed the steadiest voter support, but it has never been part of a government and only briefly in 1998-99 played a necessary role as a support party to National. Labour's junior partner, the Alliance, did not insist on many policy concessions for fear that alienating voters as NZF had done would doom both MMP and itself. In 2001, unable to resolve the tension between responsible partnership and independent identity, the Alliance split—the second consecutive junior member of a coalition to suffer that fate. Thus cautioned, the Greens, United Future, and NZF were all content to stay outside of government in 2002, but none of them was in a position to gain excessive influence, because the Labour-dominated ministry could form ad hoc majorities with the help of any one of the three. In return for a pledge of support on confidence and supply, United Future received a promise of consultation and the establishment of a Commission for the Family. The Greens lost a showdown with Clark on their signature issue, a moratorium on the release into the environment of genetically modified organisms (Bale 2003).[18]

LEARNING PAINS

When adaptation to a new system involves trial-and-error learning, the process can be painful. In New Zealand's case, difficulties of adjusting to MMP were exacerbated by the arrival in Parliament of 45 new MPs, including 12 from the previously marginalized Maori. When inexperienced members of a disadvantaged group suddenly arrive at the centre of power, it would be surprising if they all instantly respected established norms. In fact, the learning curve in New Zealand was impressively steep, on the part of both voters and politicians. As already noted, voters deserted NZF in response to its opportunistic betrayal of pre-election expectations. In particular, the Maori electorate, having awarded a sweep of their seats to NZF in 1996, returned them all to Labour in 1999—evidently concluding that the posturing and petty indiscretions of NZF Maori MPs were counter-productive. As for politicians, Labour—after spurning a pre-election pact in 1996—responded to that year's debacle by reaching an early agreement with the Alliance in 1999. After the election, the two partners formed a government on the basis of a few key principles, rather than subject the country to another long delay, such as had been required for National and NZF to reach their highly detailed agreement in 1996.

A closely related problem, which may or may not turn out to be merely an adjustment difficulty, is "party hopping" by list MPs, a practice that contributed to disillusionment with the new system during the first MMP parliament (Geddis 2002). Shortly after the 1996 election, Alamein Kopu, a member of the Alliance caucus, quit her party. Despite widespread demands that she resign from Parliament because she had been elected from the Alliance list, rather than with an individual mandate, Kopu insisted on remaining in the House as an independent. In July 1998, another list MP, Neil Kirton, similarly left NZF and also refused to resign. Later, when most of the NZF caucus quit the coalition, the votes of Kopu and Kirton were crucial to maintaining the rightist, National-led minority government. Besides infuriating Kopu's erstwhile comrades in the left-wing Alliance, the spectacle discredited the very foundations of MMP, depending as it does on the party vote.

After the 1999 election, the Labour-Alliance government attempted to fix the problem by introducing the Electoral Integrity Act, requiring any MP (whether from a list or electorate seat) who explicitly quits his or her party to also leave Parliament. When the minority coalition's support party, the Greens, refused to vote for the act, the government turned to NZF in search of a majority. Winston Peters, whose party had its own history of defections, insisted that the ban be extended to enable a party leader to oust an MP who has not explicitly quit if the leader issues a statement, agreed to by two-thirds of the party caucus, that the member "has acted in a way that has distorted, and is likely to continue to distort, the proportionality of political party representation in Parliament."[19] This draconian effort to freeze in place the intent of voters at the last election soon backfired in an unanticipated way on its chief sponsors, the Alliance. When two factions of that party became hopelessly estranged in late 2001, fear of the act compelled them to continue cohabiting, in bizarre ways too complicated to relate here, the shell of their former party home, even though they intended to contest the next election as separate organizations. That farcical situation caused a new dip in poll support for MMP, helped justify Helen Clark's decision to call an early election in 2002, and contributed to electoral disaster for both former components of the Alliance. Fortunately, the Electoral Integrity Act expires in 2005. Perhaps electoral designers elsewhere can come up with a better way of preventing party hopping, or else simply rely on voters to punish defectors at the next election, as New Zealanders in fact did.[20]

NOT CONSENSUS, BUT MAJORITY RULE

The "siren songs" of the electoral reform movement were the themes of "less conflict and more consensus" (Vowles *et al.* 1995: 8). The term "consensus," with its connotation of amicable cooperation (if not perfect harmony), resulted from the popularity in New Zealand of a typology developed by the eminent political scientist Arend Lijphart (1984). Lijphart depicted pre-reform New Zealand as a nearly perfect example of "majoritarian democracy," which he contrasted with "consensus democracy." Among the key elements of consensus democracy are PR and its usual consequences, a multi-party legislature and coalition governments. Thus, many New Zealanders incautiously concluded that adopting MMP would mean moving "towards consensus." They were sorely disappointed when politics under PR remained contentious, partisan, and (at least between government and opposition) harshly adversarial.

In fact, post-MMP New Zealand retains all the other features of Lijphart's "majoritarian" or Westminster democracy—an unwritten constitution and parliamentary sovereignty, fusion of legislative and executive power, a unicameral legislature, and centralized unitary government.

Moreover, Lijphart's choice of words itself fosters misconceptions. His "majoritarian" pole should be called "pluralitarian," because FPTP typically produces governments supported by only a plurality of voters. New Zealand became more accurately described as "majoritarian" only *after* FPTP gave way to MMP, because the new voting system widened the electoral base of most legislative majorities from mere pluralities to popular majorities properly understood. The one exception is the first MMP government, in which the coalition's bare majority in Parliament rested on an electoral base of 47.2 per cent. However, that was a great improvement over the 35.1 per cent that FPTP had turned into a parliamentary majority for the preceding National government.

Applying a deeper criterion, MMP created majority rule in every instance. If one thinks of politics as organized along a left-right spectrum and accepts the ordering assumptions incorporated in Table 5-1, every MMP government included the party representing the median voter—the best available test of majority rule. In contrast, in nine of the last 12 FPTP years, governments were not supported by the median voter—Labour in 1984-87 was to the left of the median, and the National Party governments of 1990-96 were to the right.[21] The shift from pluralitarian to majoritarian government encompassing the median position has an important corollary in the moderation of government policies. The change is a substantial triumph for MMP in New Zealand, even if it falls short of utopian dreams of "consensus."[22]

VOTER TURNOUT

A disappointment with MMP is the failure of the new system to prevent a drop in voting participation. Cross-national studies show that countries with PR elections tend to have higher rates of voter turnout than those that use FPTP. Researchers explain such results by pointing to aspects of PR that should encourage turnout: fewer votes are wasted, so parties have an incentive to mobilize voters everywhere, not just in marginal electorates; and voters are more likely to find parties advocating policies close to their own views or linked to groups with which they identify. Invoking such arguments, the Royal Commission and the ERC predicted that higher turnout would be a benefit of MMP. Historically, New Zealanders had voted at a higher rate than citizens of any other FPTP country, but in 1984-90, a fall of nearly 10 per cent—from 87.7 per cent to 78.2 per cent[23]—signalled the political alienation that soon afterwards helped boost the successful drive for electoral reform. (See Table 5-2.) In 1993 interest stimulated by the referendum halted the decline, and the first MMP election in 1996 seemed to confirm reformers' hopes by attracting a modest but noticeable increase in participation, mostly due to the return to the polls of disaffected leftists (Karp and Banducci 1999). The improvement was short-lived. At each of the next two elections, turnout declined, falling to a historic low of 72.5 per cent in 2002.

Vowles (2002a) offers an explanation based on analysis of 1996 and 1999 surveys that probably applies to 2002 as well: Contrary to what might have been expected, nonvoting was not linked to disillusionment with the first MMP coalition government. Instead, its two strongest associations were to declining identification with political parties and a drop in campaign contacts with voters. PR is usually believed to result in stronger, not weaker, ties between parties and voters; but the opposite seems to have been true in the volatile setting of New Zealand's first three MMP elections. The drop in personal campaign contacts reflects a long-term, worldwide shift to media-centred campaigning that is largely independent of electoral systems. Nevertheless, MMP may have exacerbated that trend in New Zealand by diverting attention and effort to the national party vote, at the expense of the electorate organizations that formerly were at the centre of political campaigns (Vowles 2004).

POLICY AND PERFORMANCE

Ultimately, governmental institutions should be judged not by the machinations and vicissitudes of politicians and parties, but by their effects on public policy and system performance. A detailed review of such outcomes is beyond the scope of this chapter, but I can offer a few broad-brush observations. On theoretical grounds, the shift from FPTP to MMP in New Zealand could be expected to produce three main policy effects:

1. Most policies should be more stable, and changes should be less drastic, because legislation must win the consent of more "veto players"—two or more parties instead of just one—and must rest on a wider base of electoral support—a majority rather than just a plurality.
2. However, in the absence of institutions or norms requiring consensus or super-majorities, minimal majorities will suffice, so adversarial politics, winners and losers, and shifts in policy direction are to be expected.
3. As long as politics is primarily one-dimensional, the majority-rule requirement that policies must be acceptable to the median voter will be a powerful constraint, so the general tendency of policy-making should be moderate and centrist.

Government policies under MMP in 1996-2003 were consistent with all three expectations. Despite the unpopularity of the first coalition, most of the concessions NZF won in its agreement with National pulled government policy away from National's more right-wing stands toward moderate budgetary and welfare positions (Barker 1997). In 1999, power was transferred to the other side of the political spectrum. The Labour-Alliance coalition repealed National's most extreme policy, the severely anti-union Employment Contracts Act, but most of the changes it implemented were incremental, though nonetheless meaningful—for example, marginally more progressive taxation, increased pension benefits, restoration of a state-run accident insurance system, and income-based rents on state-owned housing (Bale 2003). In New Zealand, as in any majority-rule system, to the extent that politics becomes multi-dimensional, there remains a potential for policy instability, drastic changes, and minorities rule; but that danger is less under MMP than it was in the previous pluralitarian regime.[24] Since 1996, the sharpest controversies have involved cross-cutting issues advocated, sometimes in extreme form, by minor parties—e.g., hostility to immigration, assertion of Maori interests, and opposition to genetic research—but so far parties pushing such causes have either lost or won only modest concessions.

Because of its small, highly exposed economy and low growth rates during the second half of the twentieth century, the most important test of government effectiveness in New Zealand is economic performance. Business leaders were the last-ditch defenders of FPTP, largely because they believed (correctly) that it had made possible the radical economic liberalization of 1984-93. In another irony of electoral reform, the impact of MMP on economic growth has been remarkably benign, probably because of the policy consistency and incremental change that it fostered. The best indicator of broad economic welfare provided by Statistics New Zealand is RGNDI per capita (real gross national disposable income per capita), a measure of purchasing power. In the first six years of MMP (1997-2003), that indicator rose 14.12 per cent, an annual rate of 2.35 per cent. By comparison, the gain during the last six years of FPTP (1991-97) was only one-third as much: 3.88 per cent cumulatively or an annual average of just 0.65 per cent. Moreover, economic growth under MMP has been reasonably steady, whereas under FPTP there were severe fluctuations, including negative growth in purchasing power during 1990-92.[25] Defenders of the 1984-93 restructuring would contend that the economy in the decade afterwards benefited from those drastic changes, which may be true; however, it is exceedingly difficult to argue that MMP had a harmful effect.

Conclusion

There is no such thing as a perfect voting system, and overselling MMP or any other reform fosters the kind of disillusionment that afflicted New Zealand in the late 1990s. PR in that country did not usher in an era of consensus and amicable agreement; nor did it arrest, except temporarily, a trend toward disengagement from party politics and voting. If adjustment to the new system had been just a little less rapid, mistakes made before learning how to make it work might have killed MMP in its infancy. The problem of party hopping, a flaw fatal in principle if not in practice, has been answered with a remedy worse than the disease, though in the longer run new norms backed by electoral sanctions may provide a sufficient cure.

Overall, however, MMP impresses this observer as a dramatic improvement over the FPTP system it replaced. As one would expect from a list

PR method, it has produced equitable translation of votes into seats for political parties, plus much better representation of women and minority groups. It has also delivered virtues commonly, but mistakenly, attributed to FPTP—majority rule, moderation, and even (after a false start) accountability. Beneath the froth of volatile minor parties and precarious coalitions, MMP has fostered stabler policies, incremental reform, and economic progress. Besides turning to New Zealand for sauvignon blanc, yachtsmen, and Tolkien films, other Anglo-American democracies would do well to look to the Kiwis for lessons, both cautionary and exemplary, about electoral reform.

Notes

1. I am grateful to Paul Harris, Keith Jackson, and Jack Vowles for helpful information and comments.

2. For full details on New Zealand's electoral system plus election results in a handy format, see Electoral Commission (2003a).

3. Compensatory allocation distinguishes MMP from the second type of mixed system, in which allocation of list seats is independent of constituency results. These *parallel* systems, such as Japan and Russia adopted in the 1990s, do not achieve overall proportionality.

4. For the definitive history of the reform process in New Zealand, see Jackson and McRobie (1998).

5. Earlier, in 1908-35, there was a period of geographically based three-party competition. The Liberal Party, in power from 1890 to 1912, attempted to continue competing nationwide, but lost ground in rural areas to the Reform Party and in cities to the Labour Party. Reform and the Liberals (renamed the United Party) campaigned as a coalition in 1931 and 1935. After the Depression brought Labour to power in 1935, Reform and United dissolved to form the National Party.

6. The average share of the popular vote won by New Zealand's governing parties in 1954-90 was 45.3 per cent. The comparable figure in Canada for the 17 elections in 1953-2000 was even smaller, 42.6 per cent. However, because Canada's less dispersed minor parties elected more MPs, on six occasions major parties had to form minority governments dependent on minor-party support. In New Zealand, all 13 elections resulted in one-party majority governments that held absolute power as long as their caucuses remained unified.

7. In Canada, the list of inherent defects would also include exaggeration of regional political differences.

8. The distinction between inherent and contingent factors, borrowed from Harry Eckstein, is applied to the explanation of electoral systems in Shugart and Wattenberg (2001).

9. Compare the similar "wrong-winner" outcome in the American presidential election of 2000.

10. Compare the post-2000 United States National Commission on Federal Election Reform, co-chaired by former Presidents Gerald Ford and Jimmy Carter, which ruled out from the start any proposal requiring a constitutional amendment (such as

abolition of the Electoral College), and the British Independent Commission on the Voting System, chaired by Lord Jenkins, which struggled mightily to devise a plan that it hoped would be acceptable to the ruling Labour Party.

11. During this period, the Jenkins Commission in Britain dismissed MMP with the comment, "it is impossible to pretend that [New Zealand's] early experience of MMP has been fortunate." *The Report of the Independent Commission on the Voting System* (London: The Stationery Office, October 1999) 21.

12. The Alliance was an amalgamation of Greens, Democrats (formerly Social Credit), Liberals, Mana Motuhake (a Maori party), and New Labour (the latter actually Labour traditionalists who left that party to oppose its free-market policies of the 1980s).

13. Whether the Greens would qualify for seats was in doubt for a week after the election, until special votes (absentee ballots) were counted. In the meantime, the Alliance and Labour quickly completed negotiations on a coalition agreement.

14. The 1993 legislation had retained the entrenchment clause of the Electoral Act.

15. Disproportionality in Canadian elections averaged 18.0 in 1988-2000.

16. Tau Henare as quoted in Helen Bain, "'I'm not gonna change ... Hell, no, I won't change for a bunch of bloody rednecks,'" *Christchurch Press* 22 July 1998.

17. I argue elsewhere (Nagel 1994: 156) that parties seeking to be centrist on the conventional left-right dimension "are vulnerable unless their core followers' loyalty is cemented by group identities based on a second social cleavage." Another party competing for the pivotal centrist position, United Future, also confirms that prediction. The party languished through two elections with just one MP, Peter Dunne; but then leaped across the threshold in 2002 after Dunne allied with a previously futile Christian party and campaigned on a program emphasizing family values as well as moderate economic policies.

18. On the quandary of a small party, see Bale and Dann (2002).

19. The Electoral (Integrity) Amendment Act 2001, as quoted in Geddis (2002: 564).

20. And as Geddis (2002: 571) advises.

21. This result is similar to eye-opening findings about PR and FPTP systems generally as reported by Powell (2000). The irony of Powell's analysis is that systems founded on the "majoritarian" vision do *less* well than PR in actually delivering majority rule. Application of the median-voter test in his work and in my argument above depends on a one-dimensional conception of politics—inadequate for many purposes, but a useful first approximation.

22. In Canada, the currently dominant Liberal Party only wins electoral pluralities, but it occupies the median position on both major political dimensions (the conventional left-right spectrum and linguistic/regional issues). Therefore, the virtue of MMP in producing majority rule for New Zealand may not speak to the present needs of Canadians. Indeed, as my colleague Brendan O'Leary has suggested to me in conversation, Canadians may worry that electoral reform might upset the median equilibrium now maintained by Liberal rule. That concern may be allayed by Powell's findings about the general superiority of PR in producing median-voter outcomes, but the question requires careful consideration in Canada's two-dimensional setting.

23. Official statistics from New Zealand measure "turning out" literally by including two categories of would-be voters whose ballots are disallowed. Adjustments

should be made before attempting comparisons to countries that base turnout figures only on votes actually counted.

24. For a multi-dimensional interpretation of the tumultuous politics that led to electoral reform, see Nagel (1998).

25. Author's calculations using data from several Statistics New Zealand web pages and the 1993 *New Zealand Official Yearbook*. Figures are for years ending in March. Annual rates are arithmetic averages, rather than compounded rates. Comparisons for the more familiar index, GDP per capita, are qualitatively similar but less sharp for the periods cited above. Differences are even more dramatic if one takes 1994 as the year when the impact of MMP was first felt. (As politicians jockeyed for position in anticipation of MMP, the major parties suffered significant defections, resulting in coalition or minority governments from September 1994 onward.) Average growth in RGNDI per capita in 1994-2003 was *seven* times as high as over the preceding six FPTP years, 1988-94. (The indicator is not available before 1988.) GDP per capita actually shrank between 1988 and 1994.

CHAPTER 6

Making Every Vote Count in Scotland: Devolution and Electoral Reform

Peter Lynch

Introduction

In 1999, the five million people of Scotland gained a parliament of their own and with it a measure of institutional and policy autonomy from central government in the UK. The Scottish Parliament gained legislative as well as administrative responsibility for policy areas such as agriculture, education, environment, health, local government, law and policing, tourism and economic development. Indeed, in its first four years of existence, Parliament passed over 60 pieces of legislation. Passing its own laws symbolized a return to Scotland's pre-Union history—it was independent from England before 1707—but the opening of Parliament also reflected the existence of autonomous Scottish institutions and a distinct civil society after Union, especially in the nineteenth century (Paterson 1994). In time, such distinctions in education, law, and religion led to a measure of government recognition. The UK government created a cabinet minister for Scotland in 1886 (the Scottish Secretary) followed by the development in the twentieth century of the Scottish Office, which administered a range of policy areas from Edinburgh.

One expression of the enhanced institutional autonomy brought by devolution was the adoption of a system of proportional representation (PR) for electing the members of the new parliament. During the 1990s, the issue of electoral reform became intertwined with that of devolution. This linkage was characterized by a constructive dialogue over a wide range of constitutional reforms between the Labour and Liberal Democrat parties. In Scotland, the debate centred on the design of the new devolved legislature and the means by which its members were to be elected; PR was part of a positive alternative to Westminster-style politics and the first-past-the-post (FPTP) electoral system which was seen to produce one-party dominance based on a minority of the vote. From 1979 to 1997 one-party dominance came in the shape of a Conservative government elected on the basis of electoral support from the south of England and which was deeply unpopular in Scotland where it was perceived to govern against the interests of Scottish voters. Constitutional reformers naturally sought to prevent the introduction of unpopular measures, such as the Conservatives' poll tax, in designing the devolved institutions, including the electoral system. European-style electoral systems came to be seen as the means of producing European-style coalition governments, putting an end to single-party governments with a majority of the seats but only a minority of the vote.

The choice fell on the additional member system (AMS), also known as mixed-member proportionality (MMP), which was developed in Germany. Of the 129 members of the new Parliament, 73 are elected under FPTP and 56 elected proportionately and correctively from regional lists. Moreover, the new electoral system in Scotland has brought changes. After two elections—1999 and 2003—AMS has produced a more fragmented six-party system. Independents and single-issue candidates have been elected, and split-ticket voting has become more common as some small parties built their support on the second (additional-member) vote. Moreover, electoral reform is set to be introduced for local authorities in Scotland in the shape of the single transferable vote (STV) used in Ireland, meaning Scottish voters will gain experience of a fourth type of electoral system.

The Context of Electoral Reform

Electoral reform became a more serious political issue in the years following the 1992 general election. Labour's failure to defeat the Conservatives brought a period of dialogue between Labour and the Liberal Democrats over the governmental prospects of the centre-left. While dialogue at the UK level was minimal in the years that Neil Kinnock and John Smith led the Labour Party, in Scotland, discussions had been taking place since 1989 through the medium of the Scottish Constitutional Convention. When Tony Blair became Labour leader in 1994, he and his Liberal Democrat counterpart Paddy Ashdown entered informal and formal discussions over future cooperation, prospects for coalition and the "big tent" politics of the centre-left overcoming a Conservative Party that had governed since 1979.[1] One concrete result was the establishment of the Jenkins Commission to examine the case for electoral reform at Westminster, which reported in 1998 (Jenkins 1998).

The discussions also produced cooperation on constitutional reform first via regular discussions between Labour's Robin Cook, who was Shadow Foreign Secretary at the time, and the Liberal Democrat's Robert MacLennan; then through the creation of the Joint Consultative Commission on Constitutional Reform, which published a cooperation agreement on March 5, 1997; and finally, after the 1997 general election, through the establishment of a cabinet committee on which sat several Liberal Democrats. Labour and the Liberal Democrats have continued to cooperate over freedom of information, House of Lords reform, devolution, and inclusion of the European Convention on Human Rights into UK law (through the Human Rights Act).

As is well known, the Jenkins Commission report recommended a limited version of AMS (Jenkins 1998), but the report and its proposals were shelved by the government. Labour's landslide victory in 1997 obviated the need for coalition with the Liberal Democrats at Westminster since New Labour's success in taking previously safe seats in the south of England from the Conservatives reversed existing territorial patterns of voting and resolved Labour's post-1979 unelectability as a government. As this electoral outcome was largely repeated in 2001, electoral reform at Westminster was erased from Labour's reform agenda; nevertheless, it became an important aspect of the various devolution schemes implemented from 1998 onwards.

Thus, despite having taken electoral reform off the menu at Westminster, the House of Commons was busy considering a variety of devolution schemes that included proposals for electoral reform. The Scotland and Wales acts of 1998 each instituted the AMS in these territories, while Northern Irish devolution was accompanied by the STV. The Welsh version provided for fewer additional members than Scotland, with 67 per cent of the Welsh Assembly members elected by FPTP compared to 57 per cent in Scotland. In addition, the AMS electoral system was also adopted for the Greater London Authority in 2000, its version including a 5 per cent threshold for additional members intended to block extremist parties such as the British National Party.[2]

Millions of voters now had the prospect, for the first time, of experiencing alternatives to the Westminster FPTP system. At the same time, regional list PR was adopted for the 1999 European Parliament elections for which the UK was divided into regions that coincided with existing and proposed regional assembly boundaries, with voters choosing among parties in their region. As a result, 11 Liberal Democrats, three UK Independence Party, two Green, and two Plaid Cymru MEPs were elected along with Labour, Conservative, and Scottish National Party (SNP) candidates—a considerable novelty at

European elections in the UK. As we shall see in Scotland, a change in the electoral system meant a change in the party system.

The Origins of the Scottish Electoral System

The Scottish electoral system was designed on a cross-party basis through the deliberations of the Scottish Constitutional Convention. The convention was established in 1989 to design a program for devolution as well as to build broad support for a Scottish Parliament. Participants included representatives of two of the four main parties—Labour and Liberal Democrats—as well as a range of local authorities, trade unions, and civic organizations. The diversity of its make-up meant that the convention itself contained multiple actors pursuing varied interests and outcomes. Each was committed to the establishment of a Scottish Parliament but had different perspectives on many aspects including its size, its powers, and the appropriate system for electing its members. In relation to the electoral system, the political parties' views carried the most weight, though the issue was of concern also to the trade unions and, especially, women's organizations whose representatives favoured proportional electoral systems to enhance women's representation and facilitate gender balance.

The convention met from 1989 to 1995 and published two sets of proposals for devolution. In the interval, it established a Constitutional Commission to examine the workings of the electoral system for the Parliament; its conclusions were left out of the first set of the convention's proposals (Scottish Constitutional Convention 1990). The proposals merely set out a series of general principles to guide any future choice of electoral system, reflecting the lack of agreement within the convention itself at this stage. These principles took the form of expectations that the electoral system produce results:

1. in which the number of seats for various parties is broadly related to the number of votes cast for them;
2. that ensure, or at least take effective positive action to bring about, equal representation of men and women and encourage fair representation of ethnic and other minority groups;
3. that preserve a real link between the member and his or her constituency;
4. that are as simple as possible to understand;
5. that ensure adequate representation of the less populous areas;

6. that place the greatest possible power in the hands of the electorate (Scottish Constitutional Convention 1990).

Putting these principles into practice was to prove a challenge for the convention, the parties, and subsequently the voters. The choice of an electoral system was problematic because of the opposing preferences of Labour (supporters of FPTP) and the Liberal Democrats (supporters of STV). As the Liberal Democrats were the only other major party involved and would not agree to any devolution scheme that did not involve electoral reform, they had an effective veto power over the devolution package itself. Without Liberal Democrat support, the convention would lack legitimacy and any semblance of cross-party support: factors which were seen as central to delivering devolution in the 1990s (cross-party divisions over devolution in the 1970s led to defeat in the 1979 referendum). The Liberal Democrats not only made detailed analyses of the effect of various electoral systems on electoral outcomes in Scotland—using computer modelling to simulate general elections using AMS, Alternative Vote (AV) and STV—they were also able to assess the effect of the size of the Parliament itself in determining the match between votes and seats for each political party. Initially, the Liberal Democrats proposed "STV+": a hybrid system using STV topped up by using party lists covering the whole of Scotland (Scottish Liberal Democrats 1991).

The Liberal Democrat's proposal was rejected, the convention opting instead, in 1992, for a German-style AMS system of FPTP seats with a PR top-up list on regional boundaries. AMS was seen to be advantageous from a number of different perspectives. For Labour, it retained single-member districts from which, given its strength on the ground in Scotland, it was sure to benefit overwhelmingly. For the Liberal Democrats, it contained a PR element that, if operated effectively, would enable a party's share of the vote to be reflected closely in its share of the seats. For others, there was the prospect of top-up lists enhancing gender balance and ethnic minority representation.

However, while the convention arrived at a consensus on the principle of AMS, it was unable to agree upon the details of the system. A special Constitutional Commission was established in 1993 with the mandate of examining the details of the electoral system and provisions for gender balance. It proposed a parliament of 112 members—with 72 elected by FPTP and 40 on regional top-up lists. The 72 FPTP members would be elected on existing Westminster constituency boundaries, while the European Parliamentary constituencies were to be used for the 40 top-up members; this meant five additional members of the Scottish Parliament (MSPs) for each region. A dual ballot system would operate in which voters were asked to cast their vote for both a constituency member and a closed list of regional candidates.

There was also disagreement within the commission over the degree to which the top-up lists were to be corrective. While the AMS procedure is based on the principle of using the top-up lists to "correct" the unfair alloca- tion of seats on the FPTP system, Labour members of the commission and the convention tried, ultimately without success, to undermine the principle. They wanted Labour to receive, above their existing (disproportionate) allocation of FPTP seats, a proportion of regional list seats that reflected their share of the regional vote (similar, in effect, to the Japanese system—see Chapter 8). In relation to gender balance measures, and lacking powers to influence this issue itself, the commission proposed that the parties commit themselves to achieving 40 per cent representation of women as well as fair representation of ethnic minorities within five years of the Parliament's crea- tion (Scottish Constitutional Commission 1994). However, actually ensuring parties complied with this proposal was, and remains, impossible as will be explained below.

The final agreement on the electoral system was achieved following a pe- riod of intense bargaining and negotiation in the convention. While the AMS proposal was accepted, there was disagreement on the size of the Parliament and the balance between FPTP and additional members. The Constitutional Commission's suggestion of 112 MSPs was endorsed by Labour, but opposed by the Liberal Democrats because the small size of the Parliament hindered efforts at proportionality. For example, if the 1992 general election result was repeated in a 112-member parliament, Labour would remain overrepresented (45.5 per cent of the seats on 39.1 per cent of the votes) with its three main opponents underrepresented. The Liberal Democrats analyzed the seat-votes gap by simulating the results using five to nine additional MSPs per region. With nine additional members the seat-vote gap was almost completely removed, which led the Liberal Democrats to propose this option, that is, a parliament comprised of 145 members: 73 FPTP members[3] and 72 additional members (nine MSPs in each of the eight European constituencies). However, this proposal was not acceptable to Labour, which wanted a smaller parliament and to retain the FPTP element as the dominant part of the electoral system (thus maintaining its partisan advantage). The two main parties compromised on the final number of MSPs and proposed a parliament of 129 members with 73 FPTP members and 56 additional MSPs (seven per region) elected propor- tionally and correctively using the d'Hondt system (Scottish Constitutional Convention 1995). The system, therefore, preserved a constituency or local

link between members and voters through the FPTP element as well as ensuring that the additional members came from regional constituencies rather
than all of Scotland.

The convention's proposals may have gained support from two of the
major political parties, local authorities, trade unions, and civic organizations,
but this was no guarantee of their adoption. The parties represented at the
convention were in the opposition and not in a position to implement its proposals for devolution or electoral reform. It was only when the unsympathetic
Conservative government at Westminster was ousted in Labour's landslide
election victory in 1997 that devolution was brought into play. It is notewor-
thy how much Labour's devolution policy in office followed the blueprint
of the Scottish Constitutional Convention. Conceivably, in its devolution
proposal to be put to a referendum in September 1997, the government could
have disregarded or amended parts of the convention scheme. Instead, it not
only adopted the electoral system proposed by the convention for Scotland, it
adopted it for Wales and also subsequently for the Greater London Authority
and the (yet to be implemented) English regional assemblies (Office of the
Deputy Prime Minister 2002).

The New Electoral System in Practice

While designed in the abstract, the Scottish electoral system has now been
implemented in two elections, the outcomes of each of which were influenced
by the nature of the electoral system. Moreover, the effects on the outcome
of the 2003 election have led to some debate over future changes to the AMS
electoral system itself. I shall first describe the main effects of the system on
the results of the two elections in terms of representativeness and patterns
of support for the parties. I will then address the impact of the electoral
system on the party system as a whole, and, finally, its effect on the issues of
gender balance and ethnic minority representation, two major objectives of
electoral reform envisaged in the deliberations of the Scottish Constitutional
Convention.

COMPARING OUTCOMES IN 1999 AND 2003

The first notable effect of AMS elections on the outcomes of the two Scottish
elections of 1999 and 2003 (see Tables 6-1 and 6-2) is that, despite the top-up
feature, the Scottish electoral system retains a FPTP advantage for Labour,
which was able to gain 43.4 per cent of the seats in 1999 and 38.7 per cent in

Table 6-1
Result of the Scottish Election 1999

Party	% 1st Vote	Seats	% 2nd Vote	Seats	Total Seats
Labour	38.8	53	33.6	3	56
SNP	28.7	7	27.3	28	35
Conservative	15.5	0	15.4	18	18
Lib Dems	14.2	12	12.4	5	17
Others	2.7	1	11.3	2	3

2003. The SNP was significantly disadvantaged due to its regional dependence, with 27 per cent of the seats in 1999 and 20.9 per cent in 2003. This meant that, in 2003, the SNP won about two-thirds as many votes as Labour but obtained just over half the seats. There was no significant gap between the level of votes and seats for the other parties in either of the two elections. In addition, in both of these elections new political forces gained representation. In 1999, a former Labour MP, Dennis Canavan, was elected as an independent in a FPTP constituency, while the Scottish Green Party and Scottish Socialist Party gained an MSP each through the regional lists. In 2003, the phenomenon spread (see Table 6-2), with two independents, one anti-hospital closure candidate, a member of the Scottish Senior Citizen's Unity Party, seven MSPs from the Scottish Green Party and six MSPs from the Scottish Socialist Party getting elected. Thus the level of support for "others"—meaning individuals/parties outside the big four—increased on the first vote from 2.7 per cent in 1999 to 9.8 per cent in 2003, but more dramatically from 11.3 per cent on the second vote in 1999 to 22.3 per cent in 2003. At this point, more than one-fifth of voters were supporting (and electing) non-traditional political forces. While the Scottish Socialists stood both FPTP and regional list candidates, the Greens and the Scottish Senior Citizen's Unity Party competed solely on the lists, appealing successfully for the second vote.[4] As voters came to understand the workings of AMS, they learned to take advantage of the effect of the size of the regions (seven seats per region) to break the electoral monopoly of the four main parties. It remains to be seen the extent to which the disalignment is permanent, as opposed to a response to the specific situation confronted in 2003.

It is clear that the Scottish party system now differs from that at Westminster as a result of the electoral system generally and, specifically, in the way in which electors utilized the second vote in the 2003 Scottish election. The results of the two elections illustrate the evolution of multi-level

Table 6-2
Result of the Scottish Election 2003

Party	% 1st Vote	Seats	% 2nd Vote	Seats	Total Seats
Labour	34.6	46	28.7	4	50
SNP	23.7	9	20.4	18	27
Conservative	16.6	3	15.1	15	18
Lib Dems	15.3	13	13.5	4	17
Greens	0	0	6.7	7	7
SSP	6.2	0	6.5	6	6
Others	3.6	2	9.1	2	4

electoral patterns in Scotland. Simply put, the SNP is more popular in Scottish than UK elections and Labour is less popular, while the Conservatives have been able to attain an electoral presence in Edinburgh that FPTP has denied them in Westminster in recent elections. The 1999 election made the SNP the official opposition and ended one-party dominance by giving birth to a Labour-Liberal Democrat coalition government. The 2003 election went further, bringing multi-party politics to Scotland, with a six-party chamber representative of a wider spread of the party families typical of continental European democracies (Beyme 1985) and very much at variance with the Labour-Conservative duopoly at Westminster. One can say, thus, that there has been some decoupling of voting in Scottish and UK elections (Hough and Jeffery 2003), though nothing of Canadian proportions.

THE NEW SCOTTISH PARTY SYSTEM

Two obvious party system effects are evident from the results of the two Scottish elections. First, because the electoral system ensures that a party cannot win a majority of the seats on a minority of the vote, coalition governments have become the order of the day. So far, both coalitions have involved Labour and the Liberal Democrats. The parties negotiated a four-year program for government after the 1999 and 2003 elections, comprised of policy commitments and formula for allocating government portfolios. While 1999-2003 witnessed some divisions between the two coalition parties, it was, overall, a period of considerable stability in which internal conflicts were resolved through compromise and which is likely to continue under the current coalition due to the policy affinities among the two parties as well as their determination to work constructively. Nevertheless, the institutional shape this will take has been changing. If the fragmented party system persists, subsequent elections may see results in which simple two-party coalitions give way to three or more party coalitions which could make Scotland more difficult to govern—depending on the policy stances of the parties involved.

Gender and Ethnic Minority Balance

The electoral system has not been responsible for the improvement in gender representation in the Scottish Parliament alone; rather, it created incentives and fostered a climate that affected the selection decisions of the parties. Though neither the Constitutional Convention nor the government could implement gender balance, the political parties could. In 1995, Labour and the Liberal Democrats agreed upon an Electoral Contract, which stipulated that they would try to select equal numbers of male and female candidates in winnable seats (Scottish Constitutional Convention 1995). Despite this, however, gender balance measures were rejected by the delegates at the Liberal Democrat conference. A similar outcome occurred in the SNP, when the leadership's attempts to introduce gender balance measures were defeated. Only in the Scottish Labour Party were gender balance measures approved and implemented. Labour's controversial scheme, which entailed a number of male activists losing out, involved the twinning of constituencies to ensure that equal numbers of men and women were selected, especially in safe seats. The gender outcomes were dramatic: in 1999 exactly 50 per cent of Labour MSPs were women, which brought the total to 37 per cent of the Parliament (48 women out of 129 MSPs). This level increased slightly to 39.5 per cent in 2003 (51 women MSPs), in contrasts with the 18 per cent of women MPs at Westminster. The Labour women members of the Scottish Parliament were joined by women from the SNP, Scottish Green Party, and Scottish Socialist Party. Very few sat on the benches of either the Conservatives or Liberal Democrats. The performance with regard to ethnic minorities was far more disappointing as none were elected, since they were placed too low on the regional lists or were selected for unwinnable FPTP seats in 1999 and 2003.

THE ISSUE OF HAVING TWO CLASSES OF MSPS

One consequence of the electoral system in practice has been the perception that there are two classes of MSPs. Because Labour and Liberal Democrat MSPs were largely elected by FPTP in single districts in 1999 (and again in 2003), while, especially in 1999, most of the SNP and Conservatives were elected through the regional lists, the distribution of FPTP and list members took on a definite partisan dimension. These electoral patterns generated partisan conflict, the first coming immediately after the 1999 election in the parliamentary debate over office allowances for MSPs. Labour MSPs sought to restrict the level of office allowances for list members to prevent them opening office premises in (their) FPTP constituencies and using constituency service to build a political base for future FPTP contests in the constituency. Since most of the list MSPs were defeated FPTP candidates, they—especially list SNP members—could be expected to seek to generate a "presence" in the constituency and potentially threaten the sitting Labour MSPs. The latter were therefore determined to minimize the resources available to the list MSPs, claiming that because FPTP members would deal with the bulk of constituency case grievances, the smaller workload of list MSPs justified smaller allowances. In what was, basically, a political turf war between Labour and its main opponents, a compromise was reached setting allowance levels that did discriminate between the FPTP and list MSPs, but not to the extent proposed by Labour (Lynch 2001: 54-56).

The resolution of the allowance question in 1999 was not the end of the matter. Again as a result of partisan divisions, there were a series of disputes between the two types of MSPs over handling case work. Some Labour MSPs complained that list MSPs were cherry-picking constituency cases—taking an interest in the most visible cases and neglecting others. This problem led Parliament to establish a set of principles to govern constituency relations between FPTP and list MSPs. These principles stated that:

1. Scotland has a multi-member system of representation, and each constituent is represented by eight MSPs. Constituents can choose any of these eight MSPs as their representative. Regional MSPs should inform constituency MSPs when they take up a case.
2. All MSPs are equal—whether they are from a constituency or the regional list.
3. MSPs should not "poach" cases from each other: regional MSPs can only deal with cases from their region, constituency MSPs can only deal with cases from their constituencies.
4. The wishes and interests of individual constituents and their locality should determine the allocation of representational duties and whether a constituency or list MSP becomes involved (Scottish Parliament 1999).

The question remains as to whether such FPTP-list conflicts were generated by the AMS electoral system itself or by the patterns of party representation in the constituencies and lists. Early research on the activities of FPTP and list MSPs found each type of MSP gave priority to constituency service and case-work, though the workloads of constituency MSPs were somewhat higher in relation to the level of casework, surgeries, and constituency correspondence (FPTP members reported that 42 per cent of their time was spent on constituency work compared to 35 per cent for regional list members; Cowley and Lochore 2000: 183); however, later surveys found similar levels of workload between the two types of MSP in relation to constituency service (Lundberg 2002). This suggests that, without the partisan dimension to the FPTP and list MSPs, conflicts between the types of representatives might have not have become political issues.

Democracy and Administrative Efficiency under AMS

The main result of the AMS electoral system, as expected, has been to introduce a measure of PR that has brought the votes attained by the various parties and the allocation of seats far closer than conceivable under the Westminster election system. The possibility of a Scottish government formed by a single party with a parliamentary majority based on a minority of the vote has been eliminated. Coalition has become the norm, with Scottish governments established between two parties that shared 54.3 per cent of the first vote in 1999 and 49.9 per cent in 2003. These provided a majority in each election, albeit a narrow one in 2003. Contrast that with Labour's 167-seat majority at Westminster in 2001 based on 42 per cent of the vote. In addition, the proportional system has been rendered compatible, through AMS, with the British tradition of constituency service and links between elected members and their local districts, such members comprising 57 per cent of the Scottish Parliament.

The two Labour-Liberal Democrat coalitions were able to govern in a stable fashion. The decision to establish a four-year program of agreed policies gave the coalition a clear long-term direction, since difficult issues were dealt with in advance in setting out the parties' programs for government negotiated in 1999 and 2003. In addition, the government established special independent inquiries and commissions to resolve specific potentially problematic policy issues. An inquiry into student finance was provided for in the program for government in 1999, while a commission into the reform of the electoral system for local government was set up during the term and reported in 2002.

Internally, the system of cabinet committees ensured continuous policy discussions between the two parties on sensitive issues, a process enhanced by the role of the deputy first minister, whose brief was to represent the interests of the minority Liberal Democrats in monitoring all policy proposals and documents within the executive. There were consequently very few disputes during the coalition's first four years of Parliament's existence, which led to its being reconstituted following the 2003 Scottish election.

So far, experience shows that concerns over government instability as the outcome of the electoral system were misplaced. The same is true of concerns over voter incomprehension in the face of the complexity of AMS. In fact, there was little evidence that voters found the two-ballot system unduly difficult. For instance, the Scottish Parliamentary Election Survey of 1999 found that only 10 per cent of voters found filling in the ballot papers very or fairly difficult, whereas 41 per cent found it not very difficult and 49 per cent not at all difficult. Even when it came to the more complex matter of how second vote seats were allocated, 48 per cent of voters reported difficulties with understanding the seat allocation, but 52 per cent did not (Paterson *et al.* 2001: 69). There is of course a low level of voter comprehension of more technical aspects of the electoral system, such as the number of seats that could be won on the first and second votes and the existence of special thresholds (Paterson *et al.* 2001: 72), but these are detailed matters of concern mainly to electoral specialists, not to the general public. Most important, they did not prevent the public from taking part in the elections. Furthermore, overall, there was little evidence that voters perceived any of the shortcomings critics associate with PR systems such as government instability or giving too much power to small parties (Paterson *et al.* 2001: 76). Indeed, when comparing the movements in the second vote between 1999 and 2003, it appears evident that voters understood the potential of the second vote in relation to split-ticket voting. For some, the second vote became a second choice for a non-traditional party or independent that had some likelihood of electoral success.

Conclusion

There are a few clear lessons that can be drawn from the experience of the AMS electoral system in Scotland. First, in terms of the design of the system, a level of cross-party consensus was important, as was negotiation and compromise. And it cannot be doubted that the Scottish electoral system was developed during a period of reaction to the political experiences of the 1980s and progress toward devolution, that is, during a set of quite unique circumstances. Second, without bringing instability, the AMS electoral system led to the fragmentation of the party system and also to conflicts between the two different types of MSP, resulting largely from the fact that Labour's strength assured it of most FPTP seats and, thus, very few compensatory ones from the lists—leaving few FPTP seats for others who then generally depended on election from the list seats.

The Scottish experience thus challenges other countries that may adopt its model of AMS to look into ways of building in mechanisms to prevent the latter scenario. Indeed, after the 2003 election, the Labour Party began to examine moving away from AMS towards the Irish STV system, which is based on preferential voting in multi-member constituencies, to end the system of two classes of MSP and to reduce the fragmentation of the party system. Finally, while a new party system has emerged and coalition politics have become the norm in Scotland as a result of the new electoral system, electoral turnout has declined. Turnout in 1999 was 58.16 per cent for the FPTP vote and 58.07 per cent for the regional vote; it declined to 49.43 per cent and 49.41 per cent in 2003. These are worrying numbers, but as the turnout at the Westminster election in 2001 was the lowest since 1918, we must look to changes in UK-wide, if not universal, attitudes to politics and participation more than devolution or the Scottish electoral system. However, it remains a depressing fact that devolution and electoral reform were unable to turn back the tide of voter apathy.

Notes

1. For extensive discussion of the issue see Ashdown 1999.
2. Wales has 40 FPTP seats and 20 additional members in five regions. In London, the Greater London Authority has 14 FPTP members and 11 additional members.
3. The Liberal Democrats proposed one MSP each for the Orkney and Shetland islands, which received one MP at Westminster.
4. Other small parties developed similar strategies unsuccessfully, such as the fishing party in northeast Scotland, the Scottish Peoples Alliance, and the UK Independence Party.

CHAPTER 7

Electoral Reform in South Africa: An Electoral System for the Twenty-First Century[1]

Murray Faure[2] and Albert Venter[3]

Introduction

In 2001 the president of South Africa appointed an Electoral Task Team, popularly known as the Slabbert Commission, to report on electoral reform. It duly reported in March 2003. In this chapter, after providing an overview of the present system, we present and analyze the changes proposed by the Slabbert Commission as well as a parliamentary bill that was drafted in response to the commission's report. The recommendations and provisions of the bill serve as a take-off point for our own proposal, namely for changing the present electoral system of pure party list proportionality to a mixed-member proportional system (MMP) which combines single-member constituencies (SMCs) with party lists. The main argument underlying our proposed reforms is that in the present electoral system there is a serious lack of accountability. Hence, our proposals are aimed at enhancing the answerability of public representatives.

We make this argument in full awareness of the remarkable successes that the present system has registered. But South Africa cannot afford to rest on its laurels. The longer it retains its present electoral system, we fear, the more its shortcomings will become institutionalized with the negative implications these hold for democracy. While the present electoral system was, on balance, an appropriate electoral system for South Africa's transition to democracy, the time has come to move toward an electoral system appropriate for the needs of the coming years, namely, accountable government and consolidation of democracy.

South Africa used the British first-past-the-post (FPTP) system of electing representatives to Parliament for more than 80 years. It remained essentially unchanged since its implementation at unification in 1910 until it was replaced by the new electoral system set out in the 1993 Interim Constitution and implemented in the subsequent election of April 1994. By the end of the 1980s it had become clear that South Africa was irrevocably moving towards some major form of political transition, which entailed a new electoral arrangement. The five years that preceded the adoption of the Interim Constitution in 1993 witnessed intensification in the debate on electoral options for the new South Africa.

While the proposals for electoral reform in this period differed over various technical details, a remarkable degree of consensus characterized the debate in at least two aspects. The first was that the old FPTP system was patently unfair since it overrepresented large parties, especially the ruling party in the system. This led to agreement on the second point of concurrence among participants in the debate at the time, namely, that *acceptable options for electoral reform had to provide for some form of proportional outcome of elections.* After the adoption of closed party list proportional representation (PR) in the 1993 Interim Constitution and its being put to its first test in the election of April 1994, the electoral reform debate resumed. On the one hand, experience of the new system in practice needed to be assessed; on the other, the country was to move towards its Final Constitution, which, in principle, left the door open for adjustments to, amongst others, the electoral system.

It became evident in 1995 during the deliberations of the Constitutional Assembly that the 1994 PR list system would not be changed in time for the 1999 general election. However, the public and academic debate regarding the type of electoral system continued, focusing on the 2004 election. Many roundtables and workshops were organized, all of which received quite a few alternatives proposed by experts.[4] In essence, the alternatives on the table amounted to three: retain the status quo of the party list system, introduce multi-member constituencies (MMCs), or have a system combining list PR and SMCs. In 2001, on the initiative of the minister of home affairs, the president appointed an Electoral Task Team (ETT) to report on electoral reform. This initiative was the result not only of the debates regarding electoral reform, but also of the fact that South Africa's interim Electoral Act, product of compromises during the drafting of the 1993 Interim Constitution, had lapsed. The task team duly reported in March 2003. Before analyzing and evaluating its report, we need to examine the existing electoral system.

Table 7-1

The Allocation of Seats in the South African National Assembly

National Lists		200 seats
Provincial Lists	Eastern Cape	27
	Free State	14
	Gauteng	46
	KwaZulu-Natal	38
	Mpumalanga	14
	Northern Cape	4
	Limpopo Province	20
	North-West	17
	Western Cape	20
Total		400

South Africa's Present Electoral System

Constitutional arrangements provide for a bicameral parliament composed of a 90-member indirectly elected National Council of Provinces (NCOP) and a 400-member National Assembly. Each of the nine provinces has a delegation, consisting of ten members, which represents that province in the NCOP. In general, these provincial delegations reflect the relative strength of political parties represented in the respective provincial legislatures. The members of the National Assembly, who represent the ordinary voting public, are elected on the basis of a closed party list PR system. Two hundred members are elected using national party lists, while the remaining 200 members are elected on the basis of provincial party lists. Each province is entitled to a fraction of the 200 members in accordance with its relative population size—this is equivalent to about half the number of members of the individual legislatures (the members of the provincial legislatures are elected from provincial lists comprised of a minimum of 30 and a maximum of 80 members).

The Ballot

Each voter is accorded two ballots—one for the election of members of the National Assembly and one for electing members to the legislature of the province in which the voter is resident. Only the names of the contesting political parties are reflected on the ballot. The voter is bound to the order of candidates on the various party lists as decided by the party leadership. No candidate preference is provided for, and the only differentiation that voters can exercise is to vote for different parties that contest the National Assembly and the provincial legislatures respectively.

The system uses both national and subnational (regional, provincial) party lists. The election of 200 National Assembly members from national party lists corresponds to the method used in the Netherlands and Israel. It uses the whole country as one very large MMC, while the election of the other 200 National Assembly members according to party lists from the nine regions/provinces can be compared to extremely large versions of the MMCs used in most European countries. Seats are allocated proportionally at both a regional and a national level in terms of the Droop quota,[5] but the national allocation is corrective, taking into account distortions in the regional allocations. Finally, the threshold (the minimum votes required to win a seat) is extremely low.[6] Hence, neither smaller parties with regional support nor those with a country-wide level of support (i.e., lacking a regional base) are disadvantaged by this method.

Elections in South Africa are held under the auspices of an independent Electoral Commission (IEC), which is prescribed by the Constitution. While the electoral system does not provide for representative constituencies, the voters' roll is kept by the municipalities according to a geographically based electoral district system. One could name these "registration districts": voters resident in these districts register and exercise their votes in them. Limited provision is made for postal voting. South African public servants in foreign missions can vote offshore as can South Africans who registered to vote while resident in the country if they are overseas at the time of an election. South Africans who have not registered to vote cannot register to vote—and therefore cannot vote in elections—while they are in foreign states.

Elections take place once every five years. Since 1994, there have been two general elections for the National Assembly and provincial legislatures (1994 and 1999), with the third due on 14 April 2004. There have also been two rounds of municipal or local government elections (in 1995 and 2000). Since 1994, provincial government elections have taken place simultaneously with national elections, but this is not a legal requirement. Provinces operate under a parliamentary system of government, and it is possible for a provincial executive to lose the confidence of the legislature prematurely and thus be forced to go to the electorate for a fresh mandate before its five-year term of office has expired. While unlikely at this point, over time such an eventuality should result in provincial elections not coinciding with parliamentary elections. Participation in the 1999 general election was calculated at an impressive 86 per cent of registered voters. However, there is a considerable underregistration of potential voters due to poverty, ignorance, and apathy. If measured against voting age population, the participation rate was a respectable 68 per cent, which compares favourably with other newly democratized states (Lodge 1999: 205).

Since the electoral system is strictly proportional, the outcomes for participating parties have been likewise. The low threshold has led to a proliferation of smaller parties, with 13 parties winning representation in the National Assembly in the 1999 general election. However four parties predominate: most important by far is the African National Congress (ANC) with 66.5 per cent of the vote in 1999, followed by the Democratic Alliance with 12 per cent of the vote, the Inkatha Freedom Party with 8 per cent, and the New National Party with 5 per cent. As a result of ANC policy, 30 per cent of the members of various legislative assemblies are women. This is also known as the 2:1 rule: at least one woman for every two men.

During a parliamentary term, MPs are constitutionally prohibited from crossing the floor on the grounds that they do not carry a personal mandate from a geographic constituency. Their mandate from the electorate is a party mandate; MPs who switch parties lose their seats. An exception to this rule came in 2002 in the form of an amendment to the Constitution to make "party hopping" possible. Hopping is restricted to one or two "windows of opportunity" in the five-year term of office of the national, provincial, and local government assemblies. This is determined by the president based on his "reading of party politics" in the various assemblies. Such party hopping took place towards the end of 2002.

The Need for Reform

From almost ten years experience we can observe that the absence of an individual mandate from a specific geographically delimited constituency or voting district has led to a deficiency in the public accountability of public representatives as well as lackadaisical performances by politicians and public servants. In addition, the system places an inordinate amount of power and influence in the hands of the leadership of all parties, which can lead over time to nepotism. In our judgement, the lack of individual representation could, in due course, undermine the legitimacy of electoral democracy, since the electorate will come to perceive their representatives to be of little effective use in meeting the needs and promoting the interests of communities and local districts.

Our reading of the massive literature that has developed around the issue of electoral system reform (see Faure 1999) is that scholars are agreed that the present system is legitimate, all-inclusive, and highly proportional, allowing representation for even very small parties. Because it does not waste votes, voters need not vote strategically. Moreover, it eliminates the problems of gerrymandering associated with constituency delimitation under FPTP. Finally, the double ballot provides some small measure of vote differentiation with regard to national and provincial matters. A consensus also exists on the shortcomings of the system: it is impersonal, strengthens the hands of party bosses and their party bureaucracies, and does not provide for sufficient accountability on the part of representatives. The latter shortcoming is viewed as the most serious since it effectively suppresses communication between voters and representatives. The MPs are responsible to their parties, but insufficiently responsive to the needs of voters.

In 2001 the wide expression of these views in various scholarly debates and workshops led President Mbeki to appoint, on the recommendation of Minister of Home Affairs Buthelezi, a task team (the ETT) to inquire into and report on the shortcomings of the present electoral system and to recommend reforms and adjustments. The task team was led by Dr. Frederik van Zyl Slabbert, a trained sociologist and well-connected businessman, who had served as leader of the liberal Progressive Party opposition in the whites-only Parliament. The team's main tasks was to find a way to make public representatives more accountable to the electorate, while maintaining the proportional outcome of elections (a constitutional imperative). The task force solicited public submissions, held a well-publicized and well-attended Electoral Reform Workshop in September 2002, and released its report in March 2003.[7]

The Report of the Electoral Task Team and the Draft Electoral Systems Bill, 2003-2004

Reduced to their essentials, the ETT's majority report recommended the introduction of 69 multi-member constituencies which would return 300 of the members of the National Assembly, with the remaining 100 members elected on a closed party list system. These seats would be used to compensate for any distortions in party representation accumulated in the multi-member constituencies. The boundaries of the 69 constituencies would be drawn along existing provincial, municipal, and metropolitan boundaries. In other words, no special delimitation would be needed. Representation at the constituency level, as well as on the national lists, would be through a closed party list PR system. The number of representatives per constituency would range from a maximum of five seats (in metropolitan areas) to a minimum of three (in rural, sparsely populated areas). Each representative would correspond to roughly 60,000 voters in the multi-member constituencies.

The government's immediate reaction to the ETT report was to maintain the status quo in the 2004 election, with the newly elected government to review it and make a decision in advance of the 2009 polls. To those who attended a workshop organized by Slabbert in September 2002 at Newlands, Cape Town, it was clear that the ANC was in no mood to change the existing national electoral system. Numerous ANC speakers at this workshop emphasized the benefits of the status quo, mainly ensuring gender representation and maintaining stability through strict party discipline. ANC speakers refused to see the lack of accountability in the present pure list system as a serious drawback.[8] Moreover, it was also clear that the IEC had no appetite for engaging in major reforms to the electoral system, fearing it would taint administrative capacity.

Nevertheless, despite the ANC's attitude, the minister of home affairs (who was leader of the Inkatha Freedom Party in "coalition" with the ANC) published a draft Electoral Systems Bill in March 2003. We surmise that this was done on his own initiative, since the cabinet had already made its position clear on the issue of electoral reform shortly after receiving the ETT's report. As far as we can ascertain, the draft bill has not been tabled in the National Assembly and thus has had no status other than inviting comments before July 1, 2003.

The bill is clearly inspired by the Slabbert Report. It proposes that the whole territory of South Africa be demarcated into electoral constituencies (voting districts) by Municipal Demarcation Boards. The area of each municipal district council will become a constituency for the purposes of an election, while areas with metropolitan councils will be divided into constituencies. Each district council constituency must have at least three seats and not more than seven seats, while metropolitan constituencies should ideally have four seats, but not more than five seats and not less than three seats. (These numbers differ since a formula is prescribed in terms of which quotas of seats are calculated for each constituency.) In total, 300 seats will be allocated to these multi-member electoral constituencies, leaving 100 to be allocated to party lists. As in similar systems, the results of a constituency election is declared first and any disproportionality of the final results is compensated for by allocations from the party list seats. However, the allocation of seats per constituency in fact proves to be a complicated process. Recalculations would be needed in certain cases, depending on the final total number of votes cast, which would slow down calculation of the final allocation of seats. Moreover, where surpluses are yielded in terms of the Droop calculation of the allocation of seats to parties, these surpluses compete with each other. In terms of the Droop formula, highest remainders are allocated through a process of transitive ordering.

The bill outlaws crossing the floor, with no provision for by-elections, since vacancies will be filled from national or constituency party lists registered with the IEC prior to the relevant election. If, as in the past, national and provincial elections are held on the same day, a voter will receive four ballot papers in each constituency:

1. a National Assembly ballot paper for the constituency party list vote;
2. a national ballot for the National Assembly party list vote;
3. a provincial legislature ballot for the constituency; and
4. a provincial party list ballot.

All the ballots will reflect the names of the political parties with no provision for personal candidacies. As it proposes, in effect, a type of closed party list system on a multiple scale, the bill does not recommend a personal system of representation on the constituency level, that is, no real personal bond between the representative and the constituency. Party constituency lists are similar to the national list of representatives, with no provision for voters having the right to change the party's priority regarding its list of candidates through preferential voting or panachage (that is, voting for candidates from different parties instead of for the set list of one party). The bill in effect proposes a much more complicated proportional electoral system to administer and understand, yet provides little improvement over the existing closed party list PR system. The drawbacks remain, since no direct bond between voters and their public representatives is provided for in the still large multi-member constituencies (with about 450,000 voters per constituency) elected from lists of up to seven representatives selected by the party leadership.

The bill does not take into consideration other proposals to enhance accountability that are contained in both the Slabbert report and the electoral systems debates. For instance, no provision is made to oblige parties to make public the sources of their funds, internal party democracy is ignored, and there are no provisions for electors to recall representatives. In sum, this bill does not pass. It is an obfuscation of the issue and should be rejected out of hand. Fortunately, it is unlikely to become law in its present format. In the first place, the Inkatha Freedom Party, which is led by Mr. Buthelezi, the minister (by invitation of the president in view of his prominence in South African politics) responsible for introducing the bill, carried only 8 per cent of the national vote in 1999. Second, the governing ANC has been at loggerheads with Buthelezi over the administration of his department. Most importantly, the ANC does not support any form of electoral reform at present, and the ANC government has already decided to shelve the entire matter and to maintain the present closed party list system until after the 2004 elections—at which time Mr. Buthelezi may no longer retain his home affairs portfolio. (He has held the position since 1994, and the department is reported to be in an administrative bind, *inter alia* due to his wrangling with the ANC.) Since the bill is mainly Buthelezi's initiative, his departure would probably mean that the new government will not give it priority after the elections.

Recommendations for Changes to the Present Electoral System

Rejection of the Buthelezi initiative should not end the discussion over changing South Africa's electoral system. As a contribution to that discussion, we put forward the following proposal for a different electoral system. After examining the country's experience with the present PR list system over a period covering two general elections, we argue for a system that combines multi-member proportionality with a single-member constituency (FPTP) electoral system, 50 per cent list seats / 50 per cent constituency seats, similar to that in Germany and New Zealand where it is called MMP (mixed-member plurality). An MMP system would best serve South Africa and should be introduced as soon as possible. The change would not be a radical one as this system has already been in use for local government elections in the country since 2000.

The present system was ideally suited for the needs of the transitional politics that South Africa has experienced during the past few years. The electoral arrangements have engendered inclusiveness, simplicity, fairness, transparency, and administrative straightforwardness, as well as minimizing conflict over demarcation of constituency boundaries and the need for "grand" or "oversized" coalitions (unlike South Africa's former Government of National Unity). Nevertheless, democratic consolidation requires that the electoral system foster a higher degree of accountability by representatives, encourage the electorate to express a more sophisticated range of needs and choices, and allow for the voters to "get rid of the non-performers."

When it comes to electing and allocating candidates to the National Assembly, our proposed electoral system is similar to those used in the Federal Republic of Germany, Hungary, New Zealand, and the Welsh and Scottish assemblies, as well as local and metropolitan government (municipal) councils in South Africa itself. Our proposal goes further than a mere change in the system of representation in order to enhance individual accountability of public representatives. The dual FPTP and PR list system can be termed *a proportional system of representation with a geographic element.* The outcome of such electoral arrangements comply fully with section 46(1)(d) of the Constitution which requires an electoral system which "*in general, results in proportional representation.*" A mixed or parallel system of PR list and FPTP would not, in our opinion, be constitutional since it does not assure a proportional outcome.[9] More specifically, we propose that:

1. the South African National Assembly be composed of 400 seats, 200 of which be allocated to single-member (geographically delimited) constituencies;
2. the remaining 200 seats be allocated according to national closed party lists;
3. two ballots be used—one for the national PR lists and one for constituency candidates;
4. the Droop quota be used for allocating seats for the national PR lists;
5. seats in constituencies be allocated by way of a plurality (relative majority) of votes.[10]

Each voter will thus have two ballots, one for a candidate in a constituency and one for the ordered national party lists. Both votes are cast on the same day on the same ballot. Voters are allowed to split their votes, that is, they may vote for one party's candidate in their constituency and another party for the PR lists. Candidates can be on both ballots, meaning that a candidate that loses in a constituency can still win a seat in the National Assembly via the PR list vote if he or she ranked high enough on the list of a party that draws sufficient votes. Constituency elections are decided on a simple plurality or relative majority winner-takes-all basis. Overall proportionality is guaranteed by using only the votes cast for the national party lists to determine the proportion of party support in the National Assembly. No legal threshold (like the 5 per cent *Sperklausel* in Germany) is required. The only minimum is the natural mathematical threshold as applied to the number of seats. This threshold is 0.25 per cent (100 per cent divided by 400). In real elections this differs slightly from party to party due to the use of the Droop allocation. After an election, the constituency results are declared immediately and the parties know at the outset how many constituency seats have been captured. Thereafter, the results of the list PR vote is used (1) to determine overall proportionality, and (2) to function in a compensatory manner in allocating list seats to correct the disproportionality in the outcome of the 200 constituency results.

In addition, the principle of the free mandate for members of the National Assembly should be introduced for those MPs elected from constituencies to protect the rights (freedom of belief, opinion, etc.) guaranteed by Chapter 2 of the Constitution. This principle is an important consequence of guaranteeing individual rights to citizens. If it is introduced, it will loosen the grip of party bosses on the conscience of representatives, and it could lead to a more realistic expression of issues and opinions in constituencies by candidates/ representatives. (Internationally France, Germany, and the Netherlands are well-known examples of states which prohibit an imperative mandate.)[11] Our preference would be that all members of the National Assembly should have a free mandate to vote according to their conscience, but we are willing to accept that members elected on the PR list category (the "party ticket") should be prohibited from "crossing the floor" in the National Assembly. At a minimum, however, National Assembly members elected from constituencies must be able to resign from their party but still retain their seats in the National Assembly. Unlike members elected under the "party ticket" subject to stricter party caucus control, constituency MPs should also be allowed to vote on sensitive moral issues (e.g., euthanasia, abortion, the death penalty) according to their conscience. The introduction of a free mandate in this way would be a sound corrective and input for moral reasoning within the complex of party political ideology. To reduce instability and the possibility of "vote buying" in the various assemblies, we propose further that constituency MPs who change parties must face a by-election within six months of this change in party affiliation in order to test their popular mandate.

Section 42(3) of the Constitution states that "The National Assembly is elected to represent the people to ensure government by the people through the Constitution." Present electoral arrangements, however, do not place any obligation on political parties to select candidates for their lists by way of democratic procedures. Practices for doing this differ from party to party, and in some instances party leaderships have more discretion in this than in others. We believe that requiring parties to conform to democratic practices will strengthen the bond between ordinary party members and candidates.

Democracy certainly entails that people should select their representatives and leaders competitively in order to restrain, control, empower, and influence them. If not stated in the Constitution, at a minimum, this should be a requirement in the Electoral Act.

To further strengthen the accountability of constituency-based representatives the introduction of the right of recall of such representatives by the electorate in the constituency should be considered. To eliminate frivolous recall initiatives, the conditions for such a recall should be stringent. Conditions could be the number of signatures required to validate a recall initiative, the number of times in the term of office of an MP that such a recall can be undertaken, the grounds for a recall, and appeals to the courts to check the validity of a recall, and so on.[12] We are convinced that, if sound and reasonable recall procedures can be introduced, it will have a wholesome effect on the quality of representatives that are put up as constituency candidates, the service delivery in constituencies, and accountability in general.

At present there is no legal obligation on political parties in South Africa to make public the sources of their funding. This is clearly incompatible with the South African constitutional principle of a democratic and open society. Closed party books inevitably can lead to concealment of bribery, nepotism, and favouritism. We therefore propose that political parties be obliged by law to lay open to inspection in Parliament audited statements of accounts and revelation of the source of any donations exceeding R20,000.00 per annum (ca. US$3,000.00).

Consequences of the Proposals

In general, our proposals for changes to the electoral system will give each party currently represented in Parliament, including the small parties, the same number of seats. The mathematical or "natural" threshold will double, from 0.25 per cent of the vote to 0.5 per cent of the vote. In practice, that would mean that a party should obtain circa 90,000 votes to claim a seat. The inclusiveness of the previous system will, in our opinion, be maintained. The number of voters per geographical constituency will be approximately 100,000 — that is, 20 million voters represented by 200 constituency seats, which is not out of the ordinary in democracies. In our judgement, the proportional element in the electoral system will mitigate against gerrymandering, since what is gained in gerrymandering will be corrected through the compensatory allocation of seats.

The strategic splitting of votes as provided for in our proposal is an extremely effective method of reconciling national and local issues. The present system also allows for a differentiation in the double ballot, but candidates on the provincial lists of the present system are often just as "far removed" from local matters as those candidates on the national party lists. In our proposal, voters can vote for a candidate on the basis of his or her knowledge of and commitments to the constituency, while simultaneously participating in a nation-wide "opinion poll" to determine how many overall seats each party should have in the National Assembly. No pure majoritarian or pure PR list electoral system can accomplish such a trade-off. The past two general elections have amply demonstrated that voters understand the double ballot system of voting, and in this sense our proposed voting procedure is not more complicated than that of the present system, yet will yield much better results. How good these results turn out to be will be a matter of practice as much as theory.

In a parliamentary system, whether using the PR list system or the constituency FPTP system, the ordinary MP is strongly bound to the party and its policies. Nevertheless, there are countervailing aspects built into the FPTP system, which also tie FPTP representatives to their constituents. First, the party's choice of candidate, service delivery, and the preferences of voters are all related to one another, and party leaderships will have to put up "best" candidates in each and every constituency that they contest, that is, not necessarily loyal supporters of party bosses. Second, the MP faces the problems of all his or her electors throughout the five-year term of office, problems which thus find their way into party concerns and which could have a moderating influence on extremist party political views. Third, the local MP acts as a conduit between the various interest groups in civil society and the government. Local business associations, professional associations, and municipalities — in short the whole gamut of civil society — could use the MP to gain access to governmental structures and decision makers. Fourth, the MP can act as ombudsman for his or her constituents *vis-à-vis* government structures, primarily for party supporters, but also for non-party constituents. Fifth, the MP will have a vested interest in canvassing support from local card-carrying members of his or her party in order to secure reselection to the party candidacy for the next general election. Sixth, the constituency-based MP has the advantage of receiving the symbolic approval and mandate of the constituency at election times.

In our judgement, provincial legislatures should also be elected on the same basis as the National Assembly, that is, half the seats for each provincial legislature should be elected on a FPTP constituency basis and half from closed ordered PR lists. The result is that South Africans would vote under the same electoral system at all three levels. Hence, our proposed electoral system should not be more complicated than the current list PR system. The allocation formula (the Droop quota) is the same as the one currently used, and there is only one category that needs to be allocated—*not* ten categories (as represented by the nine provinces and the national category) that presently make up the representation in the National Assembly. Moreover, the FPTP relative majority principle of the constituency component in our proposal is conceptually simple to comprehend, unlike the more complicated methods suggested in the Slabbert and Buthelezi models.

The model that we propose goes a long way to address voter accountability; the most serious shortcoming in the present system. Making 50 per cent of representatives accountable to constituency approval along with party approval is infinitely more desirable than having party bosses and party leaderships decide exclusively on the matter. Arguments that such arrangements only make half the representatives accountable are simply misplaced and do not grasp the advantages if compared to the status quo. Indeed, this system shall have a wholesome effect on accountability for all representatives, not only those elected from constituencies. It focuses accountability on one representative responsible for constituency matters, whether from the governing or opposition party. This is very different from the Slabbert/Buthelezi model in which the geographical area of constituencies is much larger: a five-member MMC will have approximately five times as many voters as a single-member one. Collective responsibility for the well-being of constituents is shared among a "coalition" of five representatives belonging to different parties, each with incentives to duck responsibilities. This means, in practice, that no one accepts accountability or answerability to the electorate.

In sum, our proposed model will best promote the core value espoused in section 1(d) of the Constitution: "The Republic of South Africa ... is founded on the following values: universal adult suffrage, a national common voter's roll, regular elections and a multiparty system of democratic government to ensure *accountability, responsiveness and openness.*" Moreover, it embodies electoral rules followed in established democracies: it will not exclude minorities, and it will ensure an extremely high degree of proportionality on the one hand, while its very low threshold on the other hand ensures accessibility of representation to minorities.

Conclusion

The changes that we recommend are not new—they have been mooted before, albeit in a somewhat different format by a number of scholars and electoral specialists. Based on an assessment of South African conditions in light of international experience, we are convinced that they are the most appropriate for the country's present political needs. After the ratification of the Constitution by the Constitutional Assembly in 1995, there was a general expectation that there would be further developments in, amongst others, its electoral system. The opportunity slipped away when, rather unexpectedly, it was decided in 1996 to retain the present system at least until the 1999 general election. The various roundtables once again opened up expectations for electoral reform, and the debate was carried through during the course of 1999-2002 with political parties coming out in support of a reassessment of the matter. Yet again, we risk letting the opportunity slip away.

Electoral reform, if it is to take place, should happen soon after the 2004 elections, so that the necessary changes can be implemented for the 2009 general election. Stalling and postponing will mean once again closing a window of opportunity since much work and preparation are required for a significant change to the electoral system. Now is the time for all scholars interested in this matter, along with commentators and politicians involved with constitutional and electoral matters, to combine their efforts to give South Africa a better electoral system than the fine one it has, one that will serve the twenty-first century as well as the current one served the last decade of the twentieth.

Notes

1. For a more detailed overview of the electoral systems debate see Faure (1999). We would like to thank Robert Purcell of the Konrad Adenauer Foundation for granting permission on behalf of the Foundation to selectively reproduce sections of Faure's (1999) overview of the electoral systems debate in this publication.

2. Murray Faure wishes to thank a number of colleagues who have commented on his work on electoral matters over a long period, though they do not necessarily agree with his views on electoral reform. They are Arend Lijphart, Bernard Owen, Michael Krennerich, Jorgen Elklit, Rudy Andeweg, and Ben Reilly.

3. Albert Venter wishes to thank Jorgen Elklit of Aarhus University, Roger Jensen of Odense University, and Peter Hennessy of the University of London who shared their views and insights with him on various electoral systems and their limits. The research for his contribution to this article was also made possible by a grant from the Faculty of Arts Research Committee of the Rand Afrikaans University. This bestowal is acknowledged gratefully.

4. The debates and proposals are treated extensively by Faure 1999.

5. The Droop quota in PR systems is a highest-average method of allocation used to determine how seats are awarded. The quota is ascertained by the following formula: total vote divided by the number of seats plus one, and then one is added to the product.

6. The effective threshold (which is mathematical) varies for the regional and national lists respectively, and those of the provincial legislatures are about half the size of those for the regional allocation for the National Assembly. For both the National Assembly and the regional/provincial legislatures the respective thresholds of the various regions/provinces differ, unless they have the same number of seats in comparative cases. Approximately 1/400 of the votes cast for the national party lists of the National Assembly (i.e., about 0.25 per cent) constitutes the threshold, but the number of seats already allocated regionally is subtracted from the seats won in this way, effectively making this threshold about 0.50 per cent. The threshold for the National Assembly as a whole is 0.24938 per cent.

7. The papers and debates of this workshop are available as "Electoral Task Team Review Roundtable: Electoral models for South Africa: Reflections and options"; published by the Konrad Adenauer Foundation, Johannesburg, South Africa. Seminar Report, May 2003. <http: www.kas.org.za>.

8. Both authors attended the workshop, and this analysis is based on our personal observations.

9. For a brief discussion of parallel PR-FPTP systems in Japan, Russia, and Senegal, see Reynolds 1999: 203.

10. These changes require, amongst others, that the present system will have to do away with the principle that the provinces form nine large multi-member constituencies that collectively elect 200 members of the National Assembly.

11. Germany—see section 38, paragraph 1, sentence 2 of the German Constitution. Netherlands—see section 8 of its Constitution. France—see article 27 of its Constitution. The Netherlands uses a PR list system while Germany uses a MMP-SMC system. France uses a run-off constituency-based electoral system.

12. For a discussion of the recall principle, see Cronin 1989.

CHAPTER 8

Something Old, Something New: Electoral Reform in Japan

Lawrence LeDuc[1]

Japan's long-sought electoral reforms were enacted in 1994, replacing the old multi-member district, single non-transferable vote system with a new mixed-member system for electing members of the lower house of the Diet. Under this system, 300 members are elected from single-member districts and 200 by proportional representation (PR) from party lists. This change was expected to lead to a more competitive party system, a reduction of factionalism and corruption, and enhanced democratic accountability in elections. Some even hoped that these reforms, which were accomplished with great difficulty, might thoroughly transform Japanese politics and open the door to a wider policy reform agenda. Now, after three elections held under the new voting rules, we can identify some of the effects of the changes in the electoral system on the political process in Japan as it has evolved over the past decade. Although certain elements of the new mixed-member system are quite unique to Japan, the experience over these past ten years provides important lessons for reformers in other countries, including Canada.

While the lofty expectations of some of the reformers have not been fully realized, the 1994 reforms *have* had substantial effects on Japanese politics. Though certain elements of the old politics remain in place, leading some critics to argue that the reforms have failed to achieve their goals, the Japanese party system is certainly more competitive that it was during the heyday of Liberal Democratic Party (LDP) dominance. Yet, in spite of efforts to suppress them, certain aspects of the old system—party factionalism, personalism, incumbency advantage—have permeated the new institutions, raising a classic "culture versus institutions" question in assessing the overall effects of the reforms. Japan's new electoral institutions are comparable, in part, with those adopted at around the same time in Italy or New Zealand, having some elements in common with each of them.[2] But political institutions do

not necessarily function in exactly the same way in different political environ-
ments. To understand the effects of the new electoral institutions, we must set
them in the context of relevant historical, cultural, and institutional factors
which have together shaped the present day Japanese political system.

The Path to Electoral Reform in Japan

The old system of single non-transferable voting in multi-member districts
was first adopted in 1925 and was re-established under the postwar constitution
of 1947. Under this unusual system, voters cast a single ballot for a candidate
running in a multi-member constituency, typically varying in size between
three and five members.[3] The candidates obtaining the three (or four or five)
highest numbers of votes were elected. Depending on constituency size, the
system produced a modest degree of proportionality in that it allowed smaller
parties to win at least some seats. But it also permitted the largest party to field
multiple candidates and thus to elect two or three members in a constituency.
This latter feature promoted party factionalism, in that it encouraged different groups within the powerful LDP to compete against each other in elections. It also encouraged the formation of personal constituency organizations
(*koenkai*), which became an essential element of Japanese political life under
the old system.[4]

In the politically turbulent atmosphere of the postwar period, parties
as they would later evolve did not yet exist, and candidates represented
either personal factions or small geographic configurations. Within ten years
however, Japanese politics began to consolidate around two major party
groupings—the Japan Socialist Party (JSP) on the left and the LDP on the
centre-right. By the late 1950s, Japan appeared to be well along the way towards the establishment of a stable two-party system. In the election of 1958,
the LDP and JSP between them won all but 14 of the 467 seats in the House
of Representatives. But gradually, the LDP came to dominate the system.
The JSP never again gained either the share of vote or seats (166 seats on 33
per cent of the total vote) that it achieved in 1958, and it gradually became
only one of several weak competitors to the LDP. For the next three decades,
Japanese politics was to be largely a one-party affair.

This is not to suggest that opposition to the LDP disappeared entirely.
Rather, it became more fragmented, as the various left parties split into different factions and other smaller parties emerged from time to time. The
LDP itself became factionalized, and the real political competition within
the system was more often among personalized factions within the LDP than

between the parties. While the LDP took credit for Japan's economic success in the 1970s and 1980s, it also became identified with corruption and scandal, the seemingly inevitable side-effects of long periods of one-party rule. The Lockheed scandal of 1976 and the Recruit scandal of 1988, both of which exposed endemic patterns of corrupt relationships between certain LDP politicians and private interests, brought the party into disrepute and effectively ended the careers of a number of prominent political figures. In the wake of these scandals, which rocked the Japanese political establishment to its core, the pressure for political reform grew more intense. Some potential leaders supported a reform agenda as a matter of principle; for others, the rhetoric of reform meshed well with their own political ambitions. As a result, the cause of reform moved steadily up the national political agenda.

Nevertheless, many obstacles lay in the path of change, and years of inter-party negotiation preceded the 1994 reforms. The LDP itself had long shown an interest in electoral reform, but for different reasons than its opponents. As early as 1955, the LDP government of Ichiro Hatoyama proposed moving to a system of single-member district representation, a proposal again taken up in 1973 by the government of Kakuei Tanaka. In both of these instances, strong protests from the opposition parties stalled the initiatives. The opposition parties quickly realized that a British/Canadian style system of single-member districts would simply serve to consolidate the dominant position of the LDP and make it more difficult to mount an effective opposition. As is seen in Figure 8-1, the share of the total vote won by LDP candidates was steadily declining, even though it was still able to dominate the system. In 1976, at the height of the Lockheed scandal, the party's share of the vote dropped to 42 per cent, and it quickly became clear to all concerned that a system based entirely on single-member districts would simply allow the LDP to gain majorities of seats in the House of Representatives on even smaller pluralities of the vote, just as has happened in other first-past-the-post (FPTP) systems such as New Zealand (before 1996), the United Kingdom, or Canada.[5] Hence, a final effort by the reform-minded LDP government of Toshiki Kaifu in 1989 following the Recruit scandal also failed. As the LDP grip on absolute power weakened in the face of the scandals in which it was engulfed, it became evident that changes in the electoral system could only be achieved by striking a bargain. When the LDP lost its majority in the House of Representatives in the 1993 election, the door to reform swung wide open.[6] Yet a compromise package put forward by the coalition government of Kiichi Miyazawa in 1993 also failed, in the process precipitating further splits within the LDP itself. The resulting collapse of Miyazawa's government brought to power a new coali-

Figure 8-1

LDP Share of Seats and Votes, 1958-93

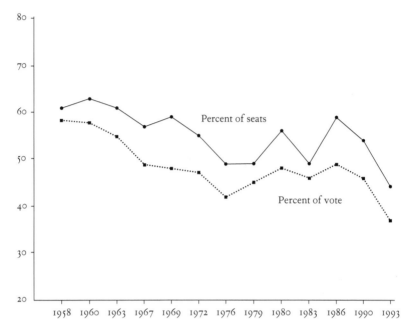

tion led by Morihiro Hosokawa of the Japan New Party (JNP). It was able to win support from all parties for a reform package based on a mixed system of representation—part single-member districts and part list-PR—for the lower house.

How did reform proposals that had previously been rejected suddenly attract such wide support after the 1993 election? The LDP, which had long favoured single-member districts, was now in a much weaker position than before. The clutch of new parties that had been thrown up by the 1993 election and the defeat of Miyazawa's coalition on a vote of confidence created new partisan interests and altered strategic calculations. Ambitious younger politicians within the LDP became more inclined to embrace the reform cause, positioning themselves against the party's discredited senior statesmen. New players such as the JNP, Japan Renewal (Shinseito), and Harbinger (Sakigake) saw their interests better served by a mixed system. Older parties such as the JSP or Clean Government (Komeito) had long pushed for a proportional component. The system which was finally adopted in 1994—300 single-member seats and 200 elected proportionally from party lists—seemed an obvious compromise.

It is important to note that the new system was to be a *parallel* model, not a *corrective* or compensatory formula as is provided in the German, New Zealand, or Scottish systems.[7] Russia, like Japan, also adopted a parallel model of mixed representation, dividing its 500 Duma seats equally between candidates elected in single-member constituencies and those chosen proportionally from party lists. South Korea uses a similar system, except that only 46 of the 273 members of its National Assembly are elected proportionally. While both *parallel* systems used in Japan, Russia, and South Korea and *corrective* ones like those of Germany, Italy, or New Zealand are often classified as "mixed" systems, these models operate quite differently. Assigning a substantial number of seats on a corrective basis helps the smaller parties to compensate for their failure to win single-member constituency seats. Assigning a small number of seats proportionally merely to "top up" a large single-member component has relatively little compensatory effect. In fact, as in the Japanese case, it allows the dominant party to gain additional seats over and above those already won in the constituency contests. The 1994 reforms in Japan quite deliberately made the single-member component the largest element in the system and avoided any compensatory formula. Further, the new electoral law allowed candidates to run *both* in districts and on party lists, thereby protecting the interests of incumbent members. At a time when the LDP appeared to be in danger of disintegration, the reforms seemed bold and ambitious by Japanese standards. However, it would later become evident that the reforms that were put in place in 1994 contributed as much to the revival of the LDP as they did toward loosening its iron grip on the Japanese political system.

Japan's New Party System

Because the political parties were in such a state of disarray at the time that the 1994 reforms were adopted, it quickly became clear that the first election held under the new electoral rules would be of critical importance in determining the shape of the new party system which was already beginning to emerge. But the first election under the new rules would not take place for two more years. In the interval, three coalition governments headed by three different parties attempted to manage the assortment of old and new forces which the 1993 outcome had produced.[8] During this interlude, leaders with quite different visions of Japan's political future attempted to forge a coherent alternative to the LDP. Some leaders such as Hosokawa of the JNP saw this alternative as essentially a conservative one, to be crafted from the breakaway factions of the LDP. Others envisioned an umbrella party of the centre-left as the princi-

Steps Toward Making Every Vote Count

Table 8-1

Results of Three Elections Under the New Electoral Law, 1996 -2003

		1996 Constituency	1996 List	1996 Total	2000 Constituency	2000 List	2000 Total
Liberal Democratic Party (LDP)	seats	169	70	239	177	56	233
	vote (%)	38.6%	32.8%		41.0%	28.3%	
New Frontier (Shinshinto)	seats	96	60	156			
	vote (%)	28.0%	28.0%				
Democratic Party of Japan	seats	17	35	52	80	47	127
	vote (%)	10.6%	16.1%		27.6%	25.2%	
Komeito / New Komeito	seats			a	7	24	31
	vote (%)				2.2%	13.0%	
Japan Communist Party	seats	2	24	26	0	20	20
	vote (%)	12.6%	13.1%		12.1%	11.2%	
Liberal League	seats				4	18	22
	vote (%)				3.4%	11.0%	
New Conservative Party	seats				7	0	7
	vote (%)				2.2%	0.4%	
Social Democratic Party	seats	4	11	15	4	15	19
	vote (%)	2.2%	6.4%		3.8%	9.4%	
Harbinger (Sakigake)	seats	2	0	2			
	vote (%)	1.3%	1.1%				
Independents / Others	seats	10	0	10	21	0	21
	vote (%)	6.7%	2.5%		7.7%	1.5%	
Total	seats	300	200	500	300	180	480
	vote (%)	100.0%	100.0%	100.0%	100.0%	100.0%	100.0%

pal alternative, to be constructed by merging the JSP with the more progressive elements of the LDP and other minor parties. The JSP of course, which was renamed the Social Democratic Party (SDP) in January 1996, continued to see itself as the principal opposition to the LDP.

Because 300 members of the new House of Representatives would be elected in single-member districts under the new system, an important strategic calculation involved nominating a single strong opposition candidate to oppose an LDP member. The LDP had long found political advantage in exploiting divisions among the various opposition parties, even as its own

Table 8-1 (continued)
Results of Three Elections Under the New Electoral Law, 1996 -2003

		2003		
		Constit-uency	List	Total
Liberal Democratic Party (LDP)	seats	168	69	237
	vote (%)	43.9%	33.8%	
New Frontier (Shinshinto)	seats			
	vote (%)			
Democratic Party of Japan	seats	105	72	177
	vote (%)	36.7%	36.1%	
Komeito / New Komeito	seats	9	25	34
	vote (%)	1.5%	14.3%	
Japan Communist Party	seats	0	9	9
	vote (%)	8.1%	7.5%	
Liberal League	seats			b
	vote (%)			
New Conservative Party	seats	4	0	4
	vote (%)	1.3%	0.3%	
Social Democratic Party	seats	1	5	6
	vote (%)	2.9%	4.9%	
Harbinger (Sakigake)	seats			
	vote (%)			
Independents / Others	seats	13	0	13
	vote (%)	5.7%	3.1%	
Total	seats	300	180	480
	vote (%)	100.0%	100.0%	100.0%

a. Komeito candidates ran as part of the New Frontier (Shinshinto) grouping in 1996.
b. The Liberal League merged with the DPJ prior to the 2003 election.

share of the vote declined. This advantage would be even greater under the single-member districts of the new system, if an LDP candidate faced four or five weak opponents. As a general rule, the larger the number of candidates contesting a particular constituency, the smaller the total share of the vote required for the LDP candidate to win the seat. Thus, the period leading up to the crucial 1996 election was one of forging new alliances between the players from the other parties, hoping to construct a single strong opposition party from the remnants of the old party system. But these efforts were often hampered by personal ambition. Tsutomu Hata, who was briefly prime minister during the period of coalition governments (see note 7), struggled for the leadership of the new opposition party Shinshinto (New Frontier) against Ichiro Ozawa, another ambitious former LDP politician with a strong personal following.[9] Shinshinto was formed in December 1994 by a merger of nine other parties, including Shinseito (Japan Renewal) and Hosokawa's JNP. A former LDP prime minister, Toshiki Kaifu, became Shinshinto's first president, temporarily eclipsing the ambitions of Hata and Ozawa, and providing the new party with a strong and experienced figure behind whom reformers from various parties and factions could unite. Only a month before the 1996 election, Yukio Hatoyama and Naoto Kan formed Minshuto—the Democratic Party of Japan (DPJ). Hatoyama, who had previously been a member of Sakigake, sought to attract the support of other incumbent members of smaller parties, often recruiting them to run as potential DPJ candidates in the forthcoming election. The pre-election period thus involved some consolidation of the fragmented party system, but it also assured that the opposition to the LDP remained divided. The political futures of prominent figures such as Ozawa or Kan depended to a considerable degree on the performance of their newly created parties in the first election held under the new electoral rules. To make matters even more complicated, the LDP would once again be fighting the election as the incumbent government, Ryutaro Hashimoto having replaced Murayama as head of the multi-party coalition government in January 1996 (see note 7). Seemingly, *all* of the parties would attempt to carry the reform banner into the election.

As might have been expected, the election that finally took place in October 1996 produced a further rearrangement of the parties. The renamed JSP (now the Social Democratic Party), fell from second to fifth place in the party standings. Ozawa's New Frontier emerged as the main opposition to the LDP, while the Kan/Hatoyama Democratic Party came a distant third. But most surprising was the renewed strength of the LDP itself, which, although still short of a majority, easily remained the largest party in the slightly reduced (500-seat) lower house. The LDP would continue in power, requiring only token support from its former coalition partners (SDP and Sakigake) and a handful of independents. Over the next few years, defections from other parties and the return of independents gradually restored the LDP to a parliamentary majority.

It is clear that the LDP's success in the 1996 election came not merely from its performance in the single-member constituency seats but also from

strength in the list vote. With just under 39 per cent of the vote in the constituencies, the LDP had, not surprisingly, won 169 of the 300 single-member
seats, competing against a divided opposition. But because the new system,
unlike those of Germany or New Zealand, makes no attempt to use the list
vote to compensate for such distortions in the constituency total, the LDP was
able to obtain an additional 70 seats, based on the 33 per cent share of votes
that it won on the second (party list) ballot. Further, because candidates who
failed to win a constituency seat could be elected on the lists, the LDP was
able to protect many of its incumbent members.[10] The broom of reform swept
lightly indeed in the first election following the 1994 changes.

In the second election, which took place under the new electoral law (June
2000), the LDP again held its position while witnessing a further fragmentation of the opposition. Hata and Ozawa's New Frontier had collapsed in
1998, its members drifting to other parties, including Kan and Hatoyama's
Democratic Party, which emerged from the 2000 election as the principal
opposition. Sakigake also disappeared entirely from the political scene, while
Ozawa re-emerged to lead a new Liberal party. A newly reorganized Komeito,
the Buddhist-affiliated Clean Government Party which had fielded candidates
as part of the New Frontier grouping in 1996, returned to put forward its own
slate under the label "New Komeito" in 2000. Compared to 1996, the LDP in
2000 was slightly stronger in the constituencies (41 per cent) and somewhat
weaker in the party list vote (28 per cent), leaving its seat total nearly unchanged. In fact, the LDP government, unencumbered by coalition partners,
had taken the opportunity to slightly reduce the proportional component of
the new system from 200 (of 500) seats to 180 (of 480). Its continued dominance of the FPTP component of the system thus assured the party's success
even as voters were gradually learning to use the "second vote" portion of the
ballot to support other parties.

The most recent election (November 2003) — the third held under the new
electoral rules — saw some further consolidation of the parties, but it again
displayed the continuing strength of the LDP. In fact, the total number of
seats won by the LDP has remained little changed in each of the three elections which have taken place since the reforms came into effect (Table 8-1).
The LDP still gains its largest share of seats in the constituency contests, but
it has been competitive in the list vote as well. In fact, the LDP percentage in
2003 on the list part of the ballot was, at 34 per cent, its best showing in any
of the past three elections. While some LDP partisans were disappointed that
the party failed to regain its absolute majority status, its dominant position in
the system does not appear to have significantly eroded.[11] With the continued

support of New Komeito, which gained three seats over its previous total, the LDP's hold on the reins of government appears more secure than ever. Under Junichiro Koizumi, who became prime minister in 2001, the LDP has straddled the issue of reform and played off the party's various factions against each other. This strategy is reminiscent of those employed successfully in previous periods of crisis when the party's dominant position was threatened.

The real story of the 2003 election, however, was the unexpectedly strong showing of the DPJ, under its newly chosen leader Naoto Kan.[12] Outpolling the LDP in the list vote, and winning 177 seats in the House of Representatives (a gain of 50 seats from the previous election), the DPJ finally seems to be emerging as a serious rival to the LDP. This was certainly the interpretation given to the strong DPJ gains by most of the news media following the election.[13] It is important to note, however, that these DPJ gains came about, not at the expense of the LDP, but rather as a result of the decline of other parties. This suggests not so much the slippage of the LDP as the consolidation of smaller parties of the centre and left around the DPJ. The dismal showing of the SDP, together with the poor performance of the Communists, who lost more than half of their seats, may foreshadow the disappearance of a genuine left alternative in Japanese politics. This consolidation of the party system, if it lasts, may eventually produce a real challenge to LDP hegemony. But the seeming emergence of a two-party system in Japan does not necessarily herald a future change of government. And, even if an opposition party does one day take power, the shift is more likely to be to another catch-all party of the centre rather than to a left alternative, as previously represented by the JSP or SDP.

Japan's electoral reforms were both the product of, and the catalyst for, the many changes in the configuration of the Japanese party system over the past decade. The LDP lost its monopoly on power temporarily in the early 1990s, partly through defections of some of its reform-minded members and partly through the loss of electoral support in the face of corruption scandals. Had its grip on the political system not so weakened, it is doubtful that the reforms that were enacted would have taken place at all. But the reforms, once in place, merely accelerated changes in the configuration of the opposition parties which had already begun to occur. As in Italy, it was necessary to forge new alliances of the existing parties in order to effectively contest the single-member constituency seats.[14] But many of those alliances proved to be unstable, and the task of forming a credible opposition to a reinvigorated LDP could not be accomplished in a single election. Further, the LDP proved more than able to adapt to the new realities of Japanese politics, sometimes co-opt-

Figure 8-2
The Japanese Party System Before and After the 1994 Reforms[a]

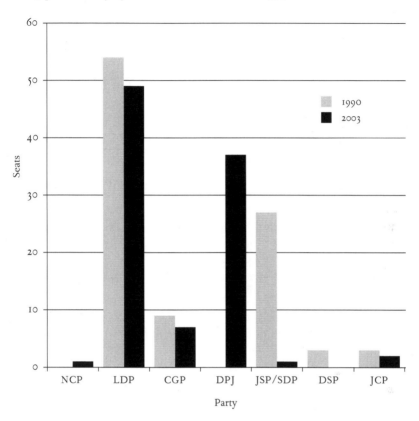

a. As measured by party shares of seats in the House of Representatives.

ing the reform agenda itself, and always taking full advantage of its traditional strength in the constituencies. While the Japanese party system in many ways looks very different today than it did before the reforms (Figure 8-2), the one element that remains constant is the strong position of the LDP. The staying power of its latest rival, the DPJ, has yet to be fully tested.

Assessing the 1994 Reforms

Supporters of electoral reform in Japan had essentially two goals, which were not necessarily consistent with each other. First, they sought to break the hold of the LDP on the system by creating conditions conducive to the development of a more formidable challenger to the LDP than the JSP had proven to be. To some degree, a Westminster-style system of single-member districts served this interest, since it forced competing parties to forge new alliances or at least to agree to support a single opposition candidate. But reform along these lines served the interests of the LDP almost as well. The party was well positioned to win single-member FPTP seats, particularly in those instances where it faced a divided opposition. Other supporters of electoral reform in Japan sought greater proportionality for its own sake and were less concerned with the defeat of the LDP. As a multi-party system began to emerge in the early 1990s, new voices were raised in favour of a more proportional electoral system. As in New Zealand, the idea that a party could continue to dominate the political system while winning increasingly smaller shares of the total vote became increasingly unacceptable and strengthened the position of the reformers.

The compromise adopted in 1994 was perhaps the best available given these differing interests and the relatively weak position of some of the parties involved. But subsequent events have clearly shown that the reforms did less to increase the competitiveness of the party system than might have been predicted at the time they were enacted. Table 8-2 shows that Japan remains one of the more disproportional electoral systems, in spite of the addition of a proportional component in 1994.[15] The overall level of disproportionality declined slightly in 2003, in part because of the improved performance of the DPJ.[16] But other mixed systems, such as Germany or New Zealand, perform much better in this respect, both because the proportional component is larger and especially because it is used to correct the distortions of parliamentary representation in line with the list vote, thereby offsetting some of the advantage which the largest party typically enjoys in FPTP seats.[17] Even though it was in a weak position at the time that the reforms were adopted, the LDP was nevertheless able to effectively use its needed support as leverage. By holding out for a larger single-member component and by limiting the effects of the list seats on the overall distribution, the LDP protected its interests well in the face of reform pressures that conceivably could have led to the demise of its position.

It is interesting to speculate on how the Japanese party system might have evolved if the proportional component of the House of Representatives had been larger or if it had been applied in a corrective fashion. In Germany, for example, where both of these conditions apply, the position of the third and fourth parties has been much stronger in recent years, because they have been able to gain a larger number of seats through the second (list) vote. In the

Table 8-2

Disproportionality of Seats and Votes in Japan and Other Countries[a]

	UK 2001	Canada 2000	Japan 2003	Australia 2001	Germany 2002	Sweden 2002
Total Seats	659	301	480	150	603	349
P1	41	41	34	37	39	40
	63	57	49	45	42	41
	22	16	15	8	3	1
P2	32	26	36	38	39	15
	25	22	37	43	41	16
	-7	-4	1	5	2	1
P3	18	12	14	6	9	13
	8	4	7	9	9	14
	-10	-8	-7	3	0	1
P4	2	11	8	5	7	9
	1	13	2	0	8	9
	-1	2	-6	-5	1	0
P5	1	9	5	5	4	8
	1	4	1	0	0	9
	0	-5	-4	-5	-4	1
Disproportionality Index	20	17	16	13	5	2

a. Five largest parties only. Percent of seats minus percent of votes.

most recent (2002) German election, for example, the Greens won a total of 54 seats with 8.6 per cent of the vote, and the Free Democrats (FDP) won 47 seats with 7.4 per cent. In Japan, by contrast, the Communists (JCP) won only 9 seats in the 2003 election with a similar percentage (7.5 per cent) of the second (list) vote.[18] Even New Komeito, with a vote share in 2003 nearly twice as large (14.3 per cent), did not fare as well in its seat allocation (34 seats) as the two minor German parties. The level of competitiveness between the two major parties in Germany has also been tighter, because the electoral system has effectively prevented either of them from becoming dominant. Gerhard Schroeder's SPD-Green coalition barely survived defeat in the 2002 election, even though the SPD share of the second (list) vote (38.5 per cent) was higher than the comparable percentage obtained by the LDP in 2003 (33.8 per cent). This is because no party in Germany is able to dominate the constituencies as the LDP does in Japan and because the larger and correctively applied proportional component helps to maintain a better balance between the two larger parties, in addition to assuring that the minor parties are represented in proportion to their shares of the vote.[19]

As the reform process unfolded in Japan, party interest played a key role, both in opening the door to reform in the first place, but also in constraining some of its effects. Unlike New Zealand, where the political parties effectively lost control of the reform process, the reforms adopted in Japan were a product of inter-party bargaining. The LDP undoubtedly knew that its traditional strength in the constituencies would protect it against any threat that might have been posed by the addition of a proportional component, particularly if the latter was sufficiently small and was used only to supplement the seats won in the constituencies rather than to rebalance the entire system. Parties and candidates, particularly those in the LDP, have shown great adaptability under the new system, but voters have been slower to adjust to the new institutions. Practices such as dual candidacies, inheritance of parliamentary seats, and the maintenance of personal campaign organizations have not been eliminated under the new regime. In fact, many of these practices, which flourished under the old system, have survived under the new electoral rules.

Japan's experience teaches us that electoral reform can be accomplished and that it can have a transformative effect on the party system and on many other aspects of parliamentary politics. But it also warns us that "reform" has many shades of meaning. The details of any reform proposal are of critical importance, and it is sometimes difficult to assess the full effect of any new set of electoral rules until they have actually been in operation over a period of two or more elections. When parties or leaders negotiate a package of proposed reforms they invariably act to protect their own partisan interests inasmuch as it is possible for them to do so. If and when the major political parties in Canada begin to get serious about electoral reform, we might well expect that they will try to do the same. Indeed, we should not be surprised if they seek to discard the New Zealand (mixed-member proportional) model currently being considered in several provinces in favour of something that looks more like the Japanese model. While "compromise" of the type achieved in Japan could perhaps improve the chances for reform, it might also render it less effective in the long run. Supporters of electoral reform in Canada, and in the provinces, should weigh these risks carefully.

Notes

1. I would like to thank Masahiro Yamada, Henry Milner, Daizo Sakurada, and Michael Donnelly for their comments and suggestions on an earlier draft of this chapter, and Jillian Kovensky for her work on a related project.

2. For an exploration of this comparison, see Sakamoto (1999). See also Shugart and Wattenberg (2001).

3. In later years, there were also a few districts with as many as six members or as few as two.

4. On the practice of Japanese politics more generally throughout this period, see Curtis (1988). See also Ishida and Krauss (1989).

5. In the 1997 federal election in Canada, for example, the Liberals won a parliamentary majority (155 of 301 seats) on a mere 38 per cent of the total popular vote.

6. The LDP won 223 of 511 seats in the 1993 election. In the House of Representatives following that election, the JSP held 70 seats, Japan Renewal 55, the Clean Government Party (Komeito) 51, JNP 35, Democratic Socialist (DSP) 15, Communist (JCP) 15, and Sakigake 13. Other minor parties and independents held the remaining 34 seats.

7. See Chapters 2, 5, and 6 in this book. See also Shugart and Wattenberg (2001) for a more extended discussion of these variations and their applications in a number of other countries.

8. Morihiro Hosokawa of the JNP formed an eight-party coalition government in August 1993 following the election. This coalition was succeeded by a minority government headed by Tsutomu Hata of the Japan Renewal (Shinseito) party, following Hosokawa's resignation in April 1994. Hata's government, which consisted mainly of Shinseito and Komeito (Clean Government) members, lasted only two months before it was replaced by a broader coalition headed by Tomiichi Murayama of the JSP. Murayama's government, which included LDP members, lasted until January 1996, when Murayama was succeeded as prime minister by Ryutaro Hashimoto of the LDP.

9. Ozawa defeated Hata in the contest for the leadership of the party held in December 1995.

10. For a discussion of the methods used to rank (or leave unranked) candidates on the party lists, see McKean and Scheiner (2000).

11. Due to defections from other parties, and the support of some independents, the LDP will in fact control a majority of seats in the new House. The disbanding of the New Conservative Party following the election, and the defection of its four elected members to the LDP, in itself gives the LDP a majority of the 480 seats.

12. Kan defeated Hatoyama in a leadership contest held in December 2002.

13. See for example the report in *The Economist* (15 November 2003): 23-25.

14. On the effects of the 1993 reforms in Italy, see Bull and Rhodes (1997) and d'Alimonte (2001).

15. The index employed in table 2 is one-half of the absolute values of the percentage of votes minus the percentage of seats obtained by the five largest parties, as measured by total votes cast. This is one of several commonly used measures of disproportionality. For further discussion of this and other comparable measures, see Gallagher (1991).

16. The value of the Disproportionality Index for Japan, computed for the five largest parties in the 2000 election, is 21. For the 1996 election, the value of the index is 18.

17. I use the party list vote in making this calculation. If the percentage of the vote obtained in the constituencies, or an average of the two, is used instead, the system would appear somewhat less disproportional. This makes a much larger difference for Japan than it would for many other countries with mixed systems, because the LDP vote has tended to be so much higher in the single-member seats (see Table 8-1).

18. The German Bundestag is slightly larger — 598 seats compared with 480 in the Japanese House of Representatives. Half of the Bundestag seats (299) are allocated to single-member constituencies and half (299) are assigned proportionally according to the party vote shares on the second (list) ballot. The proportional component is assigned correctively, thus compensating for a party's failure to win constituency seats in proportion to its vote. In the 2002 German election, for example, the Greens won only one of their 54 seats in a constituency. Parties are allowed, however, to keep any constituency seats won *above* their proportional allocation, and the size of the Bundestag may rise above its normal size of 598 to accommodate these.

19. That is, so long as they come above the minimum threshold for representation of 5 per cent of the total vote cast. The East German-based Party of Democratic Socialism (PDS) fell below this threshold for the first time in 2002, and therefore received no corrective seats. It did however win two constituency seats. In previous elections, the Greens and FDP have also occasionally fallen below the five per cent threshold.

CHAPTER 9

Lessons from France: Would Quotas and a New Electoral System Improve Women's Representation in Canada?

Karen Bird

Historically, the bulk of the arguments for electoral reform in Canada have focused on the need to correct regional disparities in parliamentary representation and to achieve a closer proportionality between the number of votes cast for, and the number of seats held by, each party. Yet the concept of proportionality applies to the descriptive or demographic composition of elected bodies as well. Even where representatives are chosen through fair and democratic elections, it is often said that legislative assemblies remain "unrepresentative," and in particular, that they are underrepresentative of women, ethnic minorities, and the poorer and less-educated. This concern is not new, but the problem has come into closer focus in recent years. Positive developments concerning the rights and political involvement of women and cultural minorities make their absence among the political elite all the more striking.

Of particular concern today is the political underrepresentation of women. Women achieved the right to vote and run for federal office in Canada federally beginning in 1918 and in most provinces between 1916 and 1925.[1] Yet today, Canadian women are still not halfway to being proportionately represented. In December 2003, women held 62 of 301 seats in the House of Commons (20.6 per cent) and 150 of 735 seats (20.4 per cent) across all 13 provincial and territorial legislatures. Women fare only a little better in Canada's major cities. In the ten largest cities, women held 72 of 267 council seats (just under 27 per cent), while only one of those cities (London, Ontario) had a female mayor. The proportion of women in the Canadian House of Commons exceeds the world average of just 15.3 per cent of legislative seats in the lower house, yet it remains below that of most western European countries. In com-

parative terms, Canada places thirty-sixth in the world for the representation
of women in national parliaments (Inter-Parliamentary Union 2003).

Women's underrepresentation deserves particular attention within the
context of potential reform of the Canadian electoral system and representative
institutions. Reform of the electoral system is no guarantee that Parliament
will become numerically or substantively representative of women. Many
supply-side constraints—including responsibility for childcare and domestic
duties, lack of time, money, or professional experience—will continue to ham-
per women's access to political office, even under the most woman-friendly
electoral rules. So will the general culture of attitudes toward women affect
whether or not voters are prepared to support female candidates. Electoral
reform alone cannot substitute for widespread social reform intended to ensure
equality of men and women in all areas of life, not just in politics. Still, it is
clear that electoral systems do significantly affect the potential for more representative parliaments. They do so by facilitating or constraining the efforts
of political parties to select candidates who reflect the composition of the
electorate.

This chapter will examine two types of electoral reform intended to increase the number of elected women: proportional representation (PR) and
gender quotas. I begin the chapter by describing the main features of PR and
quotas in terms of their expected effects on the election of women. The focus
then shifts to France, the first country in the world to have introduced parity
legislation requiring an equal number of male and female candidates. In the
popular press and among feminist non-governmental organizations (NGOs),
the French parity law is often presented as a model reform toward increased
political representation for women. Yet closer inspection of the French experience should lead us to a more careful assessment of the conditions under
which quotas can be expected to be effective. Since introducing parity in
2000, France has experienced three sets of elections, each run under different electoral rules. Looking at each of these elections, I describe the ways in
which parity and the electoral system interact—both with each other and with
other institutional and cultural factors including the party system, formal and
informal party rules, incumbency rates, and cultural attitudes about the role
of women—to produce strikingly different results for women. The French
experience provides some important lessons for Canada and other countries
considering electoral reform as a means of increasing the number of elected
women. In the face of traditional party resistance to electoral reform, neither
PR nor quotas *alone* is sufficient to improving women's political representa-

tion. I conclude the chapter by offering several recommendations for improving women's political representation in Canada.

PR and the Political Representation of Women

Electoral systems based on multi-member districts and PR tend to produce more descriptively balanced tickets, and more demographically representative legislatures, than majoritarian or plurality systems based on single-member or first-past-the-post (FPTP) districts. There are a number of reasons why this is so. First, the incentive structure of the nominations process is quite different within a multi-member district than within a single-member district. Given the transparency of party lists within a multi-member district, party selectorates understand that presenting a list that includes all social groups—men and women, easterners and westerners, farmers and merchants, students and elderly, and so on—can broaden the appeal to voters. Ticket-balancing may also be necessary to assure the continued support of different factions within the party. Under FPTP, it is more difficult for voters to tell whether women and members of other groups are absent or underrepresented among a party's candidates, and so there is less incentive for parties to balance their tickets. Moreover, because of the strictly zero-sum nature of selection decisions under FPTP, nominating a female candidate means that the party must explicitly deny the aspirations of a man in the same district. A further, crucial element in the incentive structure is the degree of control maintained by the central party in the candidate selection process. Under FPTP, the process tends to be less centralized. Where control rests in the hands of the local constituency party, local interests and preferences often take priority over the need to produce a balanced ticket at the national level.

A second reason why PR tends to be better for women is that the party list tends to shift the campaign focus toward the party programs and away from the personal characteristics of individual candidates. This is advantageous for women, who tend to be judged more strictly on the basis of their physical appearance and their personal lives and whose political styles often diverge from the typically gladiatorial style associated with male candidates (Huddy and Terkildsen 1993). Even where voters do not demonstrate any particular bias against female candidates,[2] the same cannot be said of party selectorates. In FPTP elections that pit single candidates against each other, party selectorates are more likely to pass over women, believing they are taking an electoral risk if they deviate from the norm of the white, male, professional candidate (Norris and Lovenduski 1995).

Finally, the process of contagion in the nomination of women appears more likely to occur in PR systems than under FPTP. Contagion is a process by which parties adopt policies initiated by other parties. Matland and Studlar (1996) have examined this effect by looking at whether centrist parties tend to increase the number of female candidates in cases where they face a serious challenge from left-wing parties that have already implemented gender quotas. They found that contagion occurred under the PR system in Norway, but not under FPTP in Canada. The explanation, they suggest, is that the costs to nominating a woman in a PR system are lower, while the potential gains are higher. Because the party has several candidates under a PR system, it can choose a woman without having to deny nomination or renomination to a man. The gains may be greater because, in PR systems, even a small increase in votes caused by adding women to the ticket could result in the party winning more seats.

Within PR systems, there are electoral variations that can further enhance the representation of women. One such variation is open list voting. Rather than vote for the entire list, this rule allows voters to specify one or more candidates of preference within a single party's list or to vote for candidates across party lines. Candidates who receive more personal preference votes move up the party list and thereby become more likely to fill one of the seats allotted their party. These rules create opportunities for collective political mobilization and enable women's (or other) associations to organize electoral support for the candidates who best represent their interests. The "women's coup" in the 1971 Norway municipal elections is an example of the effective use of this strategy.³ Open list voting is also a feature of local and national elections in Denmark. Because of this voting system, and because of the capacity of ethnic minority candidates to mobilize voter support within their ethnic communities, parties have found it advantageous to include ethnic minority candidates on their lists. Many of these candidates have been elected as a result of the high number of personal votes they receive from minority voters. In addition to producing virtually proportional representation of ethnic minorities in some cities, this system has the further benefit of promoting political participation among marginalized groups (Togeby 1999).

The claim that PR facilitates the entry of women into elected office in established democracies has been confirmed in a series of studies. In their study of stable democracies, Darcy, Welch, and Clark (1994: 142) conclude that, "on average twice the proportion of women (20.2 per cent) are currently elected to list PR systems as compared to FPTP (10.2 per cent)." Based on her study of 23 democracies, Wilma Rule (1987) suggests that whether elections are run using some form of PR or using a single-member district system is the most important predictor of women's levels of political representation. Of the top ten countries as of December 2003 in terms of women's representation, all but one utilized various forms of PR in national elections.

Despite these findings, it is important not to overstate the independent influence of this feature of the electoral system. More women are elected in some FPTP systems (like Canada and Australia) than in some highly proportional party list systems (such as Israel and Greece). Indeed, it is not really the proportionality of the system *per se* that matters for women, so much as the fact that there are lists and that parties place women in eligible positions on those lists.[4] Whether women are elected in PR systems depends on a number of contingent factors, including the existence of quotas, formal and informal party rules concerning recruitment and selection, district and party magnitude, cultural attitudes toward women, and pressure from women's groups.

Gender Quotas

More than 30 countries have passed national legislation or made constitutional provisions for gender quotas in the selection of candidates. In more than 50 countries, political parties have established rules or targets to include a certain percentage of women as candidates. But are quotas effective as a means for increasing the number of elected women? As promising as they appear, there is little evidence that quotas *alone* have had a significant effect in increasing women's political representation in those countries that have adopted them. Surprisingly, the percentage of parliamentary seats held by women in countries that have a constitutional provision or a law establishing gender quotas for election to the national legislature is actually *lower* than the percentage of seats held by women in countries without quotas.[5] Clearly, the passage of quota legislation is less important than the nature of those quotas, and the manner of their enforcement.

Gender quotas take very different forms from country to country. In most cases, the quotas are imposed during the candidate selection process, requiring parties to *nominate* a minimum number of women or men. More rarely, quotas apply to the numbers of *elected* men and women, a process that may require the use of reserved seats and separate electorates for men and women.[6] The required number of women varies as well. Usually a quota is intended to produce a critical mass of female parliamentarians—at least 20 per cent and sometimes as high as 40 or 50 per cent.

Quotas also work differently under different electoral systems. While they are most easily applied within a list-based PR system, they can also be used in FPTP elections. Where elections are run according to lists, quotas require all parties to include a minimum percentage of women on their lists. Some systems impose the rule of the "double quota" to ensure that a proportionate number of women are placed in eligible positions and not relegated to the bottom of the list. In France, for example, lists for municipal elections must include an equal number of men and women, and there must be three men and three women (in any order) for every six consecutive positions on the list. For elections based on single-member districts, the quota applies to the whole class of a party's candidates across all districts. One of the difficulties in making quotas effective under FPTP is that there is a tendency for parties to nominate women disproportionately to electoral districts where the party is weak and unlikely to win.

Quotas applied within a PR system are also more effective because they are more enforceable — the most important feature of any quota system. Political parties tend to view quotas as interfering with the usual prerogatives of the party organization to select their own candidates, and, without strong enforcement mechanisms and penalties, they will often fail to abide by quota rules. Not all sanctions are equally effective. The best approach is to make non-compliant lists ineligible for election, but this sanction can be applied only in list-based PR systems. In other cases, financial penalties may be imposed. Parties that fail to meet the quota requirement may have their public financing reduced, or parties that meet or exceed quota requirements may have their funding increased. As we will see in the case of France, financial penalties for non-compliance with parity in elections to the national legislature were designed by the governing party to have a decidedly *selective* effect. The law imposed greater financial incentives toward compliance upon smaller parties than upon larger parties. As a consequence, while the parity law did increase the number of female candidates among smaller parties, it had little effect on the gender distribution of seats held by the winning parties.

The French Experience Under *Parité*

In June 2000 France became the first country in the world to require by law an equal number of male and female candidates for most elections. For France, where women did not enjoy the right to vote until 1945 and where the level of representation of women in politics (about 5 per cent at the national level until 1997) has been one of the lowest among democratic states, parity seemed positively revolutionary. This new law has now been applied in five different sets of elections: municipal elections, held throughout France in March 2001;

Senate elections in September 2001; legislative elections held in June 2002; regional elections held in April 2004, and European elections in June 2004.

THE ORIGINS OF THE PARITY LAW

At first glance, France would seem to be an unlikely country to introduce quotas for women in politics. The modern French constitution is based on principles of strict individual equality, and there is usually deep resistance to any measure that allows differential treatment on the basis of group membership. Yet, parity has been an exception. From an obscure idea promoted by a handful of leftist feminists in the early 1980s, parity gained sufficient cross-party support to produce a constitutional amendment in 1999 and a revised electoral law in 2000. The advocates of parity effectively clothed the concept in the legitimating fabric of French republicanism, by arguing that women are not a minority and so not akin to ethnic and other groups who might demand measures to increase their level of political representation. Rather than establish a quota for 30 or 40 per cent female candidates, they argued that men and women, as equals, should share 50/50 in political life.

Quotas had already been tried and rejected as a means of increasing women's role in French political life. This occurred in 1982, after Gisèle Hamili, a feminist and Socialist-aligned member of the National Assembly, introduced an amendment to limit to 75 per cent the number of candidates of the same sex who may appear on any list for municipal elections. The law passed, but the quota was never applied. Rather, it was reviewed by the *Conseil constitutionnel* (roughly the equivalent of a Supreme Court) and declared incompatible with the terms of the constitution, particularly with those articles guaranteeing equality and non-discrimination in access to public office and the non-divisibility of the sovereign authority of the body politic. The 1982 constitutional decision served to renew and radicalize the parity movement. It forced advocates to develop a more fundamental criticism of sexual inequality within the representative system. If a quota was not acceptable for the Constitutional Court, neither was it adequate for women themselves who represented half of the population and therefore merited fully half of all representative seats.

At the same time, a series of European and international initiatives on women's place in politics (including the Beijing platform and resolutions passed by the Council of Europe) focused attention on the fact that French women remained in a fundamentally backward position in politics, both in comparison to other domains where they had made progress, and in comparison to women in other European countries. On January 1, 1997, women occupied just 35 of 576 seats (6.1 per cent) in the French National Assembly and 18 of 321 seats (5.6 per cent) in the Senate, no improvement over 1945, the first year they were eligible to vote and run for national office. Never before the legislative elections of May-June 1997 (when the Socialist Party adopted a voluntary quota of 30 per cent female candidacies) had women held more than 7 per cent of seats in the French Parliament.

Political resistance to parity remained strong through the 1980s and early 1990s. The foremost source of resistance lay among sitting members fearful of losing their seats. There was also the old division among feminists themselves as to whether women should be treated differently or identically to men and whether special measures tended to help women or to stigmatize and humiliate them. Finally, there was resistance among classical republicans (including many French constitutional experts) who argued that parity would undermine the French idea of equality and universality of treatment for all individuals.

Opposition to parity began to thaw in the late 1990s, when elite women began to mobilize across rigid party lines. In a significant step, in June 1996, ten of France's most prominent female politicians from across the political spectrum published a manifesto, "Pour la parité," demanding constitutional reform to allow parity.[7] The precipitating event was the victory of the Socialists, under Lionel Jospin, in the legislative elections of June 1997. Jospin's government included a number of women who publicly favoured quotas. Furthermore, Jospin was one of the few men in French politics personally convinced that parity was philosophically and politically appropriate. His wife played an important role as well. A respected philosopher, Sylviane Agacinski had written several articles and a book (1998) advocating parity. Jospin pressured reluctant deputies to support the constitutional amendment that would pave the way for parity legislation. The Socialists governed in "cohabitation" (from 1997 to 2002) with the moderate right-wing President Jacques Chirac. Chirac was clearly less disposed to the idea but had read the polls that showed that ordinary men and women favoured parity. At the end of the decade, parity was receiving wide public attention and apparent popular support as a measure that would renew the political class and modernize and relegitimate French democracy.

An amendment to the Constitution of the Fifth Republic was ratified on June 28, 1999 by a joint congress of the two legislative chambers. Whereas the constitution had previously been interpreted as forbidding any preferential treatment of candidates on the basis of gender or any other category, it now states (Article 3, paragraph v) that "the law favours the equal access of men and women to all electoral mandates and elective functions" and (Article 4, paragraph ii) that political parties "contribute to the application of this principle through conditions determined by the law." The constitutional amendment was followed on June 6, 2000 by a parity law that was approved three votes short of unanimity.

The parity law applies to municipal elections in towns of at least 3,500 inhabitants, to legislative elections, regional elections, Senate elections (in larger departments where three or more senators are elected by PR methods), elections of representatives to the European Parliament, and to elections to an assortment of legislative councils in overseas French territories. The law does not apply to presidential elections, nor to departmental or regional elections, nor to Senate elections in smaller departments (where elections are run using FPTP). Moreover, the law applies differently depending upon the voting methods used for each type of election.

PARITY ROUND I: MUNICIPAL ELECTIONS

The first elections run under the new rules were municipal elections, held across France in two rounds, on March 11 and 18, 2001. Here, parity proved highly effective. In cities and towns with over 3,500 inhabitants, the percentage of seats on local councils held by women increased from 25.7 per cent to 47.5 per cent. So popular was the idea of recruiting more women to electoral lists that even in those small towns where parity was not required by law, the percentage of women elected to council increased from 21 to 30.1 per cent.

The effectiveness of the parity law in municipal politics is due to the electoral rules applied at this level. What matters most for women in these elections is not the rule of proportionality — French municipal elections apply a *semi*-proportional method of translating votes to seats[8] — but the existence of lists and the strict enforcement of "double parity" on those lists. The law requires an equal number of men and women on every list and specifies the placement of men and women throughout the list, so as to ensure that parties do not relegate women to losing positions. Parity must be achieved for the first six candidates on the list (three women and three men in any order) and every subsequent six. Any list that fails to meet these requirements is ineligible and will not be presented to the voters. Where elections are run according to such rules, parity among those elected to office is virtually assured.[9]

Parity produced a dramatic increase in the number of women in council (as illustrated in Figure 9-1 and Table 9-1). However, it did little to increase the number of female mayors. The head of the winning list is usually named mayor by the newly invested council, but very few lists placed a women at

Table 9-1
Women in French Municipal Government Following 2001 Elections

Municipalities		Percentage Women			
Size of Town	Number of Towns	Mayor	Adjunct Mayor	All Adjuncts	Council
Less than 3,500	33,971	11.2	18.5*	23.2*	30.1
3,500-8,999	1,638	6.2	23.0*	35.4*	47.4
9,000-29,999	717	7.1	32.0*	37.0*	47.3
30,000-99,999	196	8.2	30.0*	42.5*	47.8
100,000 or more	36	11.1	30.6	39.5	48.6
Arrondissements (Paris, Marseille, Lyon)	37	24.3	27.0	46.4	48.4
Total 3,500 +	2,587	6.7	26.3*	36.5*	47.5

* Where indicated, figures are the author's estimates based on analysis of a sample (n=1,567) of city councils from across France. All other figures represent the whole population of councils for municipalities of a given size. There are 36,558 municipalities within metropolitan France (excluding overseas territories), each with its own mayor and town council.

the top. Just 6.7 per cent of mayors (in towns over 3,500) chosen after these elections were women, compared to 4.4 per cent in 1995. Women did better in smaller towns, where 11.2 per cent of mayors are now women, compared to 7.8 per cent in 1995. Parity rules do not apply in these towns, but their small size and reduced political stakes make it easier for women to gain access. Nor is parity required in the composition of the local executive. The long-standing practice has been that the top candidates on the mayor's list form the executive. The second candidate (following the mayor) on the winning list becomes the *premier adjoint* (adjunct mayor), the third becomes the *deuxième adjoint*, and so on. Yet in 2001, mayors typically named to top executive positions *men* who appeared well down the list of candidates, while passing over women in the top six.[10]

PARITY ROUND II: SENATE ELECTIONS

The next application of the parity law was to Senate elections, held on September 23, 2001. There are two types of election to Senate. In departments (national administrative districts) represented by three or more senators, those seats are allocated proportionally using lists. In smaller departments, electing fewer than three senators, seats are filled using plurality rules and FPTP.[11] Parity applies only to the former, but for those elections, the rules are

Figure 9-1
Female Mayors in French Municipalities, 1995 to 2001

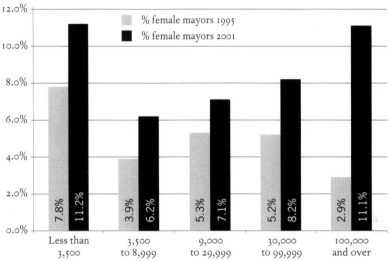

Population of Municipalities

strict. Every list must contain an equal number of male and female candidates (within a margin of one), in alternating order. As with European and municipal elections, any list that does not comply is declared ineligible and will not be presented to voters.

One-third of the French Senate is renewed every three years, and in September 2001, 102 seats were up for election, of which 74 were filled using PR methods and following parity rules. Among the 74, the number of women increased from five to 20 (27 per cent), while in the seats using FPTP and exempt from parity requirements, there was no increase in the number of women elected (there remain just two women among these 28 seats). In total, of the 102 senators elected, 21.6 per cent were women, compared to 6.9 per cent before these elections.

Conditions for the election of women in those Senate seats governed strictly by PR and parity rules seemed ideal. Yet just 27 per cent of senators elected to those seats were women, compared to over 47 per cent for municipal seats where similar rules applied. Why? The feature most disadvantageous to women in these elections was small district magnitude. In general, where district magnitude is small, and parties can win only a few seats per district, they are less willing to go deep enough down the list to elect women. Of course, the parity law in French Senate elections required parties to list men and women in alternating order. So even with very small party magnitudes, election results should still approach parity. But many parties were able to evade parity, and thereby secure the re-election of their (male) incumbents, by creating more than one list. Before parity, a party would present a single list of candidates for election in a department, from which it might hope to elect several senators. Virtually all incumbent senators were male. Facing re-election under parity rules, many male incumbents anticipated losing their position on the list to a woman, being relegated to an unelectable third or fifth place. To secure their re-election, male senators formed independent lists, placing themselves at the top and a woman in second position. Parity was respected, strictly speaking. Women comprised almost half (45.5 per cent) of all candidates in Senate elections where PR and parity rules applied, but only 24 of those 499 female candidates were placed on the top of a list.

PARITY ROUND III: LEGISLATIVE ELECTIONS

The most important test of parity was its application to the legislative elections that were held in two rounds on June 9 and 16, 2002. The impact of parity here was minimal. The National Assembly now includes 71 women among its 576 members (12.3 per cent), up just nine (from 10.9 per cent) since the previous pre-parity elections. This still leaves France near the bottom among European countries for the number of women in Parliament. Just how a country can elect so few women to national office, despite a law requiring that 50 per cent of all candidates be female, requires some explanation.

In the passage from principle to law, parity yielded to fundamental political interests. As we have seen, for both municipal and Senate elections, where there was a way around the spirit of parity, incumbents usually took it. Nowhere did this prove more true than at the locus of political power in France, the National Assembly. Deputies were beholden by their party leaders to support parity in principle. But they were successful in translating that principle into a weak law—weakest of all where it concerned their own re-election. Indeed, from the beginning of debates over constitutional reform and parity legislation it was clear (on this there was no debate) that there would be no change to the existing majority run-off system of election to the National Assembly. Every major French party stood resolutely opposed to any reform of the current electoral system.[12] They understood that while a proportional or semi-proportional system of election would benefit women, it would also reward minor and more extreme parties at the expense of larger ones.

Moreover, it was apparent that sitting deputies (almost all of them men) feared having their nominations passed over in favour of women. A revealing indication of deputies' natural opposition to parity is found in a poll conducted by the French newspaper *Le Monde*.[13] Taken at an early stage in the public debates over parity, the poll results were published on International Women's Day in 1997. At the time, the Right held a majority in Parliament, and the government was making it known that it would consider quotas as a means of bringing more women into politics. Of the 312 deputies who responded to the poll, 59.2 per cent answered that they were opposed to a system of quotas to ensure better representation for women. On the key question of whether they supported a constitutional amendment inscribing the principle of parity between men and women in elected assemblies (without which quotas would again be invalidated by the Constitutional Court) 75.6 per cent were opposed. Opposition to a constitutional amendment was higher on the right than the left, but even Socialist deputies were more likely to oppose than support a constitutional measure. While deputies on the right and left ultimately did vote for both the constitutional amendment and the parity law, we can infer that they did so under pressure from their party leaders and on some assurance that the legislative changes would not cost them their seats.

The law they designed allows more flexibility in the application of parity to legislative elections. It *incites* parties to nominate an equal number of male and female candidates by withholding from delinquent parties a portion of their annual state subsidy. Unlike at the municipal and Senate levels, no party can be disqualified for failing to nominate an equal number of male and female candidates. As suggested above, financial penalties are not particularly effective in ensuring compliance with parity. Under the new law, the parties found themselves having to balance two competing incentives: (1) to present a maximum number of female candidates and therefore minimize the financial penalty; and (2) to avoid alienating male incumbents and hopefuls who might run as dissidents against the party's official candidate, potentially splitting party support and increasing the probability of victory for opposing parties. It is clear from Table 9-2 that for the major parties—those who were the real contenders to form the government—the prevailing motivation became the need to protect incumbents. Incumbency acted as a significant barrier to the implementation of parity. In fact, the only parties that followed the spirit of parity were those with few or no sitting deputies.

The candidate selection strategies of the two major parties—Chirac's Union pour la majorité présidentielle (UMP) and the Socialists—are most interesting in this respect. As the challenging party, the UMP had fewer sitting deputies than the Socialists, and so incumbency should not have posed so great an obstacle to the implementation of parity. Yet in France, the notion of incumbency should be interpreted broadly. The UMP selected as candidates those (mostly male) incumbent deputies, as well as former incumbents who had lost their seats in the Socialist victory in 1997. In the manner typical of French politics, most ex-deputies had continued as mayor, regional councillor, etc., and this local implantation was claimed to be key to winning back their old legislative seat and carrying the party to national victory. Female candidates, without the benefit of local or national incumbency, were seen as more risky, even if this cost the party dearly in revenues. In a number of cases, the UMP rejected highly qualified women in favour of less impressive incumbent men.[14] In total, the party nominated women to fewer than 20 per cent of the districts where it ran a candidate, and (with women comprising just 10.3 per cent of its legislative caucus) it appears that these women were nominated disproportionately in electoral districts where the party was weak.

The Socialist Party outperformed the UMP on parity compliance, nominating women in 36 per cent of the districts it contested (though with women holding just 16.4 per cent of the party's legislative seats, the Socialists too appear to have nominated women disproportionately in unwinnable electoral districts). A distinct advantage for the Socialists was that a higher proportion of its incumbents were female, a result of long struggles by the women's movement within the party.[15] Still, the party's performance on parity is less than commendable, and it is clearly inconsistent that the party responsible for the constitutional revision and the passage of the parity law could not uphold the principle.

For smaller parties, on the other hand, the need to present a maximum number of female candidates and therefore minimize the financial penalty became an overriding incentive in these elections. As is demonstrated in Table 9-3, the design of the parity law — specifically the application of the financial penalty — makes it virtually impossible for small parties with few incumbents to avoid parity, while allowing major parties far greater prerogative in candidate selection.

There are two portions of a party's public subsidy, only the first of which is affected by the parity law. The first portion is calculated on the basis of the number of votes a party receives in the election (it is equal to approximately 1.55 Euros per vote). The second portion is calculated on the basis of the number of parliamentary seats that a party wins in the elections (equal to about 45,125.00 Euros per seat). For parties that do not achieve parity, the first portion of their subsidy is reduced by an amount equal to half of the difference between the percentage of male and female candidates nominated by the party. For example, with 20 per cent female candidates and 80 per cent male candidates, the difference between male and female candidates for the UMP is 60 per cent. The first portion of the party's annual subsidy (about 13.4 million Euros) is thus reduced by 30 per cent (roughly 4 million Euros). This is a substantial financial loss. However, larger parties can make up ground on the second portion of the funding formula, which is based on the number of seats they win. Because smaller parties are unlikely to win seats in Parliament, virtually all of their funding depends upon the first portion, leaving them little choice but to respect the parity law. With no seats in the National Assembly, it is no surprise that the Front National felt financially compelled to present an equal number of male and female candidates, even though it was one of the few parties to publicly oppose the parity law. For larger parties, the parity law gives rise to calculations over the fiscal and political consequences of more female candidates versus more male candidates. As Amory de Saint-Quentin, a member of the national selection committee for the UMP, explained quite candidly (Fabre 2002: 9), "It is more profitable to have men elected than to have female candidates defeated."

Parties are listed in descending order, according to the percentage of their candidates who were women. Parties indicated in italic type elected at least one representative to the National Assembly in June 2002. Tables 9-2 and 9-3 are adapted from the Rapport au Premier Ministre: "Application de la loi du 6 juin 2000 dite 'de la parité' aux elections legislatives de juin 2002."

To understand the failure of parity in these legislative elections, we must also take into account the French presidential elections held two months earlier. To the great consternation of the traditional parties, Jean-Marie Le Pen, the leader of the extreme right-wing Front National, finished in second place after the first round of these elections, pitting him against incumbent president Jacques Chirac in the run-off ballot.[16] The response of the traditional parties in the run-up to the legislative elections in June was to form left- and right-wing alliances in order to avoid splitting the vote. The fear was not that FN candidates would win legislative seats. They have not held any seats in Parliament since the PR system was discarded as the method of election to the National Assembly in 1988. It was rather a push on the moderate right to avoid the risk of splitting the vote and allowing the left — devastated by Jospin's humiliation in the presidential election — to return in force. Facing a unified party of the right, parties on the left reached similar accords.

The moderate right, uniting inside Chirac's UMP, fielded common candidates in 542 of France's 576 electoral districts. On the left, electoral accords

Table 9-2

Women Candidates in French Legislative Elections 2002

Political Party	Number of Candidates	Number of Female Candidates	% Female Candidates	Difference between % Male and % Female Candidates
Lutte Ouvrière	560	281	50.18 %	−0.36 %
Ligue Communiste Révolutionnaire	427	214	50.12 %	−0.24 %
Les Verts	456	227	49.78 %	0.44 %
Front National	565	276	48.85 %	2.30 %
Mouvement Pour la France	284	134	47.18 %	5.64 %
Chasse, Pêche, Nature et Traditions	405	186	45.93 %	8.16 %
Pôle Républicain	404	181	44.8 %	10.40 %
Diverse extreme left parties	290	128	44.14 %	11.72 %
Parti Communiste Français	496	218	43.95 %	12.10 %
Diverse extreme right parties	103	43	41.75 %	16.50 %
Diverse ecological parties	930	388	41.72 %	16.56 %
Mouvement National Républicain	563	231	41.03 %	17.94 %
Parti Socialiste	465	168	36.13 %	27.74 %
Diverse regionalist, autonomist, and nationalist parties	149	49	32.89 %	34.22 %
Other unclassifiable parties	779	237	30.42 %	39.16 %
Parti Radical de Gauche	52	14	26.92 %	46.16 %
Rassemblement Pour la France	81	18	22.22 %	44.44 %
Diverse left parties	270	59	21.85 %	56.30 %
Diverse right parties	415	83	20.0 %	60.0 %
Démocratie Libérale	20	4	20.0 %	60.0 %
Union pour la Majorité Présidentielle	542	108	19.93 %	60.14 %
Union pour la Démocratie Française	188	37	19.68 %	60.64 %
Total	8444	3284	38.89 %	22.22 %

Table 9-2 (continued)
Women Candidates in French Legislative Elections 2002

Political Party	Number of Deputies Elected	Number of Female Deputies Elected	% Female Deputies Elected
Lutte Ouvrière	0	0	—
Ligue Communiste Révolutionnaire	0	0	—
Les Verts	3	1	33.33 %
Front National	0	0	—
Mouvement Pour la France	1	0	0 %
Chasse, Pêche, Nature et Traditions	0	0	—
Pôle Républicain	0	0	—
Diverse extreme left parties	0	0	—
Parti Communiste Français	21	5	23.81 %
Diverse extreme right parties	0	0	—
Diverse ecological parties	0	0	—
Mouvement National Républicain	0	0	—
Parti Socialiste	141	23	16.43 %
Diverse regionalist, autonomist, and nationalist parties	0	0	—
Other unclassifiable parties	0	0	—
Parti Radical de Gauche	7	1	14.29 %
Rassemblement Pour la France	2	0	0 %
Diverse left parties	6	1	16.67 %
Diverse right parties	9	2	22.22 %
Démocratie Libérale	2	1	50.0 %
Union pour la Majorité Présidentielle	355	36	10.14 %
Union pour la Démocratie Française	29	1	3.45 %
Total	576	71	12.3 %

Table 9-3

Financial Penalties Imposed by Parity Law in French Legislative Elections 2002

Political Party	Number of votes received first round	First portion of subsidy, before penalty	% Parity penalty	Amount withheld
Lutte Ouvrière	304,081	472,448 €	0	0
Ligue Communiste Révolutionnaire	320,610	498,129 €	0	0
Les Verts	1,145,781	1,780,188 €	0	0
Front National	2,873,391	4,464,359 €	1.15 %	51,340 €
Mouvement Pour la France	202,831	315,137 €	2.82 %	8,87 €
Chasse, Pêche, Nature et Traditions	422,448	656,353 €	4.08 %	26,779 €
Pôle Républicain	308,664	479,568 €	5.20 %	24,938 €
Diverse extreme left parties	82,218	127,741 €	5.86 %	7,486 €
Parti Communiste Français	1,267,688	1,969,594 €	6.05 %	119,160 €
Diverse extreme right parties	63,696	98,964 €	8.25 %	8,165 €
Diverse ecological parties	297,304	461,918 €	8.28 %	38,247 €
Mouvement National Républicain	278,268	432,342 €	8.97 %	38,781 €
Parti Socialiste	6,142,654	9,543,780 €	13.87 %	1,323,722 €
Diverse regionalist, autonomist, and nationalist parties	93,300	144,959 €	17.11 %	24,803 €
Other unclassifiable parties	217,027	337,193 €	19.58 %	66,022 €
Parti Radical de Gauche	389,782	605,600 €	23.08 %	139,773 €
Rassemblement Pour la France	94,222	146,392 €	22.22 %	40,697 €
Diverse left parties	355,363	552,124 €	28.15 %	155,423 €
Diverse right parties	1,005,880	1,562,826 €	30.0 %	468,848 €
Démocratie Libérale	108,824	169,079 €	30.0 %	50,724 €
Union pour la Majorité Présidentielle	8,619,859	13,392,589 €	30.07 %	4,027,151 €
Union pour la Démocratie Française	1,236,353	1,920,909 €	30.32 %	582,420 €

were signed and common candidates nominated for 34 electoral districts, while partial accords were reached in another 136. Competition was fierce for these nominations, given that each party brought its own candidate to the table. In numerous cases, women who had been given the nod and begun campaigning unofficially months before were abruptly withdrawn and replaced by male candidates chosen by accord. Few women on either the right or the left complained loudly about this, as most placed the party's interest first. The

Table 9-3 (continued)
Financial Penalties Imposed by Parity Law in French Legislative Elections 2002

Political Party	First portion of subsidy, after penalty	Number of deputies elected	Second portion of subsidy	Total subsidy
Lutte Ouvrière	472,447 €	0	0	472,447 €
Ligue Communiste Révolutionnaire	498,129 €	0	0	498,129 €
Les Verts	1,780,188 €	3	135 375 €	1,915,563 €
Front National	4,413,019 €	0	0	4,413,019 €
Mouvement Pour la France	306,250 €	1	45,125 €	351,375 €
Chasse, Pêche, Nature et Traditions	629,574 €	0	0	629,574 €
Pôle Républicain	454,631 €	0	0	454,631 €
Diverse extreme left parties	120,256 €	0	0	120,256 €
Parti Communiste Français	1,850,434 €	21	947 625 €	2,798,059 €
Diverse extreme right parties	90,799 €	0	0	90,799 €
Diverse ecological parties	423,671 €	0	0	423,671 €
Mouvement National Républicain	393,561 €	0	0	393,561 €
Parti Socialiste	8,220,058 €	140	6,317,500 €	14,537,558 €
Diverse regionalist, autonomist, and nationalist parties	120,157 €	0	0	265,116 €
Other unclassifiable parties	271,170 €	0	0	608,363 €
Parti Radical de Gauche	465,828 €	7	315,875 €	781,703 €
Rassemblement Pour la France	105,695 €	2	90,250 €	195,945 €
Diverse left parties	396,701 €	6	270,750 €	667,451 €
Diverse right parties	1,093,978 €	9	406,125 €	1,500,103 €
Démocratie Libérale	118,355 €	2	90,250 €	208 605 €
Union pour la Majorité Présidentielle	9,365,437 €	355	16,019,375 €	25,384,812 €
Union pour la Démocratie Française	1,338,490 €	29	1,308,625 €	2,647,115 €

media were preoccupied as well by the massive reorganization of the French party system. Without criticism from women within the parties, without media criticism, and with minimal public attention to these elections (the abstention rate, at 39.7 per cent, was the highest ever), the parties felt little constraint to respect the parity law. At the end of the day, parity and women's place in politics receded to a very dim corner of the political landscape.

EVALUATING THE FRENCH PARITY LAW

For those advocating better representation of women in politics, the French parity law presents a number of general lessons. First, and most clearly, the impact of quotas on women's access to political office varies dramatically depending on the electoral methods applied and the enforcement mechanisms used. Quotas are particularly difficult to enforce where elections are run using single-member districts. They can work very effectively under a list-based system of election to multi-member districts, but only if the district magnitude is fairly large. Lists are what matter most for women, along with the assurance that they will be included in electable positions on those lists. Less important is whether the system of election is truly proportional in terms of translating votes cast into party seats.

Beyond these institutional factors, there are particular elements of the French party system and political culture that continue to pose important obstacles to women's access to politics. The concentration of power among incumbents, most of whom hold mandates simultaneously at the local and national level, makes it especially difficult for women to break through (Sineau 2001). In their recruitment practices, major parties continue to view female newcomers not as a symbol of political renewal but as a relative risk. Hence, where parties do choose female candidates, they try to avoid this perceived risk factor by selecting women from families with party connections and a history of holding political office. Thus, contrary to predictions that women will rejuvenate politics and bring it closer to the ordinary citizen, the French system tends to draw political women from a small elite. Furthermore, despite parity, attitudes about the roles of men and women tend to marginalize women within traditionally "feminine" sectors of government, where they are responsible for dossiers largely confined to education, children, and social affairs. And women are less likely to pursue politics as a life-long career, or to accumulate several political offices simultaneously, in part because they continue to carry out the majority of domestic tasks. The personal costs of political success for women are particularly high. Women who have been elected to office for more than one term are far more likely than comparable men to be divorced or single and to be childless.[17]

The French results also shed light on the idea that women's access to politics tends to improve under left-wing governments (Norris 1987). The French story reveals repeated collusion between major parties on the right and left to pass the weakest kind of quotas for women. French women have fared better under the Socialist Party than under the traditional right, largely because of the influence of a strong women's caucus within that party. However, we should not rely on left-wing parties to always pursue their ideological objectives.[18] Sustained feminist mobilization within *all* parties is one key to ensuring political and public attention to the problem of women's political underrepresentation.

The degree of resistance to gender quotas within the corridors of power and, thus, the central importance of the candidate selection process for the advancement of women cannot be overestimated. Especially where the political stakes are highest, dominant parties and political incumbents will avoid passing strict quota laws for women and will exploit loopholes in any existing laws. Even where parity measures are passed, feminist mobilization within political parties remains the most crucial element for ensuring that women are selected as candidates

Still, there is cause for muted optimism for women in France. Parity's effect at the municipal level is especially significant. Women almost doubled their numbers on town councils throughout France. And there was surprising willingness for parties to nominate women as mayoral candidates in some of the largest cities. Local office will prove a useful training ground for women who may seek national office in the future, and, as female mayors and deputy mayors become a common fixture, female nominations to highly competitive legislative elections should increase as it becomes clearer to parties that there is no electoral penalty associated with female candidates (Matland and Studlar 1996).

Lessons for Canada?

Electoral reform to reduce the barriers to women's participation in political life was one of many topics taken up in 1991 by Canada's Royal Commission on Electoral Reform and Party Financing (the Lortie Commission). Yet, the results of the Lortie Report were disappointing for women. From the outset, the Lortie Commission excluded reform of Canada's FPTP system.[19] Quotas and other incentives for parties to select more female candidates were considered, but the commission made only a meagre recommendation that was promptly rejected by every major party.[20] Today, the prospects of electoral reform favourable to women appear little better, at least at the federal level, where electoral system reform is simply not on the legislative agenda. However, the present constitutional challenge to the Canada Elections Act, which argues that our present system of FPTP violates the equality rights of women as well as of supporters of minor parties, could change that (see

Chapter 15). Prospects are better at the provincial level. Still without significant public mobilization, it is unlikely that any governing party will undertake reform that could lead to it losing a substantial share of its parliamentary seats.

The outlook for quotas or incentives to promote the selection of more female candidates looks bleak too. Presently only one party, the NDP, has stipulated a set of affirmative action guidelines for promoting the nomination of women and other underrepresented groups as candidates, but under FPTP and the high degree of control over candidate selection exercised by local constituency associations, it has found it difficult to enforce its own guidelines. And the party system is less accommodating to the representation of women and women's interests since before 1993 when all three parties were committed to increasing the representation of women (Young 2002). Hence, Canadian feminists need to follow a mid-term goal of mobilization outside of Parliament and within the political parties, following the route taken by feminists in France. Even within a democratic culture hostile to affirmative action type policies, the mobilization of feminist leaders in France led first to the adoption of voluntary quotas within parties and then to the introduction of parity legislation.

None of this is to suggest that we lose sight of the long-term goal. If the prospects for electoral reform in Canada do become more positive, it is important to consider carefully what kind of reforms would be most hospitable to women. The French experience with parity provides several lessons. The most direct and effective reform would be the implementation of a list-based proportional or semi-proportional representation electoral system, accompanied by double parity, with severe penalties for non-compliance. Ineligibility for non-compliant lists is best. Financial incentives and penalties are less effective.[21] A high district magnitude is also necessary for achieving a representative outcome. In a system with three or four major parties, this requires districts with at least eight seats to increase the probability that a party can win two or more seats in a district. Ticket-balancing becomes viable and likely to produce parity only when a party expects to win two or more seats. For both of these reasons — to overcome anticipated resistance to gender quotas from male incumbents, and to ensure adequate district magnitudes (especially in small provinces like PEI) — it would be advisable to increase the size of the House of Commons. A second choice would be a mixed-member proportional system (MMP), created by *adding* supplementary seats elected by list to the present assembly under the conditions specified above.

The evidence from France suggests that a more proportional electoral system, along with enforceable quota requirements, would be a positive development for women in Canadian politics. But it will not happen without the strong mobilization of women, working inside and outside of political parties to convince Canadian parties and voters that politics must reflect the diversity of their society.

Notes

1. The latest province to grant female suffrage was Québec, where the right to vote in provincial elections was delayed until 1940. Some Canadian women *and* men — including First Nations, Japanese Canadians, Chinese Canadians, and Indo-Canadians — were denied the vote even later than this.

2. There is considerable evidence that female candidates do as well as male candidates when facing the voters directly in FPTP elections (Darcy and Schramm 1977; Welch and Studlar 1986; Hunter and Denton 1984).

3. In municipal elections in Norway, voters cast their ballot for a list, but are allowed to strike names from that list. Frustrated by the unwillingness of parties to place women in eligible positions on their lists, women's organizations called on voters to systematically strike male names from their party's list in order to move women up into positions of eligibility (Matland 1997; 1991). Matland notes, however, that, in general, open lists in local elections in Norway have hurt women, as voters tend to strike from the list more female than male candidates.

4. French municipal elections are list-based and, under parity, have produced almost an equal number of male and female councillors. However, the electoral system is deliberately *semi*-proportional in its translation of party votes into seats. See below, note 10.

5. On average, women hold 15.8 per cent of parliamentary seats in countries with quotas, compared to 16.9 per cent of parliamentary seats in countries without quotas. Data drawn from the International Institute for Democracy and Electoral Assistance (IDEA), Global Database of Quotas for Women, October 2003.

6. In India, for example, 33 per cent of seats in all local bodies are reserved for women according to the Constitutional Amendments 73 and 74. Women and men vote in separate ballots for these elections. In Bangladesh, until 2001, a system of reserved seats for women was used, where 30 seats out of 330 were reserved for women. These seats were filled through indirect election by the 300 directly elected MPs.

7. The manifesto was signed by leading women from across the political spectrum. It was published in the magazine *L'Express*, 6-12 June 1996.

8. The system in France works as follows. Fifty per cent of council seats are given to the list that wins a majority of votes (after the first or second round). The *remaining* seats are then distributed proportionately among all parties, including the winning party. For example, a party that wins 60 per cent of the votes following the second round would receive half of all seats, plus 60 per cent of the remaining half (for a total of 80 per cent of council seats). A party that receives 20 per cent of the vote would receive none of the first half, plus 20 per cent of the remaining half (for a total of just 10 per cent of council seats). It is justified as promoting more stable governments.

9. European and a portion of Senate elections also apply double parity and the list method of voting. These elections are decided in a single round, and male and female candidates must be listed in strictly alternating order.

10. Another limitation at the municipal level is that parity rules do not apply in naming members to the governing bodies of amalgamated cities. The Public Intercommunal Cooperative Establishments (ECPI) have arguably become the locus of power in municipal government, yet women hold just 5.4 per cent of executive positions in these structures throughout France.

11. All senators are elected indirectly by an electoral college comprised of elected local and regional representatives, and MPs.

12. In 1986, elections to the National Assembly were run using PR, but the law was changed and elections reverted back to single-member majority rules in 1988.

13. The poll results were reported in "Le gouvernement envisage des 'quotas' féminins aux élections," *Le Monde*, 8 March 1997: 6.

14. Among the most notorious cases was the UMP's rejection of Françoise de Panafieu, despite her having served as deputy for the 17th legislative district, mayor of the 17th arrondissement of Paris, and as France's ambassador to UNESCO. The UMP gave the candidacy to the incumbent, despite his having reached the age of retirement. To her credit, de Panafieu ran a dissident campaign and was elected (see Clerc 2002).

15. Women were also more involved in the candidate selection process within the Socialist Party. The UMP had only one woman on its national selection committee.

16. In the first round ballot, Chirac finished first with 19.8 per cent of votes, Le Pen won 16.9 per cent, and Lionel Jospin finished third with 16.1 per cent. Chirac won the run-off ballot with an overwhelming 82.2 per cent of the popular vote to Le Pen's 17.8 per cent.

17. These patterns are described in Bird (2003).

18. The French Socialist Party was long opposed to giving women the vote because they feared that women were too closely aligned with the Catholic Church and would be influenced by the clergy to vote for the right.

19. The report claimed that women do better because parties adopt gender quotas and other measures to strengthen the position of female candidates: "In countries that use proportional representation but whose parties do not take such action, the representation of women is similar to the Canadian record or worse" (Royal Commission on Electoral Reform and Party Financing 1991, 20).

20. The Commission proposed increasing the public funding for any party electing a sufficient number of women (at least 20 per cent of its parliamentary caucus). The measure was to come into effect *only* if the overall percentage of women in the House of Commons fell below 20 per cent.

21. Financial penalties might be more effective in Canada than they have been in France, because legislative turnover is relatively high in the House of Commons. High rates of turnover open up more winnable seats for women (Young 1991). And, in a climate of regular turnover, the introduction of "new faces" is seen as a virtue, not necessarily a risk.

CHAPTER 10

The Fair Elections Movement in the United States: What It Has Done and Why It Is Needed

Robert Richie and Steven Hill

A note on terminology: For reasons tied to some of the unique challenges for reform advocates in the United States that are outlined in this article, American reformers have developed a new terminology: "full representation" is often used instead of "proportional representation," "choice voting" instead of "single transferable vote (STV)," and "instant runoff voting (IRV)" instead of "preferential voting" or "the alterative vote."

Introduction

Despite energetic reformers pushing hard for proportional representation (PR) since the early 1990s, the United States remains a unique challenge for backers of PR. The many overlapping layers of government, widespread belief in "American exceptionalism," distrust of political parties, the vast and complex nature of the country, racial tensions, and voter focus on inherently winner-take-all, personality-driven executive offices generate real obstacles to winning and preserving PR. Furthermore, even though every level of election in the United States experiences serious problems—such as extremely low voter turnout, few competitive races, regional balkanization along partisan lines that renders entire states into one-party fiefdoms, underrepresentation of racial minorities and women, and narrow debate about issues—voters' attention is dispersed among a range of government bodies, some of which they are bound to find vaguely representative—much the way one is bound to eventually win at least something in a casino. It is thus difficult to generate the kind of elite attention and persistent citizen movement necessary to overcome the numerous opportunities opponents have to block reform.

Historically, American supporters of PR have had real successes at a local level—but though important, these successes were nearly all for nonpartisan elections and their impact often poorly understood. In the past 15 years, non-winner-take-all systems have seen a steady advance in adoption at a local level—more than 100 localities have gone to the semi-proportional systems of cumulative voting and limited voting—but these gains have come exclusively as a result of lawsuits brought by racial minorities seeking fair representation under the Voting Rights Act. Although some of these adoptions are in relatively large cities—a city of more than 130,000, Peoria (Illinois), now uses cumulative voting to elect half its city council, while Amarillo (Texas), with more than 150,000 people, uses cumulative voting to elect its school board—such measures remain a distant second choice to gerrymandered single-member districts for backers of minority voting rights.

In light of these conditions and the resulting conclusion that winning PR in the United States will be a marathon rather than a sprint, the Center for Voting and Democracy (CVD)—the national PR advocacy group that we have helped lead since its founding in 1992—has pursued a combination of strategies quite different from those pursued in Canada, New Zealand, and the United Kingdom. We focus on the following priorities:

- Reform efforts to adopt instant runoff voting (the American name for the Australian winner-take-all system of preferential voting), which has been adopted in San Francisco and deliberated in more than 20 of our 50 state legislatures in 2003-04.
- Analysis and public education about the severe problems created by winner-take-all elections, particularly the most notorious impacts on voters resulting from political gerrymandering like that in Texas and California.
- Making the case for candidate-based systems of PR (choice voting, also known as single transferable vote) as a complementary means to single-member districts to promote electoral opportunities for racial minorities.
- Introducing PR to a widening circle of groups and constituencies such as women, environmentalists, and university students and otherwise becoming prepared to seize an opportunity for PR.
- Helping to build pro-democracy coalitions with groups focused primarily on other electoral reforms and on generating voter turnout.

In this article we elaborate on these less direct advocacy efforts for PR and the special conditions in the United States that gave rise to them.

The Double-Edged Sword of Opportunities and Barriers

Few nations are in need of the benefits of PR as much as the United States.

- Gerrymandered single-member districts have reduced legislative competition to historic low levels. In three national elections for the US House of Representatives since 1996, fewer than one in ten races were decided by less than 10 per cent of votes, and more than 98 per cent of incumbents were returned to office. State legislative races are often even less competitive, with both major parties fielding candidates in fewer than 60 per cent of state legislative elections since 1996.[1]
- Policy-making and majority interests can sharply diverge. More than 40 million Americans do not have health insurance, and a majority of American workers now make less income in real (inflation-adjusted) dollars than they did 20 years ago, even as they work 160 hours more a year. By one estimate, Congress is now on the same page as the American people only about 40 per cent of the time, when it comes to issues of health care, crime, welfare and social security (Jacobs and Shapiro 2000: 4-5).
- Private sources supply nearly all campaign funds, with less than 1 per cent of Americans giving the great bulk of funds to candidates. Given that money's impact is very important in primaries and in tipping close winner-take-all races, candidates in turn spend a great deal of time and energy cultivating the support of these donors.
- National voter turnout is among the world's lowest — 139 in the world in average turnout since World War II, according to the Institute for Democracy and Electoral Assistance — and startlingly tilted in its class and race bias, with big drop-offs for racial minorities, the young, less well-educated, and lower-income. Voter turnout declines have been even more pronounced in local and primary elections, many as low as single digits.
- The United States's increasingly complex racial and ethnic diversity is poorly represented. Underrepresentation can be measured at all levels of government, but perhaps most starkly in the powerful Senate. In the past century, there have been a grand total of two black US senators and one black governor elected from our 50 states — who collectively

served a total of four terms. Currently the US Senate has no black or
Latino members, despite those Americans making up more than 25 per
cent of our national population.

- The relative strength of the American women's movement is poorly
  reflected in Congress, where women's representation is 14 per cent
  and where fewer states have female US House members than a decade
  ago. Women hold barely 20 per cent of state legislative seats, and their
  numbers have declined in recent elections.
- Polls generally show that a majority of Americans would like to see an
  enduring national third party, but only five of more than 8,000 state
  and federal elected representatives were elected on third-party tickets.
  When third-party candidates, like the Reform Party's Ross Perot and
  the Green Party's Ralph Nader, run, their supporters usually not only
  fail to elect their preferred candidate but in effect help elect their least
  favourite candidate.

Yet each of these conditions also creates barriers to PR:

- The lack of competitive elections, combined with generally weak party
  leaders and out-of-control campaign financing, make each incumbent
  legislator nearly invulnerable to defeat and able to wield power in their
  constituencies through patronage and pork barrel politics, directing
  government money and campaign contributions. Unless willing to look
  beyond their own short-term self-interest, they cannot be expected to
  support reforms that would undercut their power.
- The divergence of policy from majority interest creates a class of special interests, which have every incentive to thwart reform and which
  typically have won over allies in position to do their bidding.
- The disparities in campaign financing, which also tie into grave
  concerns about income disparities overall, draw the great bulk of chari-
  table contributions for reform work. Campaign finance reform and
  modest steps to expand the franchise through changes to voter registration and expanding the voter pool receive far more than $100 for every
  dollar given to supporters of changing winner-take-all elections.
- Low voter turnout means that those who potentially might benefit most
  from reform usually are not at the polls to support reform. Even if they
  are, their distaste for politics makes it hard for them to grasp the potential of reforms that typically are not discussed in major media.

- Our racial and ethnic diversity means that the white majority can feel more threatened by the potential electoral success of racial minorities than anxious to allow it—and quick to ascribe racial motivations to any concept of "minority representation," especially as most success for PR has come from the protections for racial minorities found in the Voting Rights Act. At the same time, court rulings against some district plans designed to enhance minority voting rights have contributed to leading civil rights groups being more defensive of district plans and more wary of showing openness to non-winner-take-all systems.

- The absence of elected third-party representatives, and correspondingly a votes-to-seats ratio like that of Canada or the United Kingdom that illustrates the problems of disproportionality, means that the multi-party argument for PR appears abstract. Majorities of votes for a party often produce a majority of seats in the legislature, particularly in the US House (though not always in state legislatures, and rarely in the US Senate where the Republicans enjoy a sizable "representation subsidy" resulting from equal representation regardless of population), and minor parties are not visibly deprived of many seats due to the absence of PR.

Reformers must confront other daunting challenges as well. No other nation comes close to having both federalism and the extreme presence of checks and balances at each level of government found in the United States. In Congress and in nearly every state legislature, legislation has to pass through two separate legislative houses that have essentially equal powers and then be approved by a separately elected executive. Within each legislature, bills must pass through a number of committees chaired by entrenched incumbents who have the power to kill or refine the legislation.

More than one level of government and one branch of government addresses nearly every major policy area. Voters in Takoma Park, Maryland, which is home base of our Center for Voting and Democracy, have a typically complex array of elected representatives. They include a city council and separately elected mayor for the city of Takoma Park; a county commission, school board, county executive, and several other county officers such as sheriff, district attorney, and judges; three members of the lower house of the state legislature and one state senator; a governor and several other separately elected statewide officers, such as attorney general and state comptroller; a member of the House of Representatives and two US senators; and a president. These elected officials have overlapping powers and responsibilities and are often elected at different times of the year, with separate primary elections as well.

Beyond these elected offices, there are non-elected government positions and bureaucracies that often have their own independent sources of power. Non-elected individuals with significant power can range from Takoma Park's city manager, who makes most day-to-day decisions about city policy, all the way to Alan Greenspan, the chairman of the US Federal Reserve who sets monetary policy, and the Supreme Court and federal judiciary who serve life terms after their appointments and frequently reject or redefine laws. This high number of offices cheapens the value of any single office, even the American presidency, and the many overlapping and competing levels of government muddy citizens' perceptions of what difference PR could make in elections. When individuals do focus their attention, it is far more likely to be on executives than on legislatures. In the past two years, more than half of the states holding elections for governor have changed which party holds the office, but barely a handful of state legislative chambers have changed hands. The House of Representatives has changed party control just once in 50 years, even as the White House has changed parties six times.

Within this massive and complex governmental structure, the two major parties operate as umbrella entities through which politically ambitious individuals operate. Party primaries are open to all comers in most states—at least to those with personal means and connections—and a charismatic, well-financed individual can come to represent the party without the blessing of current party leaders. The parties are vehicles, but the drivers are individuals with their own interests and their own set of private allies and funders that they develop over time. The parties have taken on clear definitions in the current political climate, but those definitions are quite different from what they were not long ago—particularly in the South, where white voters have swung sharply from being heavily Democratic to heavily Republican—and can be very different in different regions of the nation. As a result, the idea of "party fairness" in representation is less than meaningful to many Americans who look at parties with distrust.

Voter distrust of parties makes party list systems of PR a particularly hard sell in the United States. But the candidate-based PR system, choice voting (the American name for STV), presents a sizable educational challenge, as its ranked ballot mechanism for producing fair representation is less transparent. Furthermore, ranked ballot, candidate-based PR systems typically require changes to the voting equipment that is widely used to count ballots in the United States. Developing and certifying new voting equipment around the country is a byzantine, decentralized process dominated by a handful of for-profit companies that typically refuse to add public interest features like the capability to count ranked ballot elections unless specifically paid for by a county or city. Even then, they typically overcharge for building this capacity. More than one very promising reform effort in the United States has been shot down by the likelihood of the new system costing unknown amounts of money to implement.

A final challenging reality of the American political landscape is the difficulty in drawing on international examples when making the case for reform in the United States. Most Americans have an unquestioned belief that their democracy is the envy of the world. However unfounded, and whatever frustrations they might have with their own government, this does not mean that they look to examples from other nations for improvement—quite the contrary. Furthermore, the particulars of other nations' elections held under different rules are rarely tracked and understood as they typically are viewed to have little impact on Americans. (The exceptions are when the results seem "bizarre," such as the fragmented party systems of Israel and Italy.) Highly educated Americans, sadly often including political scientists, typically believe that PR inevitably results in unstable governments, that PR is the same as parliamentary government, and that single-member districts are the basic method of election all over the world, a belief reinforced by Congress in 1967 requiring single-member districts for US House races.

Raising the Reform Banner:
The Development of the Center for Voting and Democracy

It is against this backdrop that the accomplishments of the CVD need to be set. Remarkably, after a promising PR movement had important gains in the first half of the twentieth century—including adoptions of choice voting for city council in such cities as Cincinnati, Cleveland, New York, and Sacramento—PR advocacy was nearly completely dormant from 1950 until formation of the CVD at a national meeting in Cincinnati, Ohio, in 1992, with great ambitions, but almost no money or institutional support. It took years to have income stable enough to pay one staff member, and it was not until May 1999 that the PR movement in a nation of nearly 300 million people had more than two staffers. Moreover, most funding that has been received in recent years has not been explicitly for PR advocacy, but for efforts that are part of our indirect strategies for winning PR in the United States, such as alternatives to majority minority districts for racial representation, or instant runoff voting (see below).

There has been real progress. A decade ago, "proportional representation" sounded foreign and probably unconstitutional to nearly all Americans. Today, hundreds of publications (including our largest-circulation newspapers and magazines) have highlighted the case for voting system reform. Cities like San Francisco and Cincinnati held ballot measures for the choice voting method of PR in 1996 and 1991, winning 44 and 45 per cent of the vote respectively. Recent presidential candidates such as Jesse Jackson, John Anderson, Dennis Kucinich, and Jerry Brown have expressed support for PR, and higher-profile candidates like Republican US Senator John McCain and former Vermont Governor Howard Dean back instant runoff voting (IRV). One of several congressional bills designed to allow states to elect House Members by PR drew supportive testimony from the US Department of Justice, several Democratic and Republican US House members, and leading voting rights scholars.

Many American reformers still are learning the basic language of voting system reform, but the more they understand the range of possible voting systems and their likely impact, the more PR is being seen as a sensible complement to higher profile political reforms. Major constituency organizations now recognize that fair elections, like campaign financing and redistricting reforms, should be on their agenda. Organizations endorsing PR in the past five years include the Sierra Club and US Public Interest Research Group (US PIRG), two of the largest environmental organizations in the country; the American Civil Liberties Union (ACLU) and the National Organization for Women; and several state branches of the major good government groups League of Women Voters and Common Cause. These and many other leading civic and civil rights groups now regularly reference PR in their work and include speakers on it at events. At the same time, they rarely prioritize it as a focus of their work, in part because opportunities to win PR rarely seem tangible.

The CVD was launched to support PR; indeed, its initial name was "Citizens for Proportional Representation" to "resuscitate American democracy." But it redefined its program as it strategically adapted to the realities confronting its reform agenda. We now will describe the key elements of our strategy.

Instant Runoff Voting: Momentum for a Step toward American-Style PR

Many Americans—particularly elected officials—are cautious about moving away from our political traditions and practices, but will act if current electoral rules are transparently in need of reform or reform seems in their or their party's self-interest. These needs have been particularly clear in American single-winner elections—particularly those for executive offices like president, governor, and mayor. Third-party challenges typically are strongest in these high-profile races and have led to non-majority winners and debates about "spoilers." Additionally, many primary and local elections employ traditional runoff elections that are expensive and cumbersome to run. Moreover, voters disproportionately focus on these single-winner races and can better understand the case for change.

IRV (the American term for preferential voting, or the alternative vote), though not a form of PR, would provide both better majority representation and minority participation than plurality voting. Australia has used IRV for parliamentary elections for 80 years, and Ireland uses it to elect its president. With IRV, voters rank candidates in order of choice, and the ballot count simulates a series of runoff elections. If no candidate wins a majority of first choices, the last-place candidate is eliminated. Ballots cast for that candidate are redistributed to each voter's next choice in the next round of counting. This process of elimination of weak candidates continues until a candidate wins majority support among voters in the decisive round of counting.

IRV would resolve much of the controversy over "spoilers" in elections, a concept that has been well understood by many Republicans because of the effects of Ross Perot's independent presidential candidacies in 1992 and 1996 and by many Democrats because of Ralph Nader's Green Party candidacy in 2000. When compared to traditional runoffs, IRV saves money for taxpayers and campaign cash for candidates by combining two elections into one. Because of these more obvious benefits, IRV has spread much more quickly through the American political landscape than PR. In 1997, Texas became the first state in decades to consider a statute on IRV. In 1998, a charter commission in Santa Clara County (California) placed an amendment on the November 1998 ballot that allowed IRV to replace runoffs in future county elections when the voting equipment was ready. In 1999, legislation to enact IRV for statewide and federal offices passed the New Mexico state senate and was for the second time considered seriously in Vermont. In 2000, Utah Republicans adopted IRV for their convention elections and in 2002 used it to nominate several members of Congress. In 2002, San Francisco voters adopted IRV for all major city elections, while Vermont participants in 53 out of 56 town meetings voted to support IRV for gubernatorial elections. In 2003 and 2004, at least 20 states debated IRV legislation, and presidential candidates Howard Dean and Dennis Kucinich regularly advocated it on the campaign trail.

Advocates of PR in the United States see IRV also as a potential stepping-stone toward choice voting (STV), the ranked ballot form of PR. Because of the unpopularity of political parties, as well as exceptional circumstances of our federalism, most PR advocates see candidate-based systems as more politically feasible than the party-based ones used elsewhere. Forms of PR using small multi-seat districts (three to five seats) can fit well within our current political culture. Indeed, Illinois demonstrated just how well such a system could work. From 1870 to 1980, Illinois used the semi-PR system of cumulative voting in three-seat districts to elect the lower house of its state legislature. Voters had three votes, but had the option to put all three votes on one candidate. If about 25 per cent of voters supported only one candidate, that candidate was sure to win; over 50 per cent gave a party two seats; and at least 75 per cent of votes were required to be able to sweep the district.

This relatively minor modification of winner-take-all rules had a very positive impact on Illinois politics. Nearly every constituency had two-party representation, more moderates were elected, and cross-pollenization of ideas between parties was not uncommon. Although the great majority of one-seat House districts now are safe for one party, there are relatively few areas where at least 25 per cent of voters are not ready to support another party. The system fostered not only a different partisan mix in Illinois, but also a different mix of representatives from within parties since mavericks could and did buck their party leadership. In Illinois, most constituencies typically had two representatives reflecting two major factions within the majority party, as well as a representative from the smaller party who would often bring different experiences and views than representatives of that party where it was in the majority. Women won more seats than comparable states with single-member districts, and in places with substantial numbers of African Americans, black legislators regularly won, including several black Republicans, something unheard of in Illinois and many states today.[2]

The limitations of cumulative voting in three-seat districts—it does not benefit political minorities below 25 per cent support and creates incentives for parties to limit candidates and competition to avoid splitting votes—are overcome by choice voting, which also has the political benefit of building on a rich history. In the first half of the twentieth century, two dozen American cities adopted it through ballot measures. The system nearly always accomplished its objectives—giving more diverse representation and breaking up the power of political urban machines—but faced determined resistance by persistent opponents. Despite the idea having attracted the support of retired Supreme Court justices, the founder of the League of Women Voters, US senators, and, more quietly, President Franklin Roosevelt, its opponents' persistence paid off when they were able to take advantage of the election of controversial minorities—such as Communists in New York City during the Cold War and African Americans in Cincinnati—to reverse most gains.

IRV does not necessarily lead to choice voting, but it removes two barriers to choice voting's adoption: the educational hurdle of introducing the new concept of ranking candidates in order of choice and the inability of most current voting equipment and election administrators to be able to run ranked ballot elections. IRV can give third parties a stronger presence and even sometimes allow their voters to play the role of kingmaker with their lower rankings. This in turn makes it easier to show how winner-take-all elections are unfair to supporters of these parties. Hence, implementing IRV can be a step in preparing to tackle the more formidable challenge of winning PR.

The IRV Victory in San Francisco

San Francisco became the first major American city to adopt IRV to elect its local officials by a comfortable 55 per cent-45 per cent margin in March 2002, overcoming negative editorials in the daily newspapers, attacks from Mayor Willie Brown, and well-funded opposition from the downtown business community as well as from well-connected political consultants concerned about losing opportunities for making money from the eliminated runoff election. The CVD organized a grassroots effort that reached enough San Francisco voters through extensive literature drops and phone calls to head off the late and high profile attacks. The campaign also garnered endorsements from a range of leading civic players, including Assembly Leader Kevin Shelley—since elected California's Secretary of State—leading 1999 mayoral candidate Tom Ammiano, and significant organizational backers.[3] In the end more than 60 per cent of Latinos and African Americans supported the change, and pro-IRV arguments seemed to find a footing in all major constituencies.

The result reversed a 56 per cent-44 per cent defeat for choice voting in 1996, which would have applied to the Board of Supervisors. Our case was a strong one. The city had held local elections every November (city-wide offices in the odd years and members of the Board of Supervisors on even years, with both sets of offices having staggered terms), with a December run-off election if no candidate received a majority in November. This process generated clear problems. First, each runoff in San Francisco costs taxpayers at least $2 million. Second, runoffs put candidates under great pressure to raise money quickly, giving greater access for special interest contributors and undermining campaign finance reform. Third, voter turnout dropped: in 2000, it declined by 50 per cent between the first and second round, and the December 2001 runoff for City Attorney—the city's second most important office—generated a paltry 13 per cent turnout. By producing a majority winner in a single election, IRV maximizes turnout and saves taxpayers the cost of paying for two elections and candidates the need to raise extra cash quickly.

In comparing why IRV was successful here, but failed (by margins of nearly two-to-one) in Eugene, Oregon, in 2001 and in the state of Alaska in 2002, we have learned some lessons. The first is that there must be a widely agreed-upon problem to fix. In the defeats of IRV in Eugene and Alaska and choice voting in San Francisco in 1996, there was no potential cost saving of millions of dollars resulting from reducing the number of elections. In contrast, IRV in San Francisco folded the December runoff into the November general election, allowing proponents to draw support from more moderate and conservative voters and to gain enough interest from the Department of Elections to keep it neutral in the campaign, while winning strong support from progressive voters who perceived that holding just one election helped their candidates by boosting turnout and reducing the impact of campaign contributions. There were sensible arguments for Eugene to go to IRV, but not ones that could hold up to a negative campaign funded by opponents who wanted to use the initiative to mock the city council. In Alaska, there was a history of third-party spoilers that hurt Republicans, but that problem sent a mixed message—Republicans were divided about whether it was good to allow third parties to potentially build support under IRV, while the Democrats were mobilized to oppose IRV as a power grab by Republicans. Election administrators were loudly opposed to IRV in both Eugene and Alaska because of new perceived burdens on them.

In addition, we learned to avoid focusing too much on process. In contrast to Eugene, the San Francisco campaign focused on the simply stated benefits of IRV rather than on the mechanics of the electoral system—its website was called "improve the runoff"—and stress was put on saving money and making the election process more efficient. The name "instant runoff voting" wasn't even used on key pieces of campaign literature, which said instead "Vote Yes on Proposition A." Once process is raised, a cautious voter will shift to a "no" vote unless they come to understand that process. A related lesson was that a serious campaign required serious resources. The Eugene city campaign spent less than $5,000, and the Alaska statewide campaign spent some $50,000. Once confronted with negative attacks and fervent opposition, that amount was far too little to allow an adequate response. In San Francisco, advocates spent $70,000, and the CVD devoted tens of thousands of additional dollars in staff time to the effort.

There is an important postscript to the San Francisco story: powerful reform opponents do not give up easily. IRV is still alive in San Francisco, but it was not implemented in 2003 on schedule. In August 2003, a Superior Court judge ruled against forcing the city to use IRV for the November mayoral elections despite finding that the San Francisco Department of Elections was breaking the law for failing to implement IRV, characterizing its efforts since passage of the charter amendment as "fumbling" and "haphazard." The judge gave the department permission to postpone implementing IRV until 2004 because he feared that, with time running out before the November election and the pressures of the statewide gubernatorial recall election in October, the department could not be relied on to implement IRV fairly. It was a classic Catch-22. The various government agencies charged with fulfilling the law had dragged their feet to the point where, when finally they were sued for not implementing it, the judge ruled that it was too late for that year.

Opponents had seized upon distrust of hand ballot counts, instead requiring that IRV be implemented on election equipment that had to be reconfigured. This meant that, suddenly, several new players entered the picture. The vendor had to modify its equipment and receive federal and state certification for the change. The Department of Elections had to develop a plan and timeline for the vendor that was adequate for getting IRV on time and to negotiate a contract. The Board of Supervisors had to appropriate funds for the contract. The Secretary of State had to certify the new equipment. The opponents who spent more than $100,000 at the ballot box to block IRV likely spent even more on public relations and legal fees in interfering with each step in this process. With none of the players doing their job—despite steady pressure from IRV proponents—the opponents ultimately achieved their goal: a mayoral runoff at the end of 2003 won by the well-financed candidate backed by the business community.

Looking ahead for IRV, there are incremental gains poised to be won in several legislatures, including requirements that new voting equipment be required to support ranked choice systems, and at least two ballot measures in cities that have reasonable chances to pass in 2004. The presidential race may again raise the "spoiler" controversy, and the argument for IRV over runoffs is stronger than ever. New data from the CVD show that voter turnout decreased in the decisive round in 82 out of 84 runoffs in federal primaries from 1994 to 2002, by an average of more than a third, and campaign finance abuses are particularly pronounced when candidates have to raise money for a second round of election.

Strategies for the Present—and Future

Many Americans are discontented with electoral politics, but few associate that discontent with one of its root causes: winner-take-all elections. To get people interested in PR, its advocates must convince them that winner-take-all elections are fundamentally inadequate for American politics in the twenty-first century. To that end, we have taken the lead in exposing the impact of winner-take-all elections on five pillars of a robust democracy: participation, representation, political discourse/campaigns, legislative policy, and national unity, most recently and fully in a book by one of us (Hill 2002). The central argument is that the geographic-based, two-choice/party characteristics of the winner-take-all system is fundamentally flawed and antiquated. This is particularly true as a result of the application of new technology (such as computer mapping of votes used for precise redistricting, and polling and focus groups used in campaigns for slicing and dicing the electorate). In addition, shifting regional and racial demographics have further exacerbated the negative effects of winner-take-all politics on each of the five democracy pillars. It becomes increasingly clear that without moving toward PR, campaign finance reform, the Voting Rights Act, and other such democratic reforms, on their own, cannot bring the needed improvements.

The CVD has for nearly a decade released regular reports on the roots of lack of competition and distorted representation in US House elections in its on-line reports Dubious Democracy and Monopoly Politics. Introduced in 1997, the simple spreadsheet methodology of *Monopoly Politics*, based entirely on past federal election results in the district and whether it was an open seat, set out a path now being followed by prominent analysts (like Charlie Cook's *Political Report*), who pick nearly all House races early on in an election cycle. This has drawn attention to the greater impact of single-member districts and redistricting on determining winners than to more publicized factors like campaign finance inequities. One effect of this information has been to highlight the fact that since many campaign donors know in advance which candidate is going to win, their money is in fact given to buy access to the legislators, not to buy the elections themselves. The report also helped quantify how many potentially vulnerable House incumbents were boosted in the 2001-02 redistricting, helping to explain why this redistricting was so much less competitive than the post 1991-92 redistricting, with barely any gains for women or people of colour.[4]

To draw attention to the issue of redistricting, the CVD has established an ambitious, 50-state project to track redistricting around the country, posting news articles from every state on a regular basis in a public interest guide to redistricting. These efforts contributed to redistricting becoming somewhat of a "cause célèbre" among national analysts and editorial pages—it is mentioned frequently as the source of the problems that we ascribe to winner-take-all elections. The next phase is for PR advocates to take advantage of the resulting attention to redistricting reforms to draw attention to just how limited those reforms can be. The challenge is to demonstrate that reform of winner-take-all is the lynchpin to breaking down polarization and balkanization, opening up representation, expanding discourse, and spurring more turnout.

A key aspect concerns minority representation. Without substantial numbers of African American voters in districts, very few African American candidates win; Asian Americans, Latinos, and Native Americans face similar hurdles. Dependence on redistricting to improve the representation of African Americans and other communities of colour results from three factors: white voters' general preference for white candidates; the fact that people of colour are in the minority in most areas; and near exclusive use of winner-take-all elections. But the latter can be changed. With PR systems, voters in a minority position can gain the representation of which they currently are deprived. As American society grows increasingly diverse and communities of interest increasingly develop along non-geographic lines, "full representation" (i.e., PR) is drawing even more attention.

Full representation has a history of electing racial minorities in the United States. When Cincinnati used choice voting to elect its nine-member city council from 1925 to 1955, a cohesive grouping of voters comprising 10 per cent of the electorate could fill a seat. Both major parties pursued the African American vote in efforts to control the council. At least one African American candidate consistently was elected every election, despite the fact that African Americans made up well under 20 per cent of the population. In Peoria, Illinois, where African Americans are one-fifth of the population, African American candidates have won one of five city-wide seats since a proportional plan was adopted before the 1991 elections.

Cumulative voting and limited voting also have been used effectively in nearly two dozen Alabama localities for a decade in the wake of a sweeping decision in a voting rights case. In 1995, then-Texas Governor George W. Bush signed legislation to allow school districts to adopt cumulative voting and limited voting, and more than 50 Texas jurisdictions have now settled voting rights cases with cumulative voting.[5] Indeed, the most dramatic recent example of the impact of PR for minority rights comes from that state. In May 2000, the Amarillo Independent School District for the first time used cumulative voting to fill seats on its school board.[6] African Americans and Latinos in Amarillo together comprise nearly one-quarter of the city's population, but no African American or Latino candidate had won a seat on the school board in decades. The change had an immediate impact. Both an African American candidate and Latino candidate won seats with strong support in their respective communities, and voter turnout more than doubled over the most recent school board election. In 2002, a second Latina candidate won, giving racial minorities three of seven seats. Racial representation had been achieved within two election cycles, nearly overnight by historical standards.

At this point, however, the leadership of minority and voting rights organizations still prefer the tried and true single-member district remedies to minority underrepresentation. Still, as the arrival of more immigrant communities leads to more complex multiracial and ethnic configurations and renders these remedies less effective, PR systems will be a natural solution to explore—especially if basic knowledge of PR becomes more widespread. As advocates of women's representation grow ever more restless with their underrepresentation, they may persuade more groups representing racial minorities to work for PR systems that enhance the opportunities for both women and people of colour.

Lack of knowledge about PR remains a major hurdle. To remedy this, the CVD and a growing number of pro-PR groups at a state level[7] pursue a range of tactics. They regularly circulate information about PR and problems with winner-take-all elections to a great number of university professors, journalists, and civic leaders; many of these in turn incorporate this information into their work and teaching. PR advocates at both a national and grassroots level regularly meet with representatives of organizations and elected officials and make presentations at these groups' conferences and board meetings. More and more groups have taken positions on PR and could be mobilized if and when serious campaigns for PR are ready to be launched. Similarly, sparked by CVD efforts, numerous colleges and universities have adopted PR or IRV for student elections.[8]

The problem is also one of coherence. Democracy in the United States falls short on a variety of measures, many of them pursued by a wide range of dedicated organizations and reformers, each championing their specific reform. Unfortunately, these all-too-often disparate efforts have failed to make significant headway in addressing the considerable failures of American democracy. Holding back progress is the fact that the biggest pro-democracy organizations do not present an overall broad analysis, nor do they promote comprehensive solutions. Instead, groups are defined by a piecemeal agenda of their own particular favourite reforms, the value of which is exaggerated to the point of hyperbole in these groups' efforts to secure more funding and attention.

To counter this, CVD has established a "Democracy USA" initiative designed to build a stronger infrastructure for a pro-democracy movement. If it comes to full fruition, Democracy USA will lead to strong, multi-issue democracy advocates in every state, able to take advantage of local and state opportunities and tap into national resources on a range of democracy issues. As a first step toward building this network, the CVD coordinated a major conference in Washington, DC, in November 2003 in which a wide range of civil rights and electoral reform organizations participated. For PR advocates, a stronger pro-democracy movement in the United States would lift all boats: too often we have not been able to take advantage of a possible opening due to a lack of activist presence on the ground in a particular state. It also would allow more people to evaluate the relative merits of different reforms. Hopefully, more would come to share our conclusion that winner-take-all elections are a fundamental barrier to full-fledged democracy in the United States and that lack of democracy, in turn, is the root cause of a Congress out of touch with the American people and their needs. Hence the absence of adequate health care, a decent quality of life, and a sane foreign policy. The strategy of linking PR to a broader reform movement was partly successful in the early 1900s, when PR was part of the progressive era of reforms of big city government and urban machine politics.

Two states are currently being targeted for a potential breakthrough on PR rather than IRV. With the help of a local foundation, the CVD has invested heavily in building on Illinois's history of cumulative voting for state legislative elections. A range of political leaders in the state support bringing cumulative voting back, including the two most recent governors (both Republican), the chair of the Republican party, the Democratic secretary of state, and the Democratic house majority leader. The legislature was persuaded to pass a bill in 2003 allowing counties to adopt cumulative voting. But the Democratic speaker is not supportive of the idea; hence, to go further, almost certainly a ballot measure would be necessary—a formidable challenge.

In 2004, PR should get a boost of attention in Washington State. Krist Novoselic, who made his name as the bass player for the rock band Nirvana, is a passionate advocate of fair elections. He is running to be Washington's next lieutenant-governor, and his campaign highlights his proposal to elect the state house of representatives by PR—at this point, he is presenting a classic party list proposal of 11-seat state legislative districts. As a neighbour of British Columbia, Washington may learn from what British Columbia's citizens' assembly decides to do on PR. One American variation of the British Columbia approach could be to convene a similar assembly, but using private funds rather than waiting for government action. This assembly's recommendation then would be introduced to voters around the state by civic groups like the League of Women Voters (which has endorsed PR in Washington) before seeking to place the measure on the ballot as a citizen's initiative. Of course, such a strategy is dependent on large financial resources, but there are large donors who can become supportive of reform: one individual in California donated more than $12 million in 2002 to a failed effort to allow voters to register to vote on Election Day.

Winning PR in the United States is indeed a challenge; yet with energy, political smarts, and a little luck, reformers should make significant strides in the coming decade.

Notes

1. See CVD's *Dubious Democracy* report on its website <www.fairvote.org>.

2. In 1995 the *Chicago Tribune* editorialized in support of cumulative voting's return, noting that "[M]any partisans and political independents have looked back wistfully at the era of cumulative voting. They acknowledge that it produced some of the best and brightest in Illinois politics." A bipartisan commission led by two of the most prominent members of the major parties, one a former federal judge and Democratic congressman and the other the recent Republican governor, in 2001 recommended return of cumulative voting for these arguments.

3. Organizational backers included the Sierra Club, Democratic Party, San Francisco Labor Council (AFL-CIO), Common Cause, National Organization for Women, Congress of California Seniors, Chinese for Affirmative Action, Harvey Milk GLBT Democratic Club, Latino Democratic Club, Green Party, *San Francisco Bay Guardian* weekly newspaper, and California Public Interest Research Group.

4. State-by-state measurements of competitiveness, voter turnout, effectiveness of votes, representation of women and racial minorities, and the relationship of votes cast for parties and seats won by parties are available for House elections since 1982 on the CVD's website (www.fairvote.org) in its *Dubious Democracy* report.

5. In 1998, a task force of the National Black Caucus of State Legislators found strong interest among African American legislators in seeing how PR might assist negotiations in redistricting. The National Conference of Black Political Scientists endorsed PR in 1999.

6. Cumulative voting was instituted to settle a voting rights lawsuit involving the Mexican American Legal Defense and Education Fund, the League of United Latin American Citizens, and the National Association for the Advancement of Colored People (NAACP).

7. These include Fair Vote Massachusetts, Fair Vote Minnesota, Midwest Democracy Center of Illinois, and Californians for Electoral Reform.

8. In at least two cases, at the University of California at Davis and the University of Illinois, PR was approved overwhelmingly in ballot measures by students.

PART III

The Provinces Show the Way: Progress toward Reforming the Electoral System in Canada

Electoral Reform and Deliberative Democracy: The British Columbia Citizens' Assembly

Norman J. Ruff

British Columbia today is undergoing its own quiet democratic revolution. The Liberal government of Gordon Campbell has introduced several significant parliamentary reforms. These include a regular annual calendar for spring and fall sittings of the Legislative Assembly, a fixed date for the annual presentation of the provincial budget to the Assembly, free votes by members, the institutionalization of government caucus committees, and, in the most innovative change implemented thus far, fixed general election dates on a four-year cycle from May 2001.

Important as these are, the most innovative and potentially most momentous component of the BC government's penchant for political reform emerged in its "New Era" election platform commitment for a review of the voting system. We do not yet know whether the outcome of this review will be the status quo or a recommended replacement for the single-member-plurality (SMP) electoral system, and, even then, whether the proposed replacement would be accepted in a referendum vote by a clear majority of British Columbians. Yet the manner of the review by a "citizen's assembly" made up of randomly selected provincial residents deciding what, if anything, to bring before a referendum is one of the most novel and ambitious innovations in deliberative democracy ever undertaken in Canada and a remarkable endeavour in itself. In his April 28, 2003 announcement on the launch of the citizens' assembly, the premier asserted both the importance of ensuring "strong public support in adopting any new model" and his belief that the results of the effort would be "the restoration of trust in our public institutions."

Origins

The BC Liberal government takes very seriously its responsibility to fulfill all of its electoral commitments in the 2001 election "New Era" party platform. An April 2003 count claimed implementation of 180 out of 201 items. They included the promises to:

- appoint a Citizens' Assembly on Electoral Reform to assess all possible models for electing members of the Legislative Assembly (MLAs), including preferential ballots, proportional representation (PR), and our current electoral system; and
- give the Citizens' Assembly a mandate to hold public hearings throughout BC; if it recommends changing the current electoral system, that option will be put to a province-wide referendum at the time of the next general election in May 2005.

Gordon Campbell had first unveiled this agenda at the BC Liberal Party's April 1999 Kelowna convention as part of his full governmental reform package. In his convention speech, the then opposition leader argued, "Democracies should be designed by the people, not for power brokers" and that "It's time we gave the people of BC the right to determine how they want to elect their MLAs." This concept resonated with the populist elements absorbed by the BC Liberal Party from BC Reform, which had earlier proposed such a randomly selected citizens' group before the 1997-98 BC Canadian Unity Panel review on the 1997 Calgary Declaration. As Attorney General Geoff Plant later reiterated in closing the April 30 2003 legislative debate on Motion 99 for the creation of the citizens' assembly, the idea of the assembly was motivated by the notion that since all politicians were considered suspect on the subject of electoral reform, it was necessary to take them out of the process.[1]

The BC Liberals' defeat in the May 28, 1996 provincial general election where they secured six less seats than the New Democratic Party (NDP) despite obtaining 37,534 more votes could not help but awaken their interest in electoral reform. In large part, however, it was the lobbying efforts of the advocacy group Fair Voting BC and its forerunner, the Electoral Change Coalition of British Columbia (ECCO-BC) that helped secure the Liberal party's platform promise. The electoral reform web that has now come to envelop political debates in the province was initially spun by ECCO-BC. Emerging from discussions first held in April 1997, the coalition was publicly launched in October 1997 with the twin goals of informing British Columbians about the range of alternative electoral systems and to lobby the provincial government to hold a binding referendum on the voting system. During its first year, the Coalition used an on-line petition to the Legislative Assembly to ·mobilize support for a provincial referendum on alternate electoral systems. Its September 1998 "Toward a New Democracy" Conference gathered together members of a broad political coalition that cut across the full spectrum of the province's politics. ECCO-BC's honourary directors included former MLA and Social Credit caucus chair Nick Loenen, former Social Credit cabinet minister and influential broadcaster Rafe Mair, Vancouver City Councillor Nancy Chiavario, Paul George of the Western Wilderness Committee, Reform Party of Canada MP Ted White, and leader of the BC Reform Party Wilf Hanni. Along with Green Party leader Stuart Parker and college mathematics professor Julian West, the BC director of the Canadian Taxpayers Federation, Troy Lanigan, played a central role as president. The Progressive Democratic Alliance, the BC Progressive Conservative Party (PC), the Marxist-Leninist Party, the BC Family Coalition, and Canadians for Direct Democracy were also represented in its board.

Though the two main parties were not part of ECCO-BC, BC Liberal Party executive director Kelly Reichert attended the coalition's launch, and, at that time, Gordon Campbell indicated his support for a referendum vote, though he insisted that residents, not politicians, should initiate change. Within four years (following endorsements from the BC Reform's breakaway Unity Party and, more belatedly, the BC NDP) all of the province's political parties were on side with the ECCO-BC objectives. The parallel organization, Fair Voting BC, emerged in October 1998 out of organizing efforts by Nick Loenen. It was a citizens' lobby group seeking political and legislative reform through the advocacy of a more proportional voting system to be achieved by referendum. With John Vegt, a Surrey chartered accountant as president, its more notable supporters included environmentalist David Suzuki, Vancouver developer Andre Molnar, and former NDP cabinet minister Norman Levi. The two complementary organizations provided joint sponsorship for a seminal "Making Votes Count" Vancouver conference in May 2000. The event contributed to public awareness of the electoral reform issue, but more importantly demonstrated to the provincial parties a real momentum behind a growing network of reformers.

The idea of a citizens' assembly as a vehicle of electoral reform was itself further advanced by a self-appointed, ad hoc constitutional reform group formed in November 1999. It was composed of four former MLAs—Loenen;

senior Fraser Institute fellow and former BC Liberal leader, Gordon Gibson; and former NDP cabinet minister Gary Lauk — who were brought together by Rafe Mair (assisted by Mel Smith, a former BC government constitutional advisor). In a February 2001 critique of the "control structure of government," they proposed that a citizens' assembly be mandated by the provincial legislature to consult British Columbians on improvements in the machinery of government, which, after being put to a referendum vote, would become the core element of the constitution of the province. Its mandate would include electoral reforms along with responsible and representative government, parliamentary reforms, direct democracy, the executive-legislative balance of power, the role and powers of the MLA, and transparency and freedom of information. Chaired by a commissioner of reform appointed as an officer of the legislature with a ten-year term, the proposed assembly would consist of 79 members elected from each provincial constituency, who would name an additional 21 members (seven from each of three regions — coast, interior, and Lower Mainland) to supply additional experience, expertise, or representation of interests.[2]

The strong support of Liberal leader Campbell left little doubt that the Citizens' Assembly would proceed after Campbell became premier with his party's lopsided May 2001 election victory. With 57.62 per cent of the vote, they secured all but two of the Legislature's 79 seats. The NDP had been reduced to a two-member rump with 21.56 per cent of the vote, and the Green Party's record 12.39 per cent secured it no seats. Green Party leader Adriane Carr upped the ante when she announced right after the vote that the party would use the BC Recall and Initiative Act to launch a citizens' initiative in favour of PR. The initiative proposed a New Zealand-style mixed-member proportional (MMP) electoral system, christened "Pro Rep," and drew New Zealand Green MP, Rod Donald, one of the main architects of MMP in that country, to an April 2002 province-wide tour in its support. Despite strong canvassing efforts in areas of Green Party strength in the Kootenays, Sunshine Coast, Vancouver Island, and the Okanagan, with 98,165 signatures, the initiative fell well short of the total 212,473 signatures required. It was criticized by some who favoured reform as a covert Green Party organizational drive that risked muddying the water for any subsequent non-partisan consideration of the MMP option. Nevertheless, the 90-day initiative campaign did keep electoral reform in the public eye and maintained pressure on the new BC Liberal government to deliver on its "New Era" platform commitment. And the mobilization of 4,000 canvassers had also recruited new activists for an increasingly visible social movement for provincial electoral reform.

For their part, in their twilight days of government, the BC NDP saw the light when the party's June 1999 convention narrowly approved a pro-PR resolution. It called on the "BC NDP to appoint a competent body to review the electoral process with a view to making recommendations on how the process might be improved with specific reference to the incorporation of proportional representation." A nine-member party review committee was appointed in the summer of 2000 and one year later presented a comprehensive discussion paper, "Reform of BC's Electoral System: An Idea Whose Time Has Come," which recommended an MMP system for BC and federal elections. It urged the party to endorse and campaign vigorously for that principle and recommended a government commission be set up to enable the legislature to debate alternative reforms and put a reform option or set of options to a referendum. Consequently, in March 2002, the new party leader, Joy MacPhail, urged the premier to proceed in such a manner so that a new system could be put in place for the May 17, 2005 provincial general election.

Shaping the Reform Process

While the new premier supported a jury-style citizens' assembly to carry out an electoral system review, the idea began to take concrete form only in September 2002 with the appointment of Gordon Gibson to delve into the specific framework that would be required. Shortly before Christmas that year, Gibson submitted a meticulous review of a strategy for the appointment, structure, and mandate for the Citizens' Assembly (*Report On the Constitution of the Citizens' Assembly*). He explored three methods to tackle the central issues in assembly selection: self-screening, screening by "Eminent Persons,"[3] and peer selection. Among the 36 recommendations was the proposal that this latter method, in which a meeting of randomly selected individuals grouped from four ridings would select representatives from amongst themselves (with the possibility of adding four members if necessary to improve representativeness), be adopted. (Gibson argued that electoral districts were an appropriate geographic unit rather than a province-wide or regional base on the grounds that they represented a settled political compromise between urban and rural BC.)

This comprehensive framework made its way through government caucus and cabinet meetings during the spring, and the government tabled its intentions in the Legislative Assembly on April 28, 2003. Unanimously approved two days later, the terms of reference accepted the Gibson approach with some modifications. Instead of a 79-member assembly with one member from each constituency, the government doubled the number to 158 members (plus a non-voting chair),[4] with the final membership selection from the initial random draw of citizens also drawn at random rather than by peer selection. The proposed budget was correspondingly increased from $4.5 to $5.5 million. An unexpected addendum required a super majority if matters advanced to a referendum. Though not set out in the cabinet-approved terms of reference, the premier's April 28 announcement asserted that in the event of a referendum vote, a new electoral model would have to receive "60 per cent of overall voter approval as well as approval in 60 per cent of the province's electoral districts." Justified as standard municipal government practice, the measure was generally regarded as a political concession to nervous cabinet partisans of the electoral status quo, as was the premier's ambiguous assurance that "It is critical that any system be designed to meet the needs of BC and meet the needs of all British Columbians in all the regions of the province. However, we do not wish to have the pursuit of the perfect drive out the good."[5]

The Electoral Reform Framework

TERMS OF REFERENCE

The terms of reference for the Citizens' Assembly mandate[6] it to "assess models for electing Members of the Legislative Assembly and issue a report recommending whether the current model for these elections should be retained or another model should be adopted." That assessment is "limited to the manner by which voters' ballots are translated into seats in the Legislative Assembly" and must "take into account the potential effect of its recommended model on the system of government in British Columbia." Any new model recommended by the Citizens' Assembly is to be "consistent with both the Constitution of Canada and the Westminster parliamentary system" and "be described clearly and in detail in its report." Its final report is due to be presented to the attorney general by no later than December 15, 2004, for tabling in the Legislature. If it recommends against retention of the current system, it must present a single replacement to be placed before the citizens in a referendum to be held simultaneously with the May 17, 2005 provincial general election.

STRUCTURE OF THE CITIZENS' ASSEMBLY

The nomination of Jack Blaney, chair of the Fraser Basin Council and former president of Simon Fraser University, as chair of the Citizens' Assembly was endorsed in May 2003 by a special Legislative Committee on Electoral Reform. This all-party (six Liberal, one NDP) committee receives interim reports from the chair as well as overseeing the selection of its chief operating officer, chief research officer, and director of communication.[7] The chair is a non-voting member of the Citizens' Assembly except on a tie and may appoint up to four vice-chairs to provide regional backup at sub-panels and public hearings. Decisions of the Citizens' Assembly are to be by simple majority, but a two-thirds majority will be required should circumstances arise where it might wish to expel a member for cause.

The Citizens' Assembly fully embodied the commitment to keep the process out of the hands of politicians with vested interests. Members or officers of the Canadian Parliament or the Privy Council of Canada, members or officers of the provincial Legislature or the Executive Council, and elected members of a local government (including a school or park board) were made ineligible. So too were candidates in the last two federal, provincial, municipal, or regional district elections or by-elections or their official representatives or agents, and immediate family members of a sitting MLA.[8]

The selection of members was intended to be as random as possible within a three-tier process. An initial invitation to participate from the chair of the Citizens' Assembly asked the recipient "to consider doing something very special for British Columbia." This was sent to a sample (prepared by Elections BC) of 15,800 people from the BC voters' list (200 per electoral district) stratified by gender and age to ensure equal numbers of men and women and a reflection of the province's age distribution of those 18 years and over.[9] From those who accepted their invitation to take part in the Citizens' Assembly, ten men and ten women per district were to be randomly selected and invited to attend their regional selection meetings held in 26 locations around the province. Low positive responses to the first sampling (1,181 positive responses and 596 acceptances to attend the regional meetings) led to another 10,000 randomly selected invitations.[10]

After a presentation on the Citizens' Assembly's organization and what was expected of members, each regional meeting held a roll call to confirm the continuing interest of those attending and (in a fine-tuning of the terms of reference) proceeded to a final selection for each district by a separate drawing from a hat of the names of one man and one woman. Though there were shortfalls from the targets of 20 would-be members per district, at least two of each gender was deemed sufficient to proceed with a selection and ensure a reserve backup. Those who did attend the regional selection meetings proved to be highly enthusiastic participants and at times tearful "losers." Much of that enthusiasm appeared to stem from the opportunity for public participation and exercise of a civic responsibility rather than any particular zeal for electoral reform. Though scheduled to be completed by November 25, 2003, the one hundred and fifty-eighth selection was made on December 8.

The self-screening element unavoidably qualified the randomness of the selection process. There are obvious social biases inherent in a person's willingness or ability to become a member. Not unexpectedly, the under-24 age group was underrepresented, and membership was skewed toward the 40 to 70 age groups, particularly for women. Nevertheless, with one major exception, the overall profile of the original 158 members was a credible microcosm of BC voters.[11] Since no First Nations members emerged "from the hat" at the local selections, the provincial cabinet gave the Citizens' Assembly chair permission in mid-December to add two chosen from among the names of First Nation voters who had made it through to the final random pool of potential members.[12] The now 160-member assembly formally commenced its sessions in January 2004, with members receiving reimbursement for their expenses and childcare assistance as well as an honorarium of $150 per sitting day.

TIMETABLE

The Citizens' Assembly's timetable follows the path sketched in Gordon Gibson's report, beginning with a learning phase (January 10-March 21), followed by a hearing phase (May-June), and, finally, a deliberation phase (September-November). The first phase took place over six alternate weekends at the Morris J. Wosk Centre for Dialogue in Vancouver. The plenary presentations supplemented by small-group discussions first established procedural guidelines as to how the members would work together. Along with assigned background readings, the research officers took the members through a discussion of values and the main system options as well as the issues in implementation of electoral reform with some emphasis on its impact on the workings of political parties and parliamentary government. They surveyed majority and plurality systems and then PR, single transferable vote (STV), and mixed systems.[13]

Phase two—the May-June public hearing phase—is to centre on consideration of public submissions made to 49 hearings scheduled for regional centres throughout the province; these hearings will be attended by four to ten Citizens' Assembly members with some overlapping, inter-regional participation. (The Citizens' Assembly office accepted submissions from the outset of its work in 2003, and all electronic submissions are viewable on its website.) This phase will conclude with a special meeting in Prince George to review the results of the hearings before a two-month summer break. The Citizens' Assembly is to allow a selected number of special presentations at full plenary sessions, September 11-12 before entering its ultimate delibera- tion phase with Vancouver meetings on alternate weekends from September to November. This timetable allows several weeks to prepare recommenda- tions due to be delivered to the attorney general by December 15, 2004. The Citizens' Assembly and its office support disband at year end.

This BC experiment in deliberative democracy is doubly unique in leaving no room for government discretion in its outcome. The Citizens' Assembly's report will be published by the chair on presentation of the final version to the attorney general for tabling in the Legislature and its proposed reform model—if there is one—will be put to voters. This would trigger a fourth post-Citizens' Assembly campaign phase in the mobilization of public support and opposition for the proposed replacement of FPTP leading up to the May 17, 2005 referendum.

Prospects

The Citizens' Assembly's contribution will consist not only of its recommen- dations on the future of the province's electoral system but also its ability to engage British Columbians in a public deliberation on the nature of their rep- resentative democracy.[14] Both electoral reform and the establishment of the Citizens' Assembly express the goal of enhancing the articulation of shared democratic principles.

It is foolhardy to predict in advance the internal dynamics of the 160- member assembly, the tone of its 2004 public hearing stage, or, consequently, which electoral model is most likely to emerge as a favoured replacement, if any, for the existing system. Yet it is fair to suggest that a shared sense of the historic significance, its "once-in-a-lifetime experience," and the opportunity for public service could generate a strong impetus for arriving at some kind of electoral reform. If so, we could see not only a consensus for change but also some unequivocal direction toward a single replacement. If legitimated in this way, it is not unreasonable to envisage public support for a Citizens' Assembly-endorsed replacement that could cross the 60 per cent threshold of support in the May 17, 2005 referendum.

Yet it could be difficult to agree on which electoral system should replace FPTP. Three options seem the most likely to emerge as the main contenders from the wide array of possible systems: preferential alternative vote (AV),

STV, and MMP. Some memory of the province's flirtation in the early 1950s with AV still permeates electoral system discussions, while the 2002 initiative campaign raised awareness of MMP. While the pioneering reform advocacy groups of the late 1990s avoided any declared preference, their leading and energetic spokesperson, Nick Loenen, has eloquently written in favour of STV. The FPTP status quo will naturally have its own defenders against all three.

As noted, electoral system reform is not entirely new to the BC political agenda (see Pilon 2000). Although today only those aged 72 years of age and older would have voted under AV in the 1952 and 1953 general elections, that experience remains a significant point of reference in any discussion of electoral options. AV requires that elected representatives obtain a majority of the votes cast in a single-member district with voters ranking their choices among the candidates. It had been adopted by the Conservative PC and Liberal partners in the 1941-51 BC coalition government for much the same reasons as in Australia—to permit the transfer of mutual voting support against a candidate of the left.[15] The Cooperative Commonwealth Federation (CCF, precursor to the NDP), which received 35 per cent of the BC vote in 1949, was contained with 31 per cent on the 1952 AV first count vote. The rise of an anti-coalition, populist protest vote in support of Social Credit, however, also undermined the system dynamic that was expected to favour the two old parties. The Social Credit party obtained 27 per cent of the vote, 27,463 less than the CCF, but, with one seat more, was able to form a minority Social Credit government. In the 1953 election, the characteristic AV bias against the now smaller Conservative PC and Liberal parties enabled Social Credit to consolidate its position as the governing party (see Elkins 1976). Having served its fundamental purpose, AV was promptly abandoned and FPTP restored. Nevertheless, 50 years later, it retains something of the aura of a familiar electoral option for some British Columbians along with two serious common misperceptions about it—that it is a form of PR and/or could assure that governments would be supported by a majority of the total vote.

Since BC's 1952-53 system is commonly referred to as a transferable vote, it has at times been erroneously confused with the more proportional STV, despite the fundamental difference in outcomes due to AV's single-member in contrast with STV's multi-member districts. Though less celebrated or remembered, STV is in fact also part of the BC electoral experience. As the preferred system of earlier reformers, STV achieved a modest, short-lived success when it emerged as a municipal option in the wake of the 1916 BC Liberal populist reforms. Five municipal councils initially adopted STV, followed by South Vancouver, Vancouver, and Victoria after local plebiscites. The impetus behind these experiments could not be sustained, however, and STV lasted for just one election in Victoria and three in Vancouver.

Overall, if there is to be change, the odds favour a form of MMP being selected in BC as it may be in other provinces. Nevertheless, in BC, STV has remained an important option in the contemporary debate. Compared to the level of party control under MMP and other systems, STV promises greater direct voter influence, a promise with resonance in the BC political scene, as indicated by the fact that in BC, unlike elsewhere in Canada, sitting members can be recalled by their electors. As noted, STV has also long been the personal preference of the province's most prominent proponent of electoral reform. Nick Loenen (1997) originally proposed an STV system with 15 districts varying in magnitude from three to ten members, and restated his position in a background paper for the 2001 ad hoc committee on the BC Constitution. At a November 2001 Fraser Institute conference, Loenen again maintained that if proportionality, choice, stable government, local representation and less party discipline were the shared objectives, then STV would be the preferred system (Loenen 2003a). In his brief to the Citizens' Assembly, (Loenen 2003b) put forth a somewhat different model, a mixed system christened "Preferential-Plus." This envisaged retention of a 79-seat Legislative Assembly with the possibility of the AV in nine of the existing more rural, single-member electoral districts and 14 STV multi-member districts each incorporating three to seven seats.[16]

Though designed to meet BC's particular geographic and political context, this hybrid is reminiscent of the 86-year-old recommendations of the first Speaker's Conference on Electoral Reform in the UK in 1917. This would have introduced STV for Britain's urban boroughs with three or more members and AV for the other less urban constituencies.[17] Coincidently, that particular mixture also attracted the personal attention of Lord Jenkins, chair of the 1997 UK Independent Commission on the Voting System. Its attraction lay in preserving links with a single representative in areas where this probably had more meaning while introducing some proportionality and more boundary stability in big cities where such links were less of an issue. Ultimately, however, the commission backed away from this hybrid, partly since it thought it would be difficult to explain convincingly and partly because it would have been unfair to the Labour party in particular.[18] This concern could perhaps also enter the BC debate; in any case, the continuity and echoes of "Preferential Plus" with earlier deliberations are a reminder that the issues and options in electoral reform do not come to us *de novo*.

In the wake of New Zealand's 1993 adaptation of the German MMP
electoral system, which was followed in turn by the Scottish Parliament and
Welsh Assembly, MMP appears to have overtaken STV as today's reform
system of choice (Shugart and Wattenberg 2001). As it gains even more
familiarity, MMP will gain favour over FPTP. Nevertheless, its possible
impact on regional representation from what have become paternalistically
termed the "heartlands" will continue to be a major concern. It is likely that a
more refined version than BC Green's design, one which can offer a "made-
for-BC" adaptation of some of the regional features of the German and
Scottish models, including perhaps a preferential, open party list vote, may
prove necessary to muster Citizens' Assembly and voter support.

The likely consequences and advantages and disadvantages of each
electoral model have come to be well known to the members of the Citizens'
Assembly. Much of its direction will depend on which underlying democratic
values are agreed upon by its members and how much weight they attach to
them. As noted above, if any distinctively BC preoccupation can be anticipated, it may lie in a regional divide between the North and Interior and the
Lower Mainland. Although this could emerge as the crucial cleavage in the
choice of an alternative to FPTP, it takes place in the context of continuous
interaction among the 160 members over 12 months. Some observers of the
practice of deliberative democracy raise cautions about the nefarious impact
of social inequalities and personal power relations on what are intended to be
open deliberations among equals. These could also play a critical role in shaping the outcome.

In the March 21, 2004 preliminary statement issued at the end of phase one,
the Citizens' Assembly refrained from making any unequivocal commitment
to electoral reform. It asserted that they would not want to abandon FPTP
unless it was clear that "the system had deficiencies that detracted from the
evolution and maintenance of healthy democratic politics in the province"
and that they were convinced there was an alternative that spoke to those
deficiencies (Citizens' Assembly 2004). Nevertheless, after careful synopses
of the strengths and weaknesses of the current system and the defining values
of electoral systems, the statement appeared to take on a reformist tone. In
asking for submissions, the Citizens' Assembly said it wanted to hear if British
Columbians shared its conviction about the importance of effective local representation and if they agreed with it that a more proportional system would
better reflect their basic values.

The BC Citizens' Assembly is as much a bold experiment in deliberative
democracy as an instrument of electoral system review. Even if that review

unadventurously opts for maintenance of the electoral status quo, reformers may be able to take some consolation from the workings of the Citizens' Assembly as a laboratory for the power of public dialogue and as another possible path toward democratic renewal.

Notes

1. BC, it should be noted, had experienced politically motivated voting reform when the BC government implemented the preferential ballot for the 1952 election to keep the CCF, forerunner of the NDP, out of power. See below.

2. A Report on the Need for Certain Constitutional Change in British Columbia and a Mechanism for Developing Specific Proposals, reproduced in Gibson 2003.

3. Under self-screening, the first person randomly selected from a stratified random sample to accept (after their consideration of such issues as the time commitment and complexity of the work) would become a member; screening by "Eminent Persons" consists of a larger random selection of five or six times the required number of candidates who would be asked to fill out a questionnaire to assist an assessor in gauging their suitability.

4. It was thus hoped that the selection of two members per district would obviate the need for any top-up. Joy MacPhail unsuccessfully attempted to revive this option, but the newly appointed assembly chair later indicated that he would be prepared to approach the attorney general should there be any glaring underrepresentation.

5. Premier Gordon Campbell, "Announcement of the Citizens' Assembly," (April 28, 2003).

6. Citizens' Assembly on Electoral Reform Terms of Reference, British Columbia, Order in Council 495 (May 16, 2003).

7. Appointed were Leo Perra, former president of Selkirk College, Castlegar, as chief operating officer, UBC political scientist Ken Carty as chief research officer. Marilyn Jacobson was named communication director after the first appointment was rescinded when the individual was identified as a former director-at-large of the BC Green Party.

8. Also excluded are current officers or official representatives of a registered provincial party, elected chiefs and band councillors under the Indian Act, and elected members of the Nisga'a Lisims Government along with non-Canadian citizens, under 18-year-olds, and judges, justices, or court referees. Members were expected to be "fully fluent in English" and to remain BC residents for the life of the Assembly to December 2004.

9. Since it was estimated that the number of registered voters fell short by up to 800,000 of the eligible population (with particular under representation of 18- to 24-year-old youth), a "Make Your Mark" campaign was launched to publicize the formation of the Citizens' Assembly and to improve the scope of the voters' list population before an August 22 deadline for the first random sampling.

10. The problem was that just 5 per cent responded positively from the first 6,600 letters of invitation for the 33 northern districts. Seven per cent of those letters were returned as undeliverable.

11. Profiles of all 160 are available at <http://www.citizenassembly.bc.ca/>, together with detailed information on the progress of the Citizens' Assembly.

12. Both December 22 additions were members of the Nisga'a Nation—Jacki Tait from Gitwinksihikw and Ron Walberg who resides in Abbotsford.

13. On Weekend Five, they heard from Professors David Farrell (University of Manchester, England) and Elizabeth McLeay (Victoria University of Wellington, New Zealand).

14. This is in part recognized in the Citizens' Assembly's sponsorship of an attitudinal study by University of Montreal political scientist André Blais that will trace some of the internal dynamics of the process over the 11 months of interactions among its 160 members.

15. The BC formulation retained the existing dual and three-member districts in Vancouver and Victoria but passed up the opportunity to introduce an element of PR and limited the vote to separate ballot papers for each of their component seats.

16. This model also received support in the submission by Fair Voting president John Vegt in January 2004.

17. *Conference on Electoral Reform: Letter from Mr Speaker to the Prime Minister*, Cd 8463, 1917.

18. United Kingdom, *The Report of the Independent Commission on the Voting System*, (Jenkins Report) October, 1998, Cm 4090-1, paras 102-106.

CHAPTER 12

The Uncertain Path of Democratic Renewal in Ontario

Dennis Pilon

Introduction

The victory of Dalton McGuinty's Liberal party over the governing
Progressive Conservatives (PCs) in the October 2003 Ontario provincial
election opened the door to a potential reform of the province's traditional
first-past-the-post (FPTP) voting system. Though little discussed during
the election itself, a Liberal policy document prepared well in advance of the
contest promised a "full, open public debate on voting reform" from a Liberal
government, possibly culminating in a referendum between the status quo and
"some form of proportional representation, preferential ballots or mixed system"[1] Nor is the Liberals' the only voice that has been talking about reform.
Both the provincial New Democratic Party (NDP) and Greens went into the
election with a more specific policy commitment for proportional representation (PR) in particular, though they also endorsed a public referendum as the
appropriate mechanism of change.[2] After the election the new premier wasted
little time in following up on his party's reform commitments, announcing
on the same day as his cabinet appointments the formation of a Democratic
Renewal Secretariat. Headed by the new attorney general, Michael Bryant,
who is on record as fairly sympathetic to proportional voting, the secretariat is
charged with taking up a host of potential democratic reforms, including fixed
election dates, campaign finance reforms, an increased role for backbenchers,
and internet voting. However, as its press release of October 23 put it, heading the list of tasks for the new body is "spearheading a public consultation
and referendum on Ontario's voting system."

The remarkable progress of voting system reform as a public issue in
Ontario recently—from being nowhere on the political radar screen less

than a decade ago to having multi-party support and a government-promised referendum on the question today—is both breathtaking and a bit bewildering. Observers, understandably, have been rather surprised that the Liberals, historically always one of the two main parties in the province and, as such, potential beneficiaries of the majority-inflating FPTP-system, have raised the issue of voting system reform from obscurity to government policy.[3] Indeed, despite the headlines touting the Liberal landslide at the polls, the current government's impressive legislative majority rests on a minority of the popular vote (46 per cent of the total). Bringing to the attention of the voters such anomalies in their current voting system could rebound on the Liberals in unpredictable ways, not only possibly denying them a future turn as a single-party majority government, but even casting doubt on the legitimacy of their present "majority." Clearly, the emergence of voting system reform as a political issue for two of Ontario's three major parties—one of which is presently ensconced in government and in a position to do something about it—requires some explanation.[4]

As we shall see, the arrival of voting system reform on the political agenda in Ontario is primarily a story of debate and strategy within parties, though public policy think-tanks and civil society organizations have both been influential. This chapter explores this process, looks at the proposals for public involvement and ratification that each party is supporting, and, finally, addresses the likelihood of a voting system reform actually coming to be implemented.

The Political Parties, Civil Society, and Voting System Reform

There have long been political parties in Ontario espousing some form of PR. The Greens have consistently campaigned for the German-style mixed approach to PR, in line with the system they believe helped facilitate the breakthrough of green politics there, though recently they've expressed interest in the Irish single transferable vote (STV) form of PR as well. And a host of minor parties—the Family Coalition party, the Freedom party, the Communist party—have also endorsed PR, partially out of principle but mostly out of desperation to secure some representation. Until recently, however, none of the three main legislative parties in Ontario expressed much interest in the topic, dismissing it as the concern of "losers" and "cranks" or simply ignoring it altogether. Even Ontario's traditional third party, the NDP, showed little interest in reforming the voting system, despite over half a century of chronic underrepresentation under the existing rules. In fact, since the consolidation of the modern party system in the province into a three-way battle among the PCs, Liberals and Cooperative Commonwealth Federation (CCF, the precursor to the NDP) in 1943, the question of altering the voting rules had never arisen.

The consensus in favour of the status quo began to break down with the dramatic defeat of the one-term NDP government in 1995. The following year, NDP Member of the Provincial Parliament (MPP) Tony Silipo sponsored a private member's bill to have the legislature consider PR. Though his bill went nowhere, it signalled a sharp turn in the party's thinking about voting systems.[5] After the 1944 victory for the Saskatchewan CCF, the social democratic left in Canada, like their counterparts in the UK, became staunch defenders of FPTP. Their thinking was simply that the traditional system, with its tendency to overrepresent the largest vote-getter, would eventually work in favour of the left, giving them the stable majority governing power that their adversaries had long enjoyed, which they would use to facilitate the quick passage of government policy. Efforts over the years to shift the party's position on this issue elicited hostile responses. Ed Broadbent's attempts to gain party support for a plan that would add a mild element of proportionality to the federal voting system in 1981 mobilized provincial party activists across the country against him. Delegates from Ontario no less than BC, Saskatchewan, and Manitoba voted against his motion at the 1981 convention, defeating it decisively. Efforts to add consideration of PR to the party's constitutional debates at the 1991 federal convention were also rejected. With the then-recent historic triumph of the NDP in Ontario, and the expectation of provincial party victories across the West, party elites and activists were in no mood to talk about changing the rules of the electoral game now that they appeared to be tilting in their favour.

But a great deal changed in just a few years. The crushing defeat for the federal party in 1993, followed by the Ontario party's fall from government to third place in the provincial contest of 1995, fueled a process of soul-searching on the part of both elites and activists in the NDP. Soon talk of voting system reform began emerging from all sides of the party—from left to the right, from elites to the grassroots. Silipo's efforts in the legislature and caucus were mirrored by activists at constituency meetings, the provincial council of the party, and conventions. However, the new interest in voting rules had many different—and sometimes conflicting—motivations. Voting system reform did not arise in the NDP at this time simply because the party suffered underrepresentation in 1995. A poor match between the party's vote and their seat count had long been the case, barring the exception that brought it to power in 1990. Instead, the sudden consensus around PR in the party reflected a deeper crisis in the historical trajectory of social democracy, one that left-wing parties were struggling with the world over.

After much discussion and expert consultation throughout 1996 and 1997, the Ontario NDP adopted PR as party policy at their provincial convention in 1998, though without much evident enthusiasm. As with the federal party's adoption of a similar position around the same time, the decision represented a profound break with the party's historic mission to replace the Liberals as the main alternative governing party. For some, particularly on the party's right-wing, accepting PR was simply a pragmatic recognition that the NDP's strategy had largely failed and that even when it did win power, as recent experience in Ontario demonstrated, it was constantly hobbled from carrying out its own goals by the media, which harped on its lacking majority popular support, as well as its own unwieldy coalition of supporters. Instead, these proponents felt the party should fight for PR so that the NDP could seek as much power as it could muster from the electorate and deny the other parties exclusive control of government if they could, perhaps even joining in coalitions. Indeed, they saw working in coalition as possibly also helping to discipline party activists and temper attacks from the media (Institute on Governance 1998). But the convention victory for PR was not fueled solely by pragmatism and strategic self-interest. It won with the support of a wide swathe of party activists as well, bringing together members keen on reforming democratic institutions, right-wing populists of the Harris PCs and the Reform/Alliance Party, with those working to further equity, consensus-style decision-making, and the representation of women and minority members of the party's Socialist Caucus. Still, the party's commitment to the issue remained weak, especially among elites. Neither the provincial nor federal party campaigned on voting system reform in the 1999 and 2000 elections. In fact, the issue was barely mentioned.

If traditional elites in the NDP were hedging their bets on voting reform, appeasing those keen on the issue while hoping that some return to normalcy in terms of voter support would effectively sideline it, they must have been sorely disappointed by the election results in 1999 and 2000. Support for the provincial party sank to new lows while the federal wing suffered a reversal from its modest recovery in 1997. Clearly, there would be no simple restoration of party fortunes. With the party resigned now to perennial third-party status, PR supporters gained the upper hand. In fact, in a host of forums over the next few years concerned with the future direction of the party, a commitment to voting system reform, specifically some form of PR, was often the sole point of consensus.[6] Bolstered by MP Lorne Nystrom's energetic promotion of the issue at the federal level, activists in Ontario began pressing for clearer party policy on the reform and more active promotion of a distinctive NDP plan for change. Delegates to the 2000 Ontario provincial convention voted to create a task force to sound out NDP views on the issue, specifically to come to some agreement about what form of PR should be supported and what process should be used to implement it.

Though announced with much fanfare by party leader Howard Hampton in February 2002 as an exercise in democracy itself, the task force had to grapple with many of the lingering doubts within the party about PR, particularly from those concerned about geographical representation and the role of the MPP.[7] In the end, it endorsed the German and New Zealand mixed model of PR precisely because it would retain a local link for MPPs in single-member ridings and lead to proportional results for parties via a top-up party list. The report also recommended taking the issue to the public in a binding referendum. Though generally critical of referendums, party members appeared willing to support one on the question of voting system reform, though only if it were preceded by a thorough public education process on the issue.[8] The task force report passed easily at the provincial convention in June 2002.

As the Liberals would also do, the NDP took up voting system reform as one of a number of policy commitments designed to make clear its commitment to strengthening democracy in Ontario. But here the issue also has strong roots in the party and, particularly after 1999, greater commitment from its leadership to see it enacted. More or less resigned now to their place as the province's third party, the NDP is keen for a more proportional voting system to better their legislative representation and heighten their influence on policy, inside or outside coalition governments. But PR also gained support within the party as a populist alternative to the democratic reforms of the right, as a means of furthering left-wing issues in the party, and from activists keen to further the representation of women and minorities in the legislative arena. The issue's coming to the fore also reflected the current crisis of social democracy and effective stalemate within the NDP over its future direction. In the absence of any clear consensus, either toward a Blairite "third way" or in support of a more radical anti-globalization stance, the commitment to PR represented a frank recognition that no one group appeared to have the answers.

The Ontario Liberals came to the issue of voting system reform later than the NDP and approached the question only as part of a much larger policy renewal process sparked by their loss to the PCs in the 1999 provincial election. Stung by criticism during the contest that the party had no real concrete plans for governing, the Liberals immediately set out after the election to rebuild their policy profile. Directed chiefly by party leader Dalton McGuinty, a self-described "policy wonk," the party took on a new team of policy advisors and consulted widely with academics and public policy institutes. The Liberal leader and his advisors travelled extensively in 2000, visiting think-tanks, such as the New America Foundation in Washington, DC, as well as policy groups close to Tony Blair in the UK. In May 2001 the Liberals sponsored the Niagara Conference, subtitled "Ideas for Renewal," covering a very broad array of public policy questions ranging from economics to social policy, with one section devoted to democratic reforms like internet voting, improved voter registration, and fixed election dates, as well as voting system reform.[9] The conference echoed themes that the Liberals had already encountered in their consultations, suggesting that these ideas were indeed at the forefront of critical thinking on the subject. The next step came in November 2001, when the Liberals unveiled a Democratic Charter, their blueprint for government and democratic reform. The document would form the core of party's policy in this area, one of five policy areas to be highlighted in the coming election. Among the host of suggested reforms was a commitment to a public debate about Ontario's voting system and a possible referendum about keeping or replacing it.

The question of voting system reform proved much less divisive for the Ontario Liberal party than for the NDP for a number of reasons. First, the process of policy development and change was directed from the top down, under the guidance and control of the leader and his advisors. Party members, candidates, and MPPs had much less say over the process. Second, the Liberals were committed only to sponsoring a debate about voting system reform and perhaps holding a referendum on it. They did not commit themselves to advocating, or securing the introduction of, any particular system. However media pundits quickly speculated about a hidden electoralist agenda. *Toronto Star* columnist Ian Urquart suggested that the Liberals had a particular electoral reform in mind, namely, the majoritarian transferable ballot to prevent vote-splitting between them and the NDP, a major factor in the historic PC grip on government in the province.[10] Yet publicly at least, the Liberals themselves had no clear position on the issue. McGuinty refused to state a preference. Liberal MPP Michael Bryant appeared to favour PR, speaking favourably about its potential effects at a number of conferences and on television. But individual interviews with a number of Liberal MPPs conducted in the spring of 2002 by members of Fair Vote Canada suggested indifference or ignorance about voting systems to be prevalent in the potential government caucus. Liberal politicians were much more interested in strengthening the role of individual MPPs or in the campaign finance reform aspects of their party's Democratic Charter. When asked specifically about PR, they tended to profess ignorance or appear uncomfortable with the idea.

The Liberal program presented voting system reform as a potential component of a broader set of democratic reform initiatives designed to bolster the flagging democratic legitimacy of government. Certainly, a consensus existed among public policy analysts that sinking levels of voter turnout and public participation had to be reversed, and the Liberals were clearly tapping into that. But the emergence of voting system reform as an issue in its own right in both the Liberal Party and the NDP also reflected an increasing interest in democratic institutions beyond the political arena. By the late 1990s discussions of voting system reform had crept into magazines and local newspapers, as well as community groups and associations of all kinds. From 1999 on, a host of civil society groups from across the political spectrum began exploring voting system reform, with discussion papers on the question emerging from the right-wing Canadian Taxpayers Federation to the left-wing Canadian Auto Workers.

This sudden interest in different voting systems might seem surprising at first glance, given that the recent spate of election results in Ontario appeared to deliver what supporters had always claimed were the current system's strengths. Since the fall of the provincial PCs in 1985 after 40 years in power, there had been regular alternation in government, clear policy alternatives for voters, and mostly majority government in terms of legislative results. Yet these results also served to highlight how arbitrary and unrepresentative plurality results could be, as government lurched from moderate PC, to a Liberal/NDP coalition, to a Liberal majority, to a surprising NDP majority, and finally back to the PCs (and a much more right-wing variant this time), all in the span of a decade and in a way that did not really reflect what voters wanted. The flip-flops of the Rae NDP government and the steamroller determination of the Harris PCs in the 1990s only reinforced negative public attitudes towards politics and the growing sense that Ontario's democracy was in crisis.

In 2000 a group of PR activists from all political stripes formed Fair Vote Canada (FVC), an advocacy group that sought to get the issue before Canadians, preferably in a binding referendum. Since its founding, FVC, through its local chapters, has organized numerous public meetings on voting system reform and developed contacts in all political parties to push the issue forward. In April 2002, a Fair Vote Ontario campaign was established to promote voting reform in the province. Six months later, Ontario activists released a petition endorsing the campaign and featuring high-profile support-ers from across the political and cultural spectrum, including Patrick Boyer, Ed Broadbent, Farley Mowat, Karen Kain, and Stompin' Tom Connors. By spring 2003, FVC had held public meetings with the Ontario NDP, Greens, and Liberals, the latter represented by McGuinty himself. In these meetings, FVC activists drew attention to the flurry of recent voting system changes in other democracies around the world, changes in countries similar to Canada like New Zealand and (at the sub-national level) the UK.[11] No doubt the frequency with which voting system reform began appearing in political and policy discussions, both locally and internationally, created a kind of "policy contagion" infecting Liberals and the NDP.

The rapid rise of interest in voting system reform by both the Liberals and NDP in Ontario can be explained by reference to the difficulties faced by both parties in establishing a credible, competitive public image they could take into elections. In the run-up to the 1999 election both parties confronted residues of the strong negative public reactions to their own recent turns in govern-ment, reinforced by media commentary that highlighted policy paralysis, in-decision, and incompetence. Though voters were by no means entirely happy with the Harris PCs, that government appeared to have a clear policy agenda and had in its first term shown the determination to see it through. After the 1999 defeat, both opposition parties in Ontario set out to bolster their policy profiles. For the Liberals, voting system reform was included among a host of other democratic reform proposals designed to reverse rising public cynicism about politics and declining voter participation rates, providing the party with a distinctive policy direction and attractive policy goals. Liberal commitment to voting system reform per se was much weaker. In fact, it appears to have been included because its popularity with governance think-tanks, for which it typically forms part of a larger package of democratic initiatives, meant that it added legitimacy to the party's embrace of democratic reform.

Differing Proposals for the Democratic Renewal Process

Though both the Liberals and NDP are committed to examining various voting systems and to holding a referendum as the means of introducing any reform, the two parties have different views on the advisability of reform, the process of public deliberation, and the means by which a referendum should be carried out. The key difference is on the need to change the voting system. The Liberals recognize that some important concerns have been raised about

Ontario's current FPTP approach, but in promising to sponsor a public reform process they have repeatedly underlined that they are not committed to any particular outcome. In an interview before the election, Dalton McGuinty suggested that Ontarians might decide to opt for reform or stick with the status quo and that his party would support whatever the electorate wanted.[12] By contrast, the NDP clearly favours a switch to PR, specifically some form of mixed-member system. Party policy calls for the current number of single-member ridings to be maintained and a top-up pool created by restoring those MPPs cut as a result of the PC government's "Fewer Politicians Act," returning the Legislature to its pre-1999 levels of representation, and, perhaps, expanding the number of list MPPs by up to 30 per cent of the total. Research conducted for the party suggests that even with just 30 per cent of the total seats used for top-up, reasonably proportional results could be achieved for the major parties. The decision to propose only a 30 per cent allocation to the list is defended pragmatically in the NDP's task force report as organizationally the least disruptive to current practices as well as the most inexpensive to introduce. Scottish experience with a somewhat similar approach also proved persuasive with the task force. However, it is hard not to discern political motives at work here as well, given that in limiting list seats to 30 per cent (in Scotland it is 42 per cent), such a system would offer little help to smaller parties like the Greens, which compete with the NDP for left/progressive votes. Meanwhile, the NDP is not impressed by the "alternative vote," a majoritarian system which allows for voter preferences to be registered on the ballot within single-member districts, identified by the Liberals as a possible alternative to the status quo. The NDP Task Force Report dismissed it as a "phoney reform," no doubt as its main effect would be to help the Liberals avoid vote-splitting with the left.

Despite their differences on the need for change, both the Liberals and NDP are committed to a high degree of public involvement in the deliberations over voting system reform. There are, however, differences in their idea of how to go about it. Somewhat as in BC, the Liberals have proposed using "citizen juries" to get public input into a host of policy areas, including democratic reform. A citizen jury would be composed of members of the general public, chosen at random, who would research, deliberate, and present their findings in such a way that the public could make a clear choice between two distinct options in a referendum. However, the citizen jury could also be unable or not want to recommend any alternative, and in such cases no referendum would be held.

Hence, on voting system reform, a citizen jury would consider both different voting system options and the status quo, and either recommend staying
with the present method or offer a single alternative that would go forward in
a public referendum. Voters might see a contest between plurality and some
majority system, or plurality and a form of PR, or no contest at all if the jury
simply endorsed FPTP.[13] The jury idea has been enthusiastically promoted as
less expensive than formal government commissions and more democratic, a
chance to let "ordinary citizens" make decisions. But less attention has been
paid to the details of the jury process—i.e., how members will be selected,
what kind of support they will receive to do their work, how decisions will be
made, etc.—and who might be left out of such a process. As jury proponents
hope the model will connect "the people" with policy deliberation, the details
of the selection and deliberation process—no doubt one of the first tasks of
the new Democratic Renewal Secretariat—will be key.

The Ontario Liberals' proposals for citizen juries and electoral reform appear to be following the lead of the BC Liberal government (see Chapter 11);
but there are a few important differences. The key one is that Ontario Liberals
retain the right for cabinet to review the decisions of citizen juries and possibly alter any referendum questions that are proposed. In BC, the government
cannot review, delay, or alter the wording of a citizen jury referendum question. The Ontario Liberals have also increased the tempo of the reform process, promising to hold a referendum and have the results in place in time for
the next provincial election.[14] In BC, voters will see no change before the next
provincial election as the referendum question, if there is one, is scheduled to
coincide with the new fixed general election date.

Compared to the Liberals' novel "citizen jury" approach, the proposed
NDP process for a public deliberation on voting systems appears far more
conventional. Party policy calls for an expert commission to be struck with
a mandate to research the question, consult the public, and decide what form
of PR should be offered as an alternative to the status quo in a public referendum. Thus, the NDP process would guarantee that some form of PR would
be put before the public to vote on. The commission would also function as
the supervisor for the referendum process once the campaign got underway
and, like a similar body in New Zealand, assume responsibility for a wide-
ranging public education program to bring voters up to speed on the workings of the different electoral systems. Like the Liberals, the NDP proposals
provide little detail about how the commission would be chosen or conduct
its work, or how its report would be handled by an NDP government. But
they, too, specified in their election promises that if elected to government,

reform would proceed at such a pace that if a new system were adopted in a public referendum it could be put in place before the next general election.[15] Evidently, however, with a strong majority Liberal government calling the shots, the NDP's input into such matters will be limited.

The Chances of Implementation

The election of a Liberal government in Ontario in the 2003 provincial election appears to bode well for those interested in voting system reform. The Liberals have a clear and specific policy commitment to let the public decide whether to keep the province's traditional plurality voting system or opt for something else. And the new government's strong legislative majority at Queen's Park means that little should stand in their way if they wish to make good on their many election promises. And on electoral system reform, they can even count on the support of the NDP, who also campaigned on the issue. By any tally, the numbers favour getting the reform process going as two of the three major parties in Ontario, together representing a majority of the province's voters and 79 of the 101 seats in the legislature, are publicly committed to moving on the issue. But before reformers break out the champagne, they should take stock of historical experience. Despite the recent election results, reform of the voting system in Ontario remains uncertain. Any number of developments could potentially derail the process, including concerted efforts by politicians, parties, and the media, especially in light of the low level of public involvement in the issue thus far. On the other hand, where there is public process, there is always the chance that debate over the issue may break beyond political and media control.

There are historical precedents that are relevant to the current situation. The present legislature is not the first in Ontario, nor in Canada for that matter, in which a majority of members were prepared to consider voting system reform. In 1919 a coalition of farmers and organized labour won a majority of seats in the Ontario provincial election, much to the surprise of the traditional parties and the media. Both parties were committed to voting system reform, specifically a uniquely Canadian hybrid of PR for urban areas and majority voting for rural ridings, a system that was later introduced in Alberta and Manitoba. As the coalition government had the legislative votes and fairly clear policy commitments in favour of the reforms, there seemed little doubt that a new voting system would be introduced. But it did not come to pass for a number of reasons. Chief among them was a weakening of the commitment to change the system from within the governing caucus, particularly from the farmers. The farmer-labour government had been elected on a distinct minority of votes. Most farmers could see how moves toward majority and proportional voting might weaken them politically. And they faced opposition parties adamantly opposed to any change in the voting rules, with the Conservative leader threatening to filibuster the issue indefinitely to keep it from passing.

In the end, fed up with the opposition outside and inside his own government, the premier called a snap election, which his farmer-party-led coalition lost decisively, and voting system reform faded from the political scene. A similar scenario played out at the federal level in the same period when the 1921 federal election resulted in a Liberal minority government supported by the farmer-based Progressive party. Both parties had committed to voting system reform during the campaign, but, once in Ottawa, the MPs started to have second thoughts. Throughout his first term, Mackenzie King claimed that he still supported the reform, but his large Québec contingent was staunchly opposed to any change in the voting rules. King presented a 1923 resolution that provided for a trial application of PR in a few urban centres; it failed to pass. Though pressed repeatedly about the reform over the next decade, King remained evasive or ambiguous. No reforms were ever forthcoming, despite repeated promises (Phillips 1976; Pilon 1997).

There is also a great deal of contemporary experience that can provide insight into voting system reform — the present situation in Ontario is hardly unique. A case in point is Tony Blair's Labour party, which came to power in 1997 with a promise to hold a referendum on Britain's voting system. Initially Blair moved quickly to get the voting system review process going, appointing former Labour cabinet minister Roy Jenkins as head of a commission charged with coming up with options for a referendum. But as Lord Jenkins did his work, Labour backbenchers became increasingly vocal about their opposition to any change to a proportional voting system, threatening to vote down any attempt to bring it to a referendum. After 18 years in opposition, and now strong in the polls, they couldn't see the point of changing the rules now that they had finally come to power. Meanwhile Jenkins, perhaps sensitive to the growing opposition to PR within the governing ranks, delivered a proposal for change that would only moderately alter the country's single-member plurality system, adding only a relatively minor element of proportionality. But even this modest proposal elicited damning criticism and hostility from Labour MPs. Faced with a revolt of his backbenchers, Blair shelved the report as an issue for the government to take up in its second term (Farrell 2001). Moreover, the adoption of PR systems in Scotland and Wales for the new regional assemblies appears to have only steeled the opposition within Labour to any further change.[16]

In Canada, governments elected with reform commitments have also seen backbench pressure weaken their resolve. In BC, backbenchers held up approval of the voting system jury and referendum bill for a number of months while they worked out a compromise on the fine print. In the end, a super-majority rule was added to the process, thus making reform more difficult.[17] In Québec, the Liberals had campaigned on a promise to move to proportional voting if elected. It was not a controversial position as all three major parties had promised the same thing. However, once in office, the new government began back-tracking on when a new system would be introduced. A similar result emerged in the discussion paper prepared by the Electoral Reform Commission of Prince Edward Island, which was looking at voting system reform. Though the report provided four potential models of a reformed voting system, all were skewed in such a way as to effectively prevent any parties but the two main rivals from gaining any benefit from the changes (Electoral Reform Commission of Prince Edward Island 2003).

These historical and comparative examples underline the fact that getting a legislative majority in favour of looking at voting system reform is just the first step in the process—and a shaky one at that. All evidence suggests that the new Ontario Liberal government will face enormous pressures both internally and externally to weaken its commitment to the reform process and thus either limit the effect of any reform or simply dump the idea altogether. To their credit, Liberal insiders were not unaware of this, and they claim a key reason the leadership moved so quickly to establish a clear policy profile well ahead of the election was precisely to contain the inevitable pressures that would be brought to bear once it seemed that the party was destined to govern. Nor did they seem concerned in the pre-election period about keeping Liberal members and MPPs on the same policy page. At a public meeting with Fair Vote Canada in April 2003, McGuinty responded to concerns about a British-style backbench revolt over the voting system reform issue by noting that all Liberal candidates in the coming provincial election would have to sign a written document committing them to implementing party policy. Certainly the rapid creation of his Democratic Renewal Secretariat upon attaining power would suggest that the reform agenda is still on track. Yet backbencher opposition will remain, no doubt bolstered by support from members of the powerful Ontario Liberal caucus in Ottawa who cannot be happy to see this matter advanced in Ontario.

Another factor is that the reform has drawn very little attention from the public or the media thus far. Despite efforts over the past two years by the NDP and Liberals to raise public interest in their respective democratic reform agendas, "democracy" did not become a break-out issue in either the pre-election or campaign period. Dalton McGuinty did mention his plans for a voting system referendum a few times on the campaign trail, while NDP leader Howard Hampton opened his comments on the televised debate with a plea for PR, but in neither case did media or public commentary take up the suggestion.[18] When a Liberal victory appeared imminent and in the days immediately following the election, a few reporters did mull over the implications of the Liberal promise for a vote on electoral reform, but attention to the issue was quickly overshadowed by the change of power, controversy over the size of the Conservative deficit, and the new premier's choices for cabinet.[19]

Conclusion

The real test of the Liberals' commitment will come if and when a real proposal is raised for public debate. At that point, the position that various parties and MPPs take could become decisive in how the reform process develops, or if it develops at all. After all, the only legislative party presently committed to a concrete alternative to the present plurality voting system is the NDP. The Liberals are committed only to a public debate and perhaps to a referendum, but not to a specific result. On the other hand, the PCs are on record as being opposed to both the specific NDP proposals for PR and the Liberal policy for a public and open-ended debate on voting systems.[20] A wild card in this process will be the reaction of the large Liberal caucus to the issue. Though committed to implementing party policy, this large group of mostly new MPPs are not committed to support any particular position (unlike NDP MPPs), and pre-election interviews suggest they know little about the issue. Though Michael Bryant spoke in favour of PR repeatedly in the year leading up to the election, and the premier himself suggests he has no particular bias, the views of the other Liberal MMPs are largely unknown. On the face of it, one would expect Liberals to be largely hostile to PR, which would seem to offer their NDP rivals a political lifeline just at the point at which the party appears to be on the wane. The majoritarian transferable vote system could benefit the Liberals by preventing PC gains from vote splits between them and the NDP. Hence, they might be tempted to initiate the process— farmed out to the citizen jury, the government would lose effective control, and any number of unforeseen options might emerge.

These are indeed interesting times. Ontario may be embarking on the most wide-ranging public examination and debate of its democratic institutions ever launched in the history of the province. The recently elected Liberal government campaigned on a promise to turn over the question of voting system reform to an innovative "citizen jury," a process that might ultimately let all the province's voters choose an alternative in a province-wide referendum. To be composed of ordinary Ontarians, the citizen jury would study the issue and either judge the current system to be adequate or forward a single alternative for public debate and decision. With a commanding majority at Queen's Park, and support on this issue from the NDP, the government has already begun to act, forming a Democratic Renewal Secretariat to take up this issue (along with others) as one of its first orders of business.

Voting system reform has emerged in Ontario at this time, as elsewhere, from a multiplicity of political pressures, including a marked decline in public support for and participation in the democratic system, changes in the nature of party competition, and a widespread policy crisis, particularly on the centre-left. Both the NDP and the Liberals have shown interest in a host of institutional reforms to democratic practice, including an examination of alternative voting systems, as a response to the current public malaise over electoral democracy. But voting system reform specifically has also been pushed by the competitive pressures facing both parties, with the NDP keen to avoid permanent marginalization as the province's third party, and the Liberals aware of how the traditional plurality system has placed them at a disadvantage with the PCs for most of the last century. Thus, both parties have a potential interest in alternative voting system arrangements, though not necessarily the same ones.

PR would bolster the NDP's representation and increase its influence as a potential government coalition partner. The majoritarian transferable vote would serve the Liberals' desire to prevent vote-splitting between them and the NDP from benefiting the PCs, though the party has no official position on the choice of voting system. Factors internal to the parties have also played a role in furthering the issue. In the NDP, voting system reform has emerged as a rare consensus issue as members continue to struggle over the party's strategic direction. Meanwhile, for the Liberals, the issue fits well into a larger policy strategy for the party as well as reinforcing McGuinty's leadership in the context of the evolving and widening discussion of democratic reform among academics and opinion-leading groups in civil society.

In the end, all we can say is that, literally and figuratively, the jury is out. As elsewhere, the government may find its caucus members harbouring misgivings about even opening up debate over the means by which they get elected, which could lead to delays, reduced commitments, manipulations of the process, or even abandonment of the whole initiative. With only the smallest of the three major parties actually keen on reform, and public recognition of the issue still registering at fairly low levels, the room for the government to wriggle out of its commitment or shift attention to other aspects of its Democratic Charter is fairly wide. However, this gap could narrow by the time a citizen jury reports, if the public is unhappy with other aspects of the Liberal government's record in keeping its promises.

Notes

1. Ontario Liberal Party, *Government that works for you*, policy document 5: Government: The Ontario Liberal Plan for a More Democratic Ontario (Toronto: Ontario Liberal Party, 2003) 5.

2. New Democratic Party of Ontario, *Public Power: Practical Solutions for Ontario* (Toronto: Ontario New Democratic Party, 2003) 69; Green Party of Ontario, *A Better Way to Live: Green Party of Ontario Platform 2003* (Toronto: Green Party of Ontario, 2003) 11-12.

3. John Barber, "Toronto needs electoral reform to change agenda," *Globe and Mail* (Ontario edition) 20 November 2001: A20.

4. I would like to thank members of all the Ontario political parties that agreed to speak with me about this issue, as well as those activists on this question in various civil society organizations. Of course, I bear sole responsibility for what appears here.

5. Ontario Legislative Assembly, *Orders and Notices* (Toronto: Ontario Legislative Assembly)16 April 1996.

6. Wynne Hartviksen, "Making politics matter: The shining light of PR, the rocky road of election finance reform, and the disconnect between activists and politics," *Straight Goods* 4 June 2001.

7. Press Release, "NDP Task Force Proposes PR for 'Value-Added Voting' at Queen's Park" (Toronto: Ontario New Democratic Party) 18 February 2002.

8. Ontario NDP, *Report of the Proportional Representation Taskforce* (Toronto: Ontario New Democratic Party) 23 June 2002: 14-17.

9. Ontario Liberal Party, *Ideas for Renewal*, <www.ontarioliberal.com>.

10. Ian Urquart, "McGuinty reform won't wash," *Toronto Star* 19 November 2001.

11. Fair Vote Canada, "The Fair Vote Ontario Campaign: Report to the 2003 Annual General Meeting," Parliament Buildings, Ottawa, 25 April 2003.

12. "*Pundit* interview with Dalton McGuinty," *Pundit Magazine*, 16 November 2001.

13. "*Pundit* interview."

14. Fair Vote Canada.

15. Ontario NDP, *Report* 17.

16. Roland Watson, "Prescott leads campaign to end PR pledge," *London Times* 1 March 2000.

17. See Chapter 11. The bill was based primarily on a report prepared by Gordon Gibson, though his recommendations did not include a super-majority rule.

18. CTV.ca Home News Canada, "No clear winner in Ontario leaders TV debate," 24 September 2003.

19. See coverage in the *Toronto Star* and *Globe and Mail* (Ontario edition), particularly columns by Murray Campbell, Chantal Hébert, Jeffrey Simpson, and John Ibbitson. Both papers also printed a considerable number of letters to the editor on the theme of voting system reform in the week after the election.

20. Ontario Progressive Conservative Party, *The Road Ahead: Premier Eves' Plan for Ontario's Future* (Toronto: Progressive Conservative Party of Ontario, 2003) 51.

CHAPTER 13

Twenty Years after René Lévesque Failed to Change the Electoral System, Québec May Be Ready to Act

Brian Doody and Henry Milner

Act One: 1966-1982

The modern saga of electoral-system reform in Québec can be said to begin with the 1966 provincial election, in which Daniel Johnson's Union Nationale (UN) won a majority of seats, six more than the Liberals (PLQ), despite the fact that the UN received only 40.9 per cent of the vote, compared to the PLQ's 47.2 per cent. René Lévesque resigned from the PLQ in 1967 to form what would become the Parti Québécois (PQ), replacing the more radical *Rassemblement pour l'Indépendence Nationale*, whose 1964 platform was the first in Québec to call for proportional representation (PR) (see Cliche 1999).[1] The PQ formally added PR to its program at the second party congress in 1969, and by 1970 was calling for the adoption of a German-style mixed electoral system (Parti Québécois 1970). The 1970 and 1973 provincial elections were bitter disappointments for Lévesque and his party, with Robert Bourassa's PLQ winning lopsided majorities and the PQ electing only a handful of members of the National Assembly (MNAs) despite capturing between one-quarter and one-third of the popular vote.[2] In 1971, political scientist Vincent Lemieux first introduced his "territorial proportional" electoral model before a parliamentary committee studying voting-system reform.[3] Bourassa, who had agreed after the 1970 election to the setting up of the committee, by 1972 had decided to make changes only to the electoral map.[4]

Lévesque, who came to power as head of the first PQ government in 1976, viewed PR as inherently more democratic than the first-past-the-post (FPTP) system, which he associated with the patronage he had fought against throughout his career. Soon after its election in 1976, the PQ created a Ministry of State for Parliamentary and Electoral Reform, under Robert Burns, with a mandate to clean up the election financing system. In 1977, it brought in legislation—the first in North America—to limit political-party contributions to individuals. In April 1979, Burns released his *Green Book on Reform of the Voting System* (Québec 1979) in anticipation of public hearings that were to be held later that year. Three models were proposed: (1) a variation on the territorial-proportional system; (2) mixed FPTP (two-thirds) and PR (one-third); and (3) mixed FPTP and PR (half-and-half).

The new PLQ leader, Claude Ryan, had previously advocated the adoption of a German-style mixed system while editor-in-chief of *Le Devoir*,[5] and seemed ready to collaborate with Burns and the PQ on this issue. In May, however, Burns announced that he was resigning for health reasons; by August, the public hearings were cancelled. In April 1981, Lévesque led the PQ to a second majority government despite having lost its referendum on sovereignty association a year earlier. Although the PLQ supported the PQ's renewed election-reform initiative announced in its inaugural speech in November 1981,[6] Ryan resigned as the party's leader in August 1982. After Bourassa regained the leadership of the PLQ in October 1983, he made it clear that bipartisan support for electoral reform was no longer possible.[7] The fate of Lévesque's proposals would now be in the hands of the PQ caucus alone.

Act Two: 1983-1985

At the beginning of the second mandate, the Ministry proposed that a list PR system be established in Québec. The "Moderate Regional Proportional Representation" system proposed by the new minister, Marc-André Bedard, had Lévesque's backing. This proposal would later be endorsed, with slight modifications, by a commission mandated in June 1983 by a unanimous resolution of the National Assembly and under the direction of the province's chief electoral officer, Pierre-F. Côté. The commissioners held hearings in ten cities over 19 days, during which 184 individuals and groups were heard.[8] A majority of the individuals consulted favoured changing the FPTP voting system (Québec 1984: 60-62).[9] Nearly half of those who proposed changes agreed that PR was needed to correct the systemic distortions in party representation. Forty-nine participants favoured a German-style mixed system as the best way to translate votes into seats. A certain number recommended less drastic changes such as preferential voting and the single transferable vote (STV).

The Côté Commission submitted its final report on March 28, 1984, recommending that the province adopt a "made in Québec" system of PR. Its "territorial proportional" system resembled the model proposed by Bédard the previous year. The main difference between the ministry's proposal and that of Côté was that the latter envisaged multi-member districts with as few as three seats. In determining the size and location of the multi-member districts, the electoral system was to take into account three factors: the concentration of voters in a few densely populated cities and across vast, sparsely populated regions; the presence of ethnic and cultural minorities as well as the First Nations peoples; and the pluralistic character of Québec society. The presence of large, multi-member electoral districts would, in the commissioners' view, promote greater plurality in the National Assembly, preserve governmental stability, and eliminate the possibility of a second-place party ever forming a majority government.

The commission also recommended that voters be given the final choice of accepting or rejecting candidates from party lists. Thus, while a single vote would also be a vote for a party list, voters would be given the option of selecting candidates proposed by other political parties.[10] In this way, people would vote either once for a party, or once for a party and as many times for candidates of any party as there were seats to fill.[11]

It soon became clear, however, that Lévesque could not muster sufficient support to implement the Côté proposals. The first and more obvious reason for this was that they did not have the support of a majority in the legislature. The new PLQ leader, whose principles on election reform had not changed since 1972, was uncompromising in his refusal to offer bilateral support. Moreover, the worsening electoral fortunes of the PQ—in the polls and in lost by-elections—made it easy for Bourassa to paint the effort as an opportunistic attempt by an unpopular government to save itself from electoral defeat (Fraser 1984). In addition, the government side was itself divided. It is possible that a compensatory model, such as was proposed by the PQ executive, might have been adopted had Lévesque not ruled it out. The PQ executive had presented a brief to the Côté Commission calling for a German-style compensatory system (mixed-member proportional or MMP), with one-quarter of the seats drawn from party lists to bring the overall totals closer to proportionality, thereby retaining some advantage for the party winning most of the single-member seats. At a joint caucus-executive retreat in August 1984, the cabinet failed to win support for its position. Even the fact that PQ support had sunk below 25 per cent in the polls by this point—which would have spelled electoral disaster under FPTP—could not sway the majority of MNAs. Lévesque too would not move, justifying his refusal to endorse MMP because it was being publicly identified with the party and thus partisan (Milner 1994).

A party-government committee composed of three cabinet ministers, three MNAs, and three members of the executive was set up to find a solution, but it failed in its efforts and the issue soon faded as the PQ split over whether to put Québec independence on the back burner. By the next election, in 1985, Lévesque had resigned, and his successor, Pierre-Marc Johnson, managed to *"sauver les meubles,"* winning 23 of 122 seats with 38 per cent of the vote under FPTP. Electoral-system reform was not to reappear on the Québec political agenda for another 14 years.

Act Three: 1985-Present

The November 1998 election was a major turning point in the present debate on election-system reform in Québec. The PQ won a parliamentary majority —76 seats—with only 42.9 per cent of the vote, while the PLQ, with 43.6 per cent, won only 48 seats. The *Action démocratique du Québec* (ADQ) received 11.8 per cent of the vote but won only one seat. Four years earlier, in 1994, the PQ was elected on a program that included the implementation of a mixed compensatory electoral system in the first year of its mandate, an obligation that Jacques Parizeau renounced once he became premier.[12] After Parizeau's replacement by Lucien Bouchard in 1996, the PQ program was changed at the PQ Congress in November that year, from an obligation to "examine and approve" an electoral-reform law "in the first year of [its] mandate," to a promise to do so "as soon as possible."[13] Less than two years later, the PQ's 1998 election platform seemed to suggest that such approval would only come after Québec became sovereign (Parti Québécois 1998).

In late 1998 and early 1999, the gap seemed to widen between the PQ elites, who showed little interest in electoral reform, and certain activists, for whom it was as much a part of the *raison d'être* of the party as the drive for sovereignty.[14] At a colloquium held at Laval University on January 12, various experts and veterans of previous attempts at reform called on the government to appoint a committee of "wise persons" to study various electoral models and make recommendations for reform.[15] The opposition then picked up the ball. After the PLQ caucus meeting in Pohénégamook the following week, leader Jean Charest announced his preference for a compensatory model of proportional representation and called on the PQ government to study the question.[16] At their General Council meeting held in Saint-Hyacinthe on

May 29 and 30, the PLQ endorsed the proportional compensatory system as the model to be added to their program.[17] The PQ leadership, meanwhile, saw merit in keeping to the status quo: the minister responsible for electoral reform, Guy Chevrette, said that Québec was not ready for electoral reform and that FPTP constituted the "least worst" of the options available.[18]

By the spring of 1999, ADQ members meeting in Trois-Rivières added the principle of PR to their party program, although the exact model to adopt would be subject to further study, possibly by a committee of "wise persons."[19] In the National Assembly, ADQ leader Mario Dumont proposed that the Committee on Institutions hold public hearings leading to the nomination of a committee of experts by a two-thirds vote of MNAs, followed by a year of province-wide hearings and the tabling of a report by the spring of 2000. Although the Liberals supported the ADQ motion, the PQ refused to give its consent and the motion failed.[20] While Chevrette never ruled out setting up such a committee, he maintained that it was up to the PQ caucus and cabinet to decide whether to proceed.[21] Despite growing pressure from civil society to hold public hearings,[22] no such authorization, it was quite apparent, would ever come from a government headed by Lucien Bouchard, who announced his resignation in January 2001. His successor, Bernard Landry, was sworn in two months later.

Public attention was next focused on the PQ's by-election loss in the Montreal stronghold of Mercier on April 9. While defeated by the PLQ, the PQ candidate faced two well-known advocates of electoral reform—left independent candidate Paul Cliche and the ADQ's André Larocque—which kept alive the momentum for electoral reform.[23] On May 30 a group calling itself *Mouvement pour une démocratie nouvelle* (MDN) organized a debate on democratic reform that brought together Cliche and Larocque, as well as PLQ MNA Jacques Chagnon and PQ Vice-President Marie Malavoy. The MDN was set up as a non-partisan, non-profit grassroots coalition designed to promote voting-system reform in Québec. On October 30, 2001, the Speaker of the National Assembly, Jean-Pierre Charbonneau, signed the document officially recognizing the MDN as a non-profit organization.[24] Two weeks later, the MDN founder and spokesperson Paul-André Martineau presented Charbonneau with a petition signed by 125 prominent citizens—among them former PQ cabinet minister Claude Charron, Ryan, and Jean Allaire, co-founder of the ADQ—calling on the government to hold public hearings immediately.[25] By the end of November, even the non-partisan Director-General of Elections publicly voiced support for the idea.[26] Finally, on December 19,

2001, the Commission on Institutions met to discuss the logistics of holding public hearings on democratic reform in 2002.

Thus, 18 years after the Côté Commission, three years into the government's mandate, and against his own better judgement, Bernard Landry found himself on a path not taken by any Québec premier since René Lévesque.[27] The sudden departure from the cabinet of Chevrette and Jacques Brassard, respectively ministers responsible for electoral and parliamentary reform, made it possible for Landry to elevate Speaker Charbonneau to the cabinet in January 2002 and to confer on him joint responsibility for these portfolios. To put pressure on the new minister, the MDN staged a successful public meeting in late February bringing together Ryan and Charron. By March, the government had formally changed Charbonneau's title to Minister Responsible for the Reform of Democratic Institutions and hired Larocque as deputy minister.[28] But the spring of 2002 also saw the PQ plummeting in the polls and brought some unexpected surprises in the form of the election of four ADQ members to the National Assembly in by-elections held on April 15 and June 17 and the sudden rise of that party in public opinion polls. Following on the success of its petition the previous autumn, the MDN had sent questionnaires to all the by-election candidates asking them to publicly declare their support for electoral reform, which each candidate elected in the spring of 2002 signed.[29]

On June 11, the chair of the National Assembly Committee on Institutions announced the holding of public hearings on electoral reform in ten cities beginning in October 2002, with a final report due by May 2003.[30] To assist the public in the making of oral and written submissions, the committee released a background paper and later a consultation document (Québec 2002a; 2002b). The committee met on November 14 with four expert witnesses and continued to take written submissions from the public until the end of November, though the province-wide hearings promised by Committee Chair Claude Lachance were never held.[31] Committee members and interested observers noted the unanimity of the four in favour of the mixed-member plurality (MMP) form of PR, an important milestone in the development of a wider consensus on the need to adopt a made-in-Quebec form of MMP.

Nevertheless, the Committee on Institutions was not to be the government's only forum for public consultations on electoral reform. Just days after the June by-elections, Charbonneau announced plans for an "Estates General" on democratic reform to be held in early 2003, where a wide range of reforms would be discussed. A discussion paper, entitled *Citizen Empowerment: A Paper to Open Public Debate*, accompanied by a questionnaire, was released at the end of June in preparation for public hearings scheduled for the fall

(Charbonneau 2002). The ambitious list of items to be addressed by the Estates General included:

1. the possibility of electing the head of government directly by universal suffrage;
2. the appointment of ministers who would neither sit in nor be responsible to the legislature;
3. limiting to two the maximum number of terms of a head of government;
4. holding elections on fixed dates;
5. separate elections for the members of the legislature and the head of government;
6. PR elections for MNAs;
7. allowing for citizen-initiated referendums;
8. measures to enhance the representation of regions, women, and First Nations peoples in the National Assembly;
9. lowering the voting age to 16; and
10. the introduction of a voter-identification card.[32]

Although presented as a vehicle for generating public debate, *Citizen Empowerment* clearly reflected Charbonneau's pro-reform views.

Since the deadlines for submissions to both the Committee on Institutions and the Estates General tended to coincide, the MDN encouraged its supporters to send one written submission to both committees.[33] It also circulated a petition asking citizens to endorse its four goals for voting-system reform: to ensure the best possible translation of votes into seats; to promote the equal representation of women and men; to respect cultural diversity and political pluralism; and to reflect the regions. MDN militants were well represented among those heard in the 27 public assemblies held throughout Québec and among the authors of the 237 briefs received from parties, interest groups, and private citizens.

The Steering Committee [of the Estates General], chaired by banker Claude Beland sought a wide range of geographic, gender, demographic, and cultural representation, when it selected the delegates to the Estates General from among individuals who had submitted a questionnaire or other document.[34] The PLQ refused to participate, reiterating its position on electoral reform and asserting that the government was acting illegitimately in proposing the other fundamental institutional changes envisaged (PLQ 2002). At the full Estates General held in Québec City on February 21 to 23, 2003, more than 1,000 delegates, seated ten to a table, participated simultaneously in about 100 workshops, where each of the items for reform was discussed in turn (Québec 2003a). On the last day, with the aid of hand-held voting machines, the delegates voted for the proposals of their choice (Québec 2003b). Over 90 per cent of the 825 voting delegates favoured electoral reform—of which 24 per cent preferred a pure PR system and 66 per cent favoured a mixed formula (Québec 2003c).[35] The participants in the Estates General also endorsed referenda on popular initiatives, a Québec constitution, fixed-date elections, and measures to increase the participation of women and members of cultural communities in politics. They narrowly rejected the adoption of an American-style presidential system (47 to 53 per cent). They also rejected proposals to increase regional representation, create regional assemblies, and lower the voting age to 16 (Piroth 2004).

The Béland Committee released its report on March 10, 2003, two days before Premier Landry called a general election. On the main question of voting-system reform—and despite only moderate support among delegates for the election of MNAs on a regional basis—the Béland Committee, perhaps influenced by André Larocque, recommended that Québec adopt what was essentially the same territorial proportional model proposed by the Côté Commission in 1984 (Québec 2003c: Recommendation 1: 34, 36, 62). Otherwise, the recommendations generally reflected what a majority of delegates had voted for at the Estates General.[36]

Responding to requests that the MDN had sent to each candidate during the 2003 election campaign, most PLQ candidates, including party leader Jean Charest, declared their support for electoral reform in the first two years of the next government's mandate.[37] After Charest's PLQ was elected to a majority government on April 14, Jacques Dupuis became the new Minister for the Reform of Democratic Institutions.[38] Given Landry's ambivalence on the matter, it was clear that, had the PQ won the election, the Béland Report would have been a topic for further study, at best. For their part, the PLQ dismissed the report as a whole, left open the possibility of elections on fixed dates, and turned their attention to election-system reform.

Prospects for Real Change

In September 2003, at a speech to an Institute of Research on Public Policy conference in Montréal on democratic reform, Dupuis reiterated his government's commitment to introduce a law in the spring of 2004 establishing a mixed compensatory electoral system (Dupuis 2003: 5-6). However, the minister took many observers by surprise when he said that the statutory requirements of the Elections Act made it unlikely that the new voting system could be implemented before the next election.[39] Dupuis' interpretation of the electoral law was later questioned by Pierre-F. Côté,[40] who said that it was a matter of compressing the time established by the Elections Act for public consultation on the new electoral boundaries—an assessment immediately questioned by Dupuis' top official, André Fortier.[41]

The minister also took some observers by surprise when he stated that a single-vote version of MMP was still an option under consideration (Dupuis 2003: 6). While the need for a second vote may not be so obvious from the perspective of voters and party activists already familiar with the FPTP system, the use of the two-vote system in New Zealand, Scotland, and Germany makes this option difficult to defend. The single vote—especially if there are no lists, with compensatory seats going to the "best losers" in the district seats—places the small parties at a disadvantage. It may also help the PQ more than the PLQ, since, with two votes, most observers expect less vote-splitting among current PLQ voters as compared to PQ supporters.

The minister will table a bill setting out a region-based MMP system in October (it was originally planned for May). Reports suggest that a system with 75 single-member districts based on federal election districts and 50 list seats is being seriously considered. The bill would be discussed at committee hearings in the fall and, in final form, passed in the spring of 2005. Implementation is not planned to take effect in time for the next election, due in 2007; indeed, it would be difficult to do so in the time remaining even if the government wished to do so. Among Québec's three main parties, the ADQ would be the most obvious immediate beneficiary and will be certain to support it. If its votes had been proportionally translated into seats, it would have 20 or 21 MNAs rather than four, assuring the survival of the party. The left-wing *Union des forces progressistes* (UFP) strongly favours reform: it probably has sufficient support to elect one or more MNAs. The same could be the case for the Green party and perhaps also for an Anglo-rights party. The PLQ will benefit from ending what Massicotte (1995) calls a "gerrymander *linguistique*," in which they waste many thousands of votes in the non-francophone majority districts in Montreal. The extent to which this will be achieved depends on the size and location of the regional districts. Overall, larger districts shrink the gerrymander, i.e., help the PLQ, better than smaller ones. The long-term effect of PR on the electoral fortunes of the PLQ as compared to the PQ will depend on the parties' relative ability to hold their internal coalitions together under the new incentive structures.

Steps Toward Making Every Vote Count

Neither will be able to form a majority government. It is possible the *"pur et dur"* nationalists in the PQ would split from the mainstream PQ, but this would not exclude a pro-sovereignty coalition government composed of these two, supported perhaps by the UFP and the Greens. Hence, there is no consensus among nationalist intellectuals whether such an eventuality would constitute a setback for the sovereignist cause.[42] Whatever the case, the PQ has been caught flat-footed by the PLQ initiative, refusing to participate in Minister Dupuis' consultation on the law because of its claim—after 22 years of public debate leading up to Béland's Estates General—that the PLQ has failed to consult the people.

At this point the public position the PQ will take when the bill is tabled is uncertain. The fervent hope of most of its MNAs and party officials is that it will go away, killed by foot dragging, if not outright opposition, by PLQ caucus members who like the system that elected them. This is unlikely, however, in part because the PLQ has fallen rapidly in the polls since its election, so the argument of "why bother, we can win anyway" is less credible. In addition, Québec is no longer alone in the vanguard but caught up in the momentum building elsewhere in Canada.

Nevertheless, the die is not yet cast. If they had their way, a majority of MNAs (almost all the Péquistes, and more PLQ members than they will admit) would be happy to see the initiative meet the same fate Lévesque's plan met 20 years earlier. But much has changed in Québec since that time. There is close to an elite consensus that a new electoral system is a reform whose time has come, with wide, if not deep, public support. As long as the pro-PR network remains mobilized, Québec should have a new electoral law on the books before the next election. However, we will not quite be out of the water then, for there will still be the challenge of getting it implemented.[43] As they awaited the promised release of the government's draft legislation in the spring of 2004, advocates of electoral reform in Québec could only reflect on how far they had come and how far they had yet to go.

Notes

1. Although neither the *Rassemblement pour l'Indépendance Nationale* nor the conservative nationalist *Ralliement National* won seats in the 1966 election, they won 5.6 and 3.2 per cent of the vote respectively. Independents won 3.1 per cent of the vote and two seats.

2. In 1970, the PLQ won 72 seats with 45.4 per cent of the vote; the PQ won 7 seats with 23.1 per cent; the UN 17 seats with 19.6 per cent; and the Social Credit Rally (SCR) 12 seats with 11.1 per cent. In 1973, the PLQ won 102 seats with 54.7 per cent

of the vote; the PQ won 6 seats with 30.2 per cent; the SCR two seats with 10.0 per cent; and the UN won no seats with 4.9 per cent.

3. Québec National Assembly, *Journal des débats* (1 April 1971) at B-810.

4. Québec National Assembly, *Débats* (19 December 1970) at 2622; *Débats* (30 November 1972) at 2888 and 2902.

5. Claude Ryan, "Le remède aux injustices du scrutin," *Le Devoir* 14 December 1972: A4.

6. Québec National Assembly, *Commission permanente de la présidence du conseil et de la constitution* 1981.

7. Jean-Jacques Samson, "Mode de scrutin: Bourassa s'en promet," *Le Soleil* 13 March 1984: A12.

8. It also received 60 written submissions by individuals who did not give oral testimony, while 202 individuals filled out a questionnaire, and 15 people made their views known by telephone.

9. In all, 57 per cent (263 of the 462 individuals) were in favour of changing FPTP, 20 per cent (92 individuals) were in favour of the status quo, and 23 per cent (106 individuals) did not express an opinion.

10. Seats would be attributed to each party in each district according to the D'Hondt method (successively dividing the total number of votes for each party by the number of seats it has received, attributing seats to the "highest averages"). After calculating the number of seats for each party, those parties' "list" candidates with the highest number of votes would be elected.

11. The commission also proposed that the practice of by-elections be replaced with a system of filling vacancies with the next available candidate on a party list, or with a replacement list provided by that party, if required, and that MNAs be forbidden from crossing the floor.

12. Paule des Rivières, "Le PQ et le PLQ préfèrent le statu quo au système proportionnel," *Le Devoir* 7 December 1998: A1. The election program approved by the PQ Executive Council in July 1994 contains no reference to electoral-system reform: see Parti Québécois (1994).

13. Michel Venne, "Pour un nouveau mode de scrutin," *Le Devoir* 23 December 1998: A10.

14. Although the PQ program committed the party to introduce electoral reform legislation "as soon as possible," PQ Vice-President Fabien Béchard reiterated the view of many in the party that reform of the voting system should be preceded by sovereignty: *Le Devoir* 7 December 1998.

15. Among the participants were André Larocque, former deputy minister of Democratic and Parliamentary Reform and Professors Louis Massicotte and Vincent Lemieux. See Michel Venne, *"Pour un nouveau mode de scrutin,"* *Le Devoir* 16 March 1999 : A4.

16. Michel Hébert, "Charest veut un mode de scrutin proportionnel," *Le Devoir* 22 January 1999: A10. Charest made his remarks after a three-day caucus meeting in Pohénégamook, Québec, on January 19-21, 1999.

17. Pierre O'Neill, "Le nouveau défi de Jean Charest," *Le Devoir* 30 April 1999: A4; "Charest lance une redéfinition du 'modèle québécois'," *Le Devoir* 31 May 1999.

18. Mario Cloutier, "Réforme électorale: Pas question de scrutin proportionnelle," *Le Devoir* 23 January 1999: A8. Chevrette announced that the government would introduce instead draft legislation to reduce electoral fraud through the creation of a voter's card.

19. The revised ADQ program read that "the will expressed by the voters must be the most fundamental rule for the allocation of seats between the parties" (authors' translation). Lia Lévesque, "Élection du premier ministre au suffrage universel," *Le Devoir* 13 April 1999: A4.

20. Robert Dutrisac, "La motion de Dumont sur la proportionnelle est rejetée," *Le Devoir* 28 April 1999: A5.

21. Letter from Chevrette to Jacques Chagnon, Liberal election reform critic, June 1, 1999. Cited in Cliche 1999: 55.

22. For example, reform activist Paul Cliche's book (1999). Many smaller parties not represented in the National Assembly—for example, the *Parti de la démocratie socialiste* (PDS) and the *Rassemblement pour l'alternative politique* (RAP)—adopted electoral reform as part of their programs: Cliche 1999: 55.

23. The PLQ's Nathalie Rochefort won the April 9 by-election in the former PQ stronghold. Cliche won 24 per cent of the vote. During the campaign, delegates at the Liberals' General Council meeting in Trois-Rivières on March 10 and 11 passed a resolution reiterating their party's support for electoral reform: Canadian Press, "Les résolutions des militants," *Le Devoir* 12 March 2001: A3.

24. Kathleen Lévesque, "Institutions parlementaires: Charbonneau veut faire la révolution démocratique," *Le Devoir* 10 November 2001: A5; MDN, "Actions politiques du MDN," <www.democratic-nouvelle.qc.ca>.

25. MDN, "Actions politiques du MDN"; Kathleen Lévesque, "Pas besoin d'attendre la souveraineté, croit Claude Charron," *Le Devoir* 14 November 2001: A5; Kathleen Lévesque, "Claude Ryan rejoint le camp des réformistes," *Le Devoir* 29 August 2001: A4. Other signatories included Pierre-F. Côté, former president of the *Féderation des femmes du Québec* Françoise David, writer Victor-Lévy Beaulieu, and former senator Claude Castonguay. All 14 candidates in four by-elections held on October 1, 2001 also signed the petition; see Robert Dutrisac, "La question est complexe," *Le Devoir* 5 October 2001: A2.

26. Kathleen Lévesque, "Le Québec devra réviser son mode de scrutin, dit le DGE [Marcel Blanchet]," *Le Devoir* 30 November 2001: A1.

27. Landry still considered the sovereignty of Québec as a precondition for electoral reform; Kathleen Lévesque and Robert Dutrisac, "Bernard Landry au *Devoir*," *Le Devoir* 29 May 2001: A1.

28. Kathleen Lévesque, "Réforme des institutions: André Larocque revient au PQ: L'ex conseiller de Mario Dumont sera nommé sous-ministre de Jean-Pierre Charbonneau," *Le Devoir* 13 March 2002: A2.

29. Kathleen Lévesque, "Des appuis au Mouvement pour une démocratie nouvelle," *Le Devoir* 13 April 2002: A7; MDN, "Actions politiques du MDN."

30. Mario Cloutier, "Le rapport des députés ne sera déposé qu'en mai 2003," *Le Devoir* 12 June 2002: A2.

31. The witnesses in order of appearance were Vincent Lemieux of Laval University; André Blais of Université de Montréal; and two contributors to this book, Henry Milner and Louis Massicotte. See Québec National Assembly, *Journal des débats de la Commission des institutions* 37-97 (14 November 2002) at <http://www.assnat.qc.ca/fra/publications/debats/journal/ci/021114.htm>.

32. Steering Committee of the Estates General on the Reform of Democratic Institutions, "Questionnaire" (Québec: The Committee, 2002).

33. MDN, "Press Release" (17 October 2002). To prepare for the autumn hearings of the two committees, MDN undertook two initiatives. First, the group wrote, edited, and distributed 10,000 copies of a tabloid-style newsletter on electoral reform. Second, it prepared a step-by-step citizens' guide on the preparation of written submissions and held workshops for interested groups.

34. Québec. Steering Committee of the Estates General (March 2003). The Committee also had 17 regional chairpersons, each of whom was responsible for organizing the public meetings held in his or her respective regions.

35. Tommy Chouinard, "Oui massif à la proportionnelle," *Le Devoir* 24 February 2003: A1.

36. Where the committee showed the most innovation was on matters relating to governance and the role of the individual MNA, with recommendations to require the approval of certain prerogative appointments by more accessible parliamentary committees, to increase MNAs' accountability in their ridings and to relax party discipline on votes in the legislature except on matters of confidence, to promote open and participatory governance through the separation of legislative and executive powers, and to use new technologies to promote good governance practices. The committee also recommended the creation of a national council on citizenship and democracy to monitor the quality and evolution of democratic life in the province.

37. MDN sent letters to all candidates for office in 125 ridings asking them to declare their support: see MDN. "Actions politiques du MDN." See also Kathleen Lévesque, "Béland demande à Charest de réformer rapidement le mode de scrutin," *Le Devoir* 17 April 2003: A3.

38. On April 14, the Liberals won 46.0 per cent of the vote and 76 seats, the PQ 33.2 per cent of the vote and 45 seats, and the ADQ 18.2 per cent of the vote and four seats.

39. Kathleen Lévesque, "Retard dans la mise en œuvre d'un nouveau mode de scrutin: Ce n'est pas le PQ qui bousculera le PLQ," *Le Devoir* 12 September 2003: A3; Kathleen Lévesque, "Un retard qui surprend même certains libéraux," *Le Devoir* 13 September 2003: A2; Tommy Chouinard, "Le Mouvement pour une démocratie nouvelle demande à Jean Charest d'agir avec célérité," *Le Devoir* 19 November 2003: A3. Dupuis's comments on the timing of the law's implementation were not part of the minister's prepared text.

40. He was speaking in November to the Annual General Meeting of MDN. Tommy Chouinard, "Pierre-F. Côté contredit le gouvernement Charest," *Le Devoir* 21 November 2003 : A3

41. Tommy Chouinard, "Nouveau mode de scrutin: pas avant décembre 2007," *Le Devoir* 22-23 November 2003: A3

42. See, e.g., Michel Venne, "Les élections autrement," *Le Devoir* 26 February 2003.

43. In February 2004, a group of four individuals, represented by well-known Montreal lawyer, Julius Grey, went to court to contest the constitutionality of Quebec's electoral system in order to put additional pressure on the government to act.

CHAPTER 14

Prince Edward Island's Cautious Path toward Electoral Reform

John Andrew Cousins

Introduction

Prince Edward Island has taken a cautious step toward electoral reform. In December 2003 the Prince Edward Island Commission on Electoral Reform—in the person of Commissioner Norman Carruthers, the retired Chief Justice of the province—proposed that PEI's first-past-the-post (FPTP) electoral system be modified to incorporate an element of proportional representation (PR), preferably as a mixed-member proportional (MMP) system. The commissioner made it clear that any reform must be preceded by a public information campaign, a "citizen's assembly," and a referendum, but equally left no doubt that, in his view, PEI would benefit from a modified voting system.

The Carruthers Report came on the heels of a provincial election in September 2003 in which the incumbent Progressive Conservatives (PCs) won 23 seats in the Legislative Assembly—85 per cent of the elected members—and the remaining four seats went to the opposition Liberals. The popular vote told a different story: just over 54 per cent voted PC, while nearly 43 per cent voted Liberal, and about three per cent supported the New Democratic Party (NDP). In other words, nearly 46 per cent of the electorate was represented by only 15 per cent of the members of the Assembly. Such distorted results have become routine in PEI elections since the late 1980s, providing valuable ammunition to those who have been making the case for electoral system reform—the most recent expression of which is the Carruthers Report. After exploring the history of the PEI electoral system and its effects, this article will describe recent developments in the campaign for reform.

The Legislative Assembly—Past

PEI's Legislative Assembly first sat in 1773, with 18 members (MLAs) elected at large from across the colony's three counties. Subsequent Election Acts expanded the Assembly to 24 seats in 1838, then to 30 in 1856. Under the 1838 Election Act, each county was divided into three districts, with two members each, plus two members more for each "county town." Members of the upper house—the Legislative Council—were appointed during most of the colonial period, but its 13 members were elected after 1862 (MacKinnon 1951: 34-53, 102-103, 210-214). PEI attained responsible government in 1851 and joined Confederation in 1873 without significant disruption to the voting system.

The 1893 Legislature Act imposed a sweeping change on the institutions of representation. It created a single house—the Legislative Assembly—with 30 members elected from 15 dual-member ridings, a councillor, and an assembly-man. Only property-owners voted for councillors, which they could do in any constituency in which they owned property worth $325.00 (MacKinnon 1951: 215). The property-based franchise reflected the assumption that property-owners had a distinct stake in public affairs in a province of small farms where most political controversies involved the land (Milne 1982: 42-52). Those that did not often involved religion. The interests of the roughly equal Catholic and Protestant populations were also reflected in the dual-member system, in which members of the different denominations were generally spared from competing directly for seats (MacDonald 2000: 20, 373; Clark 1973: 299-300). The essential features of the dual-member system remained virtually unchanged until 1963, when the Election Act abolished the property-ownership eligibility requirement. It also added a constituency, expanding the Assembly to 32 members (Clark 1973: 295, 308-11).

The Legislative Assembly—Present

PEI has recently undergone a further dramatic reform of the legislative system, ending the system of dual ridings. In 1993, in *MacKinnon v. Prince Edward Island* (1993), the PEI Supreme Court (Trial Division) held that the seat distribution provided inadequate representation to many voters on account of large variances in population among the districts, thus violating the right to vote under Section 3 of the Charter of Rights and Freedoms. To take advantage of the time the Court gave it to remedy the legislation before the order took effect, the government appointed the Election Act and Electoral Boundaries Commission, which held public hearings in 1993 and 1994. A point of contention was the system of dual constituencies. As one historian has put it, the dual constituencies were a "vestigial remnant" of the nineteenth-century bicameral legislature that had survived "at first mainly because they made it easier to avoid religious confrontations in electoral contests, and, in the end, because they entrenched the political influence of rural areas" (MacDonald 2000: 373). The commission recommended 30 single-member districts to replace the dual constituencies; the Assembly ultimately adopted a private member's scheme for a 27-seat legislature. Thus, starting with the election of 1996, PEI was divided into 27 single-member districts.

The Political Culture

PEI's political culture and resulting party system, as it developed through the nineteenth and twentieth centuries, could be called "traditionalist" (Adamson and Stewart 2001: 302-20). It was marked by the dominance of the Liberal and PC parties. There was little explicit ideology in PEI politics aside from appeals to farm interests. The low ratio of MLAs to voters provided for close interaction between MLAs and their constituents. Presently, the population of approximately 140,000 elects 27 MLAs, about one member per 5,000 residents. This may be compared, for instance, to neighbouring Nova Scotia, where a population of about 940,000 is represented by 52 MLAs, about one member per 18,000 people.

Recent elections have seen wider gaps between the popular vote of the two leading parties than was usually the case in the past. In the 18 elections between 1923 and 1986, a gap of ten or more percentage points between the Liberal and Conservative/PC vote occurred only four times. When it did, the opposition suffered disproportionately. The most extreme distortion took place in 1935, when the popular vote, which favoured the Liberals by 58-42 per cent, gave them all 30 seats. In recent elections such wide gaps have become far more frequent. In the five elections between 1989 and 2003, ten-point gaps have occurred four times: in 1989, 1993, 2000, and 2003. The number of opposition members elected on each occasion is telling: one (1989 and 2000), two (1993), and four (2003). Only in the close election of 1996, when there was a difference of only 3 per cent in the vote of the two leading parties, was a respectable number (nine) of opposition members elected.

Party loyalties on PEI have been likened to religious affiliation—and politics to a "blood sport" (MacDonald 2000: 21; Milne 1982: 59-67). Third parties were a marginal factor in the popular vote and won no seats until the NDP won a single seat in 1996 (see Robb 1982). In the four elections between

1989 and 2000, the NDP's popular vote rose to 5 per cent in 1993, to 7.9 per cent in 1996, and finally to an all-time high of 8.4 per cent in 2000, falling to a more traditional level of 3 per cent in 2003, a symptom of a weakening of the traditional political culture.[1]

Reforms in the 1990s

It is in the context of an electoral system that fails to transform the popular vote coherently into seats and which decimates the opposition that the present debate on electoral reform on PEI began. In hearings before the 1993-94 Election Act and Electoral Boundaries Commission a few speakers suggested PR, though nothing came of the idea. One newspaper editorialized that "daydreams of a system that more accurately reflects the wishes of all voters" should be forgotten because it would be uncertain which constituencies MLAs would represent.[2] In its 1994 report, the commission praised the MMP system, but deemed it inappropriate for PEI "at this time." MMP would be a "major departure from traditional British and Canadian electoral approaches," and its implications had not been widely discussed by the political parties or the public. Further, there were technical details to be considered; for instance, "the role of political parties in selecting list candidates, the accountability of list candidates to the public and the method of apportioning seats to political parties following each election" (Elections Commission 1994: 20). Skepticism of party lists remains a pillar of opposition to PR.[3]

The Special Committee on the Election Act

Though the commission did not regard PR as an alternative to the FPTP system in 1994, electoral reform became a live issue in the late 1990s, after several disproportional elections: 30-2 in 1989, 31-1 in 1993, and 26-1 in 2000. In 2000 the Legislative Assembly established a Special Committee on the Election Act, comprised of five MLAs, to consult public opinion and report to the legislature on several issues of significance to the electoral system, including the question of PR. For the first time, PR entered the mandate of a legislative body on PEI. After conducting public hearings, the Special Committee noted in its April 2001 report that a recurring theme was the "establishment of a system of proportional representation through use of mixed member PR ... or some other system to more closely reflect the percentage of popular vote with the percentage of seats in the Legislative Assembly" (PEI 2001: 3). Out of 15 oral or written presentations, seven called for the establishment or study of a PR system (PEI 2001: 7).

In their briefs, PR supporters emphasized two adverse consequences of distorted and one-sided majorities. First, because votes do not translate into seats, large numbers of voters were in fact wasting their votes. Moreover, inflated majorities meant few opposition MLAs. The absence of a "strong and viable Official Opposition" in a position to acquire the experience it might later need to govern, critics of FPTP argued, is a recipe for deficient government (PEI 2001: 8-9).

The Special Committee restated the reservations of the 1994 commission, but with a qualifier. There had been significant changes in electoral systems elsewhere since 1994, the report noted, such as reforms carried out in New Zealand and the United Kingdom. New Zealand had moved to a German-style MMP system, and similar systems had been designed for the new Scottish and Welsh assemblies. "One could hardly argue," the committee observed, "that PR electoral reforms in those jurisdictions ... resulted in instability in government!" (PEI 2001: 10). Hence, while it was inappropriate to recommend such a "significant departure from our traditional electoral system based on this set of hearings," PR merited further examination. The Special Committee recommended that Elections PEI, the provincial agency responsible for administering elections, investigate PR, paying particular attention to the systems used in jurisdictions "of reasonably comparable geographic size and population to Prince Edward Island" (PEI 2001: 12-13).

The Elections PEI Report

About one year after the Special Committee on the Election Act declared that PR deserved further study, the Chief Electoral Officer, M.H. Wigginton, submitted a *Report on Proportional Representation* to the Legislative Assembly. Remarking that PR takes many forms, the report insisted that any PR scheme to be implemented on PEI must be a "made in Prince Edward Island system ... made for Islanders, to be used by Islanders" (Elections PEI 2002: 1). After reviewing several types of electoral systems and setting out three alternate scenarios for a reformed PEI system, the chief electoral officer recommended that "any binding decision for one system over another system should be left to a provincial referendum, preceded by an impartial campaign of public education about the issues involved in the choice" (Elections PEI 2002: 14).

The Prince Edward Island Commission on Electoral Reform

In the Speech from the Throne opening the session of the Assembly in November 2002, the government committed itself to appoint "an independent commission to consult on and consider Prince Edward Island's electoral system ... so that it continues to reflect what Islanders require of their legislature" (PEI 2003b: 1). In January 2003 Premier Pat Binns appointed retired Chief Justice Norman Carruthers as head (and sole commissioner) of the Prince Edward Island Commission on Electoral Reform. Commissioner Carruthers's mandate was to carry out a "complete, independent and accountable examination of Prince Edward Island's electoral system."[4] Moreover, the mandate explicitly included a review of alternative electoral systems. Hence, before consulting the public, the commission released a discussion paper on "The Major Electoral Systems Found around the World and Four Models" (PEI 2003a). These assessments of the world's electoral systems were reproduced in the commission's Report, released in December 2003.

In the Report, FPTP, the existing system, received close attention. FPTP, the commission noted, had the advantage of maintaining a direct link between the voter and the representative. It tended to create majorities by inflating popular vote pluralities into electoral majorities. It reinforced the two-party system, created weak oppositions, underrepresented women and minorities, and allowed power to concentrate in the executive (PEI 2003a: 2-4). Unstated, but not unnoticed, was FPTP's great advantage of familiarity.

The report examined briefly other plurality/majority systems, including the alternative vote (potentially even less proportional that FPTP); the "two-round" (or run-off) system (expensive, in that it typically requires two elections); and the block vote (also disproportional). FPTP, it appeared, had more to recommend it than did other plurality/majority systems (PEI 2003a: 4-6). The semi-proportional systems—parallel voting and the single non-transferable vote—were portrayed as forms of a compromise between true proportionality and the disproportional results of FPTP elections (PEI 2003a: 13-15).

PR has long been the goal for most advocates of electoral reform on PEI as elsewhere. The commission classified PR systems into categories: list-based PR, STV, and MMP. The pure list system—akin to those used in Israel and the Netherlands—had two significant drawbacks: a tendency to produce coalition governments and a failure to provide a strong geographical link between a member and the electors. STV, though it represented "a means of ensuring proportional representation while still allowing people to vote for individual candidates," had the drawback of an "excessively complicated" vote counting process (PEI 2003a: 9-10). MMP, on the other hand, combined the strong points of both PR and FPTP, proportionality and the link between voters and members of the Assembly (PEI 2003a: 12).

After releasing the Discussion Paper, in May and June of 2003 the commission heard oral submissions at seven public meetings across the province. The presenters were individuals and organizations, including the national lobby group Fair Vote Canada, the Council of Canadians, the PEI Advisory Council on the Status of Women, the NDP and Green Parties, and several MLAs, as well as organizations representing Acadian groups, municipalities, and organized labour. The commission also met with First Nations leaders and community organizations and received a number of written briefs (PEI 2003b: 5-8, 34).

When it came to recommendations, the commissioner stated that "the time has probably now arrived for more modifications to the electoral system to ensure it remains responsive to the expectations and demands of the twenty-first century" (PEI 2003b: 82), adding that:

> The voice for reform is becoming louder all the time as is illustrated by the formation in this Province of the advocacy group, "Every Vote Counts," and by the many letters and guest opinions that appear in the daily media.... The interest in this Commission is another indication of the growing desire for change.... The 2003 election results can be considered a one-sided result along with the 1989, 1993 and 2000 election results so one cannot say this trend has corrected itself. (PEI 200b: 87)

In some jurisdictions, FPTP creates regional disparity in party representation; in others, the guiding purpose of adopting PR is to make the legislature more closely resemble society, especially in terms of the representation of women. The latter has been noted as a benefit of moving away from FPTP and is certainly not a negligible factor for many of those who support PR in the province (PEI 2003b: 31-33). The commissioner acknowledged these concerns in his report, stating that changes to the system should result in "increased representation for women in the legislative assembly" and that there should be discussions with PEI First Nations people to determine whether they should have a designated MLA (PEI 2003b: 101).

Not surprisingly, the commissioner found no willingness to eliminate district MLAs. He commented in September 2003 that "If there's one thing people have told me, it's that everyone wants to retain their district member of the legislature"[5] (PEI 2003b: 83). (This was indeed the conclusion in his report three months later.)

The commissioner was in no doubt that PR was the likeliest candidate for a reformed system. Of the PR systems, MMP was the most attractive, although he did not dismiss the single transferable vote out of hand (PEI 2003b: 95-98). He wrote that a split of about two-thirds district seats and one-third list seats would, in some people's view, "provide a degree of proportionality, ensure a number of members in the opposition and ... enable third parties to get elected" as well as making it "easier for women to get elected" (PEI 2003b: 92). As an example, the commissioner described a possible outcome of the 2003 election under an MMP system. If there were 21 FPTP members and ten list seats, the PCs would have elected 18 MLAs and the Liberals 13, assuming that the threshold for claiming list seats was higher than the NDP's 3.2 per cent of the vote. But the NDP's falling below the threshold was not a foregone conclusion, because "many people feel the NDP vote would increase under such a system" (PEI 2003b: 92-93).

The commissioner's report set out alternative approaches to various modalities of a reformed electoral system—including whether there would be a single ballot or separate ballots for the constituencies and the lists, how the list seats should be allocated across the province, and how list candidates should be selected—while leaving the ultimate decisions to the voters. This raised the more immediate question of the process for designing and implementing electoral reform. The decision, he wrote, must be made by a binding, publicly funded referendum conducted "in a non-partisan fashion" in which there is "an educational component which allows both sides of the issue to be explored." Overseeing this process he envisaged an "independent commission comprised of representatives from all political parties and the general public" (PEI 2003b: 99-100).

Conclusion

The immediate reaction from the government after the Carruthers Report was released was a cautious one. Premier Binns said he had forwarded the report to a cabinet committee for review, with a view to making recommendations for discussion in the spring 2004 sitting of the Legislative Assembly; he made it clear that "there needs to be considerably more discussion and debate before any decisions are made on an alternative electoral system."[6] He was skeptical about the suggestion that the Assembly be made larger—"more members mean more expense," he was quoted as saying—and felt that there was not a "driving need amongst average Islanders today to change the electoral system"; however, he said, "[t]hat doesn't mean there isn't a better system. I think the report suggests that there are better models that will ensure that following an election ...the elected members better reflect the will of the voter." He also spoke of the possibility of a referendum before the next provincial election.[7]

In any event, the commissioner's conclusion that the question of reform ought to be carried further is, in itself, a victory for reform. The report has clearly raised the possibility of an unprecedented reform to the PEI electoral system. An MMP-based Legislative Assembly would represent a radical shake-up of political life in the province. If nothing else, it should ensure the presence of a respectable number of opposition MLAs. It would also, according to the commissioner, increase the number of women in the Assembly, and, perhaps, enhance the position of third parties. Ultimately, of course, the decision will lie with the voters. Early in his report the commissioner compares the debate over electoral reform to the campaign to win the secret ballot in the nineteenth century, which was initially regarded as a "crazy old question" and a hopeless cause (PEI 2003b: v-vi). Voters now take it for granted. Could the same be said of proportional representation a century hence?

Notes

1. Statistics on popular vote are drawn from Cousins 2000.
2. Charlottetown *Guardian* 3 April 1993: 10
3. See, for example, Tom Connor, "The push for PR," Charlottetown *Guardian*, 28 May 2003: A7.
4. Premier's Office, News Release, 21 January 2003.
5. Canadian Press, 30 September 2003.
6. Premier's Office, Press Release, 18 December 2003.
7. Charlottetown *Guardian*/Canadian Press, 18 December 2003.

CHAPTER 15

Prospects for Federal Voting System Reform in Canada

Larry Gordon

With electoral reform now on the political agendas of five Canadian provinces, can federal reform be far behind? From the 1970s through the 1990s,
serious discussion of federal reform was generally limited to the pages of
academic journals and Royal Commission reports. Today, the debate is taking
place at political party conventions, policy institute conferences, and in the
media, courts, and communities across the country.

The prospects for significant federal electoral reform are perhaps brighter
now than ever before. At the same time, the major players in the Canadian
political arena are becoming increasingly alert and, in many cases, anxious.
The political elite are well aware that rewriting the rules for elections means
recasting the political system itself. Careers, egos, and fortunes will be on the
line. Reformers currently have the momentum, but they have yet to engage
in a bare-knuckles brawl with well-resourced and politically savvy defenders
of the status quo who see their future tied to the continuation of the present
system. The timing and final outcome of this impending battle are far from
clear.

The following provides an overview of the political environment in which
this historic battle will be waged and the positions of the key actors. It concludes with commentary on the prospects for change.

Distorted Federal Election Results

One of the most glaring problems associated with Canada's electoral system
is the degree to which the popular will is distorted in the allocation of seats.
Since the post-World War I emergence of a multi-party political system in
Canada, distorted election results have become commonplace. The portion of
seats won in federal elections almost always diverges, sometimes wildly, from
the portion of the popular vote received by each party.

Since World War I, Canada has had 15 majority governments. Of those, 11 were artificial majority governments created by the voting system. One party was able to capture a majority of seats in the House of Commons without winning a majority of the popular vote. In the 1980s and 1990s, the first-past-the-post (FPTP) voting system in effect wasted an average of more than six million votes, or about half of the votes cast, in each federal election. More than six million Canadians went to the polls, marked their ballots, dropped them in ballot boxes, but gained no representation for their views. The winner-take-all system awarded political representation only to those voters who held the most popular partisan viewpoint in their ridings. The cumulative effect of these millions of wasted votes in every riding across the country is distorted election outcomes. Some parties gain far more seats than justified by their portion of the popular vote. Other parties capture fewer seats than deserved.

In 1984, Brian Mulroney's Progressive Conservatives (PCs) won 50 per cent of the popular vote, which translated into 211 of 282 seats. The Liberals and New Democratic Party (NDP) were supported by 47 per cent of the voters, but gained only 70 seats between them. In 1988, the PCs won 169 seats, enough to bring in free trade with the United States, even though their popular vote was nine percentage points lower than the anti free-trade Liberals and NDP. The perceived distortion meant a renewed questioning of the electoral system, a questioning that intensified with the electoral results of the subsequent elections.

The 1993 election spelled the end of the nine-year PC majority in Parliament, but did so through one of the most breathtaking distortions in the history of Canadian elections. Under the leadership of Kim Campbell, the newly appointed leader and prime minister, the PC vote collapsed from 5.7 million votes to 2.2 million votes. This collapse, however, was dramatically exaggerated as the PCs won only two seats. While they averaged just one seat for every million votes, the Liberals gained one seat for every 31,909 votes. The electoral travesty of 1993 was followed by another ludicrous outcome in the next election. In 1997, the Liberals formed the phoniest majority government in Canadian history. Despite winning only 38.5 per cent of the popular vote, they walked away with 51.5 per cent of the seats, thus maintaining their majority control of Parliament.

The 2000 federal election produced another long list of democratic aberrations. The Liberals gained 100 of the 103 Ontario seats with just 51.5 per cent of the popular vote in that province. Canadian Alliance founder Preston Manning had been chastised for failing to "break through" in Ontario. His party's one million votes in that province, up 19 per cent from the prior election, produced only two seats. In the western provinces, however, the fortunes of the Liberals and Alliance were reversed. In that region, the Canadian Alliance won twice as many votes as the Liberals, but gained nearly five times as many seats. Indeed, Canadians, including political commentators, are surprised to learn that the Alliance actually won more votes in Quebec than in Saskatchewan. Nonetheless, Saskatchewan produced ten Alliance MPs and Quebec none.

Such examples of electoral inequities are almost endless. The Canadian voting system blatantly violates the principle of one citizen, one vote, one value — and more Canadians are coming to notice it.

Evolution of Party Positions

The current voting reform movement in Canada is not the first. Shortly after World War I, a loose coalition of farmers, organized labour, and reformers successfully pushed for the adoption of new voting systems. Many major Western cities, as well as the provinces of Manitoba and Alberta adopted a variety of new voting systems (Pilon 1999). The electoral reform debate also reached the House of Commons. Having adopted a policy supporting proportional representation (PR) at their 1919 policy convention, the Liberals found themselves forming a minority government just two years later. They subsequently tabled a bill to test PR in a number of urban districts. During the House debate, Liberal Prime Minister Mackenzie King said: "I have no fear of the consequences as regards proportional representation being wholly in the interest of good government ... I believe proportional representation will help to give to holders of all shades of opinion a feeling that at least they have had an opportunity to gain expression for their views in the House of Commons."[1] Nevertheless, despite both the Liberals and Progressives having policies in favour of PR, the bill was defeated 90 to 72.

By the mid-1920s, Canada's first voting reform movement had reached its high water mark. Many of the municipal and provincial reforms were eventually dismantled. In the federal political arena, the issue emerged briefly a decade later. In 1934, fearing the newly formed Cooperative Commonwealth Federation (CCF) would gain advantages from the FPTP system, the Liberal Party once again promised to introduce PR. After winning a solid majority and with the CCF threat receding, the Liberals once again lost interest in reform (Pilon 1999: 114-16).

Serious renewed interest in the federal parties didn't re-emerge until the 1980s and 1990s. Within the NDP, proponents of PR ran into staunch opposition for many years, as the party had formed numerous provincial governments, often with artificial majorities created by the FPTP system. But in the latter 1990s, beset by hard times, the NDP embraced the general principle of PR, and, at their 2003 convention, adopted a clear policy calling for a referendum on a mixed-member proportional (MMP) system for Canada. Newly elected party leader Jack Layton said he would make a national referendum on proportional representation a requirement for support of any future minority government.

The political right has been even slower to move. Despite their devastating loss in the 1993 election, where more than two million votes produced only two seats, the PCs hesitated to develop a strong policy on electoral reform. In 2002, the party finally adopted a new democratic reform package. The official policy statement summarized the problems with the FPTP system and called for a commission to study voting system reform and report to Parliament. The birth of the Reform party in the early 1980s seemed to herald the emergence of a new champion for democratic reforms. With a platform calling for parliamentary reform and increased direct democracy, the Reform Party (later the Canadian Alliance) also became the first modern party, with seats in Parliament, to call for a national referendum on voting system reform. The party leadership, however, never actively promoted the electoral reform policy.

The real obstacle has, of course, been the Liberals. Having become Canada's "natural governing party," thanks to the current voting system, the federal Liberal Party remains as silent as possible on the issue, with a few, sometimes amusing exceptions. In 1984, Energy Minister and Liberal leadership contender Jean Chrétien told the media in Brandon, Manitoba, that proportional representation would help reduce Western alienation. "If I were the prime minister," Chrétien said, "I would do that [introduce PR] right after the next election."[2] As Canadians will remember, Chrétien subsequently won three elections and served as prime minister for ten years, without finding the time to mention, let alone introduce, PR.

During the 2003 Liberal Party leadership race, two contenders did acknowledge the voting reform issue. John Manley, then finance minister, said he favoured consideration of the alternative vote.[3] Sheila Copps, then heritage minister, said that she was ready to set up a task force on voting system reform. Paul Martin, the runaway winner of the leadership race, remained silent on the voting reform issue. While repeatedly proclaiming the need to address Canada's "democracy deficit," Martin carefully framed the issue as one of parliamentary, rather than electoral, reform.

Despite Liberal efforts, the momentum has not been stopped. On September 30, 2003, in the first vote in the House of Commons on PR since 1923, the NDP tabled a motion calling for a national referendum on the issue, which triggered a spirited debate. NDP MP Lorne Nystrom said the referendum was an urgent priority because "we are literally sleepwalking toward a crisis in democracy in our country." Liberal House leader Don Boudria defended the FPTP system, calling it "a pillar of our institutional framework since pre-confederation times." Canadian Alliance MP Ted White countered that Boudria's "sad attitude" reminded him of Animal Farm "where some of the animals are more equal than others."[4] The motion was supported by a surprisingly diverse coalition of NDP social democrats, Canadian Alliance conservatives, Bloc québécois separatists, and two very bold Liberal MPs. The PCs surprisingly did not support the motion, instead voting with the Liberals to defeat it. PC MP Inky Mark said the party opposed the motion because no clear alternative was being presented and not enough public discussion had occurred.

In the absence of electoral reform, the recent marriage of convenience between the Canadian Alliance and the PCs was consummated. The merger objective was to end the occurrences of Liberals being elected because the two conservative parties split the right-of-centre vote in the current system of single-member ridings. The new Conservative Party of Canada has yet to take a formal position on electoral reform, though the caucus adopted a position saying a new Conservative government would consider electoral reform, including PR.

Federal Agency Calls for Mixed-Member Proportional System

Sometimes support for electoral reform comes from unexpected quarters. Such was the case in New Zealand in 1986, when the Royal Commission on the Electoral System delivered their surprising recommendation to scrap the FPTP voting system and adopt an MMP system. While reform advocates had welcomed the appointment of the commission, "most were either pessimistic about the outcome or cynical of the government's motive," according to political scientist Peter Aimer. Once the commission made its recommendation, however, "the genie was out of the bottle," and reformers suddenly had new momentum (Aimer 1999: 149-50). Will a similar white knight emerge from within the Canadian federal government?

The Law Commission of Canada is an independent federal agency established to "engage Canadians in the renewal of the law to ensure that it is relevant, responsive, effective, equally accessible to all, and just."[5] The Law Commission studies and makes recommendations to Parliament on areas of law that relate to emerging social, political, and economic concerns. In 2001 it launched a major democratic renewal project to engage citizens in a discussion on the need for electoral reform. After an initial round of targeted forums with academic experts and civil society leaders, the commission issued an extensive discussion paper, with several dozen questions on democratic values, the nature of political representation, and the various types of voting systems that Canada might consider. After another round of public consultation and further research, commission staff and a project consultant prepared a final report, which was submitted to the justice minister and subsequently tabled in the House on March 31, 2004.

The Law Commission called for the scrapping of Canada's FPTP system and the introduction of an MMP system, which would have two-thirds of the seats filled by constituency MPs elected in local ridings. The remaining one-third of the seats would be filled by list MPs to ensure overall proportionality. But it goes further than just setting out principles: it even spells out boundaries for the regional districts from which the list MPs will be elected. While the government is not compelled to act on the commission's recommendation, the report will undoubtedly create waves in Ottawa political circles and draw increasing media attention to the issue.

Charter Challenge Underway

Another development in the legal arena also has potential to accelerate federal electoral reform. On May 1, 2001, Joan Russow and the Green Party of Canada filed a case with the Superior Court of Ontario. With assistance from the University of Toronto's Constitutional Test Case Centre, the claimants charge that the Canada Elections Act, and specifically the FPTP voting system, violates the Charter of Rights and Freedoms. Russow is a former Green Party leader and candidate.

The claimants charge that the current voting system violates two sections of the Charter. As explained by the University of Toronto's Test Case Centre:

> Section 3 of the Charter protects the right of every citizen of Canada "to vote in an election of members of the House of Commons or of a legislative assembly." This, of course, means

more than simply the right to mark an "X" on a ballot and put it in a box—otherwise, there would be no obligation to count the votes at all. They could be discarded, or count for nothing. At a minimum, the right to vote in the Charter places an obligation on the government to ensure that votes are counted in a way that is consistent with the democratic nature of our system of government. As the Supreme Court has said in earlier decisions, the right to vote means that the votes of citizens must count equally, as far as possible, so that each citizen has a 'parity of voting power' in comparison with others.[6]

Nonetheless, in the Supreme Court's earlier decision on the Saskatchewan Electoral Boundaries case, the justices ruled that the application of voter equality can be tempered by the right to effective representation. In the case of Saskatchewan riding boundaries, the Court accepted urban ridings having nearly twice as many voters as the least populated rural riding. The Court ruled that the need for effective representation of those rural voters justified the two-to-one weighting differential.

Knowing that the Court has taken a very broad interpretation of voter equality, the claimants have emphasized that voter inequities created by FPTP systems far exceed those created by differential riding sizes. For example, in the 1993 federal election, the voting system created a 32:1 weighting differential between votes for the Bloc québécois and PCs. The Bloc gained one seat for every 34,186 votes, compared to the PCs who gained one seat for every 1,093,211 votes (Beatty 2001: 51-2).

The other section of the Charter that FPTP violates, according to the claimants, is the guarantee of the right of equality.

Winner Take All systems make it harder for women to get elected than election systems that are based on the principle of proportional representation. Most of the established democracies in the world use some variant of proportional representation and many of them have twice as many women legislators. In Canada, roughly one in five legislators is a woman. In countries which use a more proportional system, the percentage is generally twice as large...

The Supreme Court has repeatedly said that a violation of equality happens not just when a law discriminates on its face, by making a distinction between black and white persons, for example, but also when it has the effect of putting a certain group of people at a disadvantage, and by so doing, demeans their dignity. That is exactly what happens under the Canada Elections Act.[7]

In June 2003, in the *Figueroa* decision, the Supreme Court ruled on another electoral system case launched by the Communist Party of Canada, striking down a law that would have required small parties to run 50 candidates before being eligible to issue tax receipts for political donations.

> "There is already reason to be concerned that the most influen-
> tial parties will dominate the public discourse and deprive their
> opponents of a reasonable opportunity to speak and be heard,"
> wrote one justice. "Legislation that augments this disparity
> increases the likelihood that the already marginalized voices of
> political parties with a limited geographic base will be drowned
> out by mainstream parties."[8]

The justices realized that the rationale for their ruling leads directly to questions about the legitimacy of the FPTP system. Perhaps, to counter that expectation, the majority stated that the decision on which electoral system to use belongs to Parliament and is "not one in which the court should involve itself." But as one legal expert wrote later, that statement "is at odds with the whole thrust of the majority's decision."[9]

The Charter challenge against the FPTP system may take as long as four or five years. The case must go through the Ontario Superior Court and then the Ontario Court of Appeals before reaching the Supreme Court. The federal justice minister has the power to refer cases directly to the Supreme Court but, not surprisingly, has declined to do so. It is thus difficult to assess the long-term effect of the legal case against FPTP. Some legal experts are quite skeptical about the chances for success. Expecting the Supreme Court to strike down the voting system, said one legal expert, is "dreaming in technicolour." But one might have said something similar about the *Figueroa* ruling, or the fact that the Law Commission would take such a clear-cut stand. Regardless of the legal ruling, however, the case will undoubtedly increase public awareness and add to the mounting pressure for reform.

Public Opinion on PR

Public opinion polls over the past decade clearly indicate that Canadians support the general principle of proportionality, or fairness, in electoral systems.

These findings, however, are prior to any extensive public debate on the pros and cons of various systems. As one expert summarized, "public support for proportional representation is a mile wide and an inch deep."[10]

One of the more comprehensive surveys was the February 2001 Ipsos-Reid poll commissioned by the Institute for Research on Public Policy. Survey respondents expressed preferences that would likely require trade-offs in choosing a voting system. While 64 per cent supported the concept of proportionality, 71 per cent also stated a preference for strong majority government. When asked about a trade-off between "strong majority government" and PR of the parties, 60 per cent choose proportionality and 36 per cent "strong majority government" (Bricker and Redfern 2001: 23).

The poll also discovered a shocking level of misunderstanding about how the current voting system works: "Fully 50 per cent of our respondents believe that a candidate must get a majority of all votes cast in a riding in order to win a parliamentary seat. And 47 per cent believe that a political party must win a majority of all votes cast in order to form the government." While the pollsters noted university graduates were more likely to understand how the system works, still about one-third believed that successful candidates and governments needed true majority support under the current system (Bricker and Redfern 2001: 23). Nevertheless, pollsters Darrell Bricker and Martin Redfern summarized the findings as follows: "While recognizing the embryonic state of this debate and the low level of awareness among many Canadians, it is nonetheless striking that a solid majority of Canadians support the implementation of a PR system" (Bricker and Redfern 2001: 22-24).

Another public opinion poll released in June 2001 by the Canada West Foundation (CWF) showed public support for PR is even stronger in the four western provinces. Slightly more than 71 per cent of western Canadians support PR. The CWF survey also found that a strong majority of supporters for each major political party supported PR; for instance, more than eight in ten Canadian Alliance supporters favour it. The lowest level of support came from Liberals and the NDP, where six in ten supported proportionality.[11]

The February 2003 Vector Poll on Public Opinion reinforced the earlier findings of the Ipsos-Reid study.[12] Sixty-four per cent of the respondents supported the idea of changing to a proportional voting system. The regional breakdown showed majority support in all regions, from a high of 69 per cent in the western provinces to a low of 51 per cent in Atlantic Canada. Similar to the CWF survey, the poll also found majority support by supporters of all parties, from a high of 76 per cent of Alliance supporters to a low of 59 per cent by Liberal supporters. The Vector Poll also probed the perceived trade-offs between proportionality and single-party majorities. When asked "would you be more likely to favour or less likely to favour proportional representation... [if it] usually meant a coalition of parties, not a single party, would form the government," 50 per cent responded "more likely," 36 per cent "less likely," and 7 per cent said "it depends."

While most polls have focused on PR, a 2002 survey jointly released by the Association for Canadian Studies and the Environics Research Group/Focus Canada examined comparative attitudes about other alternatives. When forced to choose between PR, preference voting, or FPTP, respondents are far from any consensus. Support for proportionality stands at 34 per cent, FPTP at 33 per cent, and preference voting at 25 per cent.[13]

In sum, surveys show significant public support for the idea of PR, but poor public understanding of how voting systems work.

Emergence of Citizens Groups

Another indication of growing civic pressure for electoral reform is the emergence of numerous advocacy groups. In recent years, provincial reform groups have been formed in BC, Québec, and PEI.

On the national level, Fair Vote Canada (FVC) was formally launched in April 2001 at a founding conference held in the Parliament buildings. FVC was structured as a multi-partisan citizens' campaign to press for: 1) a national consultation on a more proportional voting system, and 2) a national referendum in which Canadians would choose the best voting system. FVC has subsequently become a national centre for voting reform advocacy, working closely with provincial reform groups. The campaign has been endorsed by a wide range of organizations, such as the Canadian Labour Congress, Canadian Taxpayers Federation, and Canadian Federation of Students. The campaign is also supported by an advisory board of 33 prominent Canadians from a wide variety of backgrounds and all points on the political spectrum. Included in the advisory body are current and former MPs from the Liberals, PCs, Alliance, and NDP.

FVC has mounted an ongoing public education and media relations program. Chapters are being established across the country. Its call for a national referendum has been endorsed by more than 100 political scientists from 34 Canadian universities. FVC has also held a parliamentary press conference with the opposition parties to call for reform and recently released the Dubious Democracy Report on the shortcomings of the current voting system.

Prospects for Change

With a confluence of events and forces unique in Canadian history, the prospects for federal electoral reform have never been better. Public opinion polls show tremendous citizen frustration with the political system and support for the principle of PR. Five provinces—including Ontario, Québec, and BC—are now examining voting system reform. Federal political parties are developing positions. National and provincial citizens' groups are pressing for PR.

Without question, electoral reform is on the political radar screen. But how will the story play out? While the political and public dynamic in the successful New Zealand reform process offers valuable insights, one key element will likely be different in Canada. In New Zealand, largely due to the strong recommendation from the Royal Commission, the debate was framed as a choice between FPTP or PR. In Canada, rather than trying to defend the status quo, the opponents of proportional representation will likely promote a competing "reform": the alternative vote (AV) or single-member district preference voting. Many who oppose PR fully appreciate that the AV would largely preserve the status quo, while providing a veneer of "reform."

As other chapters in this book make plain, one or more provinces will likely lead the way in adopting a more proportional voting system, probably within the next few years. As soon as one of the big three—Ontario, Québec, or BC—adopts a new system, we might expect a domino effect. With major provinces embracing "fair voting," the federal government would be hard pressed to deny Canadians a voice in a process to consider changing the federal voting system.

Provincial reforms, however, will not be the only point of pressure. In New Zealand, the reform movement was boosted quite unexpectedly by the report of the government's own Royal Commission. The recent report and MMP recommendation from the Law Commission of Canada may accelerate the national debate. The Charter challenge on the constitutional validity of the FPTP system could create additional momentum.

And, finally, the political landscape may be changing. New forces will be at work in the Canadian political arena. If the newly formed Conservative Party of Canada and a reinvigorated NDP begin to chew away at the right and left sides of Liberal support, the possibility of a minority federal government increases. A minority federal government, as observers have long noted, would likely provide the most fertile ground for substantive and far-reaching democratic reforms.

At the very least, a true public debate will soon begin in earnest. While this is not likely to develop in time for the 2004 election, Prime Minister Paul Martin's majority looks less certain at the time of this writing due in particular to polls showing a resurgence of the Bloc Québécois. If the election does produce a minority government, by the time this book is published, the issue of electoral system reform may have leapt onto the federal political arena.

Though the introduction of a more proportional voting system for federal elections is far from guaranteed, the odds have certainly improved. Several years ago, no one would have foreseen the possibility of Canada actually adopting a new voting system in the not-too-distant future. Today, the spectre of electoral reform is becoming increasingly visible on the political horizon Could it be that the days are numbered for Canada's seemingly unchangeable FPTP electoral system?

Notes

1. Hansard, 19 February 1923: 422.
2. "Chretien seeks proportional vote in federal politics," *Globe and Mail* 9 May 1984.
3. Studies have shown the Alternative Vote, or single-member district preference voting, used in Australia, would likely be very advantageous to the federal Liberal Party, perhaps even more advantageous than FPTP.
4. Debates of the House of Commons, 30 September 2003.
5. Law Commission of Canada, mission statement, appearing on web site: <http: www.lcc.gc.ca>.
6. University of Toronto, Faculty of Law, Test Case Centre at <http: www.law-lib.utoronto.ca/testcase/>; Electoral System Charter Challenge FAQ: "How does Canada's electoral system violate the right to vote?"
7. Test Case Centre, Electoral System Charter Challenge FAQ: "How does Canada's electoral system violate the right of equality?"
8. Justice Frank Iacobucci, quoted in "Communists win right to party," *National Post* 28 June 2003.
9. Colin Feasby, "Seems our entire electoral system may be unconstitutional," *Globe and Mail* 3 July 2003.
10. Paul Howe, former research director, Institute for Research on Public Policy (IRPP) in a presentation at the founding conference of Fair Vote Canada, 30-31 March 2001, Ottawa.
11. Canada West Foundation, "Institutional Reform—Survey Data: Building a New West," Fact Sheet, 6 June 2001.
12. Vector Poll on Public Opinion in Canada, February 2003, with questions on PR commissioned by the Canadian Labour Congress.
13. Jack Jedwab, Executive Director, Association for Canadian Studies, summary paper: "Electoral Reform and Donor Disclosure," Ottawa, August 2002.

New Brunswick Mission, Mandate, and Terms of Reference

Mission

To identify options for an enhanced citizen-centred democracy in New Brunswick building on the values, heritage, culture, and communities of our province.

Mandate

To examine and make recommendations on strengthening and modernizing our electoral system and democratic institutions and practices in New Brunswick to make them more fair, open, accountable, and accessible to New Brunswickers.

The Commission on Legislative Democracy will seek the views of New Brunswickers on:

- fairer, more equitable, and effective representation in the Legislative Assembly;
- greater public involvement in decisions affecting people and their communities;
- more open, responsive, and accountable democratic institutions and practices;
- higher civic engagement and participation in the democratic processes in New Brunswick.

Terms of Reference

Specifically, the Commission on Legislative Democracy will focus on the following areas:

ELECTORAL REFORM

1. To examine and make recommendations on implementing a proportional representation electoral system for the New Brunswick Legislative Assembly, and to propose a specific model best suited for our province that ensures fairer representation, greater equality of votes, an effective legislature and government, and a continued role for directly elected MLAs representing specific geographic boundaries.

2. To examine and make recommendations on future steps, including amendments to the Elections Act, required to give effect to a new proportional representation electoral system.

3. To examine and make recommendations on the principles and procedures to guide future changes to New Brunswick's electoral boundaries, including the number of constituencies to be represented in the Legislative Assembly, that will be referred to a Representation and Electoral Boundaries Commission.

4. To examine and make recommendations on instituting fixed election dates for provincial general elections while proposing a fixed election date and procedures best suited for our province.

5. To examine and make recommendations on increasing voter turnout in provincial general elections, particularly amongst young New Brunswickers, and improving accessibility to the electoral process in New Brunswick by modernizing our electoral laws while reinforcing the democratic rights and responsibilities of New Brunswickers to vote.

LEGISLATIVE REFORM

To examine and make recommendations on enhancing the role of the Legislative Assembly and MLAs in decision-making while ensuring greater accountability of MLAs to their constituents and to New Brunswickers. To examine and make recommendations on enhancing transparency and accountability in appointments to government agencies, boards, and commissions.

DEMOCRATIC REFORM

To examine and make recommendations on enhancing direct democracy by proposing a New Brunswick Referendum Act that sets out the rules and procedures for allowing province-wide, binding referendums on significant public policy issues.

To examine and make recommendations on enhancing public involvement in government and legislative decision-making.

To fulfill its mandate, the Commission on Legislative Democracy will:

- seek the views of New Brunswickers through public hearings and submissions;
- hold other meetings and forums as required;
- conduct research and analysis as required that is appropriate to all aspects of the Commission's mandate;
- report no later than December 31, 2004.

Websites on Electoral Systems in the Democratic World

Canada

- Fair Vote Canada: <http://www.fairvotecanada.org/> (see Chapter 15).
- The Edible Ballot Society: <http://edibleballot.tao.ca/>. An irreverent site by Canadian activists who are critical of winner-take-all elections and suggests various ways to protest them—including unique culinary approaches. They support a variety of electoral reforms, including proportional representation.
- Law Commission of Canada, Discussion paper on electoral reform in Canada.<http://www.lcc.gc.ca/en/themes/gr/er/discussion_paper/executive.asp>.
- Law Commission of Canada. Voting Counts: Electoral Reform for Canada <http://www.lcc.gc.ca/en/themes/gr/er/er_report/er_report_toc.asp>.
- Québec: Mouvement pour une démocratie nouvelle: <http://pages.infinit.net/mdn>. A very useful site for those interested in the Québec movement (see Chapter 13). Mainly in French.
- British Columbia: Fair Voting BC: <www.fairvotingbc.com> is Nick Loenen's useful website. Also note Citizen's Assembly on Electoral Reform: <http://www.citizensassembly.bc.ca/public> (see Chapter 11).
- PEI Electoral Reform Commission: <http://www.gov.pe.ca/electoralreform/index.php3>.

United States

- The Center for Voting and Democracy: <http://www.fairvote.org/>. A non-profit educational organization located in Washington DC. The Center is the leading organization in the United States dedicated to educating the public about alternative elections systems.

- PR Library: <http://www.mtholyoke.edu/acad/polit/damy/prlib.htm/>.
  A source of information on proportional representation elections, including
  beginning readings, in-depth articles by scholars and activists, an extensive
  bibliography, and a guide to related Web sites. This site has been created by
  Professor Douglas J. Amy, Department of Politics, Mount Holyoke College,
  and was used to locate a number of the links listed here.
- Californians for Electoral Reform: <http://www.fairvoteca.org/>. Much
  useful information about PR and especially on how to organize an effective
  campaign for PR in your community.
- Midwest Democracy Center: <http://www.midwestdemocracy.org/>.
  A Chicago-based group advocating electoral reform, including PR. Good
  section on the campaign to bring cumulative voting back to Illinois.
- "Representation and Democracy": <http://www.giantleap.org/envision/
  rep.html>. A collection of PR-related articles by journalist and activist (and
  contributor) Steven Hill.
- Proportional Representation Voting in Cambridge Municipal Elections:
  <http://www.cambridgema.gov/~Election/prop-voting.html>. Cambridge
  is the only city in the United States currently using a fully proportional representation system. This site contains information about the use of the single
  transferable vote there.

Other Countries

- Electoral Reform Society: < http://www.electoral-reform.org.uk/>.
  Founded in England in 1884, the ERS is the longest continuous PR organization. This site contains good information about the single transferable vote
  (STV), the ERS's preferred form of PR. There is also an excellent analysis of
  the recent report issued by the Jenkins Commission that recommends a new
  voting system for British parliamentary elections.
- Charter88: < http://www.charter88.org.uk/voting/index.html>.
  An independent organization in the United Kingdom that supports a number
  of political reforms, including a change to more proportional elections.
- Fairshare: <http://www.fairsharevoting.org/>. Scotland's campaign for
  electoral reform for local government in Scotland. It campaigns for the implementation of the Kerley proposals for STV for Scottish local elections.
- Proportional Representation Society of Australia:
  <http://www.prsa.org.au/>. Like the ERS, this organization is a long-estab-
  lished proponent of PR, especially the single transferable vote (called "Hare
  Clark quota preferential voting").
- Electoral Reform Coalition of New Zealand:
  <http://www.stvnz.org/index.htm>. This organization led the successful
  fight to bring mixed-member PR to New Zealand. They are now on a campaign for using STV for local elections.
- Changing Democracy <http://www.jackwebster.com/vote/index.htm>
  has a useful collection of materials and interviews on New Zealand MMP
  gathered by Ed Watson.

Sites with Useful Information on Voting Systems

- International IDEA: <http://www.idea.int/>. The International Institute for Democracy and Electoral Assistance is located in Stockholm; its overall objective is to promote and advance sustainable democracy worldwide and to improve and consolidate electoral processes. This site has descriptions of several important books and studies produced by IDEA that are of relevant reading for those interested in PR. They include the *International IDEA Handbook of Electoral System Design* by Andrew Reynolds and Ben Reilly, an internet-available report on "Global Voter Turnout," and *Obstacles to Women's Participation in Parliament*, by Nadezdha Shvedova.
- The Jenkins Report: <http://www.fairvote.org/library/geog/europe/jenkins.htm>. Released in the United Kingdom in the fall of 1998, this is the path-breaking report of the commission appointed by Prime Minister Tony Blair to study possible changes in the British voting system. The detailed report analyzes the advantages and disadvantages of various elections systems and concludes by recommending that a public referendum be held to choose between the traditional single-member district plurality system, and a new two-vote system that would add a degree of proportional representation to British elections.
- Elections: Results and Voting Systems: <http://www.barnsdle.demon.co.uk/vote/vote.htm/>. This site contains detailed descriptions of various PR voting systems, allocation formulas, etc.
- Electoral Systems of the World: <http://worldpolicy.org/globalrights/democracy/table-pr.html/> lists the voting systems used by every democratic country in the world.
- <http://www.uni-augsburg.de/bazi/pprll.html>. A detailed literature list on proportional representation, including some links, maintained by Professor Dr. Friedrich Pukelsheim, Inst. für Mathematik, University of Augsburg.

References and Suggested Readings

Adamson, Agar, and Ian Stewart. 2001. Changing party politics in Atlantic Canada. In *Party politics in Canada*, ed. Hugh G. Thorburn and Alan Whitehorn. 8th ed. Toronto, ON: Prentice Hall.

Agacinski, Sylviane. 1998. *Politique des sexes*. Paris: Seuil.

Aimer, Peter. 1999. Electoral system change in New Zealand. In Milner, ed. 145-55.

Amy, Douglas J. 1993. *Real choices/new voices: The case for proportional representation elections in the United States*. Rev. ed. 2002. New York, NY: Columbia University Press.

Anduiza. Eva P. 2002. Campaign and participation in the Spanish election of 2000. Paper presented in workshop 22 at the European Consortium for Political Research (ECPR) Joint Sessions. Torino, Italy. 22-27 March.

Ashdown, Paddy. 1999. *The Ashdown diaries, Volume One 1988-1997*. London, UK: Penguin.

Bakvis, Herman, and Laura G. Macpherson. 1995. Quebec block voting and the Canadian electoral system. *Canadian Journal of Political Science* 28, 4: 659-92.

Bale, Tim. 2003. Pricking the south sea bubble: From fantasy to reality in Labour-led New Zealand. *Political Quarterly* 74: 2, 202-13.

——, and Christine Dann. 2002. Is the grass really greener? The rationale and reality of support party status: A New Zealand case study. *Party Politics* 8,3: 349-65.

Barker, Fiona. 1997. Negotiating with New Zealand First: A study of its coalition agreements with National and with Labour. In Boston et al., eds., 247-73.

Beatty, David, 2001. Making democracy constitutional. *Policy Options* (July-August): 50-53.

Bennett, Stephen E. 1998. Young people's indifference to media coverage of public affairs. *PS: Political Science and Politics* 31: 539-42.

Beyme, Klaus von. 1985. *Political parties in Western democracies*. Aldershot, UK: Gower.

Bilodeau, Antoine. 1999. L'impact mécanique du vote alternatif au Canada: une simulation des élections de 1997. *Canadian Journal of Political Science* 32: 745-61.

Bird, Karen. 2003. Who are the women? Where are the women? And what difference can they make? Effects of gender parity in French municipal elections. *French Politics* 1,1: 5-38.

Bjorklund, Tor. 2000. The steadily declining voter turnout: Norwegian local elections 1963-1999. Paper presented at the Naples conference arranged by Della Societa Italiana di Studi Elettorali. 19-21 October.

Blais, André, and R. Ken Carty. 1990. Does proportional representation foster voter turnout? *European Journal of Political Research* 18,2: 167-82.

——, and Stéphane Dion. 1990. Electoral systems and the consolidation of new democracies. In *Democratic transition and consolidation in Southern Europe, Latin America and South East Asia*, ed. D. Ethier. London, UK: Macmillan Press.

——, and Agnieszka Dobrzynska. 2000. The choice of electoral systems: Interests versus ideas. Unpublished manuscript.

——, E. Gidengill, R. Nadeau, and N. Nevitte. 2002. *Anatomy of a Liberal victory: Making sense of the vote in the 2000 Canadian election.* Peterborough, ON: Broadview.

Bogdanor, Vernon. 1984. *What is proportional representation? A guide to the issues.* Oxford, UK: Robertson.

Boix, Carles. 1999. Setting the rules of the game: The choice of electoral systems in advanced democracies. *American Political Science Review* 93: 609-24.

Boston, Jonathan. 1998. *Governing under proportional representation: Lessons from Europe.* Wellington, NZ: Institute of Policy Studies, University of Victoria.

——, Stephen Levine, Elizabeth McLeay, and Nigel S. Roberts, eds. 1997. *From campaign to coalition: New Zealand's first general election under proportional representation.* Palmerston North, NZ: Dunmore Press.

Bowler, Shaun, Elisabeth Carter and David M. Farrell. 2000. Studying electoral institutions and their consequences: Electoral systems and electoral laws. Paper presented at the International Political Science Association (IPSA) Conference. Québec, Canada. August.

——, Todd Donovan, and David Brockington. 2003. *Electoral reform and minority representation: Local experiments with alternative elections.* Columbus, OH: Ohio State University Press.

Brady, David W. et al. 1979. The decline of party in the US House of Representatives, 1887-1968. *Legislative Studies Quarterly* 4, 3: 381-407.

Bricker, Darrell, and Martin Redfern. 2001. Canadian perspectives on the voting system. *Policy Options* (July-August).

British Columbia Citizens' Assembly. 2004. Preliminary statement to the people of BC. Vancouver, BC (21 March).

Bull, Martin, and Martin Rhodes, eds. 1997. Crisis and transition in Italian politics. Special issue of *West European Politics* 20.

Burkett, Tony. 1985. The West German deputy. In *Representatives of the people? Parliamentarians and constituents in Western Democracies,* ed. Vernon Bogdanor. Aldershot, UK: Gower.

Butler, David, and Donald Stokes. 1969. *Political change in Britain: Forces shaping electoral change.* New York, NY: St. Martin's Press.

Bystydzienski, Jill M. 1994. Norway: Achieving world-record women's representation in government. In *Electoral systems in comparative perspective: Their impact on women and minorities,* ed. Wilma Rule and Joseph F. Zimmerman. 55-64. London, UK: Greenwood Press.

——. 1995. *Women in electoral politics: Lessons from Norway.* Westport, CT: Praeger.

Cairns, Alan C. 1968. The electoral system and the party system in Canada, 1921-1965. *Canadian Journal of Political Science* 1: 55-80.

Campbell, Rosie. 2002. Gender and voter turnout in the 2001 British general election. Paper presented in workshop 22 at the ECPR Joint Sessions. Torino, Italy. 22-27 March.

Canada. Task Force on Canadian Unity. 1979. *A future together: Observations and recommendations.* Ottawa, ON: Minister of Supply and Services.

Charbonneau, Jean-Pierre. 2002. *Citizen empowerment: A paper to open public debate.* Québec, QC: Secretariat for the Reform of Democratic Institutions.

Chiche, Jean, and Florence Haegel. 2002. Les connaissance politiques. In *La démocratie a l'épreuve,* ed. G. Grunberg, N. Mayer, and P. Sniderman. Paris: Presses de Sciences Po.

Church, Stephen, and Elizabeth McLeay. 2003. The parliamentary review of MMP in New Zealand. *Representation* 39,4: 245-54.

Clark, Marlene-Russell. 1973. Island politics. In *Canada's smallest province: A history of PEI,* ed. Francis W.P. Bolger. 289-327. Charlottetown, PEI: Prince Edward Island Centennial Commission.

Clerc, Christine. 2002. Droite: les révoltées de la parité. *Figaro* 28 May: 5.

Cliche, Paul. 1999. *Pour réduire le déficit démocratique: Le scrutin proportionnel.* Montréal, QC: Rénouveau québécois.

Colliard, Jean-Claude. 1978. *Les régimes parlementaires contemporains.* Paris: Presses de la fondation nationale des sciences politiques.

Comrie, Margie, Annemarie Gillies, and Mary Day. 2002. The Maori electoral option campaign: Problems of measuring "success." *Political Science* 54,2: 45-58.

Coulson, Tony. 1999. Voter turnout in Canada: Findings from the 1997 Canadian election study. *Electoral Insight* 1,2: 18-22.

Courtney, John C. 1980. Reflections on reforming the Canadian electoral system. *Canadian Public Administration* 23,3: 427-57.

——. 2004. *Elections: Canada's democratic audit.* Vancouver, BC: University of British Columbia Press.

Cousins, J.A. 2000. Electoral reform for Prince Edward Island: A discussion paper. Charlottetown: University of Prince Edward Island and Institute of Island Studies, October 2000.

——. 2003. Electoral reform for Prince Edward Island. Charlottetown, PEI: University of Prince Edward Island and Institute of Island Studies; *Canadian Parliamentary Review* 25,4 (Winter): 22-31.

Cowley, Philip, and Stephen Lochore. 2000. AMS in a cold climate: The Scottish Parliament in practice. *Representation* 37, 3/4: 175-85.

Cox, Gary W. 1997. *Making votes count: Strategic coordination in the world's electoral systems.* Cambridge, UK: Cambridge University Press.

Cox, Karen, and Leonard Schoppa. 2002. Interaction effects in mixed-member electoral systems: Theory and evidence from Germany, Japan and Italy. *Comparative Political Studies* 35: 1027-53.

Cronin, T.E. 1989. *Direct democracy: The politics of initiative, referendum and recall.* Cambridge, MA.: Harvard University Press.

Curtis, Gerald. 1988. *The Japanese way of politics.* New York, NY: Columbia University Press.

D'Alimonte, Roberto. 2001. Mixed electoral rules, partisan realignment, and party system change in Italy. In *Mixed-member electoral systems: The best of both worlds?*, ed. Matthew Soberg Shugart and Martin P. Wattenberg. 323-50. Oxford, UK: Oxford University Press.

Dalton, Russell J. 1996. *Citizen politics: Public opinion and political parties in advanced western democracies.* Chatham, NJ: Chatham House.

Darcy, R., and Sarah Slavin Schramm. 1977. When women run against men. *Public Opinion Quarterly* 41: 1-12.

——, Susan Welch and Janet Clark. 1994. *Women, elections and representation.* 2nd ed. Lincoln, NB: University of Nebraska Press.

Dekker, Hank. 1999. Citizenship conceptions and competencies in the subject matter 'Society' in Dutch schools. In *Citizenship and education in twenty-eight countries: Civic knowledge at age fourteen*, ed. J. Torney-Purta, R. Lehmann, H. Oswald, and W. Schulz. Amsterdam: Eburon-IEA.

Dobell, W.M. 1981. A limited corrective to plurality voting. *Canadian Public Policy* 7: 75-81.

Donnelly, M.S. 1957. Parliamentary government in Manitoba. *Canadian Journal of Economics and Political Science* 23,1: 20-32.

Dupuis, Jacques. 2003. Réforme des institution démocratiques: un project en trois axes. Notes from a speech to a conference organized by the Institute for Research on Public Policy (IRPP), Montréal, 10 September. *Policy Options* (October): 5-8.

Duverger, Maurice. 1955. *Droit constitutionnel et institutions politiques.* Paris: Presses Universitaires de France.

——. 1986. Duverger's law: Forty years later. In *Electoral laws and their political consequences*, ed. Bernard Grofman and Arend Lijphart. 69-84. New York, NY: Agathon Press.

Elections Commission. 1994. *Changing the political landscape: Report of the Election Act and Electoral Boundaries Commission.* Charlottetown, PEI. March.

Elections PEI. 2002. *Report on Proportional Representation.* Charlottetown, PEI. April.

Electoral Commission. 2003a. *The New Zealand electoral compendium.* 3rd ed. Wellington, NZ.

———. 2003b. *Annual Report for the year ended 30 June 2003.* Wellington, NZ.

Electoral Reform Commission of Prince Edward Island. 2003. Paper for discussion purposes on the major electoral systems found around the world and four models. Charlottetown, PEI. April.

Elkins, David J. 1976. Politics makes strange bedfellows: The BC party system in the 1952 and 1953 elections. *BC Studies* 30: 3-26.

Elton, David and Roger Gibbins. 1980. *Electoral reform: The need is pressing, the time is now.* Calgary: Canada West Foundation.

Ertman, Thomas. 1998. Democracy and dictatorship in interwar Western Europe revisited. *World Politics* 50: 475-505.

Fabre, Clarisse. 2002. Pour les elections legislatives, la droite a relégué la parité au second plan. *Le Monde* 10 May: 9.

Farrell, David M. 2001. The United Kingdom comes of age: The British electoral reform 'revolution' in the 1990s. In Shugart and Wattenberg, eds. 521-41.

Faure, A.M. 1999. *The electoral systems issue in South African politics.* Occasional paper. Johannesburg, SA: Konrad Adenauer Foundation. February.

Flanagan, Tom. 1999. The alternative vote: An electoral system for Canada. In Milner, ed. 85-90.

Franklin, Mark. 2002. The dynamics of electoral participation. In LeDuc et al., eds. 216-35.

———. 2003. The generational basis of turnout decline in established democracies. Paper presented at the World Congress of the International Political Science Association. Durban, South Africa, July.

Fraser, Graham. 1984. *René Lévesque and the Parti Québécois in power.* Toronto, ON: Macmillan.

Gallagher, Michael. 1991. Proportionality, disproportionality and electoral systems. *Electoral Studies* 10: 33-51.

———. 1998. The political impact of electoral system change in Japan and New Zealand. *Party Politics* 4: 203-28.

Geddis, Andrew. 2002. New Zealand's attempt to combat 'party hopping' by elected representatives. *Election Law Journal* 1,4: 557-71.

Gibbins, Roger, and Loleen Youngman Berdahl. 2000. The institutional expression of multiple identities: The electoral reform debate. In *Braving the new world: Readings in contemporary politics,* ed. Thomas M.J. Bateman, Manuel Mertin, and David M. Thomas. Scarborough, ON: Nelson.

Gibson, Gordon, ed. 2003. *Fixing Canadian democracy.* Vancouver, BC: Fraser Institute.

Goul Andersen, Jorgen, and Jens Hoff. 2001. *Democracy and citizenship in Scandinavia.* Houndmills, UK: Palgrave MacMillan.

Grönlund, Kimmo. 2003. Knowledge and turnout: A comparative analysis. Paper presented at the ECPR Conference. Marburg, Germany. September.

Grumm, John. 1958. Theories of electoral systems. *Midwest Journal of Political Science* 2: 357-76.

Hahn, Carole L., ed. 1998. *Becoming political: Comparative perspectives on citizenship education.* Albany, NY: SUNY Press.

Händle, Christa, Detlef Oesterreich, and Luitgard Trommer. 1999. Concepts of civic education in Germany based on a survey of expert opinion. In *Citizenship and education in twenty-eight countries: Civic knowledge at age fourteen,* ed. J. Torney-Purta, R. Lehmann, H. Oswald, and W. Schulz. Amsterdam: Eburon-IEA.

Hartviksen, Wynne. 2001. Making politics matter: The shining light of PR, the rocky road of election finance reform, and the disconnect between activists and politics. *Straight Goods* 4 (June 4).

Hermens, F.A. 1941 [1972]. *Democracy or anarchy? A study of proportional representation.* New York, NY: Johnson Reprint Company.

Hill, Steven. 2002. *Fixing elections: The failure of America's winner take all politics.* New York, NY: Routledge.

Hough, Dan, and Charlie Jeffery. 2003. Elections in multi-level systems: Lessons for the UK from abroad. In *The state of the nations 2003*, ed. Robert Hazell. Exeter, UK: Imprint Academic.

Howe, Paul. 2001. The sources of campaign intemperance. *Policy Options* (January-February).

———.2002a. Name the premier: The political knowledge of Canadians, past and present. Paper presented at the Annual Meeting of the Canadian Political Studies Association. Toronto. 28-31 May.

———. 2002b. Where have all the voters gone. *Inroads* 12 (Fall).

Hrebenar, Ronald J. 2000. *Japan's new party system*. Boulder, CO: Westview Press.

Huddy, Leonie, and Nadya Terkildsen. 1993. Gender stereotypes and the perception of male and female candidates. *American Journal of Political Science* 37,1: 119-47.

Hunter, Alfred A., and Margaret A. Denton. 1984. Do female candidates 'lose votes'?: The experience of female candidates in the 1979 and 1980 Canadian general elections. *Canadian Review of Sociology and Anthropology* 21: 395-406.

Hunter, Susan, and R.A Brisbin, Jr. 2000. The impact of service learning on democratic and civic values. *PS: Political Science and Politics* 33,3: 623-26.

IDEA (International Institute for Democracy and Electoral Assistance). 1999. *Youth voter participation: Involving today's young in tomorrow's democracy*. Stockholm: IDEA.

———. 2003. *Global database of quotas for women*. Available at <http://www.idea.int/quota/>, 30 October.

Inoguchi, Takashi. 1993. Japanese politics in transition: A theoretical review. *Government and Opposition* 28: 443-55.

———. 2000. The Japanese general election of 25 June 2000. *Government and Opposition* 35: 484-98.

Institute on Governance. 1998. The exercise of power round table: Parliament, politics and citizens: A conversation with Bob Rae. www.iog.ca/publications/xrt6.pdf.

Inter-Parliamentary Union. 2001. *Women in national parliaments*. Available at <http://www.ipu.org/wmn-e/classif.htm>.

Irvine, William P. 1979. *Does Canada need a new electoral system?* Kingston, ON: Institute of Intergovernmental Relations.

———. 1985. A review and evaluation of electoral system reform proposals. In *Institutional reforms for representative government*, ed. Peter Aucoin. Toronto, ON: University of Toronto Press.

Ishida, Takeshi, and Ellis Krauss, eds. 1989. *Democracy in Japan*. Pittsburgh, PN: University of Pittsburgh Press.

Jackson, Keith, and Alan McRobie. 1998. *New Zealand adopts proportional representation: Accident? design? evolution?* Aldershot, UK: Ashgate.

Jacobs, Lawrence R., and Robert Y. Shapiro. 2000. *Politicians don't pander: Political manipulation and the loss of democratic responsiveness*. Chicago, IL: University of Chicago Press.

Jenkins, Lord of Hillhead. 1999. *The Report of the Independent Commission on the Voting System*. London, UK: HMSO.

Jesse, Eckhard. 1987. The West German electoral system: The case for reform, 1949-87. *West European Politics* 16: 434-48.

———. 1988. Split-voting in the Federal Republic of Germany: An Analysis of the Federal Elections from 1953 to 1987. *Electoral Studies* 7,2:109-24.

Junn, Jane. 1995. Participation in liberal democracy: What citizens learn from political activity. Paper presented at the annual meeting of the American Political Science Association. New York.

Karp, Jeffrey, and Susan Banducci. 1998. The impact of proportional representation on turnout: Evidence from New Zealand. Paper presented at the annual meeting of the Australasian Political Science Association. Christchurch, NZ.

———. 1999. The impact of proportional representation on turnout: Evidence from New Zealand. *Australian Journal of Political Science* 34,3: 363-77.

Karvonen, Lauri, and Stein Kuhnle, eds. 2001. *Party systems and voter alignments revisited*. London, UK: Routledge.

Katz, Richard S. 1996. Electoral reform and the transformation of party politics in Italy. *Party Politics* 2: 31-53.

Katz, Richard S. 1997. *Democracy and elections*. New York, NY: Oxford University Press.

Kent, Tom. 1999. How to renew Canadian democracy: PR for the Commons, FPTP elections for the Senate, and political financing by individuals only. In Milner, ed. 51-61.

Ladner, Andreas, and Henry Milner. 1999. Politicization, electoral institutions, and voting turnout: The evidence from Swiss communal elections in comparative context. *Electoral Studies* 18,2: 235-50.

Lakeman, Enid. 1982. *The power to elect: The case for proportional representation*. London, UK: Heinemann.

——, and James D. Lambert. 1959. *Voting in democracies*. London, UK: Faber and Faber.

Laver, Michael, and Norman Schofield. 1990. *Multiparty government. The politics of coalition in Europe*. Oxford, UK: Oxford University Press.

Law Commission of Canada. 2002. *Renewing democracy: Debating electoral reform in Canada*. A discussion paper. Ottawa, ON: Law Commission of Canada.

LeDuc, Lawrence, and Jon H. Pammett. 2003. Elections and participation: The meanings of the turnout decline. Paper presented at the annual general meeting of the Canadian Political Science Association. Halifax, NS. 1 June.

LeDuc, Lawrence, Richard G. Niemi and Pippa Norris, eds. 2002. *Comparing democracies 2: New challenges in the study of elections and voting*. London, UK: Sage.

Leighley, Jan, and Jonathan Nagler. 2000. Socioeconomic class bias in turnout: Evidence from aggregate data. Paper presented at the annual meeting of the American Political Science Association. Washington, DC. September.

Lijphart, Arend. 1984. *Democracies: Patterns of majoritarian and consensus rule in twenty-one countries*. New Haven, CT: Yale University Press.

——. 1994a. Democracies: Forms, performance, and constitutional engineering. *European Journal of Political Research* 25: 1-17.

——. 1994b. *Electoral systems and party systems: A study of twenty-seven democracies, 1945-1990*. Oxford, UK: Oxford University Press.

——. 1999. *Patterns of democracy: Government forms and performances in thirty-six countries*. New Haven, CT: Yale University Press.

Lodge, T. 1999. *Consolidating democracy. South Africa's second popular election*. Johannesburg, SA: Witwatersrand University Press.

Loenen, Nick. 1997. *Citizenship and democracy: A case for proportional representation*. Toronto, ON: Dundurn.

——. 2003a. A case for changing the voting system and a consideration of alternative systems. In Gibson, ed., pp.49-68.

——. 2003b. Preferential plus: A new effective, made-in-BC voting system to elect MLAs. Submission to the Citizens Assembly on Electoral Reform. Vancouver: December.

Lopez, Mark H. 2003. Civic and social studies course taking and civic engagement. Paper presented at the International Conference on Civic Education Research. New Orleans, LA. November.

Lovink, J.A.A. 1998. Run-off elections is the reform that Canada needs. *Policy Options* (April): 45-47.

——. 2001. Run-off elections revisited. *Policy Options* (June): 43-44.

Lundberg, Thomas. 2002. Putting a human face on proportional representation: Early experiences in Scotland and Wales. *Representation* 38,4: 271-83.

Lynch, Peter. 2001. *Scottish government and politics: An introduction*. Edinburgh, Scotland: Edinburgh University Press.

Mabille, Xavier. 1986. *Histoire politique de la Belgique*. Bruxelles: CRISP.

MacDonald, Edward. 2000. *If you're strong hearted: Prince Edward Island in the twentieth century*. Charlottetown, PEI: Prince Edward Island Museum and Heritage Foundation.

MacKinnon v. Prince Edward Island. 1993. 101 D.L.R. (4th) 362 (P.E.I.S.C.T.D.).

MacKinnon, Frank. 1951. *The government of Prince Edward Island*. Toronto, ON: University of Toronto Press.

Magleby, David B. 1984. *Direct legislation: Voting on ballot propositions in the United States.* Baltimore, MD: Johns Hopkins University Press.

Martikainen, Tuomo. 2000. Disengagement from politics: Part 1—Electoral participation. Paper presented at Oslo Workshop, Towards Spectator Democracy. University of Helsinki. 28-29 October.

Massicotte, Louis. 1995. Eclipse et retour du gerrymander linguistique québécois. In *L'Espace Québécois*, ed. Alain-G. Gagnon and Alain Noel. Montreal, QC: Editions Québec/Amérique.

———. 1997. Bridled workhorses. Party discipline in committees of the Canadian House of Commons. Paper presented at the annual meeting of the Canadian Political Science Association. St. John's, NF. June.

———. 1998. The rise of party cohesion in the Canadian House of Commons 1867-1945: A descriptive and comparative summary. Paper presented at the Third Workshop of Parliamentary Scholars and Parliamentarians. Wroxton College, Oxfordshire, UK. August.

———. 1999. Federal countries, Elections. In *International encyclopedia of elections*, ed. R. Rose. 101-05. Washington DC: Congressional Quarterly.

———, and André Blais. 1999. Mixed electoral systems: A conceptual and empirical survey. *Electoral Studies* 18,3: 341-66.

Matland, Richard E. 1991. Institutional variables affecting female representation in national legislatures: The case of Norway. Paper presented at the 1991 annual meeting of the American Political Science Association. Washington, DC.

———. 1997. Enhancing women's political participation: Legislative recruitment and electoral systems. In *Women in parliament: Beyond numbers*, ed. International Institute for Democracy and Electoral Assistance. 65-87. Stockholm: IDEA.

———, and Donley T. Studlar. 1996. The contagion of women candidates in single-member and multi-member districts. *Journal of Politics* 58,3: 707-33.

McAllister, Ian, and Malcolm Mackerras. 1998. Compulsory voting, party stability and electoral bias in Australia. Paper presented at the ECPR joint sessions. Warwick UK. March.

McKean, Margaret, and Ethan Scheiner. 2000. Japan's new electoral system: La plus ça change. *Electoral Studies* 19: 447-77.

Mershon, Carol. 2002. *The costs of coalition.* Stanford, CA: Stanford University Press.

Milne, David A. 1982. Politics in a beleaguered garden. In *The garden transformed: Prince Edward Island, 1945-1980*, ed. Verner Smitheram, David Milne, and Satadal Dasgupta. Charlottetown, PEI: Ragweed Press.

Milner, Henry. 1994. Obstacles to electoral reform in Canada. *American Review of Canadian Studies* (Spring).

———. 1999. The case for proportional representation in Canada. In Milner, ed. 37-49.

———, ed. 1999. *Making every vote count: Reassessing Canada's electoral system.* Peterborough, ON: Broadview Press.

———. 2001. Civic literacy in comparative context: Why Canadians should be concerned. *Choices.* Montreal: IRPP.

———. 2002. *Civic literacy: How informed citizens make democracy work.* Hanover, NH: University Press of New England.

MMP Review Committee. 2001. *Inquiry into the review of MMP.* New Zealand House of Representatives. August. Available at <http://www.gp.co/NewZealand/wooc/ipapers/mpp.html>.

Morin, Richard. 1996. Tuned out, turned off: Millions of Americans know little about how their government works. *Washington Post* National Weekly Edition 5-11 February.

Nagel, Jack H. 1994. How many parties will New Zealand have under MMP? *Political Science* 46,2: 139-60.

———. 1998. Social choice in a pluralitarian democracy: The politics of market liberalization in New Zealand. *British Journal of Political Science* 28,2: 223-67.

Norris, Pippa. 1987. *Politics and sexual equality: The comparative position of women in western democracies.* Boulder, CO: Rienner.

———, and Joni Lovenduski. 1995. *Political recruitment: Gender, race and class in the British Parliament.* Cambridge, UK: Cambridge University Press.

O'Neill, Brenda. 2001. *Generational patterns in the political opinions and behaviour of Canadians: Separating the wheat from the chaff.* Montreal: IRPP.

OECD (Organization for Economic Co-operation and Development). 2001. Programme for International Student Assessment (PISA). *International Report.* Paris: OECD.

Office of the Deputy Prime Minister. 2002. *Your region, your choice.* London, UK: HMSO.

Ontario Green Party. 2003. *A better way to live: Green Party of Ontario platform.* Toronto: 2003.

Ontario Liberal Party. 2003. *Government that works for you.* Policy Document 5: *Government: The Ontario Liberal plan for a more democratic Ontario.* Toronto.

Ontario NDP. 2003. *Public power: Practical solutions for Ontario.* Toronto.

Palmer, Geoffrey. 1992. *New Zealand's constitution in crisis: Reforming our political system.* Dunedin, NZ: John McIndoe.

Pammett, Jon, and Lawrence LeDuc. 2003. *Explaining the turnout decline in Canadian federal elections: A new survey of non-voters.* Ottawa, ON: Elections Canada.

Parker, Kimberly, and Claudia Deane. 1997. Ten years of the Pew News Interest Index. Report Presented at the meeting of the American Association for Public Opinion Research. Norfolk VA.

Parti Libéral du Québec (PLQ). 2002. Mémoire présenté par le Parti libéral du Québec au comité directeur des États généraux sur la réforme des institutions démocratiques. Montréal, QC: PLQ.

Parti québécois. 1970. Le systéme électoral. Working document. Montréal: Parti québécois.

———. 1994. *Programme électoral du Parti Québécois.* Proposition du conseil exécutif national. Conseil national extraordinaire (23 July). Montréal, QC: Parti québécois.

———. 1998. *La volonté de réussir.* PQ Electoral Platform. Montréal, QC: Parti québécois.

Paterson, Lindsay. 1994. *The autonomy of modern Scotland.* Edinburgh: Edinburgh University Press.

Paterson, Lindsay, Alice Brown, John Curtice, Kerstin Hinds, David McCrone, Alison Park, Kerry Sproston, and Paula Surridge. 2001. *New Scotland, new politics?* Edinburgh: Polygon.

PEI. 2001. Special Committee on the Election Act. 2001. Final Report. Charlottetown, PEI.

PEI. 2003a. Paper for discussion purposes on the major electoral systems found around the world and four models. Charlotttetown, PEI: Prince Edward Island Electoral Reform Commission, April.

PEI. 2003b. *Prince Edward Island Electoral Reform Commission Report.* Charlotttetown, PEI: Prince Edward Island Electoral Reform Commission, December.

Phillips, Harry. 1976. Challenges to the voting system in Canada, 1874-1974. PhD diss. University of Western Ontario.

Pilon, Dennis. 1997. Proportional representation in Canada: An historical sketch. Paper presented to the annual meeting of the Canadian Political Science Association. St. John's, NF.

———. 1999. The history of voting system reform. In Milner, ed. 111-21.

———. 2000. Making voting reform count: Evaluating historical voting reform strategies in British Columbia. Paper presented to the Making Votes Count Conference. Vancouver, BC. May.

Piroth, Scott. 2004. Prospects for institutional reform in Quebec: The Estates General on the reform of democratic institutions. Paper presented at the annual meeting of Association for Canadian Studies in the United States (ACSUS). Portland, OR. November.

Plutzer, Eric. 2002. Becoming a habitual voter: Inertia, resources, and growth in young adulthood. *American Political Science Review* 96: 41-56.

Popkin, Samuel, and Michael Dimock. 1999. Political knowledge and citizen competence. In *Citizen competence and democratic institutions*, ed. S. Elkin and K. Soltan. University Park, PN: University of Pennsylvania Press.

Powell, G. Bingham. 2000. *Elections as instruments of democracy: Majoritarian and proportional visions*. New Haven, CT: Yale University Press.

Québec. 1979. Minister of State for Electoral and Parliamentary Reform. *One citizen, one vote: Green book on reform of the voting system*. Québec, QC: Éditeur officiel.

———. 1984. Commission de la représentation électorale. *Pour un mode de scrutin équitable: La proportionnelle territoriale*. Final Report. Québec, QC: The Commission.

———. 2002a. Direction des études documentaires. *Le mode de scrutin: Quelques jalons historiques*. Québec, QC: Direction des études documentaires.

———. 2002b. Committee on Institutions. *The Reform of the Voting System in Québec: Discussion Paper*. Québec, QC: Committees Secretariat.

———. 2003a. *Cahier de référence*. Secrétariat à la réforme des institutions démocratiques. Québec, QC: Ministère du Conseil exécutif du Québec.

———. 2003b. *Participation Workbook*. Québec, QC: Ministère du Conseil exécutif du Québec.

———. 2003c. Steering Committee of the Estates General for the Reform of Democratic Institutions 2003. *La participation citoyenne au cœur des institutions démocratiques québécoises*. Final Report. Québec, QC: Ministère du Conseil exécutif du Québec.

Reed, Steven. 1999. Strategic voting in the 1996 Japanese election. *Comparative Political Studies* 32: 257-70.

———, and Michael F. Thies. 2001. The causes of electoral reform in Japan. In Shugart and Wattenberg, eds. 152-72.

Reynolds, A., ed. 1999. *Election '99: From Mandela to Mbeki*. Cape Town, SA: David Philip.

Richardson, Bradley. 1997. *Japanese democracy: Power, coordination and performance*. New Haven, CT: Yale University Press.

Riker, William H. 1982. The two-party system and Duverger's Law: An essay on the history of political science. *American Political Science Review* 76: 753-66.

Robb, Andrew. 1982. Third party experience on the Island. In *The garden transformed: Prince Edward Island, 1945-1980*, ed. Verner Smitheram, David Milne, and Satadal Dasgupta. Charlottetown, PEI: Ragweed Press.

Roberts, Geoffrey K. 1988. The German Federal Republic: The two-lane route to Bonn. In *Candidate selection in comparative perspective: The secret garden of politics*, ed. Michael Gallagher and Michael Marsh. London, UK: Sage.

Rose, Lawrence E. 2002. Local political participation in Denmark and Norway: Does political knowledge make a difference? Paper prepared in workshop 22 at the ECPR Joint Sessions. Torino, Italy. 22-27 March.

———. 2003. Local political participation in Denmark and Norway: Does political knowledge make a difference? Paper prepared for presentation at the 12th Nordic conference on local government and politics, Göteborg, Sweden, 28-30 November 2003.

Royal Commission on the Electoral System. 1986. *Towards a better democracy: Report of the Royal Commission on the Electoral System*. Wellington, NZ: Government Printer.

Rule, Wilma. 1987. Electoral systems, contextual factors and women's opportunity for election to Parliament in twenty-three democracies. *Western Political Quarterly* 40,4: 477-98.

———. 1994. Women's underrepresentation and electoral systems. *PS: Political Science and Politics* 27: 689-93.

———, and Joseph F. Zimmerman, eds. 1994. *Electoral systems in comparative perspective: Their impact on women and minorities*. Westport, CT: Greenwood Press.

Russow, Joan, and Green Party of Canada
   v. The Attorney General of Canada, The
   Chief Electoral Officer of Canada and Her
   Majesty the Queen in Right of Canada.
   2001. Application record, including
   factum, filed with the Ontario Superior
   Court of Justice, 1 May. See <http:
   //www.law-lib.utoronto.ca/testcase/
   gpfactum.pdf>.
Sakamoto, Takayuki. 1999. Explaining electoral reform: Japan versus Italy and New
   Zealand. *Party Politics* 5: 419-38.
Sartori, Giovanni. 1986. The influence of
   electoral systems: Faulty laws or faulty
   method? In *Electoral laws and their political consequences*, ed. Bernard Grofman
   and Arend Lijphart. 43-68. New York,
   NY: Agathon Press.
Savoie, Donald J. 1999. *Governing from the
   centre: The concentration of political power
   in Canada*. Toronto, ON: University of
   Toronto Press.
Schmidt, Manfred G. 1997. Nomination:
   Arguments in favour of "democracies."
   European Journal of Political Research 31:
   193-95.
Scottish Constitutional Commission.
   1994. *Further steps towards a scheme for
   Scotland's Parliament*. Edinburgh: Scottish
   Constitutional Commission.
Scottish Constitutional Convention. 1990.
   Towards Scotland's Parliament. Edinburgh:
   Scottish Constitutional Convention.
———. 1995. *Scotland's Parliament, Scotland's
   right*. Edinburgh: Scottish Constitutional
   Convention.
Scottish Liberal Democrats. 1991. *The PR
   debate and the Constitutional Convention*.
   Edinburgh: Scottish Liberal Democrats.
Scottish Parliament. 1999. *Relationships
   between MSPs: Initial report*. Edinburgh:
   Scottish Parliament. 18 November.
Shiratori, Rei. 1995. The politics of electoral
   reform in Japan. *International Political
   Science Review* 16: 79-94.
Shugart, Matthew, and Martin Wattenberg,
   eds. 2001. *Mixed-member electoral systems:
   The best of both worlds?* Oxford, UK:
   Oxford University Press.
Sineau, Mariette. 2001. *Profession femme
   politique: Sex et pouvoir sous la Cinquième
   République*. Paris: Presses de Sciences Po.

Skolverket. (Swedish Educational
   Administrative Board) 1998.
   *Gymnasieskola för alla—andra. En studie
   om marginalisering och utslagning i gym-
   nasieskolan*. Stockholm: Skolverket.
Smiley, Donald V. 1978. Federalism and the
   legislative process in Canada. In *The
   legislative process in Canada: The need
   for reform*, ed. W.A.W. Neilson and J.C.
   MacPherson. Montreal, QC: (IRPP).
Smith, Denis. 1973. *Gentle patriot: A political
   biography of Walter Gordon*. Edmonton,
   AB: Hurtig.
Strate, John M., Charles J. Parrish, Charles
   D. Elder, and Coit Ford, III. 1989. Life
   span civic development and voting
   participation. *American Political Science
   Review* 83: 443-64.
Strom, Kaare. 1990. *Minority government and
   majority rule*. Cambridge, UK: Cambridge
   University Press.
Studlar, Donley. 1999. Will Canada seriously
   consider electoral system reform? Women
   and Aboriginals should. In Milner, ed.
   123-32.
Stursberg, Peter 1978. *Lester Pearson and the
   dream of unity*. Toronto, ON: Doubleday.
Taagepera, Rein, and Matthew Soberg
   Shugart. 1989. *Seats and votes: The effects
   and determinants of electoral systems*. New
   Haven, CT: Yale University Press.
Togeby, Lise. 1999. Migrants at the polls: An
   analysis of immigrant and refugee participation in Danish local elections. *Journal of
   Ethnic and Migration Studies* 25,4: 665-84.
Vowles, Jack. 2002a. Offsetting the PR
   effect? Party mobilization and turnout
   decline in New Zealand, 1996-99. *Party
   Politics* 8,5: 587-605.
———. 2002b. What happened at the 1999 elec-
   tion? In *Proportional representation on trial:
   The 1999 New Zealand general election and
   the fate of MMP*, ed. Jack Vowles, Peter
   Aimer, Jeffrey Karp, Susan Banducci,
   Raymond Miller, and Ann Sullivan.
   Auckland, NZ: Auckland University
   Press.
———. 2004. New Zealand: The consolidation
   of reform? In *The politics of electoral
   systems*, ed. Michael Gallagher and Paul
   Mitchell. Oxford, UK: Oxford University
   Press.

——, Peter Aimer, Susan Banducci, and Jeffrey Karp, eds. 1998. *Voters' victory: New Zealand's first election under proportional representation.* Auckland, NZ: Auckland University Press.

——, Peter Aimer, Susan Banducci, Jeffrey Karp, and Raymond Miller, eds. 2004. *Voters' veto: The 2002 election in New Zealand and the consolidation of minority government.* Auckland, NZ: Auckland University Press.

——, Peter Aimer, Helena Catt, Jim Lamare, and Raymond Miller. 1995. *Towards consensus? The 1993 election in New Zealand and the transition to proportional representation.* Auckland, NZ: Auckland University Press.

Wada, Junichiro. 1996. *The Japanese election system: Three analytical perspectives.* New York, NY: Routledge.

Walker, Tobi. 2000. The service/politics split: Rethinking service to teach political engagement. *PS: Political Science and Politics* 33:3: 647-49.

Wallace, John. 2002. Reflections on constitutional and other issues concerning our electoral system: The past and the future. *Political Science* 54,1: 47-65.

Ward, Leigh J. 1998. 'Second-class MPs'? New Zealand's adaptation to mixed-member parliamentary representation. *Political Science* 49,2: 125-45.

Watanuki, Joji. 2001. Japan: From emerging to stable party system. In Karvonen and Kuhnle, eds. 138-49.

Wattenberg, Martin P. 1998. Turnout decline in the US and other advanced industrial democracies. Research paper. Irvine, CA: University of California Center for the Study of Democracy.

Wearing, Joseph. 1998. Tweaking the whips: Modified rebelliousness in the Canadian House of Commons. Paper presented at the Third Workshop of Parliamentary Scholars and Parliamentarians. Wroxton College, Oxfordshire, UK. August.

Weaver, Kent. 1997. Improving representation in the Canadian House of Commons. *Canadian Journal of Political Science* 30: 473-512.

Welch, Susan, and Donley T. Studlar. 1986. British public opinion toward women in politics: A comparative perspective. *Western Political Quarterly* 39: 138-52.

Westholm, Anders, Arne Lindquist, and Richard Niemi. 1989. Education and the making of the informed citizen: Political literacy and the outside world. In *Political socialization, education and democracy*, ed. Ort Ichilov. New York, NY: Teachers' College Press.

Woldendorp, Jaap, Hans Keman, and Ian Budge. 1998. Party government in 20 democracies: An update 1990-1995. *European Journal of Political Research* 33: 125-64.

Wolfinger, Raymond E., and Steven J. Rosenstone. 1980. *Who votes?* New Haven, CT: Yale University Press.

Young, Lisa. 1991. Legislative turnover and the election of women to the Canadian House of Commons. In *Women in Canadian politics: Toward equity in representation*, ed. Kathy Megyery. 81-99. Toronto, ON: Dundurn Press.

——. 1994. *Electoral systems and representative legislatures: Consideration of alternative electoral systems.* Ottawa, ON: Canadian Advisory Council on the Status of Women.

——. 2002. Representation of women in the new Canadian party system. In *Political parties, representation, and electoral democracy in Canada*, ed. William Cross. 181-200. Don Mills, ON: Oxford University Press.

Zimmerman, Joseph F. 1994. Equity in representation for women and minorities. In Rule and Zimmerman, eds. 3-13.